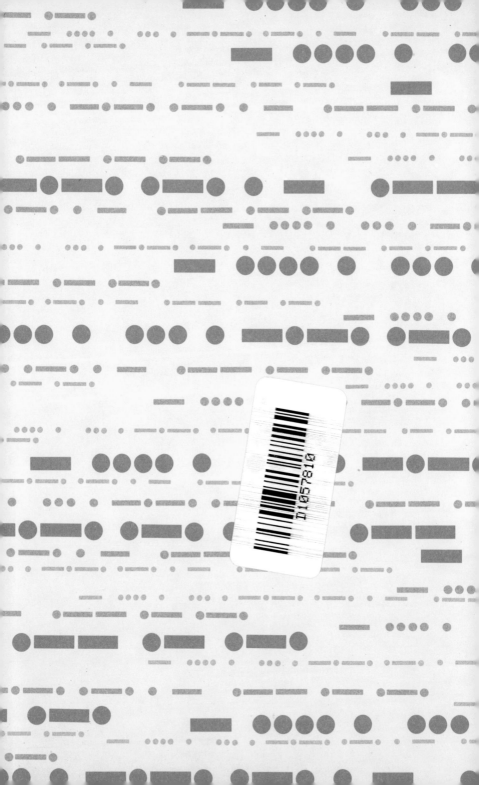

KK- 923
15 -

Reprinted 1989 from the 1943 edition
Cover design © 1988 Time-Life Books Inc.
All rights reserved.

Library of Congress Cataloging in Publication Data

Shiber, Etta.
Paris-underground
by Etta Shiber in collaboration with Anne and Paul Dupre.
p. cm.—(Classics of World War II. The secret war)
Reprint. Originally published: New York: Scribner's, 1943.
ISBN 0-8094-7258-9
ISBN 0-8094-7259-7 (lib. bdg.)
1. World War, 1939-1945—Personal narratives, American. 2. World War,
1939-1945—Prisoners and prisons, German. 3. World War, 1939-1945—Un-
derground movements—France—Paris. 4. World War, 1939-1945—France—
Paris. 5. Escapes—France—History—20th century. 6. Shiber, Etta. 7. Paris
(France)—History—1940-1944.
I. Dupre, Anne. II. Dupre, Paul. III. Title. IV. Series.
D811.5.S49 1988   940.53'44—dc 19   88-29514 CIP

Time-Life Books Inc. offers a wide range of fine music series,
including *Your Hit Parade*, original recordings from the '40s and '50s.
For subscription information, call 1-800-621-7026 or write Time-Life Music,
P.O. Box C-32068, Richmond, Virginia 23261-2068.

Paris—Underground

BY

ETTA SHIBER

IN COLLABORATION WITH
ANNE AND PAUL DUPRE

NEW YORK

Charles Scribner's Sons

1943

COPYRIGHT, 1943, BY

PRESS ALLIANCE, INC.

All rights reserved. No part of this book may be reproduced in any form without the permission of Charles Scribner's Sons

A

THIS BOOK IS
MANUFACTURED UNDER WARTIME
CONDITIONS IN CONFORMITY WITH
ALL GOVERNMENT REGULATIONS
CONTROLLING THE USE OF PAPER
AND OTHER MATERIALS

PRINTED IN THE UNITED STATES OF AMERICA BY H. WOLFF, NEW YORK

For
KITTY

AUTHOR'S NOTE

The basic facts in the book are a matter of record. Most of the names of the persons whose activities are described in this book have been changed, for obvious reasons. A few details, not already matters of record known to the Gestapo, have been recast, a few omitted, and the roles of various persons interchanged, in order to make it impossible for any use to be made of this book by the German authorities against anyone described in it.

Contents

CONTENTS

PARIS   UNDERGROUND

CHAPTER ONE

Escape from Europe

I SAID no good-bye to Europe. I was below decks when the ship began to move. Her engines were so smooth and noiseless that they must have been running for some time before I became conscious of their muffled pulsing. I hurried up on deck, expecting to find the ship coursing down the broad Tagus River, with the many-colored buildings of Lisbon piled in confusion on its shore.

But from the deck, there was already no sight of land. Behind us, I knew, was the coast of Portugal, but it was lost in the evening haze. The sea was a dirty gray. The engines of the great ship hummed soothingly, monotonously, as she plowed smoothly through the waves, America-bound at last.

The sky was overcast. As the night darkened, not a star showed to relieve the pitch blackness of the sea. Our ship alone moved in a blaze of brilliance through the surrounding gloom. All other vessels, I knew, would show no lights as they slipped silently over the black waves. But as I leaned over the side I could read the great black letters on her white hull, glowing in the light of powerful reflectors, which explained why we alone dared to pass warships, submarines and planes with every light ablaze: "Diplomat—Drottningholm—Diplomat."

For this was the return trip of the *Drottningholm*, whose safety was guaranteed by both sides, because she had taken Axis officials and correspondents to Lisbon, and was now heading back to the United States with her exchange cargo of American diplomats, consular officials and newspapermen.

I was neither a diplomat, nor a consular official, nor a newspaperman. I was a unique passenger on this official ship. I was an exchanged prisoner, released from a German cell because somewhere in the United States a prison door had swung open for some one whose return Germany desired. I was a pawn in this bargain, made through a neutral nation between the governments of Hitler's Reich

I

and my own United States. I had had nothing to do with its conclusion, knew nothing about it, until on May 17, 1942, five months
after Germany and the United States had declared war against one
another, I was told that I had been exchanged, and that I would be
sent home.

Two Gestapo agents in civilian clothes escorted me to Juvisy, the
first station beyond Paris. There we waited for five hours for the
train, until I began to wonder whether, after all, there would be any
train, whether this performance were not a police comedy, played
for some purpose I could not imagine. So long as I remained on
German territory, I could not believe the good news that had been
announced to me, that at last I was to be free and to see my own
country again. I kept myself from rejoicing until I could be certain,
for fear of bitter disappointment.

But finally the train arrived. To my astonishment, it stopped ex-
pressly for me. No one else got on; and I was to discover later that
no one else would get on during all of its slow progress across
France.

I was surprised to discover this Gestapo estimate of my importance, far greater than I would have put it myself. In my fellow
passengers, it seemed to arouse suspicion and hostility. They were
refugees from Czechoslovakia, Poland and Austria, finally allowed
to get out of German territory. It seemed to me that they reproached
me for having delayed by even a few minutes the time when they
would be at last beyond the reach of the Nazi police. Or perhaps
the silent hostility which I felt resulted from my lonely boarding of
the train. Possibly they took me for a Gestapo agent, put aboard to
spy on them. For a long while, not one of them spoke to me or
seemed to be aware of my presence.

The train was crowded. Every compartment was jammed. It was
a depressing, silent trip. Gestapo agents in civilian clothes were in
complete charge. There was not a single French employee on this
French train. The Gestapo men did not approve of animation. Once
or twice lively conversations sprang up in my compartment, or
neighboring ones. Each time one of the Gestapo men poked his
head in the door, and barked for silence. Obedience was fearful
and immediate.

But most of the refugees seemed to have little desire for talk. No doubt they felt as I did: that no relief was possible until we got out of German territory. We moved steadily ahead, through the pleasant countryside of France; but at every station we saw German uniforms and German faces, and we knew that we were still in the prison into which the Nazis have converted all of Europe.

Night fell, and the train rattled on, through a blacked-out countryside where no light relieved the gloom. I slept a little, dozing off for a few minutes at a time, and then being jerked into consciousness again as the train swayed and jolted over the bad road-bed. Our eyes were all still heavy with lack of sleep at seven in the morning, when the train pulled to a stop, and we saw the station sign through the windows: Hendaye—the Spanish border!

Faces brightened at once. Freedom seemed almost in sight, and already the universal suspicion which enshrouds every one in Nazi territory seemed to be lifting. I was asked to satisfy the general curiosity: why had the train stopped for me alone, in all France? I told them all I knew. I was an American, I had been in a Nazi prison, and I had been exchanged for some German prisoner in America.

An hour passed, then two. There was no sign of preparation to get our train under way again, to run it the few hundred yards that would get it out from under the shadow of the swastika. My fellow passengers began to show signs of nervousness. I became uneasy too. The Gestapo guards paced up and down beside the train. We were not yet out of their prison.

Finally a Gestapo agent came through the car and told us that the train would be delayed at Hendaye all morning. Any one who wished might get off and buy food in the station canteen, where either francs or dollars would be accepted.

There was consternation in my compartment. My neighbors had only brought enough food with them for the normal journey, and none of them would have any money until they got to Lisbon. I alone had money—about fifty dollars. I went into the canteen, bought enough food for all in my compartment, and came back. Some of it we shared with those in neighboring compartments.

The hours dragged slowly by. Morning became afternoon, and still there were no signs that we were going to move. All sorts of rumors began to crop up. Some persons said that Spain had refused to let any more refugee trains pass, and we would all have to go back to Paris. Depression settled over us again.

Some of the refugees spoke English, and after I had told my story, they took particular pains to be nice to me. I asked one of them if he would care to go to the canteen to buy us some more food. When he came back, he said:

"Mrs. Shiber, I found out why we are being held here. A French guard told me. It's because of you."

"Because of me?" I gasped, as the old fear that I should never be free again seized me once more.

"Yes, because of you. You're being exchanged, aren't you? Well, the Germans are waiting for the woman who was released in exchange for you, and she hasn't arrived yet. They're holding the whole train until she gets here. That's why we're all held up."

I could feel a stiffening in the attitude of those about me. They could hardly blame me, they knew it was not my fault—yet it was because I was with them that they were not yet certain of release, that they were still being held interminably in this train under the eyes of their jailers. I knew they wished I had not been with them. Their silent reproach seemed intolerable to me. But I could do nothing except sit in my place and pretend not to realize how ardently they wished me elsewhere.

Night came on again, and we slumbered uncomfortably in our crowded compartments. Morning dawned. Some of the men went to the canteen to ask news on our progress. They could learn nothing.

"How these people must hate me!" I thought. "I'm all that stands between them and freedom. Why don't the Germans take me off the train, and let it go on without me? They could send me on later, when the exchange prisoner arrives."

I hadn't the slightest idea whom I was being exchanged for, except that it was a woman.

About noon, the station was suddenly gripped in a feverish activity. The platform became crowded with every possible variety of German uniform. Down the road paralleling the tracks marched small units of various uniformed groups, all going in the same direction. Then a German military band appeared. Obviously, some ceremony was about to take place.

For more than an hour, we had not been permitted to go to the canteen. But the number of our guards had decreased. No doubt some of them were curious, and wanted to see what was going on themselves. It was not difficult to slip off the train without being seen. In company with a Czechoslovak who volunteered to go with me, I got off, and from behind a freight car watched the scene.

A train was crossing the international bridge from Spain and entering the station. As it arrived, the band burst into the *Horst Wessel Lied,* the soldiers on the platform snapped to attention, and dignitaries stepped forward on the swastika-decorated quay to greet the passengers on the train. From the appearance of the official-looking group which descended, I judged that they must be the German diplomats returning from the United States; but the most honored of the arrivals seemed to be a red-headed woman of about thirty-five or forty.

As she stepped from the train, the reception committee hurried to greet her. An enormous bouquet of flowers was thrust into her arms. I was too far away to hear what was said, but it was obvious that short formal speeches of welcome were being delivered to her, and that she was answering. She seemed to be in a hurry to get out of the crowd. With brusque arrogant movements, she burst out of the group surrounding her and hastened across the platform, while the reception committee trailed after her like the tail of a comet. She passed close to the car behind which I was standing. I heard the brutal exultant laughter with which she greeted some old friends, and had a close view of her rather coarse features and wrinkled brow. I knew I had seen her before, or at least her picture; but the name escaped me.

"Who could she have been?" I asked myself, as I got back into the car. "I wonder—could that be the woman for whom I was exchanged?"

It didn't seem unlikely. For hardly had I gotten back to my place again when our guards reappeared, drove every one back into the train, and slowly it rolled out of the station of Hendaye, across the international bridge, and onto the soil of Spain. We were free!

We were not yet, however, delivered from our guardian angels. I understood now why the Gestapo men on the train had worn civilian clothes. It took us two days to get through Spain and Portu-

gal to Lisbon. During that time, neither Spanish nor Portuguese
officials set foot in the train. Our Gestapo men travelled with us all
the way through both countries.

At Lisbon, United States Consul Wiley found me in the train
after a hurried search through car after car, during which, he confessed to me later, the idea occurred to him that perhaps the Germans had double-crossed the United States and hadn't really sent
me out of the country.

He quickly discovered that I had been kept in complete ignorance
of my own case.

"Then you don't even know whom you were exchanged for?" he
asked.

"I haven't the slightest idea," I said, "except that it was a woman.
I thought it might be a woman I saw in Hendaye—red-headed,
arrogant in manner. Her face looked familiar."

"It should," Mr. Wiley said. "Her picture was in all the papers a
few years ago. You must have seen it then. That was Johanna Hoffmann."

Johanna Hoffmann! I remembered now. She was the hairdresser
of the German super-liner *Bremen*, taken off the ship by the F.B.I.,
and convicted of being a member of a dangerous German spy ring
operating in the United States. She had been in jail in America
since the autumn of 1938. Was what I had done, I asked myself,
really worth such a price?

I felt that I was really safe at last when I crossed the gangplank
from the dock in Lisbon to the deck of the *Drottningholm*. Every
one aboard seemed to share in the same care-free feeling of joy in
release from the anxieties which had beset them all for the last few
months. The happy confusion aboard the ship was even greater
than that which regularly accompanies the departures of ocean
liners. All of us had waited months for the day of repatriation. Their
common emotion made them friends at once, and I noted how utter
strangers made friends of one another at sight, all alike jubilating in
the thought: "At last! We're going *home!*"

An American newspaper correspondent stood beside me at the
railing, watching the passengers board the ship.

"I was here when the *Drottningholm* came in with its Axis passengers," he said. "There was quite a difference. You should have seen them! They looked like pigs fattened for market. All of them had tremendous trunks, stuffed to the brim. The baggage master told me that Johanna Hoffmann brought along forty trunks and handbags. When she learned she could only take three trunks, she swore like a Prussian top-sergeant.

"But look at the Americans coming aboard. Don't they all seem ragged and starving? Look at their faces—lean and spare. And their luggage. There isn't much of it, and I'll bet that there's not much in those bags. What could they have brought from the places they're coming from?

"I think we missed a bet when we let the Axis people go. We should have made our exchange on the basis of weight. That way we would have gotten two Americans for every Axis national."

The Americans were underweight, certainly. But their faces were glowing with happiness. In a matter of minutes, the Swedish ship became a Little America, a piece of floating United States territory, of the gayest type. The decks, the bar, the salons were noisy with the jubilations of men and women. Even the children were unusually boisterous, as though they too sensed the removal of restriction. I could feel their elation more strongly perhaps than they did, for, so far as I knew, I was the only one who had reached this haven from a Nazi prison cell, escorted by watchful jailers of the Gestapo.

But I felt less like celebrating. The shadow of depression still hung over me, and inspired me with a sort of vague contentment, rather than a festive air. I found a quiet corner in one of the salons and sat down by myself. An official of the American Consulate of Lisbon saw me there, and came up to say good-bye.

"Hiding, Mrs. Shiber?" he laughed. "You mustn't do that. Every one on board knows about you. They want to hear your story. After all, you're the only passenger on this ship whom we had to dig out of a Nazi prison. Or are you having trouble forgetting about all that? It will pass, you know. Everything does. In a month or two you won't be able to believe that your adventures really happened to you instead of to some one else."

"I'm a little worried about one thing," I said. "This Johanna Hoffmann woman—she's dangerous. I can't forget how she was received at Hendaye, her self-importance, the air of a conquering hero which she assumed as she shook hands with the Gestapo officers. She even clicked her heels like a Nazi soldier. I'm sure she's back in Berlin already, setting to work to do us all the harm she can."

"Why should that depress you?"

"Well, I'm responsible for her being released. I'm afraid you've made a bad bargain. She's certainly more valuable to the Germans than I am to the United States."

"My dear Mrs. Shiber," he said. "Don't, for goodness sake, worry about that. The State Department knows very well what you did in Paris. I have looked through your record, and I know, too. Suppose the British government, in the last war, had had a chance to exchange Edith Cavell. Don't you think they'd have jumped at it? And you, after all, are the Edith Cavell of this war."

I couldn't let that pass unchallenged.

"No," I said, "you're wrong there. I am not the Edith Cavell of this war, but perhaps my dear friend Kitty was. Whatever merit there was in what we did belongs to her. I only followed where she led. And she alone has paid the price. She is still in the hands of the Gestapo, if she is alive; or dead, if the sentence passed on her has been carried out. Yes, Kitty Beaurepos may well have been the Edith Cavell of this war."

He had gone, and I remained seated in the corner of the salon, lost in my own thoughts. Most of the passengers had gone into the dining room, and from where I sat I could hear them exclaiming at menus such as most of them had not seen for many long months. That first dinner on the *Drottningholm* must have been a memorable feast for them. But I had no heart for their gaiety. I sat quietly in my corner, reliving my life in Paris, thinking of Kitty—was she still alive?

Suddenly the realization came to me that we were under way.

On deck, I leaned against the railing, and looked out over the dark water, unseeingly. Kitty's face haunted me. Her beautiful sad eyes seemed to be striving to emerge from the veil of the darkness of the sea and sky. The consular official had said that every one wanted to hear my story. Well, they should—my story and Kitty's I would set it down while it was still fresh in my memory.

I went back to the salon again, settled myself before a writing table, and began to write. The account that follows is not my story alone. More than that, it is the story of my friend Kitty Beaurepos. This book is dedicated to her.

Kitty Beaurepos was the daughter of a London banker. She had received the traditional education of a young English society girl—a smattering of music and the arts, and a good deal of fine manners. She married young, went to live in Italy, had a son there. Then her husband died. Kitty moved to Paris, where she married a French wine merchant. After a while they decided to separate, on a thoroughly amicable basis.

Kitty loved Paris. She did not return to England, being financially independent as the result of an income received from her father's estate, which made it possible for her to live where she chose. But inactivity was impossible for her, and to keep herself occupied she opened a small dress shop in the Rue Rodier.

It was there that I met her, in 1925, when I visited Paris with my husband, William Noyes Shiber, on one of our annual three months' trips to France. Friends had told me of her shop, made to order for American clients like myself, of conservative tastes, and without inexhaustible pocketbooks. A deep sympathy developed between us immediately. I sensed a natural liking for me entirely unconnected with the desire of the shopkeeper to please a customer, and I reciprocated it. Thereafter I never failed to visit her on my yearly trips to Paris.

In 1933, I made the voyage to France without my husband, but with my brother Irving. His health had been bad, and the doctor had advised a cure at Aix-les-Bains. But the trip was a tiresome one, and my poor brother was not strong enough to stand it. He became so ill after reaching Paris that we could not go on to Aix.

In this emergency, Kitty was my greatest help. She secured the best medical care for my brother—but it was too late. When he died, Kitty saw at once how great the blow was to me. She not only relieved me of the care of making arrangements for the funeral, but actually came to live at the Hotel Bristol, in the Rue du Faubourg St. Honoré, where I was staying, to look after me. She let her business manage itself for a whole month, until my husband arrived.

In that crisis, I do not know what I should have done without Kitty, alone as I was in a strange city and a foreign country. I had always depended on my husband and my brother to look out for me; and without them I was lost. My husband realized at once, when he arrived, how important Kitty's aid had been to me. It seems today that he must have had a premonition when he said to her: "If anything ever happens to me, will you look out for Etta?"

Kitty laughed. "Of course I will," she said.

Three years later, in 1936, my husband died. I cabled to Kitty, informing her of his death. Within a few hours I had an answer. Kitty cabled to invite me to come to Paris and live with her. Her promise had not been lightly given. She had stretched out her strong arms to me in friendship across the ocean, as soon as she had learned that I was alone and troubled.

I read her cable with tears streaming down my cheeks. I answered in one word: "Coming."

Hardly a week later I got off the train at the St. Lazare station in Paris. Kitty was waiting for me on the platform. My first thought as I rushed towards her was: "How odd that I never noticed before how handsome Kitty is!"

She was forty then, tall, slender and wiry. As a young woman, she must have been very beautiful. Her most distinctive features were her eyes, large and brown, with a softness of expression which reflected the tenderness of her heart. Her wavy brown hair had become gently tinged with gray, which added to her air of breeding and distinction. I admired her as a woman of the world, as well as a person of kind and sympathetic character.

Kitty and I settled down together at 2, Rue Balny d'Avricourt, in an exclusive residential section of Paris near the Arc de Triomphe. It was a comfortable modern apartment of five rooms and bath on the sixth floor of a twelve-apartment building. Kitty had furnished it according to French taste, with a few modern pieces—a large divan with leather back and arms, comfortable armchairs, gay, warm, rosy colors in the living room. It was an ideal home, and I settled into it as in a haven.

Kitty and I spent three calm and happy years in that apartment. Not once was there the slightest disagreement between Kitty and myself. Her friendship never faltered. She took charge of our common existence with serene efficiency; and though she managed things so as to make me feel that I shared equally in her responsibilities, I knew that actually it was Kitty who directed the affairs of our household.

If Kitty had any problems of her own, business or personal, I never knew of them. She handled her life smoothly and without effort. The course of the rest of our days seemed assured, charming and calm, a pleasant existence for which our moderate means would suffice, spent partly in Paris and partly on the French Riviera. When we were in Paris, I made regular visits to my brother's grave. I envisaged the future as continuing indefinitely in this course, in which we two, no longer young, would end our lives in this quiet fashion.

I had counted without the war.

When Germany attacked Poland, Kitty said to me:

"This war is my war for two reasons. England is the country of my birth and France is the country of my choice. I am English by birth and French by marriage. I shall stay here. But you are an American, and your country is neutral. There is no reason why you should take the risks of war. I shall miss you if you go—but I think you ought to return to the United States."

I knew what Kitty had in mind. Every one was predicting immediate bombing of Paris as soon as the war began. She was protecting me, as she had always protected me, ever since we had first met.

"No, Kitty," I smiled back to her, "you can't get rid of me as easily as that. When I came to Paris, we entered into an unspoken compact to remain together. There was no three-year limit, and no special clause about wars. Let's forget about my going back to America. I'm legally a neutral, yes—but tell me what I can do to help your two countries."

The next day we both joined the Foyer du Soldat—the French equivalent of the U.S.O. We busied ourselves sending packages to soldiers, visiting their families, sitting with the wounded in the hospitals. We fell into a new routine, which in its turn became familiar and accustomed. The word "war" lost most of its terrors. Once again, we seemed to be caught up in a quiet enough pattern, one unlikely to lead us into perils or adventures. Even when the eight months of the "phony war" as you called it in America, or the *drôle de guerre*, as we described it in France, were suddenly ended by Germany's attack, we did not realize at once that the whole order of our existence was threatened. We were so busy, indeed, that we did not wake up to our danger until the Germans were actually hammering at the gates of Paris.

The end of our ivory tower existence came one day before the Nazis entered Paris, and here our real story begins—on the day of June 13, 1940.

CHAPTER TWO

Flight from Paris

FOR the third time, Kitty hung up the telephone with an air of resignation. For the third time, the repeated muffled ringing of the phone had told her that the friend she had called was not at home.

"All our friends seem to have left Paris already," she said. "We're the only ones left."

"I'll call the American Embassy," I said. "After all, I'm an American. They ought to be willing to tell me if the Germans are going to besiege Paris."

A startled voice answered me at the Embassy:

"Are you still in town? Don't you know that the government has moved to Tours? The Germans will be in Paris in a matter of hours —not days, hours! The city is being handed over without resistance."

For an instant, terror clutched at my heart. Then I hung up, and told Kitty what I had just heard. Pain and astonishment showed on her usually beautifully impassive features.

"No!" she cried. "No! It can't be! It's impossible! The French give up Paris without a battle! Why, only a few days ago Premier Paul-Reynaud said they would fight before Paris and defend every building, house by house. He begged the people not to flee, he told them not to listen to rumors, he said every one should stay where he was . . ."

"And meanwhile," I said, "he and his government have gotten away to Tours. That's proof enough that Paris has been abandoned to her fate. It's a pity they wouldn't tell the people. Don't they remember what the Germans did in Vienna, Prague, Warsaw—everywhere they set foot? Of course, a lot of people have gone already, but they went without really knowing what the situation was. We've just been handed over to the Germans, a million or two of us, without even being asked how we felt about it!"

I took Kitty's hand in mine, and went on:

13

"I don't intend to be handed over to the Nazis like that, Kitty!
I didn't come to Paris from New York to live under German domination. Let's try to get out before they get here."

Kitty was efficiency itself. A few seconds were always enough for
her to make a decision. Almost before the words were out of my
mouth, she was on the way to the garage to get the car.

Left alone in the apartment, I moved from one room to another
in hopeless despair. I pulled out a trunk and began to stuff our most
valued possessions in it—the things I hated above all to leave to the
Germans. But what to leave behind, what to take? The choice was
difficult.

Our five-room apartment had long been too small for all our
things. When Kitty decided to live apart from her husband, she had
taken all her belongings with her, and after my husband's death, I
brought all my movable property to Paris when I joined her.
In the years we had lived together since, we had accumulated
antique furniture, pictures, rugs, bric à brac—innumerable beautiful
things which we had planned to spend the rest of our lives enjoying.
Our closets and drawers were crammed with clothing, furs, linen,
and jewelry.

I saw at once that we could not possibly take everything we treasured, and the impossibility of deciding what to leave behind soon
brought me to a dead stop. I was standing before the almost empty
trunk, staring into it stupidly, when the door was flung open with
a bang and Kitty rushed in.

"Everybody's gone, Etta!" she cried. "Even the garage owner has
disappeared. The only one left there was the old watchman. It was
all I could do to get him to let me take the car."

She shot an accusing glance at the unfilled trunk.

"My God, haven't you started packing yet?"

And she dove into the closets like a whirlwind, throwing out a
storm of clothing which I crammed into our bags. In a sort of blind
frenzy we packed what we could, shoved everything else back into
the closets, and pushed cherished personal belongings into the
deepest recesses of bureau and secretary drawers, in a vague unde-
fined hope that they would not be disturbed. Then we snatched up

our three precious dogs, Winkie, Chinka and Mickey, and fled We locked the door carefully behind us, and took the key along—though even then we had little hope that this would protect us from looting.

Our trunk, containing only jewelry and our most necessary clothing, was stowed away in the rear baggage compartment. Our bags shared the car with us. Kitty twisted the ignition key, stepped on the starter, threw in the clutch—and we were off, on a journey to nowhere in particular. Just away. Away from the Germans we could almost feel hurrying after us.

June 13, 1940, was a Thursday—but the deserted Paris streets through which we drove gave the city a feeling of Sunday. Hardly a car was to be seen. Only a few scattered pedestrians were in the streets. They looked nervous and apprehensive, hardly reconciled to the idea of living in Paris under German occupation.

But as we turned into the Boulevard Raspail from the Boulevard St. Germain, the impression of Sunday suddenly vanished. Ahead of us, the broad avenue leading towards the southern exits from the city was jammed with vehicles. The Boulevard Raspail had become a one-way street. Both roadways, on either side of the strip of green grass in the middle, were jammed with cars heading south, running an obstacle race with one another to reach the Porte d'Orléans.

Route Nationale No. 20, the broad highway which connects Paris with the south of France, was too narrow to accommodate the stream of frightened humanity which tried to flow along it to safety. In autos, on foot, on bicycles, thousands of refugees, as far ahead as we could see, blocked the road and struggled to advance. It was easy to understand now why the streets of Paris had been deserted. All Paris was on this highway.

Forward movement was confined to a few inches at a time. Rare traffic policemen were striving desperately to win an uneven struggle against chaos. They succeeded momentarily in lining cars up abreast, all facing the same way. They didn't have to worry about traffic coming in the opposite direction. No one was trying to get into Paris, from the south. The only movement towards the city was from the other side—that of the German Army, whose forward movement seemed to be communicated through space, by some mysterious process, to this civilian horde, and to furnish the impelling force which drove it forward.

Every sort of vehicle hemmed us in—limousines, horse-drawn carts, trucks, automobiles with household goods piled high upon their tops, all slowly oozing southward. On one side of us a typical middle-class Frenchman in city clothes was pushing a wheelbarrow full of his belongings. Behind him was a luxurious automobile, and that in turn was followed by a smart carriage, with a liveried footman sitting next to the coachman.

The noise was indescribable. Every driver was honking his horn continuously at those in front of him, and those who had no horns made up for it by shouting at the top of their lungs. Whenever a foot of clear space opened in the road there was a pellmell rush to occupy it, which usually ended in an inextricable tangle of the rival vehicles.

To one helpless traffic policeman standing impotent and bewildered in the middle of the road an irate driver near us shouted: "Why don't you let us go ahead? Why don't you *do* something?"

"Do? Do? What do you expect me to do?" the policeman shouted back. "It's like this all the way to Orléans. You're lucky if you can make three or four miles an hour."

Actually, that was much more than we made. We were a helpless unit in that endless, almost unmoving stream, which stretched ahead of us, we knew, for two hundred miles. Usually, we jarred forward a foot or two at a time. When we were lucky, we moved ahead as much as a few hundred feet, as the whole line hitched itself slowly forward before lurching to another stop. After each such movement, we would have to wait fifteen minutes or half an hour before we could budge again. Then the line would creep forward once more, and then stop. Hitch forward and wait, hitch forward and wait, over and over, interminably. It seemed that we had always been trapped in this monstrous glacier-flow, that we should never get out of it again.

Kitty looked at her watch.

"Five o'clock," she said. "We started at nine this morning, and we've covered about twelve miles. We'd have gotten farther walking.

We might as well have stayed in Paris. Every one on this road will be caught by the Germans."

Night fell. The endless line of cars was still crawling at snail's pace along the road to Orléans. Kitty hailed a motorcycle policeman who came along the edge of the road from the opposite direction, making difficult upstream progress against the flood of cars.

"*C'est impossible.* There's nothing to be done, Madame," he said in answer to her question. "The road is blocked all the way to Orléans. It will be days before it can be cleared."

"Then in that case the Germans are sure to catch up with us," Kitty murmured in despair.

The policeman shrugged.

"The Germans aren't gods either," he said. "How do you expect them to get over this road? They say it's General Weygand's idea to let refugees block this highway so that the Germans won't be able to catch up to the French Army before it has had time to organize a new line of defense."

He saluted, and put-putted off. We looked at each other in dismay. Then Kitty, to my surprise, suddenly broke into ironic laughter.

"Well," she explained, "this is a pretty kettle of fish! So it's we women and non-combatants who are supposed to hold back the Germans! I suppose that's all right for me. I'm English by birth and French by marriage. That makes me a belligerent, all right. But you're an American. You're supposed to be neutral What do you mean by daring to oppose the German Army?"

And she went off into another peal of laughter—but it didn't sound much like mirth.

Morning dawned with the situation unchanged. We had spent it in the car on the highway, stopping sometimes for hours at a stretch. We dozed off fitfully once in a while, only to be awakened by a mad tooting of horns whenever a space opened up ahead of us.

That night was more unendurable than the day had been, although that had been tedious enough, because of our cramped, slow-moving progress. The hours were punctuated with unbearable sights and tales of suffering. They added to our misery as part of that tragic caravan, hungry, unkempt, aimless, travelling to an unknown destiny over impassable roads.

We heard those tales from hitch-hikers, pitiful bits of human flotsam, who crowded into the empty seats in our car and remained there until impatience drove them out to walk again, to be replaced at once by others. Under the stress of danger, they showed themselves in their true colors, without pretense—some selfishly thinking only of their own safety, others generous and kind, anxious to help those caught in the same dire straits as themselves.

The soldiers, in particular, were wonderful. I saw many of them giving bread and food from their packs to children, though they themselves were on emergency rations. Whenever a civilian car broke down—and they broke down frequently, overloaded and overtaxed as they were—there was always a soldier on hand to fix it, or try to fix it.

But during the night, there were few incidents to relieve the awful monotony of this interminable progress. We sat straight upright in the car, our dogs curled uncomfortably in our laps. Occasionally our tired eyelids would close, our heads drop forward—and the movement would jerk us back again to uncomfortable consciousness. No lights beckoned us forward, or helped us to find our way. The blackout was complete.

In the unfathomable darkness about us, we could hear the trudge of tired feet as thousands of refugees plodded doggedly by our motionless car, but we could see only those who brushed against it. Gradually, as the light grew stronger in the east, we began to make out their dim figures as they passed—mostly civilians, but some limping wounded soldiers, evacuated from the hospitals of Paris. If they wanted to escape the Germans, they had to do it on foot. Ambulances only had space for the gravely wounded.

Nine o'clock! We had been on the road for twenty-four hours— and we were still in the outskirts of Paris. We stopped at a roadside restaurant, and bought a small piece of Camembert cheese with bread and butter for the equivalent of 75 cents. I remember arguing with Kitty that it was a ridiculous price. She laughed at the idea that prices had any importance at such a time. We shared the food with the dogs. They were obviously hungrier than we were, and less worried.

We hitched forward again, start and stop, start and stop, for another half-mile or so. It brought us to an inn, in front of which an excited group was shouting and gesticulating.

"What is it?" called Kitty, as our car ground to one of its periodical stops. "What's happened?"

A man on the edge of the crowd answered.

"*C'est terrible!* The Germans are in Paris," he cried. "The radio has just announced it. That scoundrel Ferdonnet—you know, the traitor of Stuttgart—made the broadcast himself. He even had the nerve to apologize because it didn't happen on June 15, as he predicted a month ago, but on June 14, that the advance guard of the German Army entered Paris."

The line ahead of us hitched forward again, and though the Frenchman was still talking, we had to move on. I looked at Kitty. She had crouched down over the wheel and was looking intently ahead, her lips very tight. I didn't dare speak.

Instead, I tried to realize the news I had just heard, for though I had been prepared for it, I hadn't really let myself believe that it could come. Now it had happened, and the brutal fact was like a slap in the face. I tried to imagine what it would be like in Paris, the beloved Ville Lumière, under German domination, with Nazi soldiers goose-stepping down the Champs-Elysées. The very idea sent a cold chill down my back.

"And what's going to happen to us?" I asked myself.

For the first time, I realized that our situation was hopeless. We had left almost everything we owned behind us in Paris, and the Germans were already in possession there. We were slowly creeping along towards an unknown destination, and it did not even seem likely that we would reach it. If only we could proceed towards it, whatever it was, so long as it would take us out of reach of the Germans!

The long line had come to a standstill again. Some distance ahead of us, the highway curved to the right, and we could see a motionless line of vehicles stretching ahead of us for a mile or more. It was clear that an hour or two of tedious inching forward would be necessary to take us even as far ahead as we could see.

"My nerves won't stand much more of this," Kitty said suddenly. "The Germans are in Paris, and we aren't sixty miles from there. That means they can catch up to us in two or three hours."

"But how can they if the road is blocked?" I objected.

"You don't believe that stupid policeman, do you?" Kitty answered. "If I know the Germans, they're quite capable of using any means to sweep us off the road if they want to use it for their own troops and tanks."

"But what can we do?" I asked. "Hadn't we better leave the car, and go ahead on foot? At least we could get off the road then—if they come."

"No," Kitty said. "I've a better idea. The next time we come to a crossroad, I'm going to get off this accursed highway and try to cut through the country by the back roads."

As we were still motionless, Kitty got out her Michelin road map, and checked the routes. We found that besides the main National Road we were on, another chain of roads led south from Paris, almost parallel with it. From time to time, a crossroad connected the two. Although the other was indicated as a narrow country lane, probably in bad repair, we figured that it was likely to be jammed also, but not as congested as the main highway. In any case, it would be less likely to receive attention from the Germans. We thought that by shifting to this road, and perhaps criss-crossing from one to another as necessity demanded, we might be able to put another 150 miles between ourselves and the Germans in the next twenty-four hours. Then we could breathe freely again.

Kitty turned into the first crossroad, not much more than a dirt path winding between plowed fields on either side. A great feeling of relief seemed to affect not only us, but even the car, as for the first time it was able to speed forward unimpeded.

The deep ruts showed that this was a road ordinarily used only by peasant carts. But it was dry and hard, and as there were hardly any other cars on it, we were able to make forty miles an hour. We would have felt happier, though, if we had been making that speed southward, instead of in a direction which took us no farther from Paris.

We came shortly to another road leading southward, and on checking with the map, found it to be parallel to that which we had left. To our delight, no traffic was in sight. We turned into it and sped along, congratulating ourselves on finding this means of escape, and wondering why we had not thought of it before.

Rows of waving wheat rushed by us on either side. The road was bumpy, and we were pretty well shaken up, but we didn't care. Every minute carried us farther away from the Germans, and that was all that counted.

Our good luck didn't last long. After a few miles, the road turned to the left, and once again we were running in a direction which didn't take us away from Paris.

And then the blow came. Ahead of us, the road filled with automobiles—pouring *towards* us. As the first cars reached us, people shouted from them: "Turn back! Turn back! The Germans are behind us!"

Kitty applied the brakes, and the car stopped with a jerk. I pulled out the Michelin map, and set to studying it again. I found a road a little way back which took a southwesterly direction, and we decided to try that. But we had only been on it for a few moments when another horde of refugees came rushing towards us, crying once again that the Germans were behind them. By this time we had become quite bewildered, and even the map was no help to us. We neither knew where we were, nor in what direction we were going. All we could do was to follow the others. The next time we came to a highway sign, I checked with the map once more, and discovered that although our speedometer showed that we had covered 200 miles, we were only twelve miles south of the spot where we had left the main highway.

Night overtook us again, and as the complete darkness of the nationwide blackout covered us, we realized that we would have to abandon our plan. During the day we had been able to orient ourselves, but with darkness and the blotting out of landmarks, we lost our sense of direction completely. We were in deadly fear of turning in the wrong direction and running straight into the Germans.

We bowed to the inevitable. We decided to get back to the main highway while we still had a chance of finding it.

CHAPTER THREE

The English Pilot

IT WAS already dark when we reached the national road again, but we knew in advance we were coming to it, for we could hear the nerve-racking cacophony of the honking horns, at first faintly, and then louder and louder as we approached. We guided ourselves by the sound, for we had lost all sense of direction. We didn't know at what point we were rejoining the road, or how far we were from Paris.

We had reached a point about a hundred yards from the road when we heard a faint hum which rose swiftly in a fierce crescendo over our heads. With a jerk, Kitty stopped the car--so suddenly that I felt that she must have been expecting that sound and dreading it.

The hum became a roar, as the airplane passed by just ahead of us, and from the roar emerged the staccato tat-tat-tat of a machine gun. We could see the hulk of the plane in a denser black against the dark sky, and the flame spitting from the nozzles of its guns, as it swept over the crowded road, pouring death into the trapped ranks below.

In a matter of seconds, the crowded highway was emptied of its human freight. Terror-stricken drivers turned their cars off the road, into trees, into ditches, over the fields. Some of them overturned, and their occupants squirmed out and ran in panic from the road, or threw themselves into ditches. Only a few cars remained in the road, stalled, motionless. The figures in them were motionless, too. They had not joined the mad rush to get off the road because they were dead. They had been mowed down indiscriminately, men, women and children, by the sudden hail of death that had rained down upon them out of the sky.

Twenty minutes later several more planes swooped low over the road, but there was little for them to do. No one had attempted to get back on the highway. Only the stalled cars of the dead still remained for targets.

We had thrown ourselves into a roadside ditch with other refugees, and stayed there through the second attack. For some time, we didn't dare venture out. We remained lying in the dirt, apprehensively scanning the sky in the direction of Paris, wondering whether it was over, or whether more planes might suddenly roar down upon us if we emerged from our shelter.

I felt Kitty's hand squeeze mine. I looked towards her. Her eyes were wet with tears.

"Don't be afraid, Kitty," I said. "God will protect us."

Kitty shook her head.

"I'm not afraid. That's not why I'm crying. I can't help it when I think of those poor people—here, and in Poland, in Belgium, in Holland, the poor innocent refugees on whom the Boches turned their machine guns to clear the roads for their armies. I read about it in Paris, of course, but I didn't really believe it. I didn't want to believe it. I thought it was propaganda. I didn't think even German officers would be capable of ordering the massacre of innocent people. I didn't think German soldiers would be brutal enough to obey such orders. But it's true. We've seen it ourselves. We've seen them shooting down harmless, unarmed, helpless civilians!"

Kitty was silent for a moment. Then she added, almost under her breath, as though she were talking to herself:

"How does a young German flier feel, I wonder, when he opens fire on terror-stricken women and children—like us?"

All about us there was a ghostly silence. We knew that there were hundreds of people nearby, hugging the ground in fear like ourselves, but we might have been alone in this unknown open country. Then we heard a woman groaning somewhere in the dark, not far away. From her moans, we judged that she had been wounded. But no one offered to go to her aid. No one dared move.

It seemed ages before first one or two, then dozens of men and women began to creep cautiously out of the ditches. They stood up, looking first towards the sky, and began to collect their scattered belongings. Some of them stood aimlessly in the fields, as though at a loss what to do. They had been going somewhere, they didn't quite know where, running from a danger behind them. And now the danger had caught up to them. They stood still, trapped, deprived of motion, with nowhere to go, nothing to do. And we were trapped with them.

From the darkness the noise of many motors made itself heard; and suddenly, with a rush, the German Army was upon us.

They were motorcycle troops, rushing southward at breakneck speed, driving forward through the dark with complete assurance that the planes ahead of them would have swept the road clear, like great brooms. Without slowing up, they swung around the few stalled cars still standing motionless in the road.

There was something inhuman about those riders in their dark gray uniforms. They seemed like part of the machines they rode, as cold and as unfeeling. They looked neither to the right nor to the left as they roared by. I don't know what we had expected from the Germans, but certainly not this, certainly not that they would ignore our very presence. It was more fearsome than if they had dismounted from their motorcycles and arrested us, almost more fearsome than if they had fired on us. This passage of mounted automatons who seemed not to see us at all imbued us with a chill far greater than any we had felt even during the confused panic of the airplane attack. I thought I had been frightened then. It was nothing to the deep-buried fear that clutched at the pit of my stomach, and twisted and turned in my flesh.

But there was nothing we could do. We could only wait. We stood by our car, just before the point where the crossroad entered the highway, and watched.

Light armored cars followed the motorcycles. Sitting bolt upright in them were more lifeless statues, very young soldiers, almost boys. Stiff and morose, they were dragged forward by the iron monsters in which they rode like victims to a sacrifice rather than triumphant conquerors. Not one of them spared even a glance for the refugees who lined the road on both sides. They were whisked by, pawns in the game of war, seemingly devoid of any human feelings, of joy or of pity.

The remnants of a French regiment sat alongside the road across from us. Half an hour before, the men beside the road and the men rushing down it might have been fighting each other. But now the battle had been adjourned, and they did not deign even to notice one another. The French soldiers sat beside the road, smoking, watching the procession of their enemies pass without seeming to see them. Their uniforms were clean. It was obvious that they had not yet been in battle. Perhaps they had been on their way to a front which had now disappeared. They had been too late, and there was no point in fighting now. They simply sat there and stared through the German soldiers passing south. And the Germans, in turn, glared forward stiffly into the empty air ahead. Nothing could have increased the effect of unreality, of a nightmare from which we must soon awake before the tension became intolerable, more than this mutual ignoring of one army by the other.

The rumble of heavier engines filled the air, and shook the earth about us. The tanks were coming. The very air seemed to have come to life and to be shouting with brazen lungs. They burst upon us, not only down the main highway, but from the crossroads, roaring upon us from the route which we had followed through the night, mercifully too slowly to reach the road before the Nazi planes swept over it. They plowed across the fields. They seemed to be everywhere, to possess the whole earth about us.

It was an interminable parade which passed before our eyes, lasting all night, and then through the day. It was five o'clock in the afternoon before the road cleared. As the rear guard of the Germany Army passed down the road and disappeared in its own dust, it dropped men off behind it. Every two hundred yards, unfolding in a regular pattern behind the moving army, a German motorcyclist stopped, and took up his position. The military necessities had been satisfied for this region. Now civilians could be attended to. At last there was some one charged with looking out for us.

The nearest motorcyclist swept up to us, and stopped, one foot on the ground, holding his machine up at an angle as its motor coughed and spat.

"You will go back to Paris," he told us in excellent French.

"But we were going the other way," Kitty pleaded. "We want to go to Nice."

The German's words were polite, but there was a sneer on his lips as he answered:

"That, Madame, is the way we are going. You will go back to Paris."

What else could we do? We turned our car into the highway, and started back over the same road we had taken southward, ages ago, it seemed, in another existence. Once again we were in the same congested stream of traffic. We moved once more at the same snail's pace, though in the opposite direction. But there was a difference now. No one seemed to be in any hurry to arrive. When the road was blocked, and there was a long wait, no horns tooted, no one shouted at those ahead to get going. Every once in a while, the motorcycle guards, obeying an order passed down the line, hustled us all off the road, into the ditches or the fields, and another motorized column would roar down the vacant lane we had left. Then we could turn back into the road again—those of us who had not broken axles or turned over in the process—and a few miles farther on repeat the same action all over again.

We passed a group of unarmed French soldiers standing by the roadside, guarded by Germans with fixed bayonets. They looked frightened, unlike fighting men. They had been taken one by one out of passing cars in which they had sought to escape.

A car ahead of us was stopped, and a squad of Germans pulled out a young man in civilian clothes. He protested:

"What are you taking me for? I'm not a soldier."

A German shouted at him coarsely:

"*Maul halten!* Do you think we're fools? You can't escape just by putting on civilian clothes, you know. Get over there with the others."

And he was shoved into the group of forlorn frightened French prisoners.

"Look," Kitty said suddenly. "*English* prisoners!"

It was a very small group, standing by the roadside, hemmed in by German guards. Three of them wore the uniform of the R.A.F. The car in which they had tried to escape was standing in the ditch at the side of the road.

By evening we reached the roadside inn where we had learned of the fall of Paris on the southward trip. We were exhausted, ready to drop. But when the innkeeper, standing in the doorway, saw us pull up and stop, he motioned us away.

"I have nothing to give you," he said, "nothing at all. A million people have been through here in the last two days. What can you expect? They have eaten everything. There is nothing left, nothing."

I started to climb wearily back into the car, but Kitty touched me on the arm. She was incomparable in such situations.

"A cup of tea will be enough for us," she said, turning her most winsome smile on the innkeeper.

"*Pensez-vous!* I have no sugar," the innkeeper said, none too graciously.

"That doesn't matter," said Kitty. "We'll take it without sugar." And she marched straight in and sat down.

It worked. The innkeeper led us into an inner room, locked the door carefully behind us, and produced not only tea, but the sugar he had denied having. Perhaps it was the effect of Kitty's disarming smile which caused him later to confess that he had a small piece of salami and a little cheese left that we might have also.

It was the first food we had tasted in thirty-six hours. We were so exhausted and so hungry that we had no thought of discussing our predicament until we had finished. But then we began to talk; and at our first words the innkeeper asked:

"You are English?"

"I'm English," Kitty answered, "but I'm a French citizen now, since I married a Frenchman. My friend here is American."

"Then you can do something for me," the innkeeper said. "I don't speak English myself, and I have some one here who speaks only English. I can't make him understand me. Could you talk to him for me? Ask him how long he intends to stay. Tell him that I am very sorry, I don't want to ask him to leave—but there are Germans all around, they are hunting for Englishmen, and—you understand —it is dangerous for me. I am likely to get into trouble if he stays. Wait here a minute. I will bring him to you."

He left the room. Kitty and I looked at one another.

"An English soldier, no doubt," Kitty said. "He hasn't a chance of escaping, of course. They're sure to get him."

When the innkeeper returned, he was followed by a tall young man with reddish blond hair wearing a leather coat, beneath which the gray-blue uniform of the R.A.F. was visible. He was very young —barely twenty, it seemed. He came up to our table, smiling as calmly as though he were surrounded by friends, miles from any danger. He sat down with us, and told us in a few words who he was and how he had come to be there.

His name was William Gray. A pilot caught at Dunkirk, he had been unable to get to the evacuating ships and return to England. But with the aid of French peasants, he had managed to work his way through the German lines and had set out for the south of France, hoping to get below the territory held by the Germans. But they had moved faster than he had, and here they had caught up with him.

"I don't want to trouble you ladies," he said apologetically, "but if you would just tell this chap for me to be patient, that I will go as soon as he can get me some civilian clothes, I will be able to take care of myself after that."

"My poor friend," Kitty said, "civilian clothes won't do you any good. We've just come from the south, and we saw the Germans taking young men out of automobiles, uniforms or no uniforms. They'll take any one of military age. And as for you, who don't know a word of French—why, you couldn't walk ten steps without being caught."

The young flier stared at us incredulously. His face reflected disappointment and dismay.

"You think there's no chance? How about cutting across the fields?"

"Oh, that's just childish!" Kitty exclaimed, almost angrily. "The Germans are searching everywhere. They'll get you before you even reach a village."

The innkeeper had been standing in the doorway during this conversation, straining his ears as though he could understand by listening more closely. Now he broke in.

"What does he say?" he asked. "Is he going to go? I'm very sorry, you know—but really, you see how it is. I can't keep him here. They may come any minute. It is very dangerous."

"Have you any civilian clothes you can sell him?" Kitty asked.

"Never in the world!" the innkeeper cried excitedly. *"Quelle folie!* Tell him he must not put on civilian clothes. I am a good Frenchman, I hate the Germans and I respect the English, but that is something I can't do for him. It will mean his death if they catch him!"

We looked at the innkeeper in bewilderment.

"But don't you understand?" he hurried on, impatiently. "Explain this to him: if he is caught wearing his uniform, he will be treated as a prisoner of war. If he is in civilian clothes, he will be considered a spy. They will simply shoot him at once."

Kitty translated. Gray sat still for a moment. He hadn't thought of that.

"I guess they've got me," he said finally. He rose, with an embarrassed smile.

"I'm sorry I disturbed you, ladies. Will you do one more thing for me? Find out how much I owe. I'd better get out of here as soon as I can. If I'm going to be caught anyway, I'd better not involve any one else."

No translation was necessary. The innkeeper saw the Englishman take out his purse, and realized that he was about to be rid of his dangerous guest. Too happy at this relief to be interested in money, he pushed aside the Englishman's hand, indicating by gestures that he wanted no payment. Also in gestures, William Gray expressed his thanks, and moved, with uncertain step, towards the door.

"What are you going to do?" Kitty asked.

He turned, still smiling, a forced smile through which his weariness and despair showed only too plainly.

"I don't know," he answered, "but please don't worry about me. I'll be all right. I hope you'll excuse me for intruding on you."

I pressed Kitty's arm.

"Don't let him go," I whispered. Kitty looked at me in surprise. "Haven't you noticed," I went on, "how much he looks like Irving —the same nose, the same chin? He looks exactly as poor Irving did when he was twenty."

Kitty had known my brother well, before that awful day when we buried him in the Père Lachaise cemetery in Paris.

"If only for the sake of Irving's memory, we can't let this boy go,"

I begged. "We've got to get him out of this. We can't let the Germans get him."

"That's all very well," said Kitty, "but how can we prevent it? What can we do?"

"I have an idea," I went on. "Our car is just outside . . ."

"But you're crazy!" Kitty exclaimed. "Don't you remember how they stopped all the cars? They'd pick him up before we got half a mile away. You don't think the German military police will let us cart him off right under their noses, do you?"

"Wait a minute, Kitty," I said. "I've thought of that. How about our luggage compartment? If we take the trunk out, he can hide there."

"All the way to Paris?"

"Yes," I said, "all the way to Paris. He'll have a better chance of giving the Germans the slip in a big city than here. We'll get him to Paris, and then figure out what to do with him there."

Kitty beamed on me with that enchanting smile which I had come to love so much in the years we had spent together. Automatically, she took over command again. I vaguely suspected her of having thought of the same plan before I uttered a word, and having simply left it to me to express what both of us desired. She hurried into the outer room, where William Gray was standing at the window, peering cautiously out towards the road.

"I say, Mr. Gray," she said, "come back here a moment. We want to talk to you."

And with that sentence, we were launched upon an adventure which a week earlier we would have dismissed as impossibly fantastic. Yet it had come about so naturally that neither Kitty nor myself realized that we had projected ourselves into a new course from which we would not thereafter be able to escape. We had closed the door on our calm unruffled existence.

CHAPTER FOUR

Running the Gauntlet

IT WAS no easy job for William Gray to stow himself away in the luggage compartment of our car, but he had to admit that it couldn't have been better arranged as a hiding place if it had been built especially for that purpose. It didn't open from the outside, like most luggage compartments. On the contrary, the opening was from the interior of the car, behind the back seats.

He was unfortunately tall, but luckily thin. He pulled himself in somehow or other, his long legs doubled up under him, and grinned at our expressions, which must have indicated our doubt that any one could ride long in so cramped a position.

"Now don't you worry about me," he assured us. "I'm quite comfortable. If by any chance the Germans find me here, you must swear up and down that you never saw me before in your lives, and don't know how I got in here. I'll say that I slipped in while you were in the inn eating. That way you won't get into any trouble on my account—in case."

We closed the luggage compartment on our passenger, and were on our way. The highway had cleared up somewhat now, and we made reasonable progress. There were guards all along the road, and three times before we reached the Porte d'Orléans, the point from which we had left Paris, we were stopped, and asked to show our papers.

We held them out with trembling hands, and our hearts were in our mouths as the guards peered into the car. But none of them made any motion to look into the luggage compartment and each time we drove on again, hearts thumping, but bursting with relief.

At the Porte itself, a more elaborate control had been set up. A German soldier assigned to inspect our car threw open the door, pushed our baggage aside and scrutinized the interior carefully, using a flashlight to illuminate every corner. His hand grazed the luggage compartment, and I held my breath. But he made no move to open it. He turned to us, and said in perfect French:

"Well, ladies, your wanderings on the French highways are over —at least, if you can prove you live in Paris. Have you your papers?"

We produced our identity cards, which gave our Paris address. Satisfied, he waved us on.

As soon as we were out of hearing, Kitty turned to me with a self-satisfied chuckle.

"Those efficient Germans aren't so smart, after all," she laughed. "Imagine! Four of them, and not one thought to look into the luggage compartment!"

"Thank God they didn't," I replied. "But after all, it's not so surprising. With a sentry every two hundred yards along the road watching every one who moves, it probably never occurred to them that any one would have an opportunity to stow some one away. Besides, the military police are only common soldiers. They've probably never seen a luggage compartment opening into a car before, and haven't any idea there would be room for a man to hide in it."

"There isn't much," Kitty said. "If we have to stop again, you'd better take a look at the poor fellow to make sure he hasn't suffocated."

A muffled voice reassured us from within the luggage compartment.

"I'm perfectly all right," William Gray said. "The only thing that worries me is that I might get you into trouble."

"Hush," Kitty warned him. "Not another word. Some one might hear you."

Although we had made better time coming back than going, still it had taken us all night to reach Paris. By the time we had cleared the bottleneck of the Porte d'Orléans, where thousands of returning refugees like ourselves were having their papers checked by the German military police, it was broad daylight. Once out of the congestion about the gate, we were able to speed along the outer boulevards at a normal pace, for the first time since we had started out. All about us we saw the signs of the German occupation.

It was with a constriction of the heart that I saw the Eiffel Tower again, for at its top, where the French Tricolor had always whipped proudly to the breeze, the Nazi swastika now flew.

German military cars rushed past us. When we reached the bridge we wanted to take across the Seine we had a long wait, until a German motorized regiment had passed over it. We went by the Louvre, and there, too, we saw the swastika flying where the Tricolor should have been.

But as we swung through the Place de la Concorde and into the Champs-Elysées, I could not restrain the feeling of joy at being back in Paris, even under the Germans, which always gripped me whenever I returned from a trip to look up that magnificent stretch towards the beautiful silhouette of the Arc de Triomphe, shining at the top of its hill against the clear blue sky.

Beneath its vault, I knew, lay the body of the Unknown Soldier, guarded by the Eternal Flame. From this point, every year, the great military parades which commemorated the storming of the Bastille, July 14, the day of French independence, took their start. I remembered how, nearly a year ago, I had seen the French Army in all its impressive might march down this broad avenue, followed by tanks which shook the ground and made the air vibrate with their roar, while from the sky behind the Arc, 600 planes swooped down above the procession. And now that mighty army had been defeated, and the avenue over which Louis the Fourteenth's horses had pelted to Versailles, the avenue over which Napoleon's victorious forces had marched into the city, was filled with hurrying German military cars, the swastika painted on their sides . . .

We circled the Arc, and a moment later the car ground to a stop in front of 2, Rue Balny d'Avricourt—home!

"At last," Kitty said, cutting the motor. "Very good. Very, very good indeed."

I was panic-stricken at the idea of getting out of the car. Somehow it had seemed safer to be sitting in it. It was our fortress.

"What do we do now?" I asked faintly.

"We must be very careful," Kitty said. "We must be discreet, and we must be on the alert every instant. Don't make any false moves —just act natural."

"Do—do I get out first?" I gulped.

I sensed imaginary Nazis everywhere, waiting to pounce upon me the moment I set foot on the ground. They might be watching us from behind lamp posts, or around the corner, or from any window in the street. They might even be waiting for us in the entrance, ready to trap us as we came in.

"Wait!" Kitty whispered tensely.

A German military guard came marching down the street, surrounding a French soldier. They have probably been searching the houses, I thought, looking for soldiers in hiding, and this is one of the poor chaps they caught.

We remained in the car, motionless. I looked at Kitty, and she seemed very pale. I wondered if she had just realized fully, as I had, at that very moment, that this adventure of ours could be very dangerous for ourselves, that William Gray was not the only one of us who risked being shot.

We waited for a few moments after the Germans had disappeared around the corner.

Kitty turned towards the luggage compartment.

"Mr. Gray! Can you hear me?" she called softly.

"Yes," came his muffled voice.

"We are going to get out now. Button up your leather coat over your uniform before you come out. I'll go first, then Etta, then you slip out, follow us into the house and get into the elevator right after us. Act naturally, and don't hesitate, whether we meet any one or not. Don't say anything now. The street is clear. Here we go!"

Briskly, Kitty opened the car door and stepped out. If I had worried about going first a moment ago, I was twice as frightened now at the prospect of being left behind. I sprang out of the car after Kitty and hurried across the sidewalk behind her. I heard the door of the car slam shut, and I knew William Gray was just behind me. I didn't dare look back. It was only a few steps across the sidewalk, but it seemed to take forever to cross it. Then we were in the familiar entry of our home, and I felt better. We were in luck. There was no one in the hall, and the elevator, of the self-service type common in French apartment houses, was, for once, empty, and waiting on the ground floor.

We got in without losing a second, fearful that some other tenant might follow behind us. The doors swung shut, Kitty pressed the sixth floor button, and the elevator rumbled slowly upward. I held my breath. My nails were cutting into the palms of my hands. I didn't dare look at either of the others.

It seemed to me that the elevator took long enough to rise to the top of the Empire State Building. At last it jarred to a stop. Kitty stepped out, fitted her key into the lock, and pushed open our apartment door. We hurried in, and I threw myself against the door and pushed the safety bolt, in a state approaching panic. For a moment, I leaned against the door. My legs seemed too weak to support my weight. Then I tottered towards a chair and sat down. It was good to sit down, safe in my own apartment, surrounded by my own familiar belongings.

Kitty's nerves must have been better than mine. She threw herself into an armchair and laughed happily.

"There, you see, Etta, everything went off very neatly," she said. "Who would believe us if we told them that we had smuggled an English aviator past hundreds of German guards into Paris, and into our apartment?"

I was still shaken.

"Thank God for our good luck," I said. "Suppose we had met some one downstairs or in the elevator? I'm certainly glad that's over. I wouldn't go through it again for a million dollars."

I wonder what I would have done if I could have had a flash of the future when I spoke those words? I thought we had come to the end of our adventure. It was only beginning.

"Oh, it might not have been so bad even if some one had seen him," Kitty said. "They might not have noticed his uniform under that coat. By the way, what's become of him?"

William Gray appeared in the doorway.

"You know, I shouldn't have done this," he said. "I didn't realize—I shouldn't have let you take so much risk on my account. I really don't know what to say. I can't forgive myself for putting you in such a position."

He looked younger than ever in his embarrassment. The expression on his face showed his genuine deep concern.

"Now listen to me, young man," Kitty said firmly. "On the road, you were planning to tell any one who discovered you that you had crept into our car without our knowledge, and let us out of it that way. Well, you can't do that now. You're in our apartment, and no one is going to make the Germans believe, if they catch you, that we don't know you and have no idea how you got in. We're your accomplices now. We're all in this together, and there's no point in worrying about water that's gone over the dam. You're our guest. Make yourself at home, and forget about how we got into this pickle. What we have to do now is figure out how to get out of it."

And with that, she swept off to her own room to tidy up, humming a gay little melody which always came into her head when she felt particularly happy, and, above all, pleased with herself.

CHAPTER FIVE

"They Are Here"

IT WAS EASY enough for Kitty to say that we had to find some way of getting out of our predicament, but it wasn't so simple to do. Here we were, two middle-aged respectable women of sheltered background, with an English pilot on our hands, in enemy territory, and our problem was to find out how he could escape and get back to England. We knew it could be done, we knew that some persons had done it, but we had no idea how to go about it.

I remembered the "underground railway" of pre-Civil War days, which spirited runaway slaves into the free states. I supposed some similar organization existed to help hidden English soldiers—but how could we get in touch with it? It didn't seem likely that any one in our quiet circle would know anything about it. We were baffled, completely at a loss. We didn't know where to turn, how to begin.

Meantime the Gestapo was conducting its search for hidden soldiers with characteristic thoroughness. House to house searches yielded many Frenchmen of military age, hiding with friends or relatives or even with complete strangers, who had taken them in just as we had taken William Gray in. Once in a while they also got an English civilian or soldier. We heard that they relished such captures particularly; so we knew that our guest would strike them as a particular prize—if they caught him.

We lived for a week in an atmosphere of almost constant terror, expecting daily that the Gestapo would get around to us. We were as careful as we could be. William never went near the window, never answered the telephone. We even refused to let him smoke his pipe, lest the odor should give him away. It irked him that he couldn't shave, since, of course, he had had nothing with him, and we didn't dare to make the unexplainable purchase of a razor.

Whenever the doorbell rang, William dashed to the bathroom and locked himself in. But we realized that this would be no good if the Germans really wished to search the apartment, and after a while he gave it up.

The possibility of a search was a real danger, not a fancy conjured up out of our fear. The Germans were doing it daily. They took a block at a time, shut off all the streets leading to it, and then went through it methodically, apartment by apartment, not forgetting the cellars and roofs, searching every nook and cranny.

It was very clear that if such a search occurred in our block, William would certainly be found—and we would be arrested along with him. As the searches continued, it became daily more evident that it was urgent to find a solution. Our immunity could not last forever.

But where could we turn for help?

Both of us had many friends in Paris, but most of them seemed to have gotten away earlier than we did, and were in the unoccupied zone. Kitty sat at the telephone for hours, dialling one number after the other, but always the regular distant hum told her that no one was at the other end of the line. Some of our friends had made no attempt to leave Paris; but, perhaps not very curiously, those who had been willing to stay behind though they knew the Germans were coming were not the ones we felt we could trust with our secret.

For by this time, the change had already taken place which split the French people into two groups—those who were pro-British and those who were anti-British, which was practically the same thing as saying those who were anti-Vichy and those who were pro-Vichy. Later, as the Germans taught the French to hate them, the pro-British element increased greatly; but in the opening days of the occupation, deceived by clever German propaganda and the studied and ordered politeness of the Germans, which masked their real intentions, many Frenchmen bowed to the act of Marshal Pétain in concluding an armistice with the Germans.

A formidable propaganda campaign was begun, attacking the pre-war régime of France, democracies in general, and the British in particular. The newspapers and the radio, all under German control, insisted day after day that the British were to blame for the defeat of France, that Britain had forced France into the war and then abandoned her to her fate when catastrophe threatened. The propagandists even went back into history, and brought out a popular-priced edition of the story of the trial of Jeanne d'Arc, to show that English perfidy had been exercised against France even then, when they burned a Frenchwoman who has since become a saint.

The continuous reiteration of this propaganda began to have its effect upon some Frenchmen. They had at first sought to explain the staggering blow which had been dealt them by some hitherto unsuspected military weakness of the French Army, or by the effect on the public morale of the broadcasts of Ferdonnet, the traitor of Stuttgart, who spoke nightly to France from Germany. But under the impact of German propaganda, Frenchmen began to discover a new scapegoat—the English. There were many of them who were ready to impute all the blame to them. And so France was divided into two camps, those who accepted this German theory which placed responsibility on the English, and those who fought against it.

Most of our acquaintances who had stayed in Paris belonged to the first group. Paris was still more or less deserted. Few persons had returned of their own free will. But once in a while we would meet some old friend in the street. If Kitty felt that he might prove sympathetic, she would hint that we had heard something about an English aviator in hiding, anxious to escape to England, hoping thus to find some one who might help us.

But the result was invariable. Always our friend's face would harden and his manner become cold. We would feel a sense of restraint between us. We knew that none of them would report us, but we knew also that they would do nothing to help us. They were afraid. We could understand that, for we were afraid too.

The only one who shared our secret was our Breton maid, Margot, who had been with Kitty for twelve years. We trusted her completely. When we returned to Paris, we sent word to her at her native village, to which she had gone some time before we left, and she returned to us immediately. She often heard our long conversations about the steps we thought of taking to help save William Gray. She never joined them, never mentioned him, but we knew she would not betray us.

Nothing useful came out of those long futile conversations.

Through them, we arrived at only one positive conclusion. That was that we had not only the Germans, but also a certain group of Frenchmen, to fear. We had to be careful everywhere, with every one. It was not safe to assume that every Frenchman was automatically the enemy of the Germans who had conquered his country.

Fearful though we were for ourselves during this period, we could not fail to be touched by the behavior of William Gray. He was so tactful, so inconsolable that his presence was causing us so much concern, and so worried, not for himself, but for us, at the fact that there seemed to be no solution to the situation, that we felt more strongly than ever that we had done right in bringing him to Paris. More than ever, we felt that we must find some way to save him.

Once we caught him tiptoeing out of the door, dressed to leave, trying to relieve us of our troubles by removing from us the risk of his presence. Kitty pulled his leather jacket off herself, and scolded him like a little boy caught in some naughtiness.

"Besides," she ended, after a torrent of scolding, "that wouldn't have solved anything. They'd have caught you before you could get off this street. Do you think it would have been hard for them to find out where you came from? No, it's just no good, my young man. And whatever you may think, it isn't courageous either. It's unworthy of you, and it's unworthy of us."

"But really," William protested, "it's cowardly of me to stay here while my very presence is endangering you every day I remain."

With typical energy, Kitty put him in his place at once.

"I never heard such nonsense!" she snorted. "Cowardly, indeed! We're perfectly safe as long as you don't leave here. Who would think to look here for a British soldier? What's the use of all the trouble we've gone to already if you're not going to let us finish the job? Ungrateful brat!"

And she smiled broadly at the boy she was berating.

"Now let that be the last of that. You're staying here until we find out how to get you out of reach of the Germans. I don't know whether it will take a week or a month or the duration, but I do know one thing—we're not going to let you out of here until we know the Germans won't get you."

There was nothing William could do except give in. He went to his room with a heart-rending smile of gratitude on his worried boyish face. As the door closed behind him, Kitty turned towards me. I had thought she was exaggerating her emotion for William's benefit, but now I could see that she was still deeply agitated, profoundly troubled by what had just happened.

"Etta," she said, "we just *can't* let him go. I wouldn't have any peace of mind for the rest of my life. I hadn't told you before, because I didn't want to worry you unnecessarily, but I hear they're shooting all the British soldiers they catch now. They treat them as spies."

"How do you know?" I asked.

"Mr. Vuillemin told me. Of course, I don't know whether he was telling the truth or not, but what reason would he have to lie? He told me about one case in Belgium where the Germans rounded up a company of French soldiers. There was a British soldier with them. He had his uniform on, but he had some civilian clothes in a bag. He had intended to use them to escape. They lined up the Frenchmen and marched them off as prisoners of war, but they charged the Englishman with having civilian clothes because he was a spy, and shot him on the spot."

A sickening wave seemed to pass through me as I imagined the bullets of a firing squad tearing into the skull of the gentle boy in the next room.

"But, Kitty, you don't think they could treat William that way?"

"I'm afraid they could," Kitty said. "That story has been haunting me like a nightmare ever since Mr. Vuillemin told it to me—and you know he isn't the sort of person to pass on mere rumors. Every time I think of it, I think of poor naïve William Gray, and I'm determined they shan't get the chance to murder him. That's why we mustn't let him slip out, Etta, even though he is willing to sacrifice himself for us. We've *got* to keep him from falling into the hands of the Germans."

But once again, it was easier said than done. Trains were running regularly now from Paris to the unoccupied zone, but there seemed to be no solution there. We could perhaps have gotten him a pass (for once the German administration established itself in Paris, anything could be had from it for a price, even a pass to the unoccupied zone), but an official pass was no guarantee he could get out. Inspection of papers at the border between the two zones was most severe, and the authorities did not hesitate to send a whole train back for the slightest irregularity. We heard of one train which was sent back to Paris three times before it was finally permitted to cross the border. And, of course, William did not speak French.

The more we heard about those trains, the surer we were that we dared not send him out of the occupied zone by that route. We learned that the Germans examined every compartment minutely, to make sure that nothing and nobody was hidden in it. Passengers were searched, uniformed female police being provided to inspect the women.

It was forbidden to carry any written document from one zone to the other, and the police made an especially rigid search for letters. They were described as arrogant, affecting contempt and disgust while they turned out the contents of trunks and handbags. They seemed to take special delight in ordering passengers to step off trains to the platform for further investigation when they reached the border at night, after every one had undressed and gone to bed in the sleepers. We were told that they showed a preference for ordering women in flimsy night dresses off the train in this fashion.

Even after inspections had been finished, trains were sometimes held for hours, without explanation, while the anxious passengers wondered what was wrong, and doubted if they would ever get safely out of German territory. Sometimes, though all papers were in order, the passengers would be told that the frontier was closed and the train couldn't go through. That usually meant a wait of several days.

That was the legal way of crossing the frontier. We were sure it would never do for William. He would have to get across it by stealth—and we had heard a thousand stories about that.

We had been told that persons crossing the demarcation line surreptitiously had to go on foot, being careful to avoid the guards on both sides of the border. At first, the penalty for being caught was only being returned to the zone you were trying to escape from. Then orders were given to open fire on any one seen trying to get from one region into the other. Some persons were killed in this fashion, and those who were only wounded were sentenced to long terms in prison.

Yet men still risked their lives to get out of German-held territory nightly. They had to sacrifice all their belongings, for of course they could carry no baggage on a trip which might oblige them to walk as much as ten miles across rough country in pitch darkness. There were volunteer guides who would take them across, and sometimes sentinels could be bribed. But here, too, caution was necessary. Sometimes a guide would lead his charges straight into the arms of the Germans and collect a reward for his services. Or a sentry would accept a bribe—and then fire on the refugees who had paid him. Nobody could be trusted.

Many ingenious ruses were used to cross the line. In one village, for instance, there was a cemetery whose main gate opened into unoccupied territory. But in the rear wall was an old forgotten door which had not served for years; and that was in unoccupied territory. Inhabitants of the village at first were surprised to note a sudden increase in the number of mourners at local funerals. But they noted also that fewer mourners returned from the cemetery than went to it; and the old-timers recalled the disused door and realized that it was serving once more.

Another story we heard was that of a doctor whose house happened to straddle the line of demarcation. His practice increased enormously—for after seeing his patients, he let them go out by either the front or back door, without inquiring by which they had entered.

But none of these stories helped us, for naturally by the time they had become common knowledge, the Germans knew them, too. They had already arrested those concerned and plugged the leaks in the frontier by the time we heard about them. We couldn't find any one who knew about any such means of getting across the border which hadn't yet been discovered. Day after day, we ran up against a blank wall in our attempts to find out how to get William Gray out of danger.

Kitty was late for supper. Margot had prepared what she could. It wasn't much. We had discovered from bitter personal experience the truth of what we had been told, that wherever the Germans appeared, food disappeared. We had an extra disadvantage. We had three ration cards in the house—but four mouths to feed.

When Kitty breezed in, I could tell at once from the look on her face that it was good news which had detained her.

"Imagine, Etta!" she burst out, before she had even taken her hat off. "I've found some one who can help us! Do you remember Chancel, of the Gueules Cassées?"

I remembered him very well. He was a big husky chap, who had suffered a face wound in the last war. The men disfigured in that fashion had formed their own association, and called it Les Gueules Cassées (The Broken Mugs). Chancel held some official position in this group, exactly what I don't remember. We had met him at the Foyer du Soldat, where we had both worked before our attempt to get out of Paris.

"I ran into him on the subway," Kitty said. "I couldn't say very much to him there, of course, for you can never tell who may be listening. They say some Gestapo agents do nothing except ride back and forth on the subways, listening to everything that's said. But the few words we exchanged gave me the impression that he can and will help us. I trust him. He's a real Frenchman, one who won't ever compromise with the Germans. I made an appointment to see him tomorrow afternoon."

We were all cheered up by even this faint glimmering of hope, and we treated our scanty meal as though it were a gala feast. For the first time, I saw a smile on William's face which wasn't distorted by some other emotion—fear, or worry, or anxiety for us. He had been particularly depressed during the last few days, and it was good to see him care-free for once.

We sat together in the living room after dinner drinking our last treasured coffee, which Margot had brought out because she sensed that this special treat would coincide with our holiday mood. We didn't talk. The silence seemed soothing, and we sat quietly, sipping our coffee, and thinking, all of us, of that interview next day which we hoped—no, which we believed—would end our troubles.

And then the doorbell rang.

Today, as I write these lines, that strident peal is months behind me, but I feel again the chill which seized my whole body and the cold perspiration which started from every pore. I don't know why that particular ring should have sounded like the trump of doom, unless it was because I knew, deep down inside me, that we were basing our happiness on the most fragile of hopes; and so an equally fragile interruption could destroy it, and plunge me back at once into the abyss of fear where I had dwelt for the past week. Or perhaps it was that there was a sharp, aggressive, urgent quality about that ringing, bequeathed to it by the finger which pressed upon the button, arrogant and unfriendly.

I can still see the pale frightened face of Margot as she slipped into the room and closed the door behind her. She almost whispered, in a colorless voice:

"The Germans are here."

Kitty was the first to recover from the icy terror which gripped all of us.

"Soldiers?"

"No, civilians."

"It must be the Gestapo," Kitty gasped.

There was an instant of silence so intense that I could hear Kitty's heavy breathing. Then she swung to me:

"Quick! Take Bill to your room. Try to hide him somewhere."

She cast a swift glance around the room.

"Take the third cup with you. Hurry!"

She shoved us in the direction of the door. As we went out, we heard her say, lifting her voice so that she could be heard outside, in a tone indicating impatience with a frightened servant:

"Don't be silly, Margot! Don't keep the gentlemen waiting. Bring them in here."

I was standing in the center of my room, straining my ears, trying to hear what Kitty was saying. I couldn't; but it seemed to me that they, in the next room, must be able to hear the beating of my heart. Each pulse sounded in my ears like the blow of a hammer.

William sat on the edge of the sofa, his head bent forward on his chest, his hands clenched. I wondered if he were praying. I remained standing only because I was petrified, my limbs too weak even to carry me to the sofa.

Kitty had told me to hide William? But how? Where? There wasn't even a closet in the room. The bathroom? Surely, if they searched at all, they would look there. What difference whether they found him here or there?

I stood still, immovable, thoughts and fears pursuing one another in my head in a mad torrent. Out of the vague indistinct familiarity of the objects about me, two of them suddenly took on sharpness and clarity as they caught my eye—the photographs, standing on my dresser, of the two men who had been dearest in the world to me—my husband, whom I had buried in New York, and my brother, who was resting here in Paris, in the cemetery of Père Lachaise.

In that ghastly moment, as if the two pictures had come to life, I could hear the very tones of their voices within me, and what they seemed to be saying was characteristic of what I had often heard them say in real life.

I imagined my husband's voice, as he would have said: "Well, Etta, you've gotten yourself into a pretty mess. But don't lose your head. There must be a way out."

And I seemed to hear my brother say, as he had said so often when he was alive:

"Don't worry, Etta. I'll fix everything up."

Even in my disarray, I could not help noticing again how much this picture of my brother looked like the young man sitting in anguish on the edge of the sofa, waiting for his executioners to come and lead him away to the firing squad. And suddenly I understood how my brother really was going to help us, how he was going to get us out of this dilemma.

I darted to the sofa, grasped William by the arm, started tearing at his clothes.

"Quick!" I whispered. "Get off your clothes, and into bed. Pretend you are very ill. Leave the talking to me."

Together we pulled off his outer clothing as I whispered my plan to him in quick short phrases. He was in bed in a matter of seconds.

I tied a towel around his head—just in time. For at that moment, I heard Kitty calling:

"Etta, where are you? This gentleman wants to see your room."

As I came into the living room, it seemed to me that the piercing glance of the Gestapo agent bored right through me. But I was strengthened for the part I had to play by the slight amusement I was able to feel, even through my terror, at the short moustache with which he had slavishly copied his master. Somehow that made him seem less terrifying, reduced the fear always induced by the word "Gestapo."

He was not alone. Two other plainclothesmen were standing in the doorway. Behind them I could see Madame Beugler, our concierge, her suspicious eyes watching every move of the German. It was easy to see that he would get no help from her.

I admired the calm with which Kitty was conducting herself. She introduced me with a smile which only one who knew her as well as I did could have realized was forced.

"This is my very dear American friend, Mrs. Shiber," she said. "She has been living with me in Paris, and finds herself an unwitting victim of the war, far from home—like yourself."

I steeled myself to be as natural as possible, while I said:

"Come this way if you want to see my room. You'll have to excuse its appearance. My brother is in bed. He's quite ill. I'm afraid he may have contracted intestinal flu, there's so much of it in town now. I hope you won't have to disturb him."

I could see surprise on the faces of both Kitty and the concierge, but fortunately the Gestapo agent wasn't looking at them. I evaded their eyes, for fear I'd betray myself, but turned towards my room and opened the door for the policeman.

He stepped across the threshold. William made a realistic invalid, with his unshaven face and the towel about his head.

"It's all right, Irving," I said soothingly. "Don't try to talk." I turned to the agent. "This is my brother," I said.

The Gestapo man darted a single swift glance at the bed.

"His papers, please," he said curtly.

I opened the drawer in my bureau where I kept all documents—

the drawer towards which it had seemed to me the eyes of my brother in the photograph were looking when, a few minutes ago, I had suddenly realized that there was a way out. I took out the red wallet which had remained undisturbed there ever since Irving's death, drew out his American passport and the green identity card issued to all foreigners in France by the police, and handed them over.

The Gestapo official flipped through the pages of the passport. He came to the picture of my brother, and flashed another quick glance towards the bed. I thanked God again for William's unshaven face, and also for the fact that the passport, issued some years back, carried a picture taken when Irving was nearer William's age.

The policeman closed the passport, and opened the identity card. "This card has expired," he said. "Why wasn't it renewed?"

"We intended to go back to America, because of the war," I said. "We would have gone long ago, if his health had been better. It didn't seem worth renewing it under the circumstances."

I knew that unrenewed identity cards were not unusual. So, apparently, did the German. He handed the card back without comment, and asked for my papers. Those, I knew, were in order, and I breathed more freely. He checked them, returned them with a frigid word of thanks, and left the bedroom. I breathed again. Our ordeal was over!

But there I was wrong. I had not counted on the methodical technique of the Germans.

Back in the living room, the Gestapo officer said to one of his aides:

"The list of tenants."

He took it, looked through it carefully. Then he turned towards Madame Beugler:

"I do not find the name of Madame's brother on this list."

I was thunderstruck. This was something I had not thought of. My knees weakened again. After all my acting, I thought, after we had apparently succeeded, were we to be tripped up by this minute detail?

It was Kitty's turn to save the situation. Mme. Beugler was obviously confused and frightened. Kitty spoke up:

"Goodness, it's no crime to forget a name, is it? Irving isn't a regular tenant here, anyhow. He has only been here since he was ill and needed some one to take care of him."

Mme. Beugler rose nobly to the occasion.

"I'm sorry, sir," she said to the policeman. "*Je suis idiote*—I forgot about the gentleman. He never asked me for a certificate of domicile, so he isn't on my list."

I held my breath for a few seconds which seemed like an age.

The Nazi sat down slowly at the table, took out his fountain pen, and put on a pair of glasses, which he drew from his pocket. This might have made him seem less formidable also—but I was too frightened to think of that at the moment. What did he intend to write, I wondered? Perhaps a warrant for our arrest?

What he did was to take the list of tenants, and add to it, in his own writing, the name of my brother Irving!

It had worked! We were saved! I wanted to shout with joy, but we were not yet alone. One of the two assistants looked perfunctorily into the closets and bathroom—and I rejoiced that I hadn't tried to hide William.

When they declared themselves satisfied that we were innocent of concealing anything or anybody, the Gestapo agent picked up his hat, and the procession started out, inspecting the entry on the way. The door closed behind them. Kitty instinctively sprang to it, and pushed the bolt.

Now I no longer had any desire to shout with joy. I had suddenly gone limp inside. Kitty leaned her back against the door, and we looked into each other's eyes in silence. Next door we heard the loud long peal of the doorbell.

In the doorway of my room appeared a pale-faced unshaven young man in his underwear, a towel tied around his head.

"What happened?" asked William Gray.

Not until we were sure the Gestapo men had left the building did we dare sit down again around the small table in the living room, from which, half an hour earlier, we had been precipitated in an instant from bliss to terror.

Without a word from us, Margot brought in a bottle of champagne and three glasses. We clinked them solemnly together as we drank a silent toast to our escape.

"How in the world did it ever occur to you to pass William off as your brother, Etta?" Kitty asked. "Had you thought of it before?"

"No," I said. "The idea had never entered my head. It must have been the danger that inspired me—or Irving. I think it was Irving. We have him to thank that we are not the prisoners of the Gestapo now."

And I told her of how Irving's photograph had caught my eye, and how I imagined that his voice had said he would help me.

"It's a miracle, Etta," Kitty said with conviction. "It's nothing short of a miracle. It's not so much that you thought of your brother's papers. The stupid thing is that we didn't think of that before, for you remember you were first attracted to William because he resembled your brother. The miracle is that that sharp-eyed Gestapo man didn't notice that the photograph on your bureau is a later picture of the man whose photo was on the passport—obviously a man twenty years older than William."

"I don't know how I looked," William said, "but I swear to you that while he was in the room I felt old enough to pass for my grandfather."

And with that, we all went off into peals of uncontrollable, almost hysterical, laugher, as our tortured nerves at last sought relief in merriment.

CHAPTER SIX

Plans for Escape

THIS experience provided us with a bitter, but a needed, lesson. Ever since we had returned to Paris with William, we had, of course, expected some such visit at any moment, but full realization of what it meant came only with the event itself. During those tense moments when we had felt the prison gates yawning before us, we understood as never before the danger we were running. They gave us new energy in our pursuit of a solution.

But at the same time that this incident goaded us on to greater efforts, it provided us with new problems. First of all there was the question of the concierge, who might now suspect our secret.

Madame Beugler had showed the greatest sympathy and friendship for Kitty ever since we had lived in the house, and we felt that we could count on her. A typical Frenchwoman, Mme. Beugler, we were sure, would be willing to help us even if Kitty told her the whole story, a part of which she must now suspect. But we thought it better not to involve her. We didn't know how much she might have believed of our story about my brother, but she would undoubtedly remember that I had buried a brother at Père Lachaise. She might have put two and two together and have penetrated our ruse, or she might have thought that I had another brother.

Whatever the case, we decided, after long debate, that we must make some explanation to Mme. Beugler.

"I tell you what I'll do," Kitty said. "I'm going to tell her that this is another brother of yours who has just arrived from Nice, and that we were hiding him because he got across the demarcation line surreptitiously. That will satisfy her. I'm sure she'll accept any explanation we choose to make."

That took care of Mme. Beugler; but another problem had now arisen, and this was one we couldn't do anything about. The Gestapo had access to French public records, and if they checked our statements against them, they would discover that the man whose papers they had inspected had been buried in Paris. It seemed evident that there was nothing we could do about that. It was rather unlikely that they would make such a check, and we decided that all we could do was to hope they wouldn't. For if they did, we hadn't a leg to stand on; we had hidden a person in our apartment by supplying him with the papers of a dead man. The proof would be clear in the municipal records and in that list of tenants with Irving's name on it.

So we gave that one up and turned to our third problem—the one which we had already found so hard to solve. How were we to get William out of the house and across the demarcation line? At least, it seemed, we had gained a little time in which to continue our efforts in this direction. William was now officially registered, under his borrowed name, as a tenant of this apartment, and it seemed temporarily safer to keep him there until we could find a legitimate reason to explain his leaving and have his name removed from the list.

If we now had more time, we had no easier problem, for we had said that my "brother" intended to leave for the United States. Suppose the Gestapo returned to demand proof that he had applied for a permit to leave, what would we do then? Or suppose the fact that he held an expired identity card were reported to the competent authorities, and a demand was made that he renew it? In that case, the discrepancies between William's appearance and the date of birth given on the identity card could hardly be missed. Close study of the photograph, too, might reveal that it wasn't a picture of William, particularly if he shaved. And for a few minutes we considered the idea of trying to change the photograph and the date of birth.

Kitty studied the identity papers carefully for some time, and then said, in a discouraged tone: "I'm afraid there's nothing we can do. It's not that I have any scruples about a bit of forgery in this case. I'd commit almost any crime short of murder to get William out of this. But we couldn't do a convincing job. For one thing, the official stamp on the card is printed partly over the photo, and we couldn't fake the stamp. All we can do now is to trust to luck."

So the upshot of our consideration of the new situation was that we must try to get William out of the apartment as soon as possible, to avoid any future comparisons between his papers and their originals; but that until we had arranged for him to get out of the occupied zone, he would probably be safer there than anywhere else.

The afternoon following our Gestapo visitation, we went to see Chancel. He lived in a modest little apartment near the Bastille, where he had remained during the period of panic when every one else was trying to get away. He was not afraid of the Germans, and judged that they would have no interest in him, a man too badly wounded in the first World War to fight again.

We took seats in his scrupulously clean typically French apartment and Kitty opened the conversation cautiously, approaching the subject with the greatest prudence; for even with Chancel, whom she trusted, she did not quite dare be too open. He sensed immediately the general trend of her talk, and smiled at her in the most friendly fashion imaginable.

"*Ma chère madame*," he said, "you don't have to be so cautious with me. I didn't change my politics when the Germans came in. Now tell me—exactly what sort of a scrape have you gotten yourself into?"

"Well," Kitty gulped, "we're hiding an English pilot in our apartment!"

Monsieur Chancel whistled.

"Well!" he said. "That's quite an exploit for two ladies like yourselves, who certainly wouldn't be taken by any one for adventuresses! You've got one advantage. You certainly ought to be above suspicion."

"Oh, but we aren't!" Kitty said. "The Gestapo came last night!"

"The Gestapo?" Chancel exclaimed. "What do you mean?"

Kitty told him of the previous night's visit.

"Ah!" said Chancel. "That's better. It may not have been the Gestapo—just a routine check-up. You wouldn't have gotten off so easily if they had any reason to suspect you. . . . But now, tell me—how did you acquire this English pilot?"

So Kitty related the whole story—how we had first picked William up, our trip to Paris and our efforts to find a way for him to escape.

"You see our situation," she ended. "We haven't the slightest idea how to get William out of occupied territory, and there's no one we can turn to for help. In all the world, you're the only person we know who might possibly be able to assist us."

"As it happens," Chancel said, in a perfectly simple and natural tone, "I *am* in a position to help you."

Kitty and I looked at each other with a mounting hope that we both restrained until we could be sure that the words really had definite meaning, that they were a prelude to a solution of our problem and not simply an expression of sympathy.

"It's a pity you didn't come to me at once," Chancel went on. "You would have saved yourselves a great deal of worry—and last night's harrowing experience, for instance. Here is what we will do: Some very good friends of mine have transformed their home into a refuge for soldiers in hiding. They're not rich, but they're fairly well off just the same. They've got a roomy house on the Left Bank in a secluded street, very well placed for the purpose.

"Both of them wanted to do something to help the soldiers of this war. The man is a veteran of the last war—he was wounded then, and still has a slight limp. He and his wife lost their only son in this war. Through some of his acquaintances, they got word around to soldiers in hiding, who were looking for a chance to escape to join the Free French, that they would take care of them until they could be smuggled out. They've got a secret room for them in the cellar, with comfortable beds and furniture, well heated, where they stay for two or three days until some of our other friends can get them across the demarcation line."

Our hearts rose at these words. He was not, then, simply a sympathetic friend, but a man who belonged to the groups we knew to exist which helped soldiers to get away. Luck had put us on the right path.

"When can we take William there?" Kitty asked.

"Immediately," said Chancel. "I'll give you the address, and you can go there at once. . . . But just a minute. He's English, you say. Does he speak French?"

"Not a word," Kitty answered.

"Mm—that's bad," Chancel said slowly. "You see, what we do is to get travelling passes for these boys—there are ways of doing that, you know—and then we send them by train to a village on the frontier. There we have other friends who own an estate on the demarcation line, which passes right through it. We get them out through that estate. But if he doesn't speak French, that wouldn't work."

"It's worse than that," Kitty explained. "He's so typically Anglo-Saxon in appearance that the first German policeman who clapped his eyes on him would arrest him even if he talked French as well as Marshal Pétain himself. He's got to be kept out of sight. The only way to get him to the frontier is the way we brought him into Paris—in hiding."

She stopped for a moment, obviously turning something over in her mind.

"Give us the address of the frontier estate," she said. "I'll undertake to get him there in our car."

"That's not so easy now," Chancel objected. "According to the new German regulations, you know, you have no right to drive or even own a car. You can't buy gasoline. You might get some on the Black Market, of course, but even then you would have to be able to prove that you were operating your car in the public interest or in that of the occupying forces. And any German policeman can pick up your driver's license."

Chancel was silent for a moment. Suddenly he slapped his hand down hard on the table.

"I have it!" he said. "You ladies belonged to the Foyer du Soldat, where we met. It's still operating, you know, even under the Germans. They're perfectly willing to have some one else take part of the job of feeding the prisoners of war off their hands. Among other things, they're collecting food and other necessities for prisoners, and visiting wounded men in hospitals. Offer your services, and the use of your car, for these purposes, and you can put the Red Cross emblem on the auto, get Red Cross armbands, and be allowed ten gallons of gasoline a week. Besides, you'll have an excuse for moving about the country, visiting hospitals and camps for prisoners of war.

That's our solution! Just leave it to me. I'll make all the necessary arrangements."

Kitty must have felt like hugging Chancel, but she compromised by throwing one arm around me and squeezing me hard.

"You hear, Etta dear!" she cried. "If Monsieur Chancel manages to arrange that for us, we'll pop William back into the luggage compartment and we won't stop till we get to the border!"

CHAPTER SEVEN

William Escapes

THE actual escape of William Gray was so uneventful as to be almost disappointing.

Our first act was to shift him to the home of Monsieur Chancel's friends. It turned out to be a beautiful house, in which every piece of furniture was an antique of considerable value. He stayed there two days. During that time, Chancel procured a permit for William to use in Vichy territory. It was made out in the name of my brother, thus automatically regularizing the situation we had created on the night of the Gestapo visit, and ending our fears for the future.

But one problem still remained to be solved: How were we to get the gasoline for the trip? We had our identification papers from the Foyer du Soldat, and we had started visiting hospitals in the Paris region, but we had not yet received our gas ration coupons.

Kitty exhausted the small supplies of our friends—mostly doctors, who helped her out by sharing with her their own limited rations. But it didn't add up to enough for the trip. Kitty conceived a plan for getting some, which she kept to herself until after she had carried it out. Not until then did she tell me of her audacious method for getting gasoline.

Wearing the nurse's uniform in which she had worked in the American Hospital of Paris, Kitty drove boldly up to the entrance of the Invalides, where the German General Staff had established its headquarters. A young officer was in charge of the guards. She marched straight up to him, favored him with one of her most winning smiles, and said: "I've completely run out of gasoline. I wonder if you could let me have enough to get home?"

She had spoken in French, but the officer evidently recognized that her accent was not that of a native Frenchwoman.

"Do you speak English?" he asked.

Kitty wasn't sure just what lay behind that question.

57

"A little," she answered cautiously, in that language. "Do you?"

"I'd rather speak English," he said. "My French isn't very good."

"You speak English very well," Kitty said, exercising her smile again, as soon as she learned that his question had had no sinister intent behind it.

"Why shouldn't I?" he asked. "I lived in England until the war broke out—spent seven years there. I studied at Oxford, you see."

"Oh!" said Kitty. "When were you there?"

"1924."

"Did you by any chance know Anthony Faulkner?"

"Anthony Faulkner!" he exclaimed. "Don't tell me you knew Tony! Why, he was my best friend!"

"You know, Etta," Kitty said to me, when she reached this part of her story in telling it to me, "when he said that, I remembered the miraculous luck we had had up to now, and I was sure that some power was helping us! Imagine, out of the whole German Army, stumbling on some one who had a mutual friend!"

Kitty told the German that Anthony was her cousin, and he laughed. "So you speak English 'a little'," he said teasingly. "The truth is you're English yourself, aren't you?"

"Yes," Kitty admitted, "but I'm French by marriage."

"You know," the German said, "war or no war, it's nice to talk English again and remember England. I was very happy there. Won't you have dinner with me tonight when I go off duty? We can talk about Tony—and England."

"He was really rather nice, Etta," Kitty told me afterwards. "For a German, that is," she added hastily. "But I really couldn't accept. Somehow it would have seemed like an awful thing to do. I told him quite bluntly, though I was afraid it would lose me the gasoline. I said: 'You don't seriously think that I could dine with a German officer, do you?'"

Kitty's remark seemed to have hurt the German's feelings a little. He stiffened a bit, but remained friendly.

"I beg your pardon," he said. "I had forgotten for a moment the painful circumstances. I appreciate your frankness. Now tell me—do you really need gasoline?"

"I certainly do," Kitty answered.

The officer called his chauffeur, who was sitting in his car at the curb.

"Siphon off enough gasoline from my car to fill this lady's tank," he ordered. The chauffeur obeyed, and as Kitty, after thanking him, got into her car, the officer said, with what she felt to be a slightly ironical smile:

"I can only hope, Madame, that you will make good use of this gasoline."

"Oh, I will," Kitty laughed back at him. "I'll put it to better use than you could ever imagine."

And that night, with the German Army's gasoline powering our car, we were off to the south with William once more in the baggage compartment.

Our trip had every appearance of legitimacy. The insigne of the Foyer du Soldat was painted on our car, and we had parcels and gifts for a number of military hospitals in different sections of the country. Our itinerary was so arranged that the first stop was at the small town on the demarcation line which split France into two parts. We found Chancel's friends without trouble and handed William over to them after a sentimental farewell—and immediately put as much distance between ourselves and the line of demarcation as possible.

When we were finally back in Paris again, savoring the pleasure of being once more in our own home, and this time alone, without fear of the police, I sat down on the sofa beside Kitty and put my arm around her.

"Thank God we got out of this adventure so luckily," I said. "It might have ended very differently. We must have had a guardian angel watching over us. I didn't want to say so to you while William was still here, but I was constantly in deadly fear, every minute of the time. I noticed that you jumped every time the bell rang, too.

"Now that it's all over, let's be careful not to get into any more adventures like that one. Whatever we do, we must avoid anything that will bring the Nazis down upon us. You will be prudent, won't you, dear?"

Kitty looked into my eyes without answering for a moment. Then she sighed, and said: "I suppose you're right, Etta."

It was about a week later that Margot, usually the most self-effacing of maids, rushed into the living room with a triumphant yell, waving a postcard as if it were a battleflag. It was from William, and the postmark was Marseilles.

This was a pleasant surprise, for we had resigned ourselves to not knowing his fate; and indeed, there was only a period of some two weeks during which we could possibly have received word from him. When the Germans first came into Paris, all communication with southern France was cut off. On July 15, mail began to pass between the two zones once more, but a fortnight later, on August 1, the Germans ended all civilian and non-official correspondence between the two regions. It was during that brief period that William's card got through.

The complete shutting off of communications with the unoccupied zone was one of the greatest hardships for families which had been split between the two regions. After August 1, it was easier for a person in the unoccupied zone to get a letter from America than from Paris. Apparently the object of the regulation was to increase the division of the populations of the two zones, which the Germans hoped would weaken French resistance to the New Order, by pitting Frenchmen against each other instead of against the Nazis.

The two zones were not completely cut off from each other, for every night persons risked their lives to cross from one to the other carrying letters to be mailed after the border had been crossed. After six months of complete cessation of communications, the rule was relaxed to the extent of allowing ready printed cards to be sent across the line. These contained a number of stereotyped sentences (I am well, ill, better. I have received, not received, your letter, etc.), and the sender was allowed only to cross out the unwanted phrases. Some families discovered through these cards that though they had been separated for months, without news of absent members, they had been living all that time within a few miles of one another on opposite sides of the border.

But William's postcard arrived on July 31, the last day when such communications were allowed. He had naturally sent a cautious message, containing a sentimental greeting, and ending with the

information that he had been reliably promised that he might soon
"visit his parents."

I knew that meant England, and I was so happy that I felt that
all our anguish had not been in vain. At the moment, I would have
been almost willing to start a similar process all over again.

Kitty wasn't home when the card came. She had gone out early
in the morning, and only came in late quite worn out. Ever since
William had left, Kitty had spent most of her time out of the house,
working her hardest for the Foyer du Soldat. In spite of her exhaustion, her face lighted up when I showed her William's card.

"Isn't that splendid!" she exclaimed. "That's the best news I've
heard for a long time!"

"For him and for us, too," I said. "Now that we know he is safely
across the frontier, we can be sure for the first time that there
won't be any unpleasant repercussions for us from this affair.
You remember we agreed that we must be careful not to get
involved in anything like this again, don't you?"

"What have you got on your mind, Etta?" Kitty asked.

"I want to know what you've got on yours," I said. "I think
you're keeping something to yourself. You might be able to hide
something from other people, but not from me—not after four
years of living together. Now today, for instance, you left home
early in the morning, and you're only back now, obviously dead
tired. You did the same thing yesterday. You aren't getting mixed
up in any more adventures, are you?"

Kitty turned to me with a tired smile.

"Don't worry, Etta," she said. "I'm not doing anything dangerous.
I just want to be helpful, to do something instead of sitting at home
idly all day, fretting and fuming."

"Now, Kitty," I said, "you aren't deceiving me in the least.
You're just trying to reassure me. You know I've never asked you
what you were doing or how you spent your time in all the years
we've lived together, but I'm worried about you now. I don't want
you to get into any trouble. You've been up to something. What
was it?"

"Oh, well," Kitty said, "I'll tell you, and you'll see it's perfectly harmless. I didn't say anything to you, because I didn't want to worry you about nothing—but if you're going to worry anyhow, I suppose I might just as well tell you what I've been doing the last two days.

"Do you remember that yesterday I drove Mme. Robert's 75-year-old mother to her home in the suburbs? Well, on the way back, I caught up with a young man trudging along the road. I had an idea he was another soldier dodging the Germans. It was the way he walked—in a hurry, but aimlessly, looking back over his shoulder every few steps. Besides he had on civilian clothes that didn't fit, and he looked tired, weak and hungry.

"I stopped beside him and asked if he wanted a lift. He noticed my English accent, and decided he could trust me. He told me he was a French officer, and that he had escaped from the prisoners' camp at Baune-la-Rolande. The clothes he had on were smuggled into the camp by a friend; that was how he got out. If he had run into any Germans on the road, he'd have been caught at once, but fortunately I met him first. So I popped him into the luggage carrier."

I let out a gasp that was almost a scream.

"Kitty! Don't tell me you've got him outside!"

"Don't be silly, Etta!" Kitty said. "I told you this was yesterday. As a matter of fact, I did think of bringing him here, but I remembered what you said about how you felt while we were hiding William, so I changed my mind. And I didn't even mention it to you for fear of upsetting you."

"What did you do with him?" I asked.

"I took him straight to Chancel, of course. Chancel got papers for him today, and now he's on his way—one more snatched out of the Germans' hands. Now are you satisfied?"

"It sounds all right," I said. "Are you sure there won't be any repercussions?"

"I don't see how there could be. Even if he should be caught, he doesn't even know who I am. I just picked him up and turned him over to Chancel. After all, it would be a pity not to take advantage of Chancel's organization when we have the chance. My heart aches when I think of all those English boys left behind at Dunkirk, still hiding somewhere in France. I'd like to find them and help them escape."

"Now Kitty," I said, alarmed, "you're not going to start hunting for escaped soldiers, are you?"

"Of course not, dear," she said. "Only, if I should happen to come across others, the least I can do for them is to take them to Chancel. It isn't likely to happen again, of course. You don't come across escaped soldiers every day."

"I certainly hope not," I said. "Look, Kitty. Let's be sensible about this. You say what you did yesterday wasn't dangerous. The boy doesn't know you. All right. But Chancel does. So do his friends on the border. They might get to them, and they might make them talk. They don't care how they do it, you know."

"They wouldn't give me away," Kitty said. "It would be easy enough for them to leave me out of it. Nobody saw me. It was so dark by the time I got into Paris that I could hardly find my way through the blackout."

"That's not the point," I said. "It's what might happen afterwards, whether you're seen or not. The Germans aren't going to let officers escape from prison camps without an investigation. They must be hunting for him right now. And if they get him, they'll move heaven and earth to trace every step of his escape and find every one who helped him. It was dreadfully dangerous, Kitty. You mustn't take chances like that. You're not the adventurous type. And you're up against a strong well-organized system. Just because a couple of sentimental impulsive women got out of one brush with it safely doesn't mean that it can be done again. It will take a well-organized French system to fight the Gestapo. It's too big a job for you, or for both of us. We were terrifically lucky the first time, Kitty, and we're not even sure we were up against the Gestapo. If the Gestapo really gets on our trail, we won't get off so easily. Remember what Chancel said! You mustn't risk your life again—because that's what you are doing, you know."

"You're a fine one to preach to me," Kitty said. "After all, you got me into this."

"I?"

"Yes, you." Her tone was serious, but she was still smiling, so I knew there was no blame behind her accusation. "Wasn't it you who suggested that we save William Gray?"

"Yes," I said, "and we've done it. Perhaps I wouldn't have had the courage if I had realized in advance what it meant. But now that chapter is closed, and I want you to promise not to get into another adventure of that kind."

Kitty had picked up a copy of *Paris-Soir* and pretended to be deeply immersed in it.

"Kitty," I repeated, "will you promise?"

"I did promise, didn't I?" Kitty said evasively. "Now, for goodness sake, let me read the paper. One would think I'd committed a crime!"

We were quiet for a time. Kitty turned the pages of her paper. I was reading a book. I had about decided that I was ready for bed when Kitty uttered a little exclamation, picked up a spoon from her saucer, and with its handle circled an item in the paper, pressing hard to leave a mark.

"Etta," she said, handing the paper to me, "isn't that interesting!"

She had been reading the "Missing Persons" column. It had become the most widely read part of the paper in France, for hardly any one was without a close friend or relative who had disappeared in the confusion of war. Six million persons had left northern France at the time of the invasion, and their only means of locating one another was through advertisements in the newspapers.

Paris-Soir, a pro-German paper since the Nazis had come in and taken it over, published several hundred such advertisements daily. The German censorship permitted it, for the Germans wanted civilians to return to their normal way of living in order that France might resume production—for Germany's benefit.

The announcement Kitty had marked read something like this:

"Jonathan Burke is looking for his friends and acquaintances. Address Military Hospital, Doullens (Somme)."

"What's exceptional about that?" I asked. "I've seen hundreds like it."

"So have I," said Kitty. "But how about that name—Jonathan Burke? That can't be French. He must be English. Perhaps he's one of the boys from Dunkirk, trying to contact friends who could help him."

"There are Frenchmen with English names, you know," I said. "You're English, but you've got a French name."

"I married mine," Kitty said. "I doubt if he got his that way. I ask you, could a Frenchman possibly be named Jonathan? Burke, perhaps, but certainly not Jonathan. I've been looking at these advertisements for days, and this is the first time I've seen an English name. There are quite a few British soldiers scattered through hospitals and prison camps in northern France, you know. Besides, Etta, I *feel* that he's British. I'm sure of it. Why do you have to argue that he isn't?"

There was a tone of momentary exasperation in her voice. Then it changed.

"I'm sorry, Etta," she said. "I didn't mean to be rude."

But she was obviously agitated. She got up from her chair and walked into the next room. I was afraid I was displeasing her, but I was really worried now, for if she had been looking through the "Missing Persons" columns for English names day after day, it was obvious what was on her mind. She was searching for more William Grays. So I followed her, although I knew she was trying to escape from me, and sat down on our deep-seated divan beside her.

"I'm only insisting because I'm fond of you, Kitty," I said. "I don't want to see you get into serious trouble—and it looks to me as though you were looking for it. Suppose Jonathan Burke *is* an English boy. We're in no position to do anything for him. He's in a military hospital—that means under guard. Picking up a man on the road, by accident, is one thing; getting him out of a guarded hospital is another. Even if we worked out some brilliant scheme to help him escape, we'd probably be caught red-handed. You can't expect such luck as we had with William twice. The Nazis weren't born yesterday."

"They aren't supermen, either, even if they think they are," Kitty said. "Some of them are lax, some are stupid, and some are just plain indifferent." She adjusted a pillow behind her back and sank back into it. "Plenty of British soldiers have gotten out of the occupied zone since the armistice, and no one has been punished for it."

"You mean we don't know whether any one has been punished for it," I said. "There are other ways in which we can help, Kitty. We don't have to go to such extremes."

"Oh, I suppose you're right," she said. "But let me do just one thing, Etta. I won't unless you agree—but it's perfectly safe. Just let me answer Jonathan Burke's advertisement. I'll tell him that we'll bring him a package if he wants to see us. Now, don't look so startled! I said 'us' because I want you to come along. I want you to see for yourself that I'm not doing anything you wouldn't approve of.

"There's no harm in that, is there? I'm sure he's an English boy, and I want to do something for him. We're allowed to take packages to them, you know—in fact, at the Foyer du Soldat we're supposed to. What does it matter if we take one to a specific soldier, instead of to just any one?"

"All right," I said. "And I'll go with you—but just for one reason. That's to make sure you keep out of trouble."

And with that settled, I went off to bed. Kitty had seemed terribly tired herself, but she didn't go to bed at once. She had something she had to do before she could go to sleep. She stayed up long enough to write a letter to Jonathan Burke.

CHAPTER EIGHT

A Trip to Doullens

A FEW days later, Kitty dashed into my room before I was up. "He got my letter, Etta," she cried. "Look! Here's his answer!"

I didn't have to ask whose. I suddenly realized that I had been waiting almost as anxiously as Kitty for Jonathan Burke's reply.

She held the cheap, soiled envelope under my nose. The cramped, almost childish handwriting suggested that it had been written under difficult conditions—in Jonathan Burke's hospital cot, no doubt.

"Well, what does he say?" I asked.

Kitty seemed to hesitate a moment about opening the envelope. Then she tore it open, unfolded the single sheet within it, and scanned it rapidly.

"I *knew* he was English!" she exclaimed triumphantly.

"For goodness sake, read it!" I cried.

"He says," Kitty read: " 'Can you help? Well, I guess! I can use some food, that's sure, and it would be splendid to have someone to talk to. Seems English is scarce around here, and I have nothing but time on my hands. You are wonderful to write to me, and I shall look forward to your visit.' . . . That's all," Kitty concluded, handing me the letter.

"Poor chap!" she went on. "There must be hundreds like him, not even able to talk to any one. How glad I am that I saw his ad! *Paris-Soir* is still good for something, even if it is a Nazi sheet. I'm sure we can manage to help the boy."

I looked at Kitty. She had a faraway look in her eyes that I had seen there before once or twice when she was particularly excited about the chances of freeing William Gray.

"Now, remember, Kitty," I said. "You promised. This is just a visit. We'll take him a package of food chat with him for a while, and that's all."

"Of course, of course," Kitty said impatiently.

"All right," I said. "That's settled, then. When shall we go?"

"We're on inspection duty at the Foyer du Soldat today," she said. "How about tomorrow?"

Tomorrow it was.

It was early in the morning of August 15 when we set out for the small town of Doullens. Our package for Lieutenant Burke contained several cans of sardines, some bread, cigarettes, and a few other things we thought he might like.

We were already in the car, about to start, when Kitty suddenly said: "I forgot something!"

She hurried back to the apartment and returned with a box covered with brown wrapping paper.

"Another gift?" I said. "What's in it?"

"It's not a gift," Kitty said. "Just something I want to leave at the Foyer on the way back."

She stepped on the starter, and we rolled through the streets of Paris. It was a beautiful day, and as we got out into the country, and moved swiftly along through fields bright with flowers, I felt elated about our errand. As we sped along, we speculated on Jonathan Burke's looks and character.

"I suppose he's wondering if we're coming at all," Kitty said. "Perhaps I should have answered his letter. He may have thought I had a momentary good impulse and then forgot all about him. He probably took me for a nosy old woman who wanted to pry into his troubles but wouldn't bother to do anything about them."

"The fact is that we couldn't do much about them," I reminded her uneasily. I sensed an air of determination, almost of recklessness, in Kitty's attitude which gave me an uneasy feeling.

We reached Amiens in good time. Doullens was about eighteen miles beyond it. Just before we reached the town, the road passed an old fortress, which we had visited on a pleasure trip two years earlier. Known as the Citadel, it dated from mediaeval times. We had been inside it, and seen its windowless cells, and the narrow slits through which its defenders had fired—the only openings through which the sun could penetrate.

It had never occurred to us that this building could possibly be put to any modern use, so we were astonished to see the Nazi swastika waving in the breeze over the Citadel, and helmeted German soldiers on guard at the entrance.

Kitty drew the car up beside a peasant woman standing by the side of the road.

"Why are the Germans guarding the Citadel?" she asked her.

Her face twisted with hate, the woman replied:

"God punish them, they've got our men in there. They've made a prison out of it. The men are shut up in those filthy holes where we wouldn't think of keeping our dogs. There's no sun, and they're all sick. There's not a day the priest isn't called in. Damn them all, I say!"

"You'd better be careful," Kitty said. "If they hear you, they're likely to arrest you too."

"I don't care if they do," said the old woman. "My two sons are in there. They had come home, they had civilian clothes on again, but the Boches came and took them away. My oldest son, that's Jean, was a sergeant. He had his discharge papers. He showed them, but they paid no attention to them. He came across the line, you see—slipped over without a pass. You understand—he couldn't get one, and he wanted to come home. I've been here since sun-up, trying to get a peep at them. But every time I get near the gate, the damned Boches chase me away."

"Poor woman," Kitty said, as we drove away. "Let's take a look at the Citadel while we're here."

She pulled up to the gate, picked up a few of the parcels we had brought with us for the hospital, and stepped briskly out of the car. "Come along," she said over her shoulder, and walked straight towards the gate. The sentry looked at our Red Cross armbands, and made no move to stop us.

Inside we passed through a low, arched hall, closed at the end by iron bars. Through it we could see the courtyard of the Citadel. It seemed to me the most sinister place I had ever seen in my life. Behind the high stone walls of the old fortress hundreds of prisoners were jammed together, surrounded by barbed wire barriers which seemed hardly necessary in addition to those thick walls and iron bars. Herded aimlessly together, the prisoners, some standing, some sitting, some lying on the ground, turned hungry, haggard faces towards the bars which separated them from us.

Kitty shuddered. "What a horrible place!" she said. "And all these people have done is to be on the losing side! No civilized country would keep the worst criminals in such a place!"

Heavy footsteps sounded in the dark corridor. A German sergeant came up to us, glanced at our Red Cross armbands, and said: "Let me see your papers, please."

He looked over them carefully. They carried the seal of the German Kommandantur, and stated that we were authorized to visit prison camps and hospitals to distribute gifts to the prisoners.

Kitty, with her disarming smile, said in German:

"We brought some packages for the prisoners. We would like to distribute them, and talk to some of the men."

The Nazi shook his head.

"You may leave the packages if you wish. Visiting the prisoners is strictly forbidden."

"But we are authorized to do so by the Commanding General," Kitty insisted. "See—it says so on our credentials."

The German still shook his head.

"The Commanding General himself has forbidden visits to the prisoners here," he said. "His order does not exempt you. Moreover, your credentials do not say that you may talk to prisoners— only that you may give them gifts."

And he shoved us towards the entrance, as though he were afraid to allow us even the brief glimpse we had had of the inside of the Citadel. In spite of our failure, I was glad to get out of the place. Kitty didn't say anything. We climbed into the car in silence, and continued toward Doullens.

The hospital was about a mile and a half from the Citadel, on the other side of the humble little town of Doullens.

We stopped in front of the hospital gate, under a spreading oak. Pulling our parcels out of the tonneau of the car, we walked towards the entrance, and passed through the arched stone gateway. Two helmeted German soldiers, standing stiffly at either side of the gate, appeared not even to see us. We learned later that the hospital, though operated by its French staff, was under the control of the German military authorities. Its patients were considered as prisoners of war, and on recovery would be confined to a prison camp—probably the Citadel.

To tell the truth, the hospital was not much of an improvement over the Citadel. It was filthy, dark and smelly, and infested with vermin. We even saw a rat scurrying through one dim passageway.

After making ourselves known to the director in charge, we wandered through the hospital on our own. No one had time to guide us, which suited us perfectly. We went into a number of rooms, talked with the soldiers, and left them the comforts we had brought.

In one room which I still remember vividly were two young Algerian soldiers, with badly wounded hands, which they were unable to use in any way. They were lying helpless and untended, on dirty mattresses, in their underclothes, without sheets or blankets. Over them swarmed hundreds of flies, not only on their bodies, but covering their faces like a living, stirring crust of black filth. They could not brush them away, and it was easy to see by the distortion of their features how intolerable was this slow, unavoidable parade of the insects over their helpless faces. They were literally gasping with thirst. Kitty and I found them some water, and made them as comfortable as we could, though there was little we could do. We brushed the flies away, but we knew they would return the instant we left.

In other rooms we found similarly bedridden men in much the same state. I was shaken by the sights I saw, gripped by the desire to help, but I knew very well that there was no way I could do much for these unfortunate men, condemned to escape from this horrible caricature of a hospital only to the more horrible caricature of a prison we had just seen—or to the grave.

Meanwhile Kitty was looking for Lieutenant Burke. She had refrained from asking for him in the prison office, not wishing to draw attention to our visit in connection with him. She had assumed that this hospital, like every other she had ever seen, would have a chart at each patient's bed, giving his name and a record of his condition. But there was nothing like that here. We were reduced to chance.

It was a relief to escape at last from the rooms and wards, and step out into the garden, where convalescent patients were allowed to roam about freely. We saw a number of them sitting about in the sun; and finally, in one corner, we noticed an English R.A.F. officer, in uniform, sitting by himself on a bench. Since most of the others we had seen were French, we judged this might be Lieutenant Burke, and we turned towards him.

He was about 27, lean, dark-haired with a small black mustache—a rather good-looking young man. His uniform was crumpled and faded, and he wore a bandage over his right eye.

As he saw us approaching, he seemed suddenly to come to life, like a puppet when the marionette master pulls the strings. A slow grin twisted his boyish mouth, and with a restrained gesture to his pale, emaciated hand, he invited us to sit down on a bench against the wall.

"How good of you to come!" he said at once, without even asking if we were the ones who had written him. "I hoped you would, but I didn't dare count on it. It's a long way from Paris, and, after all, I'm no kin of yours."

"You're a countryman of mine," Kitty reminded him.

"That doesn't always mean very much," said Lieutenant Burke, "though I guess it means more now than it did before we started fighting . . . I took a chance some one like you might see that ad when I put it in the paper. I didn't expect it to reach any one I knew already. I don't know anybody in Paris. I used to visit there in the old days—had a fine time: wonderful shows, marvelous night life. You know the sort of thing. But that was just during school vacations. I had no friends there."

As he talked, I watched him intently, and thought what a fine young man he seemed to be and how proud I would be to have a son like him. But I pitied his mother, for I knew that if I had been in her place I wouldn't be able to sleep for worry, knowing that my boy was shut up in this filthy place, under guard like a criminal . . . but perhaps she didn't know. That might be worse.

My feeling was so deep that when I asked, "Were you hurt

badly?" my voice was almost a whisper. I had to repeat the question before he understood me.

"I got a shrapnel wound at Dunkirk, Ma'am," he said.

"What a shame!" I exclaimed.

"I got off easy," Lieutenant Burke said grimly. "I left a lot of buddies back there who'll never see this world again—even with one eye."

"Did you lose your eye?" I almost moaned, but Kitty tactfully intervened to change the subject.

"We've been all through the hospital," she said quickly. "It's a filthy place. It's disgusting to think you have to stay here."

"Maybe it seems so to you," he said, "but I'm trying to stay here as long as I can. When I'm better they'll send me to the Citadel. You should see that!"

"We have," said Kitty.

"Well, then," he said, "you know there's worse places than this. I was there for two days before they brought me here. I don't want to go back there. I'd be back already if they weren't so slipshod here. They haven't found out yet that my wound's practically healed. Look!"

He pulled up the corner of his bandage. Underneath we could see a scar under the eye, completely healed. The eye itself seemed normal. He hurriedly pulled the bandage down again.

"You see," he said, "I'm perfectly fit to leave, but I'm stalling for time. There's hardly any guard—just the two men at the gate. I might be able to escape from here, but there isn't a chance of getting out of the Citadel. And I wouldn't get far in this uniform. I suppose they count on that—that, and our being weak. Otherwise they'd watch us more carefully."

Kitty got up from the bench. She walked a few steps nervously, then paced back towards us again. Suddenly she leaned over and said in a low voice into Lieutenant Burke's ear:

"Would you like me to take you to Paris?" (She seemed to have forgotten my very presence). "Will you risk it? I'm not afraid—but would you be? We can get you out of the occupied zone. We've done it before."

Lieutenant Burke clutched at Kitty's hand.

"Would I like you to take me to Paris!" he ejaculated, so loudly that he frightened me.

"Sh!" I warned him. "They'll hear us!" And I looked fearfully across the garden to the other convalescents; but no one was paying any attention to us.

"Would I be afraid?" Burke repeated. "Afraid? After this? After the Citadel I'd rather be rotting on the beach at Dunkirk, honestly dead, than rotting there while I'm still alive! What could happen to me any worse than being sent back to the Citadel? And that will happen any day now—the next time the commandant comes here to check on men well enough to go back."

"Has any one tried to escape from here before?" I asked.

"Everybody's thought of it," Burke said, "but there's not a chance. Three or four have actually gotten out of the hospital grounds— that's easy—but the highways are watched, and all of them have been picked up almost immediately. The punishment is going back to the Citadel, no matter how sick you may be. That's about the worst fate any of us here can imagine, so no one has tried to get away recently . . . You can't dodge the German motorcycle patrols. They run back and forth all the time over all the roads in the neighborhood.

"I'm willing to take any chance, Mrs. Beaurepos. I'll be back in the Citadel in a few days anyway, whether I do or not. But how can you manage it? After all, you're only a woman. I don't mean anything derogatory by that. But what can a woman do? . . . You remind me of my aunt Katherine—aristocratic, gentle, fine, wanting to help, but helpless. I know you *want* to help me. I'm sure you'd try. But, God, what can a woman do in times like these? You're just licked before you start."

The sound of his own voice seemed suddenly to embarrass him. He stopped short, and pressed his hand over the wound under his bandage, as though it itched. I noticed that his long fingers were trembling. His blue eyes seemed to gleam with the dry light of fever.

Kitty said softly:

"You are mistaken, Mr. Burke. We can get you by the motorcycle patrols, and we will."

I looked at Kitty with admiration for her firm calm tone, but also with fear. I could feel the cold terror which had only left me with the safe departure of William Gray flooding me again. I didn't know whether I wanted more to help Lieutenant Burke or to get away without finding myself committed to another adventure like that from which we had so narrowly escaped.

Kitty had taken complete charge of the situation.

"You two wait here," she said. "I'll be back in a minute."

When she returned she had the brown parcel she had gone back to get before we started out. She handed it to Lieutenant Burke.

"There are a pair of overalls in this package," she said. "Get into them without being seen. You see the branches of that tree over there, on the other side of the wall? Our car is parked under it. There are bushes covering the wall at that point. Climb over the wall there. It's not high, and the bushes will hide you. The car is unlocked. Get into the back, and behind the back seat you will find the opening of a luggage compartment. Get into it, close it behind you, and wait."

Burke seemed a little doubtful. Kitty reassured him:

"There's been another English pilot in that cubby-hole before you," she explained. "He was taller than you are, but he was comfortable enough—especially after the trip was over."

Now for the first time, Kitty looked towards me. I suppose she expected a protest, for of course she knew that I must realize now that in spite of her half-promise, she had planned all this from the beginning. When she had brought the overalls with her, when she had chosen the spot to park the car, she was already preparing her plan.

But what could I say, with Burke beside us, visibly vibrating with hope? She saw that I was not going to say anything; and it was with a lilt in her voice which showed the relief she felt that she turned back to Burke:

"Don't forget to take off your bandage. Without that, and with these overalls, you'll be all right even if you're seen. If you get into the car unobserved, the battle's won. The motorcycle patrols won't stop us."

Burke nodded, without a word. He seemed too moved to speak.

"We'll go now. We don't want it to be noticed that we have talked with you longer than with other patients. Don't be nervous if we're slow coming. We'll stay at least ten or fifteen minutes more, and make sure of being seen with others just before we leave."

Kitty held out her hand. Burke took it, then shook hands with me also, as though we were saying a routine good-bye to him. As we walked away, I saw him fumbling with the package, as though trying to verify its contents by feeling it before opening it.

We passed by several groups of French officers, some bandaged, some apparently completely recovered. We shot sidelong glances at them, wondering if they had paid any attention to our conversation with Burke. If any of them had noticed us, they evidently intended to pretend they hadn't. They ignored us completely as we passed them.

One of the hardest things I ever did in my life was to enter the hospital building again, and walk through the wards, stopping to talk to patients as though nothing had happened. I tried to appear calm and natural, but I didn't feel as though I were succeeding. I forced a smile to my lips, where it seemed frozen in place; and then I found I didn't know how to stop smiling. It seemed to me that I must be walking through the wards like a hideous grinning gargoyle, the expression on my face felt so unnatural.

Kitty seemed cool as a cucumber. As far as I could see, she was acting just as naturally as before we had found Burke. I let her do the talking to the soldiers. I didn't trust myself.

The minutes dragged by like hours. As we left one ward, I clutched Kitty's arms, and whispered fiercely:

"We've waited long enough, Kitty. For God's sake, let's get out of here now."

"Not yet, Etta," Kitty said. "He hasn't had time to change his clothes yet. Better to allow too much time than too little. Keep your chin up, and don't look so terrified! That's better. Let's see who's in here."

And she turned into another ward. There was nothing to do but follow.

As we came out of this room into the dark corridor again, a

blond young man who seemed to have been lying in wait for us outside the door limped towards us, and whispered:

"I saw you with Burke. I'm English, too. I'm sure you're helping him get away from here. Please—get me out, too. I've *got* to get away from here!"

"What's your name?" Kitty asked.

"Corporal Lawrence Meehan. Lieutenant Burke will vouch for me."

Kitty stood silent for a moment, looking at the newcomer. Suddenly she seemed to come to the decision that he could be trusted.

"Why do you want to get out?" she asked.

"God, who doesn't? But I've a special reason. It's my leg. I'm not getting proper care here, not even rest and food. It's playing me the very devil. I know it would improve if I could get out of the Germans' hands, where I could have quiet and peace of mind. But it'll never get better here!"

He was trembling all over, and looked very ill. Drops of perspiration stood out on his forehead.

"But you have a fever," I objected.

"No, no, I'm not feverish at all—really. It's only the idea that perhaps I can get away. It's worked me up a little. I'll be all right the minute I get out of here."

"Look here, young man," Kitty said, "I'll make you a promise. If the Germans don't catch us, we'll come back for you next. But we can't take you now. We can only hide one at a time in our car. If you want to get out, your best bet is to keep us from being suspected of helping Burke; otherwise, of course, we couldn't ever come back here again for you. Now, is there anything you can do to keep them from noticing that Burke is missing—or at least from finding it out long enough so that they won't connect it with our visit?"

The corporal thought a moment.

"I could do this," he said. "At six every night, a clerk goes through the wards and calls the roll. I'm not in his ward (officers and non-coms are not put in the same ward, you know), but I can manage to be there and when his name is called, I'll say he's gone to the toilet. That will be all right at night, because they aren't very particular then; they don't expect escapes in daylight. But in the morning, the check is more careful, so they're sure to find he's missing then. They'll think he slipped out overnight."

"Perfect!" Kitty smiled. "That's all we need. You take care of that, and in two days we'll be back for you. Be ready."

And she swung around and strode off without a backward look. I hesitated. I thought I ought to say good-bye, or say something encouraging to Corporal Meehan. But as I saw Kitty's back retreating down the corridor, a feeling akin to panic came over me, and I hurried off after her like a stray kitten following a possible protector.

As we reached the gate, Kitty said loudly: "Wait here! I'll bring the car around to the gate for you."

I would have protested, but I didn't dare. Instead, I stood riveted with terror between the two German sentinels, and waited for an eternity. I heard the whir of the starter as Kitty pressed it, and the answering roar of the motor.

What, I wondered, had come into Kitty? Was it just bravado? Did she take pleasure in driving the car with Burke hidden in it right up to the sentries? As the car moved towards the gate, I started forward, to make her stop a little farther away. I was deathly afraid that it might occur to one of the sentries to look into the car, and perhaps even to think of opening the luggage compartment.

"Hop in," Kitty said, and then, to my terror, instead of starting up, she beckoned to one of the sentries.

He came over to the car.

"What time do you open the gates for visitors in the morning?" she asked calmly in German. He told her.

"We may have to make several trips here," she said coolly. "Have a cigarette?"

He accepted one, and another for his fellow sentry, and struck a light for her as she produced one for herself.

"*Danke schön*," she said, and started the car.

I was about to upbraid her, when she spoke quietly, without looking towards me.

"I wanted to give him a chance to see that there was no one in the car except the two of us," she said. "Now even if they discover Burke's absence tonight, the sentry will swear up and down that our car was empty. In fact, since the other man saw him standing by it talking with us, he wouldn't dare voice a suspicion even if he had one. He'd be convicting himself of negligence."

"Kitty," I said, "you're a wonder! But what would have happened if he had poked around inside the car and decided to open the luggage compartment?"

"He couldn't," Kitty said. "I locked it. And I certainly wouldn't have admitted that the key was any nearer than Paris."

CHAPTER NINE

Ten Thousand Englishmen

As we speeded out of Doullens, a German motorcycle patrol passed us, but didn't even pause to inspect our car, with its prominently displayed emblem.

From time to time, Kitty stopped, to ask Lieutenant Burke if he were comfortable. Each time the same reply echoed from the depths of the luggage compartment:

"More comfortable than I have been for weeks, thanks. How soon do we reach Paris?"

The drive was uneventful. The only incident occurred when we had to stop because the road was blocked by the car of a German official, who had crashed into a peasant's ox-cart. He was too busy shouting at the peasant and trying to extricate his car to bother about us; and as soon as he had backed out of his predicament, we sped on unhindered.

Arrived at our building, we re-enacted the same scene that had occurred when we reached there with William. This time the danger was less, for since Burke was in overalls, he would appear to be a workman entering the house if any one caught sight of him, whereas William had been marked by his uniform.

Once in the apartment, Kitty shot the bolt. We looked at one another like two tried and triumphant conspirators, and laughed.

"Practice makes perfect," said Kitty. "Remember how excited and worried we were the first time? I wasn't a bit frightened this time."

"Neither was I," I said, not quite truthfully.

But Lieutenant Burke was a new hand at this game. He was pale, and the perspiration was streaming down his face.

"Come, come," Kitty laughed banteringly, "don't show how little trust you have in us. We're past masters at this game, you know." She rang for Margot. "Is dinner ready?" she asked, when our maid appeared.

"Yes, such as it is, Madame," Margot answered, without showing the slightest surprise at the appearance of another young man. "I found a little cheese—not much, but very good. And we have some vegetables and bread."

We sat down to dinner, and during its course explained the next moves to our guest.

"Tomorrow morning we will take you to a very beautiful house across the Seine," Kitty told him. "You'll probably be there about two days. Then you will be moved down to the demarcation line, where friends of ours will get you across. I don't know whether you'll go by train, or whether we'll have to take you. It's a rather long trip to make in the luggage compartment—though our last visitor made it. The train would be more comfortable, but then you'd have to be able to pass for French. Do you speak French?"

"Yes—*un peu*," Burke said, "but not well enough to fool any one. No one would take me for a Frenchman."

"We'll let a Frenchman decide that tomorrow," Kitty said. "Our friend M. Chancel, who will arrange the details for getting you out, will tell us what to do. You can have complete trust in him."

After dinner we sat in the living room, and Jonathan told us about himself. He had been a civil engineer before the war. He described the hell of Dunkirk, but compared it favorably to that other inferno, Doullens, whose greatest torture was the hopelessness which gripped its inmates.

"I sat in the garden most of the time after they let me get up," he said, "worrying about the future and about my family—my mother and my sister, Mary. It was some of the others there—the French patients—who asked me why I didn't put an ad in the paper. Some of them had located relatives that way. I knew I wouldn't find any relatives, but I thought, 'What's the harm?' So I did."

He sighed.

"You're both wonderful," he said. "I guess the world hasn't gone to the dogs after all. No matter where you go or what happens, you always find good people everywhere."

He lapsed into silence. His face seemed to darken. It didn't look as though he were thinking pleasant thoughts.

"What's the matter, Jonathan?" Kitty asked. "Can we help?"

"I just thought, suddenly, of other English soldiers who haven't been as lucky as I. There are supposed to be about ten thousand of them, most of them escaped from the Dunkirk area, like myself. They're hiding in woods and caves in northern France, half-starved, tracked down like beasts. If they try to slip into the villages to get food, the Germans get them. They've organized special units to hunt for them. It's a miniature war, with well-armed well-fed German motorcycle police on one side, and starved, unarmed, broken, sick men on the other."

The figure Burke mentioned was roughly the estimate we had heard from Chancel, too. His organization had been trying to find some of these men, but without much luck. Obviously, it was not easy for those who wanted to rescue them to find their hiding places, especially while their enemies were also scouring the country in search of them.

After the Dunkirk evacuation (or, as Churchill called it, the miracle of Dunkirk), several thousand British soldiers were left in France. They were caught behind the lines of the German Army moving through France, without hope of escape. The Nazis captured many of them, but others took refuge in the woods, and it was these men the motorcycle patrols were trying to round up.

As the Germans moved southward, the British soldiers had followed close behind, hoping for a chance to break through some gap in the front and get out of German-occupied territory. Some of them had been seen as close to Paris as Chantilly, practically a suburb of the capital.

But their chances of breaking through were close to zero. As the Germans occupied Paris, signed the armistice, and moved down along the Atlantic coast to the Spanish border, the front became a frontier, and the English were trapped. Then the Nazis set to work to mop them up.

These were the men whose fate worried Burke.

"There's no way of saving them," he said gloomily, "no way at all. If we were all together, and had arms, we might be able to fight our way to the coast. I'm sure England would do the impossible to get boats over to us. But we're scattered all over the place. There's no way of getting together."

Burke went to bed early. Kitty and I sat in the living room. Margot, coming in with the coffee, found us sitting there silently. The unaccustomed quiet affected her, too, and she tiptoed about the table, clearing away the dishes, as though she were afraid to make a sound.

When she had left the room, Kitty turned to me with a look of determination, as though she were about to say something, then changed her mind, and began stirring her coffee with unnecessary vigor. Suddenly she seemed to come to a decision. She laid her spoon in her saucer with deliberation, and said to me:

"Etta, you will have to go back to America."

I was so surprised that I didn't know what to say. Kitty went on:

"There's no use arguing, Etta, I've decided. I can't simply remain here, taking things easy, while this cruel man-hunt is going on. I've got to help them—the thousands and thousands of William Grays and Jonathan Burkes, some of them wounded, half-starved, dying. I know you don't approve, and even if you did, I have no right to involve you. You're an American. These men aren't your countrymen. There's no reason why you should feel as I do about it. Besides, you're ten years older than I am. I can't drag you into danger with me. But I've got to help. So you'll have to go home, and leave me to do the work I feel I must do."

"This is the second time you have tried to send me away, Kitty," I said. "The first was when war was declared. And my answer is still the same. I won't leave you."

"This time you must," Kitty returned. "Because I'm going through with this whether you're here or not; and even if you have nothing to do with it, the consequences might be just as bad for you as for me. So you'd better go to the American Embassy to-morrow and tell them you want to leave as soon as it can be arranged."

I shook my head.

"No, Kitty," I said. "I'm going to stay with you. You gave me a helping hand at the most difficult period of my life, and after staying with you through the good times, I'm not going to desert you now that bad times have come.

"You may be worried about me, and want me to go because I might get into trouble—but I'm worried about you, and I intend to stay to keep you out of trouble. I'm afraid you're going to get yourself into a fatal mess if I leave you to your own devices. You're an incorrigible idealist, Kitty, and you've got to have some one to keep you from attempting the impossible.

"That's just what it is—the impossible! Don't you remember that Burke said only a few minutes ago that there was no way of saving those men? If an English officer thinks so, what could two weak women do?"

"Two weak women saved William Gray," Kitty said. "He was caught here after Dunkirk. Two weak women are saving Jonathan Burke. He's from Dunkirk, too. Their situation was just the same as that of the other ten thousand. What would have become of William Gray by now if it hadn't been for us? What was going to happen to Jonathan Burke? The lot of the others is no more desperate than theirs seemed to be. If we got them out of the hands of the Germans, why can't we do it again? After all, we know of a way of escape from occupied territory. I believe it was God who showed us that way. It would be sinful and criminal not to use our knowledge to save as many men as we can."

I looked at Kitty's flushed face, transformed almost with ecstasy. I realized I would never be able to convince her, or to turn her aside from the work she had chosen. But I made one more effort.

"But why should you alone do this, Kitty?" I asked her. "Isn't this more of a man's job?"

"Etta," Kitty said solemnly, "no one who knows how to help these men has any right to abandon the duty of aiding them to any one else. It's like seeing a drowning man, and looking around for some one else to save him for fear of getting your clothes wet."

She sat down next to me, and bent so close that I could feel the warmth of her feverish face against my cheek.

"It wouldn't be true if I told you that I am not afraid to die," she said. "I'm no braver than any other woman, and it horrifies me to think that my life might be snapped off brutally—before a firing squad. When this horrible war is over, I'm looking forward to more beautiful years like those we have already spent together. Like you, I didn't know a peaceful moment while William was here, and whenever the elevator stopped at our floor during the night, I woke up at once. I'm really a coward. Yet if I were absolutely certain that the Germans would execute me for harboring this boy, I still wouldn't abandon him before I had made sure of his escape. And even if I were absolutely certain that they would execute me for continuing to try to save my countrymen, I would still do it—because I have to. I couldn't hold up my head again if I didn't. I couldn't enjoy a longer life gained at the expense of betraying these poor fellows today. But I don't mean to be executed, Etta. I'm going to be very careful, and I don't intend to get caught."

"All right, Kitty," I said. "If you're determined, I'll help you. There's only one thing I won't do. That's to leave you to do this alone. If you have to save soldiers, I have to stay."

CHAPTER TEN

The Gestapo Pounces

TELLING Kitty that I would help her cost me a night's sleep. Elated at my surrender, she insisted that we set to work at once to plan our campaign for helping the refugees from Dunkirk, and we talked until nearly dawn.

"The most difficult thing," Kitty began, "is how to contact these men. They have no addresses, they are living in the woods, and they are suspicious of every one. Chancel told me that his organization had tried to get food to them, but the men sent out to try to find them returned with the report that they hadn't been able to locate a single hidden soldier. They don't know, of course, whether persons looking for them are friends or enemies, so they hide from every one."

But Kitty thought she had found an answer for that.

"I've got an idea. Tell me what you think of it. I plagiarized from Lieutenant Burke, of course."

Her idea was to use the Missing Persons column, just as Burke had done. She assumed that the men in hiding would slip into villages when they could and get hold of newspapers to find out the progress of the war, and try to get some inkling of the most likely points at which to break out of occupied territory. Since they would have little to occupy their time, she thought also that they would probably read everything in any paper they got hold of. Thus they ought to see her advertisement.

"Now how about something like this, Etta?" Kitty asked, and she wrote:

"Jonathan Burke, formerly of Dunkirk, is seeking his friends and relatives. His present address is 2, Rue Balny d'Avricourt, Paris, 17."

"The way I figure it out," Kitty said, "is that all the men who were in Burke's unit will understand at once that Burke has found a means of escape, and will communicate with him. No doubt they'll pass the word on to others. When we get answers, we will go to

86

the places they indicate—that will be safer than putting anything in writing ourselves. If we only get one or two answers, we can get in touch with others by using their names, and so on."

I picked up the paper and read the wording of Kitty's advertisement carefully.

"I see two objections to this," I said. "The first is that we have to remember that not only English soldiers, but also Gestapo men will probably read this ad. It would be terribly dangerous to give our address—especially after the little experience we have had with the Nazis already. The second is that we can't use Burke's name. He's on record as a German prisoner. Suppose some one in the Doullens hospital sees it? They'll be down on us at once like a ton of brick."

"You're right," Kitty said, with disappointment in her voice. She thought for a moment.

"I have it!" she exclaimed. "We'll use William Gray's name. He's not on any German records anywhere, and he's safely out of occupied territory.

"As for the address, I know what we can do about that. There's a little café on the Rue Rodier, near where my shop used to be. It's a typical Paris *bistro,* and its proprietor is as French as they come. He's even named Durand." (What Kitty meant was that he had one of the commonest names in French, like Smith in English). "I ran into him the other day, and he rushed up to greet me with the words, 'In days like these, I'm happy to shake the hand of an Englishwoman.' I'm sure he'll let us give his address. He isn't responsible for what his customers do. In fact, he can always say that he doesn't even know who could have used it. Everybody here gives café addresses without even asking permission. I know we can trust him."

And with a sly chuckle, she added:

"Won't it be fun to help English soldiers to escape with the aid of the German-controlled newspapers?"

Kitty was so impatient to get to work that she rose early, in spite of our all-night conference, and went off to *Paris-Soir* to insert her advertisement. When she returned an hour later, she reported that she had even argued the advertising department into promising insertion of her ad in the last edition for the same day, in spite of the fact that the shortage of paper, which restricted *Paris-Soir* to two pages, often forced considerable delays in the appearance of advertisements.

She had also managed during her brief absence to talk with the café proprietor.

"It's all right," she told me. "He was wonderful. If the police make any inquiries, he is going to deny knowing who gave his address. If they leave any one there to watch who comes for that mail, he won't give it to us. We aren't to ask for it in any case. When we go there, we will simply sit down at a table and give an order, and if it's safe, he'll bring us letters without being asked. So that's all fixed."

We sat down to breakfast—for Kitty had been in such a hurry to get out that she hadn't waited for it. She prattled on happily to Lieutenant Burke about her plan, which he approved heartily.

After breakfast we were just putting on our hats to visit M. Chancel's Left Bank friends, to arrange for them to take Burke off our hands and start him on his trip out of France, when Chancel himself arrived.

The moment he entered the room, I sensed that he had bad news. He attempted to smile, but his expression was forced. It was obvious that he was laboring under some strain.

He sat down at our invitation, and we exchanged a few formal remarks while he seemed to be trying to decide just how to tell us what had happened. Finally, giving up any thought he may have had of breaking the news gently, he blurted it out.

"*C'est fini*. The Gestapo has discovered our little organization," he said.

We were thunderstruck.

"They raided my friend's house at 9 o'clock last night," Chancel continued. "They thought they were going to get all of us—and they would have if we hadn't been warned. They were just a little too late.

"A Frenchman—if you can call him a Frenchman—whom we

had trusted and let into our group betrayed us. He didn't know all of us, but he did know that we were meeting on the Left Bank last night. Fortunately one of the people he didn't know was our man in the Prefecture—the one who fixes up the exit visas for us. He warned us. Everybody got away in time, including the boys hiding there. They were the last ones to get out across the demarcation line through our route. It's no good any more, of course. The Nazis know about that, too . . . *malheureusement.*"

Chancel heaved a deep sigh.

"Now I've got to find some way of getting out myself," he said. "They know I'm in it. I didn't sleep at home last night, so they don't know where I am. I'm going to Salies de Béarn and see if I can get through there. Meanwhile, I came here to warn you not to go near my place or the Left Bank house. The Gestapo is watching both of them."

"Then they'll be here any minute!" I gasped.

"Oh, no!" Chancel answered. "You're all right. Our friend at the Prefecture is trusted completely by the Germans, and he knows everything they know. They've never heard of you, and don't know you're implicated. You're in no danger whatsoever."

Chancel rose, as though immobility irked him, and paced back and forward rapidly.

"It's too bad," he said. "Our organization is broken up, and just when it could have been most useful! In a few weeks, or a few months at the most, the Germans will have established such a perfect system of police, internment camps, and so forth, that we will find it difficult to help any one any more. In fact, by then they may have done such a good job of rounding up fugitives that there won't be any one to help. . . . Well, I'm going out, till this blows over, but I'll be back."

"You're going to risk that?" Kitty asked.

Chancel sat down again and smiled faintly:

"Yes, I'm coming back. I'll stay in the unoccupied zone just long enough to grow a beard to hide my face wounds, so the Germans won't be able to recognize me on sight. That will take three or four weeks, I suppose, and in the meantime I'll work on establishing a group to take care of men we get across the line, and smuggle them into Spain or Portugal. I'll get in touch with you when I come back."

"What a shame!" said Kitty. "And I was so hopeful of being able to get in touch with more English soldiers. I put an advertisement in *Paris-Soir* only this morning asking them to write me."

"You—what?" Chancel almost roared, as he leaped from his chair in the greatest excitement.

"I advertised for them in the paper," Kitty repeated.

"My God!" Chancel exclaimed. "That was terribly imprudent! What did you say?"

Kitty hurried to her desk, took the copy of her advertisement, and handed it to Chancel. He looked over it hastily, and said severely:

"You shouldn't have done this! Don't you realize that the Gestapo is going to read this even before the boys it's intended for? They read every line that appears in *Paris-Soir* before the paper is allowed to go to press. They're sure to spot this!"

Kitty was almost in tears. She made me think of a child whose newest toy has been taken away.

"When did you insert this ad? Is there still time to stop it?"

Kitty shook her head.

"No, it's in today's paper. They sent it to the printer while I was there. But is it really so dangerous? I've been very careful. I gave a false name and address at the paper. The address given in the advertisement is a café. I'm sure of the proprietor. He's prepared to deny he knows anything about it. I don't see how the Gestapo could possibly trace it to us."

Chancel read through the advertisement again, slowly and carefully this time.

"I beg your pardon," he said at last. "You can understand my excitement, under the circumstances. After all, this seems to be fairly safe. I must warn you of one danger, however. If replies come in, you will have no way of telling whether they are not from Gestapo agents. Therefore you must be extremely careful about answering them or acting on them. I've always been of the opinion myself that we tend to overestimate the cleverness and ingenuity of the Gestapo, but it would be a bad error to take them for idiots."

"Perhaps it isn't rescuing any more Englishmen that's our main problem just now," I interrupted. "Have you stopped to figure out what we're going to do with Lieutenant Burke?"

Kitty bit her lip. It was clear that in the excitement of plans for the future, she had forgotten entirely that we now had an unsolved problem of the past to worry about.

"Yes," she said. "I had forgotten. What advice can you give us about that, M. Chancel?"

"None," he said. "I'm sorry, but I'm temporarily unable to be of any use to you. I'm a fugitive myself now, and I don't know how I'm going to get over the frontier yet. You can be sure I'll do what I can. If I succeed in finding another way into the unoccupied zone, I'll see that you are informed. But it's very unlikely that you will have any word from me in less than a week."

He took his leave. With him, the slight courage his presence had given us evaporated. The atmosphere was funereal. We were back where we had been when we were hiding William Gray, and had no idea which way to turn to aid his escape. It seemed unlikely that the miracle of finding a Chancel would be repeated.

From the kitchen, in the deathly silence, we could hear Margot humming a Breton folk song. On the other side, we could hear Lieutenant Burke pacing back and forth. Perhaps he had sensed the predicament about which we still had to tell him.

Kitty's head turned towards the entrance. I didn't have to speak to her to know the meaning of that instinctive gesture. I, too, had heard the elevator. I realized that once again we would have to pass days of fear and trembling, when we would quiver each time the elevator stopped at our floor, or the door bell rang.

It was hardly with enthusiasm that Kitty unfolded the *Paris-Soir* when it arrived, and found our advertisement. She handed the paper to me, with a pitiful expression on her face.

"To think," she said, "that some poor fellows may answer this advertisement with the last feeling of hope they may ever experience —and we will be unable to help them."

She stared intently at the floor for a moment, as though she were discovering the design of the carpet for the first time.

"There is only one thing we can do, Etta," she said. "We must drive to the border, and find some French peasant living along the line who will agree to smuggle our protégés across. We'd better do it as soon as possible—tomorrow, if I can get gas."

Then she interrupted herself:

"We can't do it tomorrow! We have to get Corporal Meehan tomorrow. What in the world are we going to do with two of them? Goodness knows how long we'll have to keep them here!"

"But Kitty!" I protested. "You aren't going to bring Corporal Meehan here now, are you?"

Kitty looked at me in surprise.

"Why, Etta," she said, "how can you suggest that we should leave him there? We *must* go. We promised."

CHAPTER ELEVEN

"Where Is Lieutenant Burke?"

THAT night I dreamed that we drove up in our car to the hospital at Doullens. Before the gate stood the same Gestapo agent who had searched the apartment. He smiled with satirical courtesy, and said quietly: "We have been waiting for you for a long time." With that, two helmeted German soldiers raised their rifles and pointed them at us.

At this point, I awoke, so terrified that it took me nearly an hour to get to sleep again. Once more I went through the same nightmare, and woke up again at the same identical spot. I must have had that dream half a dozen times during the course of the night. When it finally came time to get up, I was worn and exhausted, hardly in shape to set out on another adventure.

But Kitty had apparently slept like a child. She had risen early, while I was still tossing through the last version of my bad dream, taken the car to the garage, and had it overhauled in preparation for the trip. When she joined me at the breakfast table, her eyes were bright and sparkling, and she was in excellent spirits. She saw at once that I was not, and said:

"If you don't feel well, Etta, you can stay home. I'll go to Doullens alone."

"I didn't sleep well," I explained. "I had a stupid recurring dream last night—that we were shot by the Germans at Doullens. You know I don't believe in dreams, but this one has started me thinking. Don't you agree that after smuggling Lieutenant Burke out of that hospital, it's suicidal for us to turn up there again, and repeat the performance?"

"Do you really think so?" Kitty asked, looking at me searchingly.

"I'm sure of it," I said. "It's quite possible they don't suspect us of having had anything to do with Lieutenant Burke's disappearance. In fact, perhaps it hasn't even occurred to them to put our visit and his escape together. But if we turn up there again, that will remind them that we visited the hospital and talked to Burke just before he disappeared. It may start them thinking. And then if another soldier disappears, the fact that prisoners have escaped twice just after our visits there is bound to seem suspicious. I'm afraid we'll be arrested almost as soon as they find Meehan is missing. And if they come here, they'll find the two men in the apartment. We'll be caught in the act."

Kitty did not answer. She sipped her tea slowly, and I could see that she was pondering what I had said. I knew how repugnant it was to her to abandon Corporal Meehan after her promise to him. I didn't like the idea either, but sober realities forced me to insist.

"Perhaps we'll be able to do something for him later," I reminded her. "But I don't think we can succeed in helping him now. Instead, we are going to imperil Lieutenant Burke, who isn't out of danger yet. In trying to save one more, we may lose both. After all, you know, in war it's often necessary to sacrifice individuals for the sake of others. If we are caught trying to save Meehan, that means that all your plans for helping many others will be destroyed."

Kitty put down her tea-cup and looked up at me.

"Etta," she said, "I can't answer you. Your arguments are perfectly sound. You are absolutely right. But I can't help it. I know it isn't logical or sensible, but I can't desert the boy. I have to keep my promise. I have no right to involve you. You see the danger clearly, and don't want to risk it. I advise you to keep out of it. Remember, I told you before I thought you ought to leave. If you don't feel as I do about this, I still think you should go. I'm going to Doullens today, and if I am caught, I don't want you to be the victim of my decision."

She rose, and went into her room. I stepped into the kitchen, and began to help Margot wrap up the gift parcels without which there would have been no excuse for appearing at the hospital. The Foyer du Soldat had supplied only a few parcels for Doullens and we had distributed them at our last trip. We had to provide new ones ourselves.

Margot helped me wrap up the packages willingly, although she had looked at us as though she thought we had taken leave of our senses when we told her to get out the few cans of sardines and the cheese we had in our pantry and make gift parcels of them. The food shortage was beginning to assume tragic proportions. A can of sardines brought a tremendous price on the Black Market, and cheese, which we could only get through our ration books, was limited to 100 grams (three and one-half ounces) per month. I felt guilty as I helped Margot stow away the provisions she had secured for us by standing patiently in line for hours. But this was all we had to give, except a few packages of cigarettes, which we added to the food.

Lieutenant Burke wandered into the kitchen. He seemed worried, and I judged that he had overheard me talking to Kitty. His door had been ajar.

"You heard what I said to Mrs. Beaurepos, I suppose," I said to him. He nodded.

"Then why didn't you put in a word and help me out?" I asked. "You agree with me, don't you? You must realize she is taking a great risk."

"Yes," Burke said slowly, "I agree—but my own position is very delicate. You got me out of Doullens, at great risk to yourself, and I have no right to seek to dissuade you from doing as much for some one else—particularly not on the grounds of my own personal safety. Meehan has as much right to a chance to escape as I have.

"But it is true, I believe, that the danger is ten times greater on the second attempt than on the first. That doesn't seem likely to deter Mrs. Beaurepos. I don't think she's going to allow herself to be dissuaded. If you can't stop her, let me give you a piece of advice. Be very careful of Major Thibaud, the chief military physician at Doullens. He's French, of course, but he's the typical military man, who accepts the orders of his superiors without question, and it makes no difference to him whether those superiors are French or German. He has been following the instructions of the Germans without a murmur. I think he would be perfectly capable of arresting you himself and turning you over to the Germans if he suspected anything."

I thanked him for the warning, picked up the parcels, and piled them on the entry table. Then I put on my coat and went to Kitty's room.

"Well," I said, "when do we start?"

"We?" Kitty exclaimed joyously. "Etta, do you mean you've changed your mind?"

"Not at all," I said. "I disapprove completely. I think you're taking an unnecessary risk and imperilling all your future plans—but if you're determined to go, I'm going with you."

Kitty threw her arms around me and kissed me on the cheek. Her brimming eyes were shining.

There was practically no traffic on the highway, and the trip to Doullens was a quick one. We passed a number of German military cars going north, but none of them showed any interest in us.

Just after we had passed Amiens, a large open truck appeared ahead of us. As we overtook it, we saw that it was full of English prisoners—about thirty of them crowded together in the body of the vehicle. Four German soldiers with fixed bayonets stood at the four corners of the truck, guarding them. They were dirty, ragged and unshaven. I judged they were some of the men who had been in hiding, and had been rounded up by the motorcycle patrols.

Kitty threw an almost panicky glance at me, and stepped on the accelerator, to get away from the distressing sight as quickly as possible.

"It's terrible," she burst out, "that Chancel's organization had to fail us at just this time, when there are so many to be helped! Did you see those poor men, worn-out and exhausted, packed into a truck without even a place to sit down, being moved about like cattle!"

She didn't speak again until the houses of Doullens came in sight. Then she said softly, almost as though she were speaking to herself:

"You said this morning, Etta, that sometimes it is necessary to sacrifice one individual for the sake of others. That is very true in times like these. How unimportant it would be to sacrifice one's own life if by doing so one could save a hundred or perhaps a thousand others!"

I looked at Kitty, but the words wouldn't come. She could read the emotion in my eyes.

"What's the matter, Etta?" she asked. "What's troubling you?"

"Nothing is troubling me," I said. "I was just admiring you."

"Oh, dry up," said Kitty. But she began humming contentedly as she guided the car through the narrow streets on the way to the hospital.

Kitty had timed our arrival so that we reached the hospital as the men were coming out into its garden after lunch. She parked the car under the same tree as before, gathered up the parcels, and we passed once more between the two sentries at the gate without a challenge.

As we walked slowly through the garden, we peered about for Corporal Meehan. We didn't want to ask for him, or even to be seen speaking to him if we could possibly avoid it. He wasn't in the garden, so we entered the building and started through the wards.

Finally we glimpsed him. He was in bed, looking very tired— much worse than when we had last seen him, but perhaps only because he was unshaven. His eyes lighted up at the sight of us, but he was clever enough to give no sign of recognition which others might have seen. We stopped at the bed of a French soldier next to his, and spoke to him for a few moments, pretending to pay no attention to Meehan. Then Kitty took my arm and steered me out into the corridor.

"We've got to distribute these parcels first," Kitty said. "Until we get rid of them, every one's eyes are going to be on us every second. Did you notice how those poor half-starved men stared at us, as though they were hypnotized? It's because they know we have food in these parcels."

We went to the main first-floor ward, and began to pass out our gifts. We had with us a ten-pound parcel which a relative of one of the patients had sent to the Foyer du Soldat for delivery to him. We found the boy to whom it was addressed, but his eyes were closed, and he seemed to be in a coma.

The man on the next bed stretched out a bony hand towards the parcel.

"It's no good giving it to him," he said. "He doesn't know what's happening, and doesn't care. He saw his brother killed at Dunkirk, and when he comes to, all he does is rave about joining him. It won't be long before he does. . . . The rest of us will go that way too unless you people can get us more packages. We can't recover our strength here because we get so little food—mostly dirty hot water they call soup. We're being starved to death."

Kitty helped him open the package and divide the contents among those in the ward—cake, chocolates and cigarettes.

When we had gotten rid of our parcels, and could move about without attracting so much attention, we passed through several wards on the way back to the one where we had seen Meehan, chatting with the prisoners, and doing our best to appear natural. Finally we got back to the room where we had seen Meehan. His bed was empty!

"How stupid!" I said. "Why didn't he wait for us? Or perhaps he went to the garden, expecting us to go there."

We went out into the garden. There was still no sign of him. By this time I, who had opposed coming in the first place, had become more anxious than Kitty seemed to be to find him. Without even thinking that this gave me an excuse to get Kitty away without letting her take the risk of engineering a second escape, I almost dragged her back through all the wards once more. Finally we gave up.

"We might as well go home, Kitty," I said. "He seems to have disappeared completely. We've wasted the whole day for nothing. And it's all his fault, the stupid fellow!"

We passed through the corridor on the way to the hospital office, where we had to sign out. "Perhaps he's in the office," I said to Kitty, as we approached it. "He might have been called there for some reason. That would account for our not finding him."

I reached for the doorknob; but just as I was about to put my hand on it, the door swung open. A man in the uniform of a major, with the emblems of the medical service on his tunic and cap, stood before us.

"*Ah, c'est vous,*" he said. "Permit me to introduce myself—Major Thibaud."

It was the man of whom Lieutenant Burke had warned us!

"I believe you ladies have honored us with your visit before," he said slowly. "It is really very kind of you—extraordinarily kind, I might say—to take so much interest in so small a hospital."

Before either Kitty or myself had time to think of a reply, he bent over and said in a low confidential tone.

"I wonder if you would be kind enough to answer just one question for me? Would you be so good as to inform me where Lieutenant Burke is at this moment?"

I felt as though my heart had suddenly stopped beating. The scene seemed to be recreating my dream. Instead of the Gestapo agent, Major Thibaud was playing his part. But the end might very well be much the same.

Even in my terror, I could not fail to admire Kitty's self-possession.

"You must be a mind reader, Major," she said. "We have been through the whole hospital twice looking for him. Was he sent back to the Citadel?"

Major Thibaud did not answer at once. He scrutinized Kitty carefully. Then he stepped back through the door, saying, "Kindly come into my office."

The doctor's office was no more prepossessing than any of the rest of it—gray, dirty and foul-smelling. We sat down before Major Thibaud's desk in chairs which he designated to us with a wave of the hand. But he did not sit down. He clasped his hands behind his back, walked over to a small window and looked out for a moment, as though in deep thought. Then he paced back and forth slowly, once or twice. The silence and the tension of waiting were unbearable. Kitty, sitting close beside me, put her hand gently on my arm, and I felt a little more courageous. Major Thibaud turned, and stopped before us.

"Our conversation will be shortened," he began, "if you ladies will be intelligent enough not to deny the obvious fact that it was you who helped Lieutenant Burke to escape from this hospital. Since his disappearance, I have of course made a careful investigation. Your names appeared on our visitors' register for the day of Lieutenant Burke's escape, and it was simply a routine measure to check on you with the Foyer du Soldat. You, Mme. Beaurepos, are British-born. I can understand your sympathy with a British soldier, and it therefore does not surprise me that after your visit one of the

very few English prisoners here should have been the one to escape.
You, Mme. Shiber, are an American, and may be assumed to have
a certain fellow feeling with another Anglo-Saxon also.

"I cannot, of course, criticize you ladies for desiring to help Lieutenant Burke to escape. However, we are not concerned here with
human sympathies, but with decrees and ordinances. You happen
to have violated the laws established by the High Command of the
occupying forces."

Kitty, who had kept silent up to now, broke in at this point.

"But I assure you, Major, we know nothing about Lieutenant
Burke's escape. We have just learned of it at this moment from
you."

Major Thibaud lifted his hand to check her protests.

"Please," he said firmly. "I am not a fool, Mme. Beaurepos. That
you helped Lieutenant Burke to escape is so obvious that I am not
going to waste time even in debating the question. Perhaps you
will realize the uselessness of your denial if I tell you that I happened to send for Lieutenant Burke to examine his eye twenty
minutes after you had left the hospital. He had gone. So had
you. There is really no sense in your denying that he went with
you."

"Pardon me," Kitty retorted. "The fact that he may have disappeared at about the same time that we left the hospital doesn't
necessarily mean that he went with us. He may have taken advantage of the distraction caused by our visit to get out; but he didn't
get away with our help or knowledge."

"Très bien," said the Major, in an irritated tone. "Persist in your
denial, if you want. We both know what to think of it, of course.
Now let me tell you what I am going to do."

He was silent for a moment, weighing his words. I could hear the
sound of Kitty's breathing.

"You liberated a prisoner from this hospital," he said deliberately,
raising his hand again to check another denial he saw forthcoming
from Kitty. "It is my duty to hand you over to the authorities,
which, in this region and at this time, means to the German Army.
I am a soldier. It is my habit to obey orders."

He paused for another instant. My heart was beating madly.

A softened tone came into his voice.

"But I am not only a soldier, ladies," he said. "I am a Frenchman. That is why I have not yet reported the disappearance of Lieutenant Burke."

I sat bolt upright in my chair, thunderstruck at the unexpectedness of this development. I could see that Kitty, too, had suddenly realized that, after all, we were perhaps not yet lost.

"I have not yet decided," Major Thibaud was continuing, "just how to dispose of this case. The occupying authorities are, as you know, very meticulous, and the completeness of their records and of their controls does not make it easy for a man to disappear without being noticed. However, every system has its weaknesses, and that of completeness of records is afflicted with some of its own. It is, for instance, not impossible that in the multiplicity of papers concerned in receiving patients, discharging them, transferring them, and so forth, there might arise cases where it would require considerable research to discover just where a certain individual represented by those pieces of paper was supposed to be. It would take, perhaps, more trouble than it would be worth. This is simply an interesting observation which I have had occasion to make in the course of my work, and I would certainly not advise any one to trust any important practical measure to this possibility."

His dry tones suddenly became sharper, as though he were issuing an order.

"I must ask you ladies to leave this hospital at once, and not to return. If you had any intention of repeating your act, I must ask your formal promise that you renounce it. I might add that failure on your part to keep such a promise would very probably be fatal to yourselves. I advise you to forget this conversation as soon as you have left here. I am quite sure that I shan't remember it myself."

Kitty rose, and held out her hand.

"Thank you, Major," she said. "I am very happy to have met another real Frenchman."

Major Thibaud took her hand without answering her compliment.

"You will pardon me," he said drily, "if I take the precaution of escorting you to your car."

I was too exhausted by the emotional strain of the interview with Major Thibaud to speak until we were several kilometers outside of Doullens. The spell was broken by a German motorcycle patrol, which passed us with much shrill hooting, and enveloped us in whirling clouds of dust.

"I wonder what will happen to that poor corporal?" I said.

Kitty didn't answer.

"I'm afraid we'll just have to forget about him," I went on, afraid that she might not yet have abandoned the impossible task of rescuing Corporal Meehan. "We can't ever go back to the hospital again."

Kitty turned her head towards me and smiled.

"It won't be necessary," she said. "Corporal Meehan is in the luggage compartment."

CHAPTER TWELVE

Nach Paris

THE expression on my face was too much for Kitty. She started laughing so uncontrollably that she had to pull the car up to the side of the road. It was contagious. I had to join in, too, and there we sat by the side of the road, two women roaring with laughter, in a country where laughter had become rare.

"How do you know he's in there?" I asked when I could speak again. "You haven't had a chance to look."

"He is if he followed instructions," Kitty said. "Let's find out."

She leaned over the back of the seat, and called:

"Corporal Meehan! Are you all right?"

His muffled voice floated back to us.

"All right, thanks," he said, "except that I hurt my leg a little getting over that wall, low as it was."

"Don't worry about that," Kitty said. "We'll fix it up when we get home. We're off to Paris now."

As we swung out into the road again, I asked:

"But how did you do it, Kitty? We didn't even speak to him!"

"You showed me the way," Kitty said with a mischievous smile.

"I?"

"Yes, when you pointed out to me this morning how dangerous it would be if we were seen speaking to the second soldier to escape from Doullens. When I went into my room, I wrote down the same directions I had given Lieutenant Burke, and slipped them to Meehan while we were at the next bed. I never intended to speak to him."

"How could you, Kitty!" I said reproachfully. "All the time I was worrying myself to death looking for Meehan, you knew that he had already gone. Didn't you trust me?"

"Of course I did," Kitty said. "But let me ask you just one question: How did you feel in Major Thibaud's office when he accused us?"

"As though I were going to faint," I answered.

"Exactly," said Kitty, "and if you had known that Meehan was already in the car, you *would* have fainted—or maybe given him away. I thought you'd be less worried that way."

"But Kitty," I said, "what will happen now? Major Thibaud knows we took Burke out. When Meehan disappears too, what will he do? He can't protect us twice. Won't he denounce us?"

"I doubt it," said Kitty. "Just put yourself in his place. Suppose he reports Meehan's escape and says he suspects us. The Germans ask why. Does he say: 'Because the last time they were here, Lieutenant Burke escaped'? Of course not. Since he didn't report that as soon as it happened, he can't report it now. In fact, he's got to protect us from being suspected of Meehan's escape, because if they get us, they'll find out about Burke, and Major Thibaud will be for it too, for not having done anything about Burke's escape. I don't know how he'll get out of it—maybe he'll report that Meehan and Burke got away together overnight. That would put the responsibility on the sentries and the German motorcycle patrols instead of his own lack of vigilance about visitors, and set the Nazis on the wrong track in hunting for them. One thing is certain: he daren't take any chance of putting the Germans on the right trail. He'd be in trouble, too, if they caught us."

It sounded convincing, and I felt better—for a few minutes. Then, just as we were passing a German military post some 50 miles from Paris, there was a loud explosion, and the car skidded to a stop.

"Did they shoot at us?" I quavered.

Kitty laughed derisively.

"Silly! Just a tire," she laughed.

"Only a tire? What luck!" said a muffled voice from the compartment.

"Keep quiet!" Kitty warned. "Whatever you do, don't come out!"

I got out of the car, too, and together we took the spare tire off the back of the car. As we slid the jack under the axle, we heard Meehan's voice again:

"Hadn't I better get out and help? I can fix it in a minute."

Kitty leaned into the back of the car as though looking for tools, and said sharply: "For goodness sake, keep quiet! There's a German post only a few yards away."

Her warning came none too soon. A German officer strolled over from the military post, and stopped a few feet away, watching us with apparent enjoyment of our plight.

Kitty, tugging at the rim of the wheel, grunted between clenched teeth: "If that Fritz doesn't go away, I'll throw the jack at him."

"Be careful, Kitty," I whispered. "Don't forget we mustn't arouse their curiosity."

Kitty muttered in French something unladylike and unprintable about the German. Several times she turned to cast a contemptuous glance in his direction. He seemed to misread her meaning—or perhaps it was the picture Kitty presented, with the high color resulting from her effort enhancing her natural handsome charm. He walked over to the car, and bowed politely. I thought he might offer to help with the tire. But no!

"I beg pardon, ladies," he said. "I wonder if you would give me a lift to Paris? I have been waiting for my car for half an hour, and it hasn't arrived yet. You are French, I suppose?"

"No, Americans," I said. I hoped this might cause him to leave us alone. Unfortunately, it had exactly the opposite effect.

"Americans!" he said. *"Sehr interessant!"* And turning towards Kitty with a manner that made it quite plain that she was the one he was interested in, he said: "I am sorry I don't speak English, but I see that you speak French very well. Please excuse me for not offering to help you, but I thought you were French, and French women have been behaving very badly towards us. I could not, of course, risk a snub by offering to help. Since you are neutrals, Americans, I'm sure you'll allow me to aid."

He waved towards the post, and a soldier trotted across the road to us. The officer said a few words in German, the soldier saluted, and taking Kitty's place, began to wrestle with the recalcitrant tire.

"Well, well, Americans!" the German officer said again, as though Americans were rare objects. He launched into a dissertation evidently intended to be complimentary to us, about the charm of

American women and the brilliance of American moving picture stars.

I didn't pay much attention to what he said. I was anxiously scanning the road, hoping his car would appear. But the soldier finished changing the tire, saluted, and returned to his post, and no car had yet appeared.

"Well, *meine Damen*," the German smiled, "I'm afraid you're in for it. You'll have to accept my company to Paris—or rather to Chantilly. You can drop me off there."

And with that he opened the back door of the car. My heart was in my mouth. I knew that Meehan must have heard and would not speak, but to any one sitting in the back seat, the slightest movement or the lowest cough would be audible. Once again, Kitty's coolness saved the situation.

"Oh, don't sit back there all by yourself," she smiled. "Come in front with us. There's plenty of room for three."

Obviously the German was waiting for nothing better. He promptly got in the front seat, placing himself between us, with one arm resting along the back of the seat touching Kitty's shoulder.

The trip to Paris I thought would never end. The German, highly pleased with himself, sat jabbering away. Our only consolation was that as long as he continued to talk a steady stream he couldn't hear any noise from the luggage compartment. He seemed to be especially obsessed with the failure of French women to appreciate the merits of German officers.

"It's so stupid of the French not to invite us to visit their families," he said. "I should very much like to get to know Paris from the inside. We want only to be friendly. Yet these cold Frenchmen hold us at arm's length—and the women are even worse."

He tightened his grip on Kitty's shoulder a trifle, and went on:

"It's so sad to see Paris under these circumstances—Paris, so famous for its good living and its handsome, friendly women. *Ach,* Paris! *Ach,* French champagne! *Wein, Weib und Gesang!* At least, Madame, I can say that one woman has been charming to me in France."

Long before we had reached Chantilly, he was obviously paying court to Kitty. When at last, after what had seemed an interminable journey, we let him off in front of the German Kommandantur at Chantilly, he said: "I thank you heartily, ladies. I hope I may have the pleasure of meeting you again—perhaps of calling to pay my respects, if you will be good enough to give me your address?"

He produced a small notebook from his pocket, and without further ceremony copied Kitty's name and address from the plate on the dashboard, which complied with the French law that the owner's name and address must be displayed on every car.

"And if you should happen to find yourself in the neighborhood of the Rue St. Dominique, in Paris, I should be flattered if you would pay me a call. Please take my card—Captain Kurt Weber, special prosecutor of the Military Tribunal . . . *Auf Wiedersehen!*"

He saluted smartly, and walked briskly to the building of the Kommandantur, where he turned and favored us with another impeccable military salute before entering. We drove off hastily.

"Etta," Kitty said to me, "I thought I'd go mad! Honestly, there were moments when I thought of upsetting the car to get rid of him. Better take a look back there and see how our corporal is getting on."

I called softly but there was no answer. I listened, and heard what seemed to be the sound of snoring from the luggage compartment. My blood curdled at the thought: suppose he had fallen asleep and started snoring while the German was in the car. Now it didn't matter.

I turned back to Kitty.

"He's gone to sleep."

"Good," she said. Then, after a moment's pause:

"What in the world are we going to do if Captain Weber takes it into his head to call while we still have Burke and Meehan in the apartment? I think he has it in mind."

I thought he had also. He had harped throughout the drive on the cool reception he had had from French women. I had heard many stories about the boycott they had applied to the invaders, some of whom had been tactless enough to insist on being received in French families.

I had heard of one case, for instance, where a German officer had agreed to sign certain necessary papers for one lady only on condition that she receive him and members of his staff in her home and introduce them to some young French women. All the Germans desired, he explained, was to be able to enter into normal relations of friendship with French persons, and she would be doing her own people a service as well as the Germans by helping to promote better relations between them.

The papers which the French woman needed were authorizations freeing her husband from a prison camp. To get them, she consented. As agreed, the German officers arrived at her home, and were introduced to a number of her friends. Anticipating a pleasant evening, they set out to make conversation. One typical exchange began like this:

THE OFFICER: Paris is a beautiful city, isn't it?

THE LADY: Yes.

THE OFFICER: Parisian women are charming. Don't you think so?

THE LADY: Yes.

THE OFFICER: Don't you like us Germans?

THE LADY: No.

The Germans left twenty minutes after their arrival.

It was safe to say, the exceptions were so few, that French women were never seen in the company of Germans. Many German women had come to Paris to join their husbands, but most of the Germans were still completely deprived of feminine company, and hungered for it. To avoid incidents and public snubs which would tend to decrease the prestige of the German uniform, they were forbidden by their own regulations to approach French women in the streets of Paris during the daytime. But at night, under cover of the blackout, the soldiers were apt to show themselves highly aggressive.

It became very unpleasant for a woman to walk through the streets of Paris at night. They were pitch-black because of the stringent regulations, and it was possible to walk into a group of German soldiers without seeing them. They thought nothing of seizing a passing woman by the arm, and when they were in packs, they would often surround a woman, repeating over and over the only French phrase most of them knew: *"S'il vous plaît, Mademoiselle."*

There was usually no real danger. A woman had only to threaten resolutely to call an officer. The German soldiers were so well disciplined that the one word "officer" (which is the same in French and German) was sufficient to tame them completely. But with the officers themselves, that didn't work. One French woman told us her method for disarming them. That was to say, "You know, of course, that I'm Jewish."

The word was passed around among Parisian women that another way of embarrassing German officers was to gaze fixedly either at their collars or their feet. One friend of ours made successful use of this trick in a subway station, where she noticed a German officer staring at her in impertinent fashion, and thought it probable that he might annoy her. They were both standing at the center of the subway platform, where the first-class car of the subway trains stop. She began looking at his feet as though there were something curious about them. He quickly became aware of the direction of her gaze, and looked down at his shoes himself. He could hardly have seen anything abnormal about them, but as the young lady continued to stare at them, he became obviously ill at ease, and shuffled about as though trying to hide his feet. When the train pulled in, he hurried into the car in such haste that she was able to get into the following second-class carriage before he noticed that she had given him the slip.

CHAPTER THIRTEEN

The Wound

IT was quite dark as we rounded the Arc de Triomphe, passing through the Place de l'Etoile. In other days, this circle had always blazed with light, and was one of the most frequented spots in Paris. Now it was dark, gloomy and deserted.

"There is only one thing to do," Kitty said, as we swung around the great bulk of the arch, dimly outlined in darkest black against a blue-black sky, "and that is to tell Margot that we are not at home to Captain Weber, and it is up to her to keep him out if he comes. We mustn't let him get inside the apartment."

She pulled up at the curb in front of our building.

"I'll go ahead to see if the coast is clear," she said. "Whatever you do, don't come up until I come back—just in case I've guessed wrong about how Major Thibaud will act. If I shouldn't come down at all, you'd better find some other place to spend the night."

But her fears were groundless. A few minutes later she was back.

"Everything's all right," she said. "Let's get him out of there."

We opened the baggage compartment. Corporal Meehan did not stir. Evidently he was still asleep.

Kitty reached in and shook him.

"Here we are, Corporal," she said. "Last stop. All change."

Still Meehan didn't budge.

"What's the matter with him?" I asked apprehensively. I was afraid some one would come along before we got him out. The street was deserted for the moment, but I knew a passerby might turn the corner at any instant.

There was a sort of moan from the luggage compartment, and Meehan stirred at last. He dragged himself out of his hiding place. He seemed to be having a good deal of difficulty in moving, which I attributed to his sudden awakening, and the cramped position he had been occupying. Kitty and I each took an arm and helped him out. We hobbled into the building, with Meehan between us, leaning heavily on our arms.

Kitty had left the elevator on the ground floor with the door jammed open, so that no one could call it before we got there. We helped Meehan in. His eyelids drooped, and he seemed about to fall asleep standing up, leaning against us and the wall.

"We'll have to get him into bed the minute we get in," Kitty whispered. "He can hardly stand. In his condition, the trip was probably too much for him."

Margot and Burke were both standing in the entry waiting for us when we opened the door. Both looked anxious.

"Everything go off all right?" Burke asked.

He got no answer. Kitty had let go of Meehan, and he had dropped heavily straight to the floor, and lay there, sprawled out and unmoving.

With an exclamation, Burke knelt down and bent over Meehan. He glanced up at us.

"He's fainted," he said. "What's the matter with him?"

"I don't know," Kitty said.

"Let's get him onto a bed," Burke said. He took hold of Meehan under the shoulders. Margot bent over to take his feet. But hardly had she touched him than she sprang up again with a scream.

"Mon Dieu!" she cried. "Blood!"

Sure enough, one leg of Meehan's trousers was soaked with blood. Burke was the first to realize what had happened.

"His leg wound must have reopened because of the cramped position and the jolting of the car," he said.

"Or when he climbed that wall," Kitty remarked. She turned to the maid.

"Margot," she ordered, "phone for a doctor at once." Then she suddenly checked herself as she realized the situation. "No, no," she countermanded, as Margot obediently moved towards the phone. "No! Don't! We can't call a doctor!"

"What shall we do?" I asked, thoroughly frightened now.

"First we'd better get him to bed," Burke said again, and bent over to lift him up. But the moment he moved him, great drops of blood dripped from the wounded leg to the floor.

"Guess we'd better let him lie still on the floor for the moment," Burke said. "He's lost too much blood already. Can't afford to lose more. The first thing is to stop the bleeding. I'll try to bandage the wound. Have you any bandages in the house?"

Kitty shook her head.

"Run to the pharmacy, Margot, and get some bandages. Whatever you do, don't tell what they're for."

Margot darted out the door.

"Etta," Kitty said, "get some towels from the bathroom—and a few handkerchiefs. They may help to bandage the wound temporarily until Margot gets back."

I turned to obey, when something happened which froze me in my tracks. The doorbell pealed, loudly and insistently.

We all stood stock still, silent and transfixed, as though we had been turned into statues. The bell rang again.

Kitty made a hopeless gesture with her hand.

"It's no use," she said. "We can't hide this. Etta, answer the door."

Never in my life have I performed any act with such reluctance as opening that door—but our fears were unfounded. Behind it was the answer to all our troubles.

I had expected to open to our visitor from the Gestapo, or perhaps to Major Thibaud, accompanied by the police. Instead, Henri Beaurepos, Kitty's husband, entered.

He stopped, astonished at the tense expressions of the little group that confronted him. Then his gaze swung downward to Corporal Meehan, lying on the floor, and he seemed to understand the whole situation in a flash, without need of an explanation. He took complete charge at once, and in a few minutes he had solved our problems like magic.

His first care was for Corporal Meehan. He phoned a doctor friend of his, whom he assured us could be trusted completely, and who had the further advantage of living close by. He was in our apartment in five minutes, and in fifteen Meehan was comfortably tucked away in bed, his wound washed and bandaged.

But the doctor did not hide from us that his condition was bad.

"He hasn't had proper care," he said, shaking his head disapprovingly. "Infection has set in, and it isn't going to be easy to treat at this stage. I'll come again in the morning, and decide whether I hadn't better have a specialist take a look at him."

When he left, Henri settled another problem for us. Kitty explained our activities, and Henri smiled at her description of our mental state, with two British soldiers on our hands, and no way to get them out of the occupied zone.

"So you let a little thing like that worry you, my dear?" he asked teasingly. "Why, it's child's play! Since the Germans established the demarcation line, I've crossed it secretly seven times. I have business at Bordeaux, and I've been going in and out to attend to it. I have a friend at Libourne—Tissier—you may have heard me speak of him; I buy his wine every year. His vineyards stretch across the line, and I pass through there. I can pass Lieutenant Burke across for you, and the wounded man too, whenever he's strong enough to travel. There's not the slightest difficulty about it."

Kitty threw an ecstatically happy look towards her husband.

"Mr. Tissier," Henri continued, "is an excellent Frenchman, and is delighted to let any one use his land to escape from the Germans. There's a slight charge, though—50 francs a person. That isn't the price Tissier puts on his services. It's a legitimate expense. It seems that the Herrenvolk, the Supermen, as they call themselves, like to make a little small change now and then. The New Order seems to bear a certain resemblance to the eastern system of government, which involves handing out frequent doles of bakshish. Tissier figures that tips to German sergeants work out at about fifty francs a head."

He grinned, and Kitty smiled back at him. I thought, as I had thought often before, that they were a curious couple. They seemed deeply in love with one another, although they had been separated for years. Ever since I had lived with Kitty, she had always talked of him most affectionately—yet much of the time she didn't even know his address. His business as a wine merchant required him to do a good deal of travelling, and sometimes months passed without his turning up, or even writing a letter. But whenever he did come to town, the day was a holiday for both of them. As far as I could see, there was no disagreement of any kind between them. They simply preferred, both of them, to live separately, and see each other only at intervals.

Henri was a fascinating companion, a good talker, who seemed to know a little about everything, and who always managed to learn what was going on within a few minutes of arriving anywhere. Although we lived in Paris, we knew very little of what was happening there. Henri, who had just come in, had heard all the news.

"I saw Goering this morning," he told us. "It seems that he and Himmler were not killed in the air raid. Too bad."

He was referring to an incident which had been whispered about Paris shortly before. A banquet had been given in a big hotel in Normandy to celebrate the arrival of Goering, at which several officers of the German General Staff had been present. For the sake of safety, no previous announcement of the banquet had been made —but the R.A.F., obviously well informed, arrived in good time to catch the party in full blast and did a little blasting of its own.

The day after, the swastika banners in Paris were draped with black. The word went around that the Germans were mourning some important persons killed at the banquet, but no one knew exactly who the victims were. Rumors were wild, as usual, some of them even suggesting hopefully that Hitler himself had been killed. Finally, they crystallized to the report that Goering and Himmler had been the victims, chiefly because Goering, always a conspicuous spectacle, hadn't been seen for several days. But here he had turned up again, alive and apparently unhurt! Henri said he had heard that the important victim had been, not Himmler, but Himmler's brother.

"I saw Goering in the Rue de la Paix," Henri said. "He was getting out of his car. He had on a light-colored eye-catching uniform, and he had brought along his field marshal's baton. I suppose he sleeps with it. When I first saw him, he was holding it in his outstretched arm like a choir boy afraid of being burned by his candle. It was a pretty ludicrous sight. I wondered that the officers with him were able to keep a straight face, but they managed. Perhaps they don't have the same sense for the ridiculous we have.

"He went into Cartier's. They tell me he bought an 8,000,000 franc necklace. I judge he can afford it. Money's no object to him. . . . He seems to prefer that his wife should wear French rather than German styles, in spite of the German claims that their fashions are sounder than our degenerate Paris modes. He goes to the best couturiers whenever he comes to Paris and personally picks out their most lavish creations for Madame Goering. He goes in heavily for silk pajamas. Incidentally, he buys them in such tremendous sizes that although Frau Goering is no lightweight, there's a suspicion that he wears those feminine pajamas himself."

The subject of Goering's purchases naturally led Henri on to the emptying of French shops by the Germans, which we had noticed vaguely, but hadn't paid much attention to, since we were too much preoccupied with our soldiers to think of clothes. Henri told us that the soldiers were buying women's clothing—particularly furs, stockings and cloth to make dresses—until most of the shops had been obliged to close for want of anything more to sell.

This was not only the result of individual purchases by German soldiers, supplied with plenty of occupation marks, but also of regular organized looting, Henri explained. It had not occurred to French citizens at first that private homes and apartments would be entered and stripped of their valuables. That, however, was what happened. Furniture, tapestries, art objects, and other valuables were taken from the homes of persons who had not returned to Paris. Specialists saw to their packing and transport to Germany. Linen was used to wrap up the confiscated objects, and thus went to Germany as well.

Henri told us one story of the caretaker of a château in the department of Seine-et-Marne who watched impotently while the building was so thoroughly cleaned out that he called to the Germans as they were leaving: "Wait a minute! You've forgotten to take the nails!"

Electric refrigerators seemed to be particularly welcome to the Nazis, Henri remarked. His refrigerator was one of the things which was missing when he returned to his home, where he found a Nazi officer had been billeted.

"I asked him," Henri said, " 'Can I count on being allowed to keep the few things which have not yet been taken away?' The fellow wasn't embarrassed at all. It apparently struck him as quite a normal question. He said, 'I think so. The specialists have already been through here. They've probably taken everything they thought worth while.'

"The way it works, you know, is that they come in directly behind the fighting troops, and pounce before you have time to hide anything. They're very thorough; you know the Germans. You're lucky not to have had their visit here. Perhaps they ran out of transportation. That's the reason they've been giving for cutting down food parcels to the prisoners of war, you know—not enough trains to handle them. But they found trains for their loot, all right."

It was well after midnight. Henri looked at his watch, and rose to go.

"You'd better stay here," I said. "Don't you know that in Paris civilians can't use the streets at night? You might get picked up by a German patrol."

Henri smiled, and produced a pass with the seal of the German Kommandantur on it.

"Five hundred francs to a German sergeant-major for this," he said. "Good for fourteen days. Want one? I can get one for you."

He picked up his hat, and moved towards the door. With his hand on the knob, he turned.

"Oh, by the way," he said, "I'm dropping in at the Prefecture tomorrow morning. I know a man there who'll give us passes in French names for your two English friends. I'll see that they're taken to the train, and that some one goes with them all the way to Tissier's place to make sure there's no trouble. You needn't worry about them. I assure you they'll be all right."

As Kitty closed the door behind him, she turned slowly, and stood there, her back pressed against the closed door. I could see the tears in her eyes as she remained there, motionless.

"Why, Kitty," I said. "If that's the way you feel, why did you let Henri go? Didn't you realize that he would have liked to stay, if you had only uttered the slightest hint about it?"

"What a naïve little woman you are!" Kitty said, smiling through her tears. "Do you really think I'm crying about Henri? It's because what has happened is so beautiful! Only a few hours ago we thought our situation was hopeless, with Chancel's organization broken up, and no way of getting our boys out of German hands. And now we have a new means of escape for them—and for others!

"Etta! perhaps there will be answers to our advertisement tomorrow!"

CHAPTER FOURTEEN

Friends or Enemies?

ARLY in the morning—well before eight—the doorbell woke me.
I knew Margot must have gone out at six to get into line at the
grocery store (which meant that she would get in about noon), so
I got up to answer the door myself.

A French boy who appeared to be about fifteen stood at the door.
"*Voici, Madame,*" he said only, handing me three letters which
he pulled out of his pocket, and immediately hurried towards the
stairs.

"Wait a minute," I called after him. "Who are these from?" But
he clattered down the stairs without answering.

I looked at the letters. They were addressed to William Gray at
Durand's café. They must be replies to our advertisement, probably
sent over to us by Monsieur Durand. I didn't like the boy's behavior,
though, and as I went into Kitty's room to give her the letters, I told
her about the curious way in which I had received them.

"Oh, don't worry about a little thing like that," Kitty laughed.
"It's all right to be cautious, but don't let your imagination run away
with you. The boy wasn't a Gestapo agent in disguise. He's probably
Durand's errand-boy."

"Does Durand know our address?" I asked.

"Of course," Kitty said. "I gave it to him."

"I think that was a mistake, Kitty," I said. "We've got to work
secretly, and no matter how much we may trust people, the best
guarantee we can have that they won't give us away is not to let
them know anything. I'd feel much more comfortable if Durand
didn't know our address. He wouldn't betray us knowingly, no
doubt, but suppose some one followed the boy?"

"You're right," Kitty said. "Perhaps that was incautious. But I'm
sure Durand can be trusted. I'll check with him about the boy, and
ask him not to send letters over any more. . . . Why don't you call
in Lieutenant Burke while I open these letters? He'll be interested."

The first letter contained only this laconic message:

Should my name be familiar to you, kindly write to this address: Mlle. Lucie Beauvais, Bergasse, Somme.   JOHN HITCHCOCK.

"Do you know him?" Kitty asked, handing the letter to Burke. He looked at the letter carefully, and then shook his head.

"No," he said, "but that doesn't prove anything. Since you used William Gray's name, he's probably from his unit. For that matter, I wouldn't even recognize the names of every one in my own regiment."

Kitty took the letter back, and she stared at it intently, as though trying to wring some extra meaning from its single sentence.

"Bergasse must be a very small place," she said, "since the name of the village is the only address you need. Probably he's some English boy who found refuge in a peasant's home—too sick, perhaps, to continue to hide in the woods—or even wounded. We'd better write to him."

"Remember what Chancel said," I broke in. "He warned us that this was the dangerous moment. The Gestapo might be trying to trap us by answering the advertisement themselves. For all we know, the Gestapo wrote this letter. We must be very careful about answering it."

"For goodness sake, Etta," Kitty said, "how could you imagine that any one named John Hitchcock would be working for the Gestapo?"

"Would you expect a Gestapo agent writing a fake letter to sign with a German name?" I asked.

Kitty was silent for a moment. Then she burst out in exasperation:

"But what are we going to do? How are we going to tell? What's the use of all this effort if we're going to distrust the letters when they come in? William Gray isn't here. We can't check with him on these names! And see how cautiously this letter is worded. He' afraid of a trap, too. Would the Gestapo write that way?"

"They might if they were clever enough," I said. "They'd want to make it sound authentic. As for the name, perhaps they're using the name of a real soldier whom they've captured—just as we used William Gray's name. But what's in the next letter?"

It was even shorter than the other. It contained no message, only an address:

B. W. Stowe
12, Rue de la Gare
Reims

Kitty handed this too to Burke.

"What do you make of this?" she asked.

He studied it for a minute, then shook his head again.

"Not much," he said. "It seems a little odd that he should give an address in Rheims. That's a fairly large city. It's an unlikely place for a soldier to be hiding."

"It seems suspicious to me," I said.

"Oh dear," Kitty said, "Etta is going to see the fine hand of the Gestapo behind every one of these letters!"

"Make fun of me if you like," I said, "but let's not underestimate the Gestapo. I can't see any way to distinguish between genuine and fake letters, and this second one seems to me even more suspicious than the first. If you take my advice, you won't answer either of them."

"And perhaps abandon two English soldiers?" Kitty asked.

I didn't answer. I could see she was becoming irritated.

"Perhaps we can find some means of checking without giving ourselves away," Burke suggested. "Do you think you could locate some one trustworthy in Rheims, or even near that small village mentioned in the first letter, who could inquire cautiously and find out who wrote those letters?"

Kitty thought for a moment, her eyes half closed.

"Perhaps I could find some one at the Foyer du Soldat who has contacts in Rheims," she said, "but it won't be so easy for a small place like Bergasse. I think we ought to go there ourselves."

"I wouldn't do that if I were you," Lieutenant Burke said. "If two foreigners turn up in so small a place and try to make inquiries, they would be extremely conspicuous. If the Gestapo has set a trap there, you would be sure to be arrested and investigated; and if they checked back here, you'd be found out."

"Yes, you're right," Kitty said, with deep disappointment in her voice.

She was silent for a moment. Then she said:

"Under the circumstances, I'm afraid there wasn't much sense in publishing that ad at all. I did want to get in touch with English boys trying to escape—but if we don't dare communicate with them after they answer, what can we do for them? The whole scheme was no good. It has only caused us worry. I'm sorry I ever started it!"

Listlessly, she took up the third envelope and opened it. She read through it hastily, then looked up at me, her eyes shining again. She passed it to me, and said softly: "What do you make of this?"

It was in French, and rather long. It went:

Dear Sir:

I am the parish priest of the village of Conchy-sur-Conche, and I am writing to you at the request of a few of my parishioners, who seem to recognize an old friend in you. According to them, I can approach you with confidence on a matter very important from the point of view of my congregation.

Our church building, the pride of our congregation, is very much in need of urgent repairs, otherwise this beautiful product of the art of the Middle Ages, the church tower, will undoubtedly collapse.

Now that our country is bleeding from a thousand wounds, it might seem that there are scores of other things to save more important than an old church; but our restoration committee (of which I hope you will also become a member) has decided that it will immediately begin a campaign for a restoration fund, since a catastrophe may be expected any day, and irreparable, irreplaceable values would be lost with the collapse of our church.

I beg you, my dear sir, to inform me immediately when and where I could look you up, or when I can expect your visit. In case it is not easy for you to travel, perhaps you can send a representative with whom I could discuss the broadening of our collection campaign.

In order to avoid any misunderstanding, may I remark that I have already secured the permission of the church and the local authorities for my collection campaign.

Asking God's blessing upon you, I am,
Yours very faithfully,
Father Christian Ravier
Conchy-sur-Conche (Somme).

I ran through it, skipping a phrase here and there, and tossed it aside carelessly.

"Just an appeal for funds," I said, uninterestedly.

"Etta!" Kitty almost screamed. "Don't you get it? It might have been just an appeal for funds if it had come in our regular mail! But it was addressed to William Gray! It was in answer to our advertisement! It's written so that we will understand, but no one else."

"Of course!" I said. "How stupid of me!"

"Listen," Kitty said to Burke, and she translated the letter for him swiftly. Then, with mounting excitement, she went on:

"You see: 'a few of my parishioners seem to recognize an old friend in you.' He must be in touch with some men of William Gray's unit; that would be about the right place, too. Then he says 'according to them, I can approach you with confidence on a matter very important from the point of view of my congregation'—that is, of these men.

"He says himself, you see, that a church restoration, which is supposed to be what he is talking about, isn't very important these days; and yet he talks of the loss of something 'irreparable, irreplaceable' and says that a 'catastrophe' may be expected any day. It's easy to see what he means by a catastrophe; the men he has there—his 'congregation'—may be discovered and arrested.

"Let's see, now; what else? Ah, yes—he asks where he can look us up or if we can come to him; and he realizes that an English soldier couldn't move about very easily, so he asks if a 'representative' can come to see him—and about 'the broadening of our collection campaign'! Why, it's easy to see what that means—saving more soldiers! And I judge that when he talks about having the permission of the local authorities for his collection campaign, he means the French administration is helping him in getting English soldiers in his neighborhood together. Why, it's as plain as the nose on your face!" Kitty concluded triumphantly.

This time I could see no objection. When Kitty said, "Well, how about it, Etta? Do you think the Gestapo wrote that letter?" I answered: "No, I don't think so, Kitty. This one looks genuine."

"Now I tell you what I'll do," Kitty said. "I'll go to the office of the Bishop of Paris, and inquire if it is correct that a collection has been authorized for the restoration of the church at Conchy-sur-Conche. I imagine that if Father Christian was so careful to make his letter appear innocent, he probably actually has some such fund, so that in case of investigation he won't be suspected. If he has, we can use interest in restoring the church as an excuse for visiting him."

The doctor was back early the following morning to see Corporal Meehan—at seven o'clock. He brought a second man with him, whom he introduced as a professor of the medical faculty, and an eminent specialist. The two doctors went into Meehan's room, and Kitty, after waiting an hour for them to come out, grew too impatient to wait any longer, and set off for the office of the Bishop of Paris to check up on Father Christian.

I couldn't understand what the two doctors could be doing so long in Meehan's room. Eight-thirty, nine, nine-thirty—and there was still no sign from them, except the occasional murmur of their voices. Once I thought I heard a low moan from Meehan.

When Kitty returned, they were still there. I could see from her excited expression that her errand had been successful.

"It's all right," she said. "There *is* a fund for the restoration of Father Christian's church. If Henri hadn't promised to come and visit us, I would have started for Conchy-sur-Conche at once!"

In her enthusiasm, she had probably forgotten momentarily all about poor Meehan. But at this moment the door opened, and the two doctors came out. Excusing themselves for a moment, they stepped into the ante-room and launched into an animated discussion.

"Goodness!" Kitty exclaimed. "Have they been with Meehan all this time?" She looked at her watch. "Why it's almost ten o'clock!"

I nodded. We both strained our ears to catch the conversation going on in the ante-room; but what we could hear was so filled with medical terms that it did us little good. We exchanged uneasy glances. Apparently Meehan's state was worse than we had thought.

Lieutenant Burke entered the living room at the same time that the two doctors came back. His mind was filled with his projected departure with Henri Beaurepos, for which he had prepared, and naturally the first thing he said when he saw the doctors was:

"Well, what's the verdict? Will Meehan be able to come along with us?"

Kitty translated the question to them. They stared at her as if she were mad.

"Strong enough to travel?" our doctor repeated. "My dear lady, there's no question of that! He has a bad case of blood poisoning. We will do what we can—but the question is whether we shall be able to save his life."

When Henri arrived an hour later, he found us once again in the same state of terror as when he had first entered to find the unconscious corporal lying on the floor. The Professor had gone, but the doctor had remained. To Henri's incisive questions, the doctor repeated some of the things he had said to us.

"Of course," he said in answer to one of Henri's remarks, rather impatiently, I thought. "Naturally, he should be in a hospital. But it's too late now. I discussed all that with the Professor. He could have gotten him into a hospital bed, although it would have been very risky—we might all have been arrested by the Germans—but he can't be moved now. There's no choice. He must stay here.

"To tell you the truth, it's a miracle that he even got here. It seems impossible that he should have been able to walk out of the hospital, climb a wall, and survive the journey in that cramped position. Did you really get him here in the way you told me?"

We assured him that we had told the absolute truth. He shook his head wonderingly.

"It's astonishing what the human organism can do!" he murmured.

Kitty uttered a sentence which had been in my mind for some time, but which I hadn't dare phrase. It seemed difficult for her to say it. I had the impression that she was forcing the words out.

"Was it—dangerous—to move him from the hospital, doctor?" she asked. "Would it have been—better—to leave him there?"

"Judging from his condition," the doctor answered, "the great pity is that you didn't move him before. He's been very badly neglected . . . I suppose it wasn't their fault. They probably have no drugs and no equipment. Most of those military hospitals are like that . . . As it is, his condition is deplorable. *Pauvre garçon!* He may have taken so much risk only to come to Paris to die!"

"It's really as serious as that?" Kitty whispered, pallid.

The doctor nodded silently.

Lieutenant Burke, sitting with one elbow on the table, and his fist propping up his chin, compressed his lips, and as he saw me looking at him, shifted his gaze unhappily and stared steadfastly at the wall. No one spoke. The ticking of a wall clock suddenly entered my consciousness, sounding startlingly loud. The doctor cleared his throat.

"I wish I could avoid bringing this up," he said. "But do you realize the difficult situation which you may have to meet shortly? Frankly, I have very little hope. We weren't able to determine exactly how long the sepsis has existed. In his feverish condition, he was only able to give us vague answers. They weren't much help. We are using sulfa injections, but the result probably depends on whether or not the infection is relatively recent, and it appears to be fairly well established. To put it bluntly, you risk being left with a dead man on your hands. How are you going to explain his presence here?"

That was something I hadn't thought of. I had been worrying about Meehan's condition because of personal sympathy for him. Now I suddenly realized what a difficult problem would be created for us if he died!

Kitty jumped up from her chair with unusual violence.

"It's hateful!" she exclaimed. "I can't stand it! How can we sit here and discuss calmly how we're going to—what we're going to do if he dies, while he's still struggling for his life in there! It's heartless! It's cold-blooded. . . . I just don't believe it! He's not going to die! I won't discuss any clever plans for saving our skins if—" She sobbed suddenly, snatched at her handkerchief, pressed it to her eyes, and ran into her room.

Henri looked after her with a sigh.

"Well, that's Kitty all right," he said quietly. "Too much heart to giving up defending those she loves even when she knows she has lost . . . Doctor, perhaps it will be better for us to settle this before she comes back . . . It seems to me we'd better not try anything as dangerous as smuggling a body out of the house. Isn't there some way we could bury him from this apartment, under a false identity?"

"You can't simply give any name you happen to hit on, you know," the doctor said. "I can deliver you a death certificate, of course. But a city doctor will come here to check the death, and you will have to show the dead man's papers. He has to represent some real person."

"Why not use my brother's papers?" I asked. "That worked once before."

"It wouldn't work this time," Henri said. "That was just a routine check-up, and no comparison was made between the papers and official records. In the case of a death, papers are always checked with the official files. Besides that, all deaths are reported to the Prefecture of Police and entered in an alphabetical file. Simply in inserting the record of this death in its correct place, the authorities would be certain to notice that the same death had been reported before . . . Besides, there's likely to be more than a routine check-up. A death from a wound is a serious matter, you know."

"One thing is certain," the doctor said. "We can't report his death under his own name. If they learned that you had hidden an English soldier here, without reporting him until his death forced you to it, we'd all be arrested. . . . How about this: suppose I made a report now that you found this man in the street, took him in and then called me—we'd have to get your other Englishman out of the way first, of course. If we report him before he dies, instead of after, we might get away with it. And, after all, it can't make much difference to him whether he dies here or in a military hospital—if they dare move him to one."

"No, that won't do," I said quickly. "Suppose they find out his real identity—and in his present state he might tell them without realizing what he was doing. When they checked up, they would certainly discover that we had visited the hospital he escaped from, and we'd be caught just the same. . . . Besides, suppose he lives? We don't want to hand him back to his jailers if there's any chance of saving him."

"*Ma pauvre dame,*" said the doctor, "that chance is unfortunately very slight. However, I agree with you. I think we should try to find some other way, if only to give him every possible chance. And as you say, that probably wouldn't save you anyway."

"I think I have the answer," Henri broke in.

We all looked towards him.

"There is only one person who could die in this apartment without causing difficulties for you," he said. "That is myself."

"How do you mean?" I asked.

"It's very simple," Henri explained. "It's obvious we can't get away with a purely imaginary identity. We have to have the papers of some real person. Secondly, it can't be some one already dead. That would be sure to be discovered. Therefore we must borrow the identity of some living person.

"The person whose identity is borrowed would, of course, be legally dead from then on, which would be inconvenient at times, perhaps, but not exactly a terrible fate. In fact, in moments like these, it might occasionally be advantageous to have disappeared from the official records of the living. After the war, I'm sure the authorities will accept an explanation and rectify the error in the official files.

"Now to begin with, it might not be easy to find any one willing to deprive himself of civil rights for the duration, but as a matter of fact, there's no question of hunting around for some one else, for the circumstances make me the inevitable choice. If you found a stranger to lend you his identity, you'd still have to explain what he was doing here. But in my case it's simple. I am legally still Kitty's husband, and it would be quite natural for me to have stopped here, coming from the south. All we need to do is to think of some plausible excuse for my having gotten an infected wound. The doctor can testify that he was called to treat me for it, but it was too late. The only papers we will need will be my passport and the doctor's death certificate."

The doctor rose.

"I think that is the answer," he said. "You can count on me. If it is necessary, I will issue the certificate, and I believe there will be no trouble. And now, if you will excuse me, I have other cases to visit."

I thought that now that the discussion was over, it might be possible to tell Kitty what we had decided without hurting her too much. I went into her room, and found her sitting on the floor, beside her bed, one arm resting upon it. Her eyes were moist, and I judged that she had been kneeling by the bed praying.

In a few words, as gently as I could, I told her what we proposed to do if it should become necessary. This time she took it calmly enough, but with unshakable faith in the future.

"Henri is a fine fellow," she said. "It is splendid of him to offer. It might cause him more difficulties than he admits. Obviously, he doesn't need a passport for travelling, since he crosses the border illegally anyhow. But how about ration cards? How about unexpected developments in the future, in case he gets into trouble, and can't produce papers? . . . But he won't have to take that chance. Corporal Meehan is not going to die, believe me. I feel it so deeply that I know it must be true. He can't die . . . I know he can't."

The doctor came again the next day, and once more spent a long time in the corporal's room. When we asked for a report, he shrugged his shoulders.

"I don't know which way he will turn," he said. "There's no perceptible change today. I'm afraid he's suffering a little more, if anything. Still, in the condition he's in, every day he hangs on is so much gain. I haven't given up hope yet."

On the following day, the doctor came out of Meehan's room much sooner. He appeared relieved.

"It's remarkable!" he said. "These new sulfa drugs are amazing! His temperature is much lower. I think we're going to pull him through!"

I took Kitty's hand.

"Perhaps you were right after all, Kitty," I said.

She smiled back at me.

"I never doubted that he'd get better," she answered.

And she was right. In the next two days, Meehan improved with startling speed. He listened for hours to adventure novels which Burke read to him, and even became definitely gay. Henri, seeing that his passport wasn't going to be needed, made his postponed departure, but Burke stayed behind to keep an eye on Meehan while we went to Conchy-sur-Conche.

This was a concession to Kitty's impatience. When she suggested that we go to see Father Christian, I protested that Meehan still needed us.

"Well, there's Margot," Kitty said. "And the doctor comes every day. Anyhow, he's out of danger."

How well I understood what caused her to say that! So many of her countrymen were still in danger, that she couldn't wait to get back to the task of saving them. Meehan was out of danger now, so she had lost some of her interest in his case. The others now seemed more urgent to her.

But I insisted that Margot had to be out of the house much of the time, buying food; so Burke volunteered to stay until Meehan could leave with him. With that settled, we decided to leave for Conchy as soon as possible.

CHAPTER FIFTEEN

A Visit to Father Christian

IT TOOK us all the next day to arrange our trip to Conchy-sur-Conche. Our travelling permit from the German Military Command had expired and had to be renewed, and we had to find gasoline for the journey. Neither of these things was too simple to fix up, and it kept both of us trotting through various official bureaus until well along in the afternoon.

On our way home, Kitty suggested that we stop at Monsieur Durand's café to ask if there were any other replies to our advertisement.

"It's quite unnecessary for you to take the trouble of coming here for your letters," Monsieur Durand said. "If anything more comes, I'll send it over to you by Emile, as before."

"I wanted to speak to you about that," Kitty answered. "Are you quite sure the boy is absolutely trustworthy? When he brought the other letters he acted so queerly that Mrs. Shiber thought his behavior rather suspicious."

Monsieur Durand smiled.

"Don't give it another thought, ladies," he said. "The boy is quite all right. He's the son of the postman, whom I've known for years. In fact——"

Monsieur Durand looked carefully about, and then, bending towards us and whispering, although no one was in sight, continued:

"*Le facteur, il est dans la combine aussi!*"

"The postman's in on it too?" Kitty echoed. "Why, what do you mean?"

"*Voici:* I told the postman to be very careful about these letters —that they weren't love letters, like most of the mail addressed to people at cafés. He spoke to the head of the sorting department at the post office, whom he knows very well, and he sees to it that these letters don't go through the German censorship. They don't try to read all mail, you know; they just check what they're interested in.

Now if they saw your adverisement, they may be looking for answers; but they won't find any, for our friend in the sorting department will keep all letters addressed to William Gray out of the
mail sack that goes over to the German censorship. Well done,
wasn't it?"

"Splendid!" Kitty agreed. But when we got outside, I couldn't
refrain from saying:

"Kitty, doesn't it worry you to know that so many other persons
of whom we know nothing are *dans la combine*, as Monsieur
Durand puts it? Not only does he know what it is all about, but so
does Emile, so does the postman, and so does his friend in the sorting department—at least four persons who share our secret, and for
all we know there may be others. For instance, the mail sorter and
the postman may not be on duty all the time. Do they pass on their
information to their substitutes? You can say what you like, but
I'm getting the cold shivers again. Suppose just one of these men,
over a drink in Durand's café, for instance, says something about the
combine loudly enough to be overheard by some other customer who
may be working for the Gestapo—they're everywhere, you know.
Just one little slip might be enough to doom us."

"Oh, don't be so nervous," Kitty said impatiently. "They're all
patriotic Frenchmen, and old friends of one another. We can count
on them. In fact, if we get into trouble, they may even help us out
of it."

We started out to see Father Christian early the next morning.

As usual, there was little traffic on the highways, and we made
good time, leaving behind us one northern village after another
whose names brought pangs to our hearts as we recognized in them
places which had figured in the communiqués of a few weeks ago,
when we had still believed that the French Army would be able to
hold the Germans out.

We didn't talk much on the way. Kitty was no doubt busy with
her own thoughts, as I was with mine. I was arguing with my fears,
disputing within myself the distrust which I could not completely
banish concerning Father Christian's letter.

There is no reason for worry, I said to myself. The letter was so convincing, so serene, so evidently honest, that it is next to impossible that it could be a Gestapo trap. But in the next instant, the response would come. But is it so impossible? Nothing is impossible when the Gestapo is concerned. Its members would be quite capable of conceiving such a trap.

"Look," said Kitty, pointing to the roadside sign: "Conchy-sur-Conche! And that must be the church steeple!"

It was my last chance to speak before we had committed ourselves. I couldn't resist telling Kitty of my apprehensions.

"There's no danger," Kitty said. "We haven't notified any one we're coming. Until we've seen Father Christian himself and have had a chance to size him up, our story is that we stopped only to have a look at the church as we were passing. Just leave everything to me."

She stopped the car in front of the church. We got out and looked up at its dilapidated steeple, with the air, we hoped, of curious and admiring tourists. The building was obviously many centuries old, and seemed to have been erected by pious artisans, inspired more by their devotion than by any knowledge of academic art. Perhaps that was why they had created a structure of lasting beauty, quite worthy of Father Christian's campaign for its restoration.

We walked about the church, hoping to encounter the priest; but no one appeared. We returned to the front.

"You get back into the car," Kitty suggested, "and keep a sharp watch for any one suspicious. I'm going inside."

But as I sat in the car on the main street of this small town of northern France, I saw nothing out of the ordinary. It was true that the town's aspect was not the same as it would have been in times of peace. Women, old men and children passed through the street, but it was immediately noticeable that no young men were visible. They, no doubt, were all in prison camps. Or were they, too, hiding in the forests like the Englishmen whom we were trying to aid?

Even middle-aged men were few. The only ones I saw were a postman and a gendarme, who passed slowly down the street as I sat in the car waiting for Kitty.

And then a young man appeared. But he was not a Frenchman. He was a German soldier. He carried no rifle, but his bayonet swung from his belt, which also supported a revolver. He walked with the uncertain gait of a man bored by inactivity, with no particular destination in mind. As he walked down the street, I noticed a curious phenomenon.

At every door, little groups were gathered, and many of the windows of the street were occupied by women, calling out the day's gossip to their neighbors. As the German moved along the street, the little groups seemed to dissolve, the heads disappeared from the windows. There was nothing conspicuous or demonstrative about this disappearance of the French before the lone representative of the invaders. They moved slowly, almost casually, so that one hardly noticed the movement itself. It failed to catch the eye. Yet one moment they were there, and the next they were not.

The progress of the German soldier along the street swept it clear of humanity as though an invisible broom were passing down the road before him. And behind him, the doors and windows filled again as he went by. He seemed to move through an automatically self-created vacuum. I could not help being deeply impressed by this silent demonstration of antipathy to the German, which consisted in refusing to remain even within his sight. The soldier himself, unless I imagined it, seemed to be sad, depressed, as though this avoidance of his person, as if he were a leper, had affected him deeply.

I had been waiting for perhaps a quarter of an hour when Kitty appeared in the church entrance with a priest by her side. I had expected from Father Christian's letter, I don't know just why, to meet a saintly old man, complete with long white beard. Instead, Father Christian turned out to be the first young man I had seen since our arrival at Conchy-sur-Conche, bright-eyed and energetic.

I judged him to be no more than twenty-eight. He was one of those Frenchmen whose classic profiles, passed through generation after generation down the centuries, remind the foreigner that France was once part of the great Roman Empire.

Kitty introduced me to Father Christian, and he suggested that we talk in the rectory, behind the church. From its architectural style, I surmised that it dated from about the same epoch as the church itself.

As we turned the corner of the building, I was astounded to see the German swastika flag waving above the entrance. Father Christian saw the expression on my face, and explained without waiting for a question.

"I'm sorry, but I can't do anything about that flag," he said. "I was in the army when the Germans entered the village. They took over the rectory for their headquarters then. I was captured before Paris, but I managed to escape, and came back here to resume my work. I asked them to hand back the rectory, but they refused. However, they did let me keep the rear part of the building, which they weren't using, and that's where I live now."

Father Christian led us through the garden into a side door towards the rear of the house. It let us into a small low-ceilinged room which looked like a warehouse compartment, for it was piled high with church paraphernalia, which, Father Christian explained, the Germans had thrown out of the rectory into the courtyard until he had moved it back into his own part of the rectory.

"We can talk safely here," Father Christian said. "The Germans are right over our heads, but they can't hear a word. Thick walls were the rule in the days when this building was put up. This room is completely sound-proof."

At first Father Christian did most of the talking. He told us that there were at least a thousand English soldiers hiding in the woods in the region of Conchy-sur-Conche, and that he maintained regular contact with them. But their hardships, he explained, were appalling.

"There isn't a day," he said, "when I am not called upon to bury one of them. They come at night, and leave the dead man beneath the cross at the entrance to the town, and there we pick the body up and give it Christian burial. And do you know, they are never marked by weapons! I have yet to see one who has died of wounds. The cause of death isn't even illness, for there are no traces of disease. The cause of death is simply exhaustion, debility. You might say that these lads in their twenties have died of old age, like men of eighty. They are completely worn out by the lives they lead, which saps their vitality before their time."

Father Christian sighed.

"There is so little we can do," he continued. "This is a small place, and even under the best of circumstances, it would be difficult for us to supply the needs of a thousand men. But today we are rationed ourselves; and besides, we must be careful not to attract the attention of the Germans. I try to keep body and soul together for these men, so far as my poverty permits. But even if we all gave up everything we possess, it would not be enough. I have already stripped every member of my congregation of clothing and food. I must say that they have all behaved admirably."

I thought of the scene I had witnessed when the German soldier passed down the street, and I mentioned it to Father Christian, adding that it seemed to me that the German looked sad, as though the ostracism to which he was subjected had made its mark on him.

"You are quite right," Father Christian said. "The Germans are depressed. Their attitude seems strange for a victorious people. It is only the very young soldiers who show a different spirit. They are arrogant and full of confidence. They try to convince the French officials, the only inhabitants who talk to them, because their duties oblige them to, that resistance to Germany is utterly foolish and futile because she will soon dominate the whole world. 'First we'll go to England,' they say, 'then to America.'

"But with the older men, it's a different story. It's already been a long and weary progress, they say, to Vienna, to Prague, to Warsaw, to Norway, to Amsterdam, Brussels and Paris. They are tired of fighting and want to go home. They tell us that England is next on the list, too. But as one of them said to me, 'And then what? I'm beginning to feel like another Wandering Jew—I'm a pure Aryan, you understand; it's just the idea that we are moving on ceaselessly from one country to another, and we can't stop. What would happen if we did?' He was afraid that if the succession of conquests ever ended, the conquered peoples would succeed in revenging themselves against the troops left to police them.

"He said to me: 'We really ought to massacre everybody, in self-defense, you understand, to make sure that some day we, ourselves, won't be massacred.'"

"What did you answer to that?" I asked.

"Oh," said Father Christian, with a grim smile, "I said, 'Cheer up. Perhaps there'll be an earthquake to wipe us all out together.'"

Kitty had obviously become impatient during this exchange.

"Let's go back to the English soldiers," she broke in. "How do they manage to keep from being caught?"

"They're very clever," Father Christian replied. "There have been several raids in this region by motorcycle patrols, but only a few men have been caught. They hide well, and they have learned to know every foot of the woods. They have a well-hidden headquarters in the forest, where they get news from the outside world by means of a radio which I smuggled in to them. Generally, the only catches the Germans make are of men so weak with starvation that they haven't strength to move.

"But I don't think they can remain hidden successfully very much longer. So far, there have been no systematic round-ups in this region, like those which have been going on north of us. There the method has been to surround whole counties with large forces, and simply close the circle. Any one hiding within it is pushed back as the lines tighten until finally the whole lot is captured without firing a shot. It's certainly only a question of time before they apply that method here, too.

"Now here is what I have done. I have made all the necessary arrangements to get these men out of here, a few at a time. I will take responsibility for getting them to Paris if you can take charge of them after that. I have already fixed it up to get identity cards for them, which will show that they have permission to go to Paris to take jobs in war factories there. This will enable them to take a train for Paris, and the chances are that they will meet with no difficulties.

"But it has to be remembered that very few of these men speak French, and therefore it is impossible to send them off alone. They must be escorted by some quick-witted person, able to speak up for them quickly in case of unforeseen circumstances. I plan to do that myself, unless it should be absolutely impossible, and I have to send some one else. I figure that it will seem much less suspicious if a priest is in charge of a group of three or four young men, handling their travelling passes, and so forth. Anyway, I will guarantee to deliver the boys to you in Paris if you can take care of them from then on. Can you do that?"

"We certainly can," Kitty answered enthusiastically, her flushed cheeks and sparkling eyes revealing her delight at the working out of her plans. "We have a five-room apartment in Paris. You can bring the boys directly to us, and we will let them rest there for a few days while we get them travelling papers to go to Bordeaux. From there we can send them across the line of demarcation through the estate of a Frenchman who is helping to get escaped soldiers out of occupied territory."

Kitty glanced at me, and continued:

"Of course, Etta, we will take care of the expenses—the railroad fares, and the 50 francs per person we will have to pay to get these men across the border."

I don't know which of the two seemed happier, Kitty or Father Christian. The young priest closed his eyes for a moment, and from the expression on his face, I thought he must be offering up an inward prayer of thanks.

"Preaching is my profession," he said finally, "and usually I don't have any difficulty finding words for what I want to say, but I'm at a loss to express the depth of my gratitude to you. If you knew the mental tortures I have suffered, as a helpless witness to the indescribable sufferings of these boys!—and then your advertisement appeared, out of nothingness, like an answer to my prayers! . . . When can I bring you the first batch?"

"When?" Kitty echoed. "Why, immediately, of course. There's no time to lose. Let them start tonight, and they can be at our place tomorrow."

"Goodness, Kitty," I interrupted. "Don't be so impatient. Remember, we have preparations to make, too. In the first place, we haven't heard yet from Libourne—from Monsieur Tissier. We have got to make arrangements with him for receiving these men and getting them over the border. Then we have to arrange with the Prefecture man about travelling passes. I think we will need at least a week to prepare."

"I'm afraid you're right, Etta," Kitty admitted with reluctance. "I think I had better go to Libourne myself, see Tissier, and prepare everything in advance. Then we'll notify Father Christian, and he can start sending the boys to us."

She paused for a moment, and then added gaily:

"But what's to stop us from taking one man back in the car with us now? How about it, Father? Do you think you could reach one of them in time to ask if he would like to come back to Paris with us?"

Father Christian smiled.

"Reaching them will be no difficulty," he said, "since there are four of them in the house now."

"In this house?" I stammered. "Here, under the same roof with the Germans?"

"Why, yes," said Father Christian simply. "What place is safer from search? They were all sick when I picked them up and brought them here. They're well again now, but I could hardly chase them back into the woods, could I?"

I was still astounded.

"Well!" I exclaimed. "I thought we were daring in taking escaped soldiers into our apartment. But you, under the very noses of the Germans! How in the world do you hide them?"

The priest rose.

"Come with me," he said. "I'll show you."

Remembering the age of the building, I imagined vaguely that we would be conducted into some mediæval hiding place, some crypt or secret dungeon, entered through a sliding panel or a secret staircase constructed hundreds of years ago. But the truth was much less romantic. Father Christian simply opened a door into a corridor, crossed it, and knocked on a door on the other side. It was opened by an elderly woman, whom Father Christian introduced as his cousin and housekeeper.

The room into which we were conducted, like Father Christian's, looked like a storeroom. The front part of the room contained an unencumbered strip hardly wide enough to stand in. Furniture removed by the Germans from the rest of the building filled the rest of it, piled up almost to the ceiling.

Father Christian closed the door carefully, and then, turning towards the mountain of furniture, said in slow and difficult English:

"Gentlemen, an English and an American lady have come to call on you."

To our astonishment, we heard the sound of movements in the

pile of furniture, and one by one, four heads protruded from it, at different heights. The Englishmen were living in the furniture, like rats in a wall. In piling it up, the priest and his guests had so arranged it as to leave living spaces within the heap, which from the outside appeared as a solid mass.

From a few inches beneath the ceiling, a young redhead of about eighteen grinned down at us. His long thin face was mottled with freckles from forehead to chin. Kitty smiled back at him, and said:

"How'd you like to come to Paris with us, son?"

He shook his head.

"Thanks, Ma'am, but I can't go. I've got a job here. Maybe one of my buddies would like to get out of here though."

I turned to Father Christian in bewilderment.

"What does he mean by a job? Doesn't he want to escape?"

Father Christian explained. The red-headed young man was a radio man, and since he had been in the house, he had devised a microphone and placed it in the ceiling, so that he could hear what the Germans were saying. As he was the only one of the four who understood German, he thought he ought to stay.

"But what use is it to listen to them here?" Kitty asked. "You can't get any information you may pick up back to England anyway."

"That isn't the idea," Father Christian explained. "It's to help the others in the woods. We've been able three times to give them notice twenty-four hours in advance that there would be a motorcycle patrol raid. It's a handy thing to know."

"But if it's so easy for you to hear what the Germans are saying," I said, "how do you know they aren't listening to you?"

"The difference," said Father Christian, "is that we know they're there, but they don't know these boys are here. Besides, they're Bavarians. They aren't as inquisitive as the Prussians. They leave us pretty much alone."

Half an hour later we were on our way back to Paris, and once more our much-frequented baggage compartment had a passenger. This time our man was Captain Jesse Handsby, the first of a series we were destined to receive through Father Christian, our new ally in the organization of escapes.

CHAPTER SIXTEEN

The Death Decree

To our surprise, the first thing we saw as we entered our apartment with Captain Handsby was Corporal Meehan, sitting up on the living room sofa, wrapped in blankets.

"What do you mean by such foolishness?" Kitty roared at him, with an exaggerated air of anger. "Don't you know that you've been at death's door? And you, Burke—and Margot, too—how could you let him do such a thing?"

Meehan grinned sheepishly.

"They did their best, Ma'am," he said. "But I couldn't stick bed any longer. I feel fine now—strong as an ox."

He looked like a very feeble ox, but we were too pleased that it wouldn't be necessary to carry out our plans for disposing of his corpse to feel too much resentment about his rashness in getting up so soon. However his body may have been, his will was strong enough. Our combined efforts couldn't induce him to go back to bed.

In spite of our difficulty in getting provisions, Margot succeeded in pampering Meehan, and the majority of the food she was able to get on the Black Market went to him. The results were quickly visible. His thin cheeks filled out again, and he quickly looked a very different man from the invalid we had rescued from Doullens. He would obviously soon be strong enough to travel, so we anticipated sending him off together with Burke and Handsby.

Frankly, we were anxious to get Handsby in particular on his way as soon as possible. His experiences hiding in the woods and then in Father Christian's house had wrecked his nerves, and he was in a constant dither about what might happen to all of us if we were caught. He jumped whenever he heard footsteps in the hall, or even in another room of the apartment itself. He paced back and forth continually, occasionally peering cautiously out of the window. We couldn't blame him, but he gave us all the jitters, and we were anxious to start him on his way for the sake of our own nerves.

It took us a week, however, to get in touch with Monsieur Valentin, the clerk at the Prefecture who had been recommended to us by Henri Beaurepos as the man who could supply us with travelling permits for our men.

Trusting in Henri's assurance that we could have perfect confidence in Valentin, we told him in detail what we were doing, and asked him to get us passes so that we could send the English soldiers from Paris to the frontier.

Monsieur Valentin listened to us gravely and attentively.

"What you are doing is very dangerous, ladies," he said, "very dangerous indeed. Possibly you don't realize quite how dangerous. I understand that the Germans intend to enforce new and drastic measures against any one who helps English soldiers to escape. However, if you two are not afraid of the possible consequences, I certainly should not be."

He told us that he would require a little time to get us the necessary papers. As a matter of fact, it took him a whole week—but when he provided the passes, we had everything we needed. He had succeeded in getting a large number of blank permits, duly signed, and stamped with all the necessary seals, so that we could fill in ourselves whatever names and details we wanted without having to make a special request to him each time we wanted to send men out.

I was the happiest person alive when the permits were at last in our hands, for Captain Handsby's nervousness had turned our peaceful home into a regular insane asylum. By now he had all of us tiptoeing about, starting at each other's movements, and imagining that Gestapo men were hiding behind every piece of furniture.

But we could not start him off yet, for we were still without word from Monsieur Tissier at Libourne; and we dared not ship the boys south until we knew that everything was ready for them at the frontier.

One morning during that waiting period Kitty and I were sitting at breakfast. She had picked up the paper, which she always read during the morning meal; but hardly had she glanced at it than she folded it hastily and made some inconsequential remark. I knew by experience that this meant that Kitty had seen something in the paper which she thought I had better not see, and I demanded to know the bad news. I almost had to tear the paper away from her to get it. As I unfolded it, Captain Handsby bent over to read it across my shoulder.

It was impossible to miss the item which had caught Kitty's eye. It was played up boldly on the front page, a German proclamation announcing that the death penalty would be imposed on any persons discovered to be hiding English soldiers or aiding them to escape.

"That means you," said Captain Handsby, turning deathly pale, "and you can depend on it, the Germans will check first on all English residents of Paris to find out who is helping English soldiers to escape. The Gestapo may be here any minute. We can't stay another instant. Our presence is endangering your lives. I'm going to leave at once. You'd better tell the others."

We were too stunned by the proclamation to stop him as he hurried into his room to get ready to go. I looked at Kitty in dismay.

"There is only one thing to do," she said. "I must go to Libourne to see Tissier at once. I'm afraid this order will frighten him out of going through with it. This decree might very well be a catastrophe. People like Tissier, who have been cooperating up to now, are likely to stop through fear. You can't expect them not to react to a threat of death."

"How about you?" I asked. "Are you forgetting that you are just as much threatened as he is? Both of us are, in fact."

"But Etta, please!" Kitty answered. "I thought we had already discussed that question between ourselves and settled it once for all. We have already considered that risk, and decided to accept it. We have been very careful up to now, and we shall be even more careful in the future. We didn't get into this entirely of our own free will. We were more or less led into it. But now that we are embarked on this course, we've got to go ahead with it. We can't desert these poor boys in the face of this threat, brutal as it is. We're up to our necks in this business, anyhow. To begin with, we have three of them here right now; and our first concern must be to get them out. We have to continue at least to that extent. We have no choice."

She was silent for a moment. Then she added softly, as though speaking to herself:

"What can happen anyway? Nobody will find out."

Since we had travelling permits for our three refugees already, Kitty decided to kill two birds with one stone and take them to Libourne with her. I was a little worried about risking that, with no guarantee that Monsieur Tissier was still willing to get them across the line, but I'm afraid I didn't argue very firmly, for the prospect of getting them out of the apartment, especially the fidgety Captain, was so pleasant that I was really in favor of their going.

And I did enjoy to the full the unaccustomed peace and quiet that pervaded our apartment with the departure of our guests. For two days I neither read the papers nor listened to the radio. I locked the world and the war out of my mind and out of my home. I tasted again the quiet I had come to Paris to find, of which I had been brutally deprived by the war.

Kitty returned at the end of that time, fresh, youthful and buoyant. I didn't have to ask her to know that her trip had turned out well.

"This fellow Tissier is a wonderful old chap," she told me enthusiastically. "He's just a simple peasant, but he's got amazing common sense. In fact, he's even a philosopher of sorts. If all French peasants are like him, I don't wonder that they're supposed to be the backbone of this country.

"He hasn't swallowed the Vichy propaganda at all—just laughs when any one mentions Pétain's new political order. 'How was it possible for us to lose the war against Germany?' he asked me, and then went ahead and answered himself. 'It was like this,' he said, 'we got our carts going on the right road, but we couldn't get anywhere because some one was always poking a stick between the spokes of the wheels. Now who did that? It's easy to figure it out. It must have been the people who profited by it—the people who are running things in Vichy now.' That's the way he figures it out, and he tells me eighty per cent of the people he knows think the same thing."

"Did he know about the death decree?" I asked.

"Of course," Kitty said, "The Germans have posted it all over

Libourne. The walls and trees are covered with copies of it. When I mentioned it to him, he just spat. He said: 'I went through the 1914–1918 war. I might have keen killed a thousand times, but I got out of it. Now another war has passed over my head, and I'm still safe. I figure I'm that much ahead of the game already, and I can't lose.' "

For the next few days, Kitty and I were alone in the apartment together, as we had been in the happy days of peace. There was no need any longer to jump whenever we heard footsteps in the corridor outside, no need to fear the ringing of the doorbell. It was a blissful interlude—so blissful that I tried to prolong it by arguing with Kitty once more about the foolishness of continuing our activities now that the Germans had announced the death penalty. I remember that I said to her:

"Kitty, now that we have gotten rid of the three men we had to get across the border before we could get out of this dangerous business, there is no reason why we shouldn't stop. Remember what Captain Handsby said—that the very fact you are English-born gives the Gestapo a reason to suspect you. That ought to be enough to decide you to give up this work. It's only natural that the Germans should keep a more watchful eye on us, conspicuous because of our nationality, than on any particular Frenchman, indistinguishable from millions of other Frenchmen.

"Father Christian hasn't sent his first group along yet. There's still time to call it off. It would be only sensible to route these boys through some French family, less likely to be suspected than us."

Kitty looked at me angrily.

"Do you know of one? If you know a French family that will take them, that can get them travelling passes, that can get them across the border—in short, that can do what we are doing—*then* suggest that we turn the job over to them. But until you can find one, *we* have to do it."

But then, as always whenever she raised her voice in our discussions, she suddenly stopped, and a conscience-stricken look appeared on her face.

"Forgive me, Etta. I didn't mean to speak so rudely. But my whole heart is in this thing. I *must* keep on. One of the things that worries me most is that I am implicating you in everything I do. I would be so happy if you would only listen to me and go back——"

I knew what she was going to say. I broke in:

"It's no use, Kitty. That's one thing I won't do. You can have a clear conscience about my share of the risk, because I refuse, of my own free will, to go back to America and leave you alone. I'll stay with you whatever happens, and if I can't convince you that you're jeopardizing your life, I'll talk to Father Christian. Perhaps he will understand, after that decree, that you're not the proper person to continue this man-saving campaign, since you're English yourself, and likely to be suspected at once."

Kitty looked at me, troubled.

"Do you really think Father Christian would be capable of letting me down?" she asked.

I had no time to answer this strange rejoinder. Margot came into the room, and said: "There's a young priest asking for you. He says his name is Father Christian."

Father Christian's arrival was the result of a letter Kitty had written him from Libourne. With her customary impatience, the moment she had learned that Tissier was still willing to cooperate, she had sent Father Christian a letter in which she said that everything was ready to begin his collection campaign for the restoration of the church, and that she would be in Paris the following day, prepared to go ahead with it. This would have been unintelligible to any censor, but Father Christian understood at once, of course, that it meant he might begin to bring his boys to our place. So here he was with four of them.

His arrival created a problem. It was just about noon, and five unexpected guests for lunch were not easy to cope with in those days of restricted rations. Margot managed somehow to make a success of it, at the price of frightful inroads on some food we had recently succeeded in getting on the Black Market at outrageous prices.

The English boys were very quiet throughout the meal. They were much more subdued than the first ones we had rescued, which we supposed was a result of their having lived the lives of hunted beasts longer than their predecessors. We knew from the grateful smiles they directed at us during lunch, however, how much they appreciated our help. Their expressions weakened my determination to try to persuade Kitty of her danger, and I began to feel almost as strongly as she did the need to continue with what we were doing.

Nevertheless my more sober judgment could not let me forget that death decree, and I spoke to Father Christian about it, half hoping that he would remonstrate with Kitty. I couldn't very well ask him to directly, now that we had four English soldiers with us. But Father Christian, like Kitty, seemed not even to entertain the idea that this edict should make any difference to him. Instead, he discussed it impersonally, like an outsider unaffected by it.

"Judging from what I've heard," he said, "the Nazis are going to get just the opposite effect from what they expect by this brutal threat. Up to now, it's happened very often when I've spoken to French people about these boys that they've shrugged their shoulders and said, 'After all, if a million and a half of our boys can stand the German prison camps, why shouldn't the English be able to?' But I've noticed a change since the new order was issued. They're coming around to the belief that if it's as important as that for the Germans to stop the English soldiers from escaping, then it's the duty of all Frenchmen to help them get away.

"Apparently the Germans have had plenty of reason for taking drastic measures," Father Christian continued. "We seem by no means to be the only ones doing this sort of thing. I hear fantastic stories about escapes of English soldiers everywhere I go. It's impossible to tell which are true and which are not—but the fact that they're being told so widely in itself indicates how thoroughly people are aroused on this point.

"*Tiens!* Have you heard, for instance, any of the stories about the exploits of Englishmen wearing German uniforms? No? Well, one has practically become standard. It varies slightly in detail, but it always concerns two men in German officers' uniforms who turn up at a peasant's house and ask to spend the night. They always leave before dawn, and the peasant finds a note from them, sometimes with money, sometimes without, reading something like: 'Cheer up. You will soon be free again. Your English friends.' Possibly all the versions of this story come originally from the same source, or similar incidents may have occurred at different places.

"Then there's another story of a group of several soldiers in German uniform who marched into a hotel under command of an officer. The officer; apparently a typical Prussian, wearing a monocle and conducting himself in arrogant fashion, demanded accommodations for himself and his men. But the woman who kept the hotel noticed him looking at her fixedly, and realized she had seen him before somewhere. After a moment she recollected his face. It was that of an *English* officer who had stopped at her hotel during the war. He saw the light of recognition in her eyes, and with an apparently careless gesture, put his finger to his lips to warn her to keep quiet. She nodded, almost imperceptibly, to indicate she understood. He gave a stiff Prussian salute, and marched his men upstairs. The following day she found a note in his room with a single word on it: *'Merci!'* "

Father Christian chuckled.

"You know, all these stories have done the Germans a good turn," he said. "Germans who aren't known to be part of local garrisons often get a fairly cordial reception from the peasants these days, in the belief they may be Englishmen in disguise.

"They don't always figure it out, though. Here's a story I can vouch for, because I know the man it happened to. He owns a small delivery truck, which he is permitted to drive to transport food. He was stopped on the road by two men in German Luftwaffe uniforms, who asked him to drive them to the Villacoublay airfield, outside of Paris. When he refused, saying that he was going the other way, one of them drew a revolver and ordered him to take them to Villacoublay. My friend had a most unpleasant trip, with an occasional nudge in the back from the revolver to remind him to keep going.

"When they got to the airfield, the officers directed my friend to turn into a small road running towards a side entrance to the field. They got out of the car and handed him a sealed envelope. 'We'll want this again if we have to come back,' they said. 'You wait here for a few minutes. If we don't come back in a quarter of an hour, open it.'

"That naturally made my friend think something unusual was up, so he watched them through the wire fence. He saw them walk through the camp to the airfield, exchanging salutes as they marched along, then get into a plane and take off. He opened the letter. Inside was a thousand-franc note and a sheet of paper, on which was written: 'Thanks. R.A.F.'

"Since I know that story to be true," Father Christian concluded, "I don't find it hard to believe the others. They would explain why the Germans thought it necessary to decree the death penalty. Helping English soldiers to escape is getting to be quite a thriving industry."

Father Christian and the four boys stayed in the apartment until seven in the evening. Then, provided with the travelling permits which we filled out for them, they walked with Father Christian to the Gare d'Orsay, where he bought their tickets and saw them aboard the train.

We had the satisfaction of seeing them leave. We went over to the station ourselves a few moments before the train was due to pull out. We exchanged no words or gestures, of course, with either Father Christian or the boys; but we could see them through the window and our hearts went out to them as the train moved slowly away, taking them to freedom.

CHAPTER SEVENTEEN

An Old Friend

WE LIVED on pins and needles for two days after sending off Father Christian's first group of soldiers. Kitty had arranged with Tissier to notify us at once when the boys arrived, and to send us a second message when they had been smuggled safely across the border. But one day passed, and then another, and there was no word from Tissier. We began to fear that something had happened to our friends on the way when Tissier turned up himself.

He was the image of the French peasant making a visit to the city, attired uncomfortably in his black Sunday suit, and obviously rather ill at ease in it. His long drooping moustache, à la Clemenceau, was continually getting into the corners of his mouth. As a dweller in Paris, it was the first time I had met so typical a French peasant. And in talking with him, I acquired a deep respect for these simple, direct, unspoiled people whose sturdy character seems to me to represent the essence of all that is best in France. It remains an everlasting mystery to me how such a man, living in so isolated a community, could manage to be so accurately informed, and, on the basis of that information, could arrive at such accurate judgments concerning the situation in France. His native common sense served him much better than the more subtle minds of much cleverer persons.

His opinion of Marshal Pétain, for instance, was characteristic:

"I'm not one of those who think the old man is a traitor," he told us. "After all, your wits can't be as sharp as you get along in life as they were in your prime. Now take me, for instance—I'm only seventy-three, much younger than the Marshal, but I often don't realize I'm being cheated in a deal until it's too late. That's what happened to this poor old fellow. They pulled the wool over his eyes. What do they expect of a man over eighty? He was fooled, and the whole country is suffering as a result. That's all there is to it."

In accordance with the habit of the French peasant, who considers it impolite to start a conversation with a blunt reference to the object of his visit, Monsieur Tissier covered most of the topics of the day before he came to the point.

"I came to Paris to do some shopping," he explained. "The stores in Bordeaux, where I used to do all my buying, never have anything any more. The Germans have cleaned them out. So as long as I had to come anyway, I decided to drop in on you ladies and tell you that you made a very bad mistake. In the future, whatever you do, don't let those boys travel without an escort."

We feared some mishap had occurred. Tissier quickly relieved our fears. But, as he pointed out, the English boys had only escaped arrest by a miracle, and we mustn't count on such good luck again.

What had happened was this:

Somewhere between Paris and Bordeaux, French gendarmes boarded the train to check the passengers. One of them spoke to one of our boys, who, of course, couldn't answer. When he discovered that there were four young men in the compartment, all provided with official French travelling permits, but none of them able to speak French, he was naturally suspicious. He ordered them off the train; but at this point the French passengers in the compartment intervened; and they were so violently indignant that the gendarme gave way, and the boys continued on their journey. But it was a close call, and they had had a good scare.

"You mustn't ever send them alone again," Tissier concluded vehemently. "Suppose an investigation were started to find out how they got travelling passes! It might lead back to your friends in the Prefecture and then to yourselves—and you know the penalty now. You must get French citizens to go with them. And you mustn't even let them sit together. Have one French boy with each English one, ready to speak up and answer questions. If you can't do that, it would be a crime to start them across France alone. The chances are against their ever getting to Libourne."

After Tissier had gone, Kitty was moody and thoughtful.

"Tissier is right," she sighed. "I hadn't thought of that difficulty before, but now that we know about it, what can we do? I have no idea where to find escorts for them. And Father Christian may arrive with more boys any day!"

Monsieur Tissier, who had arrived early, left about 11 o'clock. He hadn't been gone half an hour when Margot announced another caller—a Monsieur Corbier.

"I don't know any Monsieur Corbier," Kitty said, distrustfully. Unexpected visitors were not welcome at this period, when we feared that any moment might bring us an envoy from the Gestapo. "Did he say what he wanted?"

Monsieur Corbier spared Margot the necessity of answering. He simply opened the door, which Margot had closed behind her as she entered, and walked in. He looked rather like a doctor, for he had a black, uneven beard, a fashion still not uncommon among French doctors. He also wore thick-rimmed spectacles.

He stood still, one hand on the door knob, offering no explanation for his intrusion. Not unnaturally, we stared at him, expecting him to say something. His appearance seemed vaguely familiar to me, but I couldn't place him.

Finally he broke the silence.

"Well, my dear ladies," he said, "I think the test is conclusive. I am happy to see that you don't recognize me. I wasn't sure that these glasses and a three weeks' growth of beard would make that much difference in my appearance. But I see they do."

Kitty and I shouted almost in unison:

"Chancel!"

He chuckled at our surprise, and we had to smile, too. But Kitty, quickly becoming serious again, said: "You've come at the right time again. We've got another problem for you."

In the course of the next few minutes, Chancel explained his new activity to us. He was now working for a new organization, whose object was to smuggle out of France any Frenchmen who wanted to fight with the de Gaulle forces, and get them to England. He had come to ask us to work with him. But when Kitty explained our problem, he saw at once that he could adapt his plans to fit in with ours.

"Nothing is easier," he said, "than to get you French escorts for your boys, since I'll be sending Frenchmen out of the country just as you're sending Englishmen. Whenever you have any Englishmen to send out, let me know, and I'll provide the same number of French boys, on their way to join de Gaulle, to go with them. I suggest we conclude a sort of merger. You take care of getting the men to the frontier, and I'll have them picked up there and taken on to England. I don't know yet just which route we're going to use to do that—possibly across the Spanish frontier to Gibraltar or Lisbon, but more likely from some coastal village in southern France, where a fishing boat can take them out to an English ship. We might even send them the whole way across the Mediterranean to North Africa, and have them picked up and sent on from there."

Chancel's proposal fitted in perfectly with our needs. The problem of escorts was solved, and what was more, we would be spared the anguish of being left in doubt as to the fate of our boys after they crossed the frontier. Hitherto, we not only had no way of taking care of them after they got into the unoccupied zone, where, of course, they were still not entirely out of danger, and would be on their own in trying to get back to England, but there was not even any way by which they could let us know what had happened to them. We had given them letters of introduction to friends, and the addresses of other people they might be able to look up, but we had no reason for believing that any of them could get them out of the country. Now we had an opportunity to start the young men we wanted to help on a route of escape which would lead from the forests of northern France, not simply to the unoccupied zone, but all the way to England!

Chancel left with the promise to prepare escorts for our next group of English soldiers. He assured us that his men would be coached in advance on exactly how to meet all emergencies, so there would be no necessity of trying to make spur-of-the-moment explanations to their English comrades through the barrier of a foreign language.

"God must have sent you to us once again," Kitty said to him, as he was preparing to leave. "I was beginning to despair of the possibility of finding escorts to get our boys safely across France. You don't know what a load you've taken off my mind. Now everything will be all right."

Kitty's remark stuck in my mind. It was true, I thought, that we had experienced miraculous luck again and again. Was it all luck, or was it the guiding hand of Providence? And could we always count on such good chance? Or were we perhaps being led deeper and deeper into actions from whose consequences there could be no escape, by a capricious fate which would turn against us only when we were completely enmeshed in its toils? I remembered the verse from Job: "Great things He does which we cannot comprehend."

It was on the following Friday that Father Christian arrived with another group of four young men. I noticed at once how tired he looked. He seemed to be near exhaustion.

"You look worn out, Father Christian," I said. "Aren't you overdoing it a bit? You might have sent some one else with this group, for instance—especially as it may seem odd that you should come to Paris twice in such a short time."

"Don't worry about that," Father Christian answered, with a smile. "I'm here this time with special German permission. I've got the Germans in Conchy very much interested in my campaign for restoration of the church. After all, they live in the rectory, which can stand a little repairing too, and they figure that if I do well, they may be able to ask for a few improvements to their living quarters. They would be delighted to have me come to Paris three times a week."

He paused a moment, and then added:

"As for sending some one else, that would be easy enough. Almost any one in the village would do it. But I think I'm the best one for the job as long as I can possibly manage it. My robes provide protection that a layman wouldn't have. The only thing that worries me is that something might happen while I'm away from home that would cause the Germans to discover the English lads hidden in the rectory."

Chancel was notified that we were ready to send four more Englishmen south, and it was arranged that they should start at seven o'clock. We watched from our window shortly before the hour set, and saw Chancel's escorts arrive. They came separately and with every appearance of nonchalance. The first one strolled slowly down the street, stopped to take out a cigarette, leaned casually against a lamp post as he lighted it, and then, putting his hands in his pockets, continued to lean against the post as he smoked it. A second arrived unfolding a newspaper, slowed up as he walked as though something particularly interesting had attracted his attention, and then stopped to read it better.

We didn't wait for all four of them to appear, for Chancel had instructed us to start the English boys down one at a time as soon as his men showed up. We watched them leave the building, and couldn't help admiring the technique of the French escorts. When the first English boy appeared, the man reading the newspaper appeared to finish the article he was looking at, folded it, and started off in the same direction, overtaking him gradually, but without appearing even to notice that he was on the street. The man leaning against the post made a casual sign to the second English boy who came out, as though he were an old friend he had been waiting for, and strolled slowly and nonchalantly across the street to join him. The third pretended to ask our man for a light. And we lost sight of the fourth as he was still walking along the street on the opposite side from the English lad he was to take in tow, with apparently no interest in him at all.

Kitty turned to me when we had watched this last pair out of sight.

"Chancel certainly knows his business," she said. "This is going to work beautifully."

And it did. The process of getting our protégés out of the country was reduced to a routine which operated with clockwork precision. By the end of October, we had sent about 100 English soldiers, accompanied by the same number of French soldiers, out of the country, usually in groups of four of each. We became so accustomed to it, that we hardly thought any more of the dangers we were incurring. But realization of them was not far below the surface, as we discovered on the one day during this period when we suffered a scare—or rather two scares, for oddly enough the only two untoward incidents which occurred at this time both came on the same day, a Monday towards the end of October.

Father Christian had arrived as usual with four young charges.

We were seated at lunch, which the half-starved men bolted ravenously under the benevolent smile of Margot, who seemed positively to delight in seeing the food which she could only procure by standing in line for hours disappearing in a matter of minutes.

Kitty said something to one of the boys, who had been quiet up to then. To our astonishment, he answered: *"Ich spreche nicht Englisch, gnaedige Frau."*

A German! The thought flashed into my mind immediately: is he a spy, a Gestapo agent, perhaps, who has gotten among these boys to discover how they are escaping?

Kitty and I both cast startled glances towards Father Christian, who said calmly:

"I beg your pardon, ladies, I had completely forgotten to tell you that we have with us today Dr. Joseph Wandel, late of the German Army. Having decided that he was fighting on the wrong side, Dr. Wandel has, shall I say resigned? from the German Army, and he feels now that it would be highly advisable for him to move to some other country."

Well! He wasn't a spy—at least, Father Christian didn't think he was—but I hardly felt too happy to know that a German deserter was sitting at our table. This was even more serious than helping English soldiers to escape. Harboring a deserter would probably mean instant execution for any one caught at it.

Kitty's German is good, and I can manage with mine. We asked about Dr. Wandel's history, and he told us that he was an Austrian, who had been drafted into the German Army, but had firmly resolved to desert at the first favorable opportunity. He found it in France, and was hiding in the woods like the English soldiers when some of them stumbled on him.

"They treated me like a real comrade," Dr. Wandel said. "It was good of them to take an enemy in so freely. So I am in the same boat with them—or rather, I'm a little worse off. They might be shot as spies if they're captured—especially those wearing civilian clothes—but they can always hope to be treated as prisoners of war. I can have no such hope. If they get me, my most merciful end will be the firing squad. I was quite prepared not to be taken alive. But now I am in luck, for my good English friends told Father Christian about me, and he insisted on helping me to escape."

And he beamed good-naturedly around the table at all of us.

Of all the things that Dr. Wandel told us, the most interesting was that there had recently been an epidemic of suicides among German soldiers. It seemed hard to explain, for the German armies had been victorious everywhere, but Wandel thought it resulted from discouragement because soldiers who had been serving since long before the war had expected that with the fall of France, Britain would collapse, and they could go home; and now, after the momentary confusion which had followed the French debacle, the English were more determined than ever, and the end of the war was still not in sight.

Moreover, Wandel said, the Germans were in deadly fear of the reception they would get when they attempted to invade England. In August, the troops along the coast had seen thousands of German bodies washed up on the shore, horribly burned. They were quickly buried, and kept from the sight of most of the soldiers, but the story got around that the English had repulsed an invasion attempt by some horrible new weapon which had burned its victims alive.

We had heard rumors of this kind already from the French, but no one had been able to pin them down to much fact. Frenchmen as well as Germans had seen the burned bodies washed up on the coast, and some of them told of seeing great walls of flame rise suddenly from the waters of the Channel. There had been a vague and subtle reference to some repulse of an invading force in one of Churchill's speeches, which we heard surreptitiously on our radio, but that was all. We couldn't understand why, if the British had really thrown back the Germans, they had never publicized it; but talking with Wandel, we realized that perhaps secrecy was better, for German soldiers, not knowing the exact truth, had passed stories from mouth to mouth which must have been heavily exaggerated.

Wandel said that the German soldiers were never really sure whether an actual invasion attempt had been made or whether it was simply during practice maneuvers, but that they all had heard a story about the sea around the Nazi invasion barges suddenly bursting into flame. One theory was that the British had anchored oil drums off their coast and exploded them when the German boats reached them; but no one was quite sure how it had been done. All they knew was that at one instant they were moving forward over the sea, with the cool spray dashing in their faces; and at the next they were enveloped in a raging inferno of flames. Only those who hadn't quite reached the flaming area escaped with their lives.

After that, Wandel said, the German soldiers were so mad with terror that it was only by force that they could be persuaded to get into their boats for drill. Officers with drawn revolvers had to stand over them and threaten to shoot before they would obey. At some points along the coast, they were chained to the boats like galley slaves.

Father Christian confirmed what Wandel had said about the fear of the German soldiers whenever the invasion of England was broached. He told us that when some of the men stationed at Conchy were ordered to the coast, the younger ones wept, and kept repeating over and over a French phrase which had been shouted at them derisively by children: "*Chair à poisson, chair à poisson!*"—which means, food for the fish. One boy who had been billeted in a peasant's house, said as he left, "We'll never come back."

"But if they're so afraid," I asked Wandel, "why don't they revolt?"

"You don't know the German soldier," Wandel said. "His discipline is complete. He will permit himself to be chained into a boat which he believes is going to take him to a fiery death, or he will commit suicide to seek an easier end, but he will not revolt."

It was about five in the afternoon when we had our second shock of the day. Margot was preparing to serve tea when the doorbell rang. We had already told the boys what to do if this happened, and they hurried into my room, leaving Kitty and myself alone in the living room.

Margot went to answer the door. She returned in a moment, closed the door carefully behind her, and, deathly pale, whispered: "A German officer!"

Kitty looked quickly about the room to make sure that there were no telltale indications. Fortunately Margot had not yet set the table, and there was therefore no sign of the number of persons she expected to serve. She took me by the elbow, and said in a low voice:

"Come with me. We've got to keep him from coming in."

We went into the entry. There stood Captain Weber, the military prosecutor who had ridden into Paris with us, and had promised us, much to our dismay, that he would call.

He seemed very pleased with himself. He was rubbing his hands together in a self-satisfied manner as we came in. He had perfumed himself so strongly that we noticed the odor as soon as we entered the room. I had seen German humorous papers which depicted Prussian officers as preparing for romantic adventures by making lavish use of perfume, but I had thought it an exaggeration. Apparently it was not.

Screwing his monocle more tightly into place, Captain Weber stepped forward, all smiles, and said:

"*Ach,* my dear ladies . . . I was just passing this way, and I thought I would drop in for a moment. I hope I am not intruding."

And before we could think of some way to make plain to him that he was, he went on:

"What a beautiful place you have here! Real American atmosphere!"

And with that he stepped through the door and into the living room before either of us could think of any way of stopping him.

Kitty threw a despairing glance in my direction, and I understood what she wanted. I excused myself hurriedly, and went into my room, where I found the boys tensely straining their ears to catch the conversation. I could hear their heavy breathing, proof of their emotion.

"There's a German officer in the next room," I whispered. "I hope Mrs. Beaurepos will manage to get rid of him shortly. He probably won't look in here, because he hasn't come in any official capacity; but just to be safe, perhaps you had better tiptoe into the bathroom."

"Suppose he wants to go there?" one of the English boys asked.

At this point Dr. Wandel, who had gathered very little idea of what was going on from our whispered English, asked "*Was ist passiert?*"

I told him what had happened. He asked:

"Is he alone?"

I nodded.

"And you are sure he is not on official business? It is probable that no one knows he is here?"

"I can't be sure," I said, "but I think he has only come to pay a social call."

"*Ist in Ordnung*," he said, and a curious glint came into his eyes. "It is quite simple. If he comes into this room, he will not leave it alive. Do nothing. Just trust in me."

I was terror-stricken.

"But you mustn't—" I began.

"On the contrary, *gnaedige Frau*, I must. We have no choice. If he finds us here, I must kill him, otherwise we will all be killed ourselves. That is the only way out."

He spoke quite calmly, as though his proposal to murder Captain Weber were the most reasonable suggestion in the world. And before I could recover my poise sufficiently to translate to the English soldiers what he had said, he was trying to explain to them in his incredibly bad Engish:

"Do nothing. I do. I kill him. You—just look. I kill him *oder* he us kill."

I hurried into the kitchen, which I could reach from my room without going through the living room. Margot was there with her ear pressed to the door, trying to hear the conversation going on in the living room.

I walked over to the kitchen window, and pressed my forehead against the cold pane, trying to think of some means of getting Captain Weber out of the apartment. Suppose Kitty couldn't get rid of him? Suppose he should ask to be shown to the bathroom? Providence had gotten us out of tough spots before, I told myself; but would we get out of this one?

Providence was with us once more. While I was still in the kitchen, the bell rang again. It was Father Christian, back from a series of errands. I pulled him into the kitchen, and told him what had happened.

"Leave it to me, Mrs. Shiber," he said calmly. "I'll get rid of him for you." His eyes twinkled. "You will see the advantages of the cloth."

I led Father Christian into the living room. He stopped in pretended surprise at the sight of Captain Weber.

"Excuse me," he said. "Have I made a mistake? I thought it was today that we had our appointment."

"Oh, but it is!" Kitty cried, picking up her cue perfectly. "Captain Weber just happened to drop by."

And she introduced the two.

"I am so sorry to disturb you, Captain," Father Christian said politely, "but Madame Beaurepos, who has been very kind to some of my parishioners, has consented to go with me to see a needy family this evening. There are many sad cases at this moment, unfortunately."

Captain Weber, who had risen, showed obvious disappointment; but he tried to put the best face on the matter.

"Could I perhaps drive you somewhere?" he asked. "My car is outside."

"Thank you, Captain," Father Christian answered, "but I am afraid my parishioners would not understand if they saw me arrive with a German officer. You realize, of course, how they feel."

"Yes, indeed," said Captain Weber stiffly. "They do not yet understand that we have come to save their country from degradation." And he saluted stiffly, kissed Kitty's hand, and marched, rather than walked, out.

I followed him, and closed the door behind him. Margot, arriving uneasily from the kitchen caught me in her arms as I closed it. Otherwise, I believe I should have fallen to the floor in a dead faint.

CHAPTER EIGHTEEN

Check to the Gestapo

BY OCTOBER our wholesale traffic in escapes had run us into finan-
cial difficulties. The travelling expenses of the large number of
men we had sent out of the country, including the fifty francs per
head for getting them across the border, amounted to a substantial
sum in itself; but even more expensive was feeding them while they
were in Paris. We had only three food cards in the household, and
as we often found it impossible to obtain even the amounts of food
we were legally entitled to buy, we would have had to resort to the
Black Market even for our own needs alone. In addition, everything
the boys ate had to come from there. We had no trouble getting
food in that way, but we paid through the nose for it.

The Black Market was supplied by truck drivers, who got produce
through to the illegal vendors by turning half of each load over to
certain German officials, who in turn saw to it that the truckmen
got the gas and oil necessary to stay in business. The food which
they brought in was sold at prices varying from ten to twenty times
the legal rate fixed by the authorities. Often this legal rate was reasonable enough, but the commodities to which it applied couldn't
be found. And the lower the rate, the greater was the incentive to
divert foodstuffs to the more profitable Black Market.

The official theory was that no one in Paris was starving. Every
one had his ration card, and the quantities of food it allowed were
at least sufficient to sustain life. But in practice it wasn't possible to
get the food your card called for unless you could give up a considerable part of your time looking for it. After standing in line for
two or three hours, you might find there was no more of the article
you wanted. You would try again the next day, and the next. Eventually, you would get what you wanted—if you could spare the time
to wait for it. Margot did that job for us. Standing in line had become the major part of her work. But in many families, where every
one worked, no one had time to wait for food, and these poor people

often simply went without even the small quantity they were allowed.

The lucky ones were those who had places in the country, where they had accumulated stores of food. The only solution for the others was the Black Market, which did a flourishing business. It was a market where there were never any complaints. No one dared complain. Any protest at the high prices would have meant cutting off the only available source of surplus food. There were plenty of others ready to pay, more than could be accommodated.

The drain that purchases on the Black Market made on our small funds couldn't be remedied. Kitty's family fortune was in England, and there was no possible way she could draw on it. I had sent for money through the American Embassy, but none had yet reached Paris.

"I've got to look around for some money," Kitty said to me one day. "We'll have to give up our work for lack of funds if I don't get some assistance. I think I'll take a little trip to round up some help."

I shuddered at the thought of being left alone, and of having to take care of a group of English soldiers, perhaps, without her. But it was obvious that there was no other way. If Kitty could get to the Free Zone, she knew a number of well-to-do French families who would undoubtedly be glad to help. We had talked that possibility over several times, and Kitty was quite sure she could get contributions from them. But of course it couldn't be done by correspondence; she had to go herself.

"Very well, Kitty," I said. "I'm afraid I'll have to manage without you for a while. But don't stay away any longer than you absolutely have to. I'll be lost without you. And I think the sooner you start, the better. That will bring you back more quickly, perhaps before Father Christian turns up again."

That was a Thursday, and Father Christian's usual day for arriving was Friday. I figured that if Kitty left with the boys the following day, she might be back before the next lot arrived. It was so decided, and the next day she set off with our English soldiers, travelling in the same train, but pretending not to know them.

Left alone, I prepared to create for myself the same sort of artificial peace I had enjoyed the last time Kitty had left me alone—no newspapers, no radio broadcasts, no links, as far as I could cut them, with the world of war and politics. But this time, I was not destined to remain undisturbed.

The very first night I remained alone, the air-raid sirens sounded. I was undecided what to do, whether to stay in the apartment, or seek shelter, when the concierge arrived to tell me that a very comfortable refuge had been fixed up in the cellar of the house next door, and to suggest that I go there with her. I accepted—and that gave me an opportunity to see the remarkable reaction of the French people to an air raid by the British.

They came hurrying out of their apartments to the shelters, not in fear, but with exaltation. Some of them were singing for joy. Others embraced, with tears streaming down their cheeks. One man shouted up at the sky: "Come on! Drop your bombs! We don't care! We're on your side!" and some one else, up the street, called through the darkness: *"Vive les Anglais!"*

It was only a few days before that the hated traitor, Marcel Déat, had written in the *Oeuvre* that people were "naïve" who listened to "false rumors" about the ability of British fliers to appear over France. "Don't allow yourself to be misled," he wrote, "by this collective hallucination which seems to delude hundreds of Parisians into believing that they have seen English airplanes over the city every day. The German anti-aircraft is strong enough to see to it that not one British plane will ever cross the Channel. Those who say the contrary are liars."

It looked as though the Germans had joined the collective hallucination; for now the air-raid sirens were blowing away, as though they too had decided that there was nothing imaginary about the British planes.

It was, indeed, the real thing: not just planes, but bombs as well. For two hours, we stayed in the cellar, while outside we could hear the roar of airplane motors, the staccato barking of the machine guns, and the distant explosions of bombs. Every time we heard the dull crushing explosion of a bomb, the people in the cellar seemed to take on new life and gaiety. They didn't seem to realize that they might be killed or wounded themselves. They were too happy about this attack against the common enemy!

Some one in the shelter struck up *God Save the King,* and followed with *Tipperary.* Every one else joined in. A few knew the English words. The rest followed the tune wordlessly.

In the darkness of the cellar, where identification was difficult, and all felt free to talk, tongues were loosened, and pro-British and anti-German stories were told.

A woman sitting next to me leaned over and whispered in my ear: "See that man sitting by himself in the corner? He's the Gestapo's undercover man for this building. I'd like to see what kind of a report he'll hand in tomorrow."

Probably his report was corroborated by his fellows all over Paris. For the following night, though we heard the anti-aircraft guns open fire, and the distant sound of bombs, which we learned the next day had fallen on the airfields about Paris, the sirens did not sound; and the reason, we heard, was that the Germans had decided that it was unwise to allow Parisians to get together in the air raid shelters, where anti-German conversations could be carried on with impunity.

That night in the cellar was the first occasion when I had personally an opportunity to see how little effect the German anti-British propaganda had had. It seemed not to have registered at all on the little middle class people, the *petite bourgeoisie.* They revealed their sympathies spontaneously during that air raid.

But there had been other evidences, less striking, it is true, but significant. They were written on the walls.

Everywhere the Germans had put up anti-British propaganda posters. Again and again one passed remnants of such posters which some one had torn from the walls. Sometimes changes had been made in their inscriptions to change their meaning. For instance, one of the favorite placards showed a drowning French sailor, holding the flag of France above the waves. Its message was: "Don't Forget Oran." (That was, of course, where the British fired on the French fleet.) Very seldom could that poster be seen in its original form. Either some one would change it to "Forget Oran," or, more commonly, to "Don't forget!"

Another common poster showed a woman holding an emaciated baby in her arms in the foreground, while behind her could be seen a chubby Churchill, smoking his famous cigar, and smiling contentedly. This one was labeled "See what the blockade is doing to your children!" I once saw one of these posters with the original legend scratched out, and the substitution: "Tell us about our prisoners," while another one had been amended to read, with more appropriateness: "How about our potatoes?" (This was at the period when all the potatoes in the occupied zone had been requisitioned and sent to Germany.)

Then there was the poster which showed on a colored map the French colonies which had been taken under British control—meaning those ruled by de Gaulle. It read: "Frenchmen! Here is what the English have taken from you!" On one such poster I saw, scrawled in what looked like a child's hand, "And our bicycles?"

That referred to the fact that thousands of bicycles had been requisitioned by the Germans. They had a very simple way of doing it. They would simply stop a cyclist in the street, and ask him where he lived and where he worked. Then they would pull out their maps, demonstrate that he could get back and forth on the subway, and therefore didn't need a bicycle—and without further ado, they would make off with it.

In order to protect their posters from alterations, the Germans began to put them higher up on the walls. This made it harder to tamper with them—but it also made them harder to see. And on the space left free by their elevation, chalked inscriptions began to appear. Among the most common were "Vive de Gaulle!" "Down with Hitler!" "Death to the Boche!" and "God bless England!" Among more picturesque legends which I saw were "Doriot, you will be hanged!" (Doriot was an ex-Communist Fascist who put his terroristic anti-Semitic hordes at the service of the Nazis), "To see Venice, join the Greek Army," and "Napoleon, too . . ."

During the week I spent at home, I failed to enjoy the calm and quiet I had hoped for. Far from waiting until the following Friday to bring in his next group, Father Christian sent me three parties during the week, and three times I had to hand them over to Chancel's escorts, and start them on their way. But there were no difficulties. The system was working like a well-oiled machine.

The first two were brought to Paris by other guides than Father Christian himself, and so I assumed that he would no doubt arrive on his regular day, Friday, with a personally escorted convoy. He usually arrived at noon. So I was surprised, on answering the door a few minutes after nine Friday morning, to find it was Father Christian.

"Anything wrong?" I asked, apprehensively. His unusually early arrival seemed alarming.

"Don't worry," Father Christian smiled. "Nothing's wrong. I reached Paris with my boys last night, but I didn't bring them here because I didn't know if you could take care of so many overnight."

"Where are they now?"

"I put them up in a small hotel. I'll bring them over shortly."

I was alarmed at this change in method.

"Oh, dear," I said. "Do you think it was wise to do that—to put up English boys in a Paris hotel, where almost any one might be working for the Gestapo, from the proprietor to the guests? And how about the police registration form?"

"They didn't fill it out," Father Christian said calmly. "You needn't be alarmed. The proprietor of the hotel, Madame Henri, is one of us. We can trust her completely. She is only too happy to help."

"You mean she knows all about it, too?" I gasped. "How long have you known her?"

"Since yesterday," Father Christian answered imperturbably, and in answer to my anguished expression, hastened to add: "I assure you, Madame, there is no cause at all for worry. We priests, you know, are pretty good judges of people. I knew at once from the way she received us that we could depend on her. It was easy to see that she recognized at once that the boys were not French. I didn't have to explain anything. She understood at once. I didn't even ask, but she offered immediately to provide rooms whenever I came to Paris with young men in tow.

"It seems to me that the hotel would be a safer hiding place for us than this apartment. Comings and goings are more normal there. There is always danger that attention will be attracted to your house by the number of strange persons who go in and out. I came over now to suggest you come with me to meet Madame Henri, who is very anxious to make your acquaintance."

I shook my head decidedly.

"I'm sorry, Father," I said, "I don't want to make hers—nor extend knowledge of what we are doing to any one else. Kitty is out of town just now, so I don't know what she would say, but I hope she would agree with me on that. I think too many people are in the secret now. I certainly don't feel comfortable about any more learning it."

"But Madame Shiber," Father Christian protested, "what you don't realize is that all Frenchmen are with us! It is safe for us to ask *any one* to help. No one will betray us, unless we have the very bad luck of falling upon one of the very few persons who serve the Germans. I think, on the contrary, that we should try to gather about us more people who will be able to help us, so that we will have alternate courses of action to fit all possible future situations. From that point of view, it seemed to me that this woman, with her hotel, would be in an ideal position to cooperate with us."

"But we don't *need* any one else," I insisted. "We now have all the persons necessary to do what we want to do. Increasing the number of those who know about it won't help us any, and it will make it more likely that our secret will get out. We must keep the number of those who know it to the absolute minimum. It's the only safe way. I'm terrified whenever I think of the number of people who are in the know now. And now you want us to add Madame Henri to the list!"

"But why should you be so set against Madame Henri?" Father Christian asked, puzzled. "You don't even know her."

"Please don't misunderstand me, Father," I answered. "I have nothing against Madame Henri. How could I, since, as you say, I don't even know her? It's just the principle of the thing—the advisability of keeping knowledge of what we are doing in the smallest circle possible.

"No doubt Madame Henri is the staunchest of patriots—but if she should be arrested by the Gestapo, and if they should torture her to get information—and, you know, every one says they *do* do that—would she be able to keep silent to protect us? We will all be safer—you and I and Kitty—yes, and Madame Henri herself—if she doesn't know anything."

Father Christian seemed suddenly abashed.

"Perhaps you are right," he said. "I hadn't thought of it in that way. We are all taking risks, of course. But we are all in God's hand. I know I am doing his work. I put my trust in him, and I don't worry."

Father Christian's words calmed my fears, and the tranquillity they gave me lasted until after the new group of boys had been started on their way. Expecting no more visitors until Monday, I settled back in an easy chair, peaceful and unworried, and with the sense of satisfaction that comes from the accomplishment of good deeds. My blissful state was short-lived.

Margot came in hardly half an hour after the English soldiers had left, to tell me that a young boy had come to the door asking for Kitty. I recognized him at once. It was Emile, the boy whom Monsieur Durand had sent to our place with the letters which came to his café in answer to our advertisement.

"Well, what is it, Emile?" I asked him.

"Monsieur Durand says there is a Mr. Stove in the café who wants to talk to you, Madame."

Mr. Stove! What a queer name! I couldn't think of any one I knew, or Kitty knew, named Stove.

"What does he want?" I asked.

Emile didn't know. He hadn't seen the mysterious Mr. Stove. All he knew was that he had been told to bring me the message which he had already delivered.

Mr. Stove . . . Mr. Stove. . . . I repeated the name mentally—and then suddenly I saw the light. In French, "w" is pronounced like "v." What the boy was trying to say was "Mr. Stowe"—and that was the name which had been signed to one of the letters we had received in reply to our advertisement, which we hadn't dared answer for fear they were traps.

Hardly had I realized that when a second thought struck me like a blow in the face. How did this man know Kitty's name? The boy had said "Mr. Stove" wanted to speak to me, meaning Kitty, for he had asked for her, and assumed that I was she—yet our advertisement had contained only the name of William Gray!

For a moment, I was riveted to my chair as though I were paralyzed. I couldn't seem to gather my wits, to focus them on the problem of what to do next. I was afraid, as I have not been afraid before or since—no, not even when the Gestapo later came to arrest us. I suppose it was because I was alone, without Kitty to give me courage.

I must escape, I thought. Perhaps I could still catch the train the boys were to take, and get into the unoccupied zone, out of danger, with them. But with feminine intuition, I knew that I wouldn't do that. Suppose Kitty should return, perhaps within an hour or so, and find me gone? I began to grow calmer. After all, we had avoided other dangers before. Perhaps this one could be averted by other means than flight.

While all this was going on in my mind, Emile stood waiting before me. I thought he was beginning to show signs of impatience at my not having thought of an answer for Monsieur Durand. I got up, and said to him:

"Let's go, Emile."

I slipped on my coat and hurried away with the boy. Now that my decision was made, I wanted to get it over as quickly as possible.

I didn't accompany Emile all the way back to Monsieur Durand's café. I sat down at a table in a small restaurant a block away, and told Emile to tell Monsieur Durand to meet me there. I made it very clear that he was to give my message to Monsieur Durand without being overheard by Mr. Stowe, and that he was to tell Monsieur Durand to slip out without attracting any one's attention, that it was very important that he should not be seen.

Monsieur Durand arrived a few minutes later. Evidently Emile had done his job well. The café owner seemed both excited and surprised.

"Did you give our address to this Mr. Stowe?" I asked at once, as he sat down. It was the first thing that came into my head. It was what was worrying me most.

"Of course not," Monsieur Durand said. "Madame Kitty told me not to give the address to any one, so of course I didn't. But tell me, Madame, what has happened? What is the matter?"

"Just a minute, Monsieur Durand," I interrupted. "I'll tell you what I'm afraid of, but first I must know one or two things. How did he know Madame Beaurepos' name?"

"Oh, but he didn't!" Durand explained. "He asked for William Gray. I knew that meant you, of course, so I sent the boy around."

"But you didn't tell him who we were?"

Monsieur Durand showed his strong white teeth in a grin.

"*Pas si bête!*" (I'm not that stupid!)

I breathed again.

"Thank you, Monsieur Durand," I said. "You've done wonderfully. Now tell me all about it."

"It was like this," Durand began. "About an hour ago, this chap came in. I could see at once he wasn't a Frenchman. He beckoned to me, and I came over to his table. He asked me to sit down—said he wanted to talk to me. I sat down next to him, and he leaned over and began whispering. He said he had written a letter to William Gray and addressed it to him at my café, but that he had gotten no answer, and no one had come to see him. Now, he said, he had come here in the hopes of meeting Mr. Gray.

"I tried to pump him, and finally he confided to me, in an even lower whisper, that he was an Englishman. He said he was in great danger, and he didn't know how much longer he would succeed in keeping out of the clutches of the Germans. He said he wanted to find William Gray because he thought he might help him to escape."

"What did you say?" I broke in excitedly.

"You may be sure, Madame, that I'm not as stupid as I look," Durand answered. "I couldn't tell whether his story was true or not. I played safe. I told him that I didn't want to be mixed up in helping anybody to escape, that my customers' affairs were none of my business, and that anyway I didn't know any William Gray. I said people often gave the café as an address, and then came and asked if there were any letters for them, and that the name seemed vaguely familiar—I thought I had received some letters for a William Gray, but I wasn't quite sure. If he wanted to stay there, I told him, he was welcome to, and if William Gray came in to ask for mail, I would introduce him."

"And then you sent for me—that is, for Kitty?"

"Yes. I thought that if Madame Kitty came in, I could let her look at this fellow without his noticing her, and she could decide whether she wanted to talk to him or not."

I thought the situation over for a moment.

"What do you think of him, Monsieur Durand?" I asked finally. "You see all kinds in your café. You ought to be a good judge of people. Do you really think he's an English soldier trying to escape?"

Monsieur Durand scratched his forehead for a moment in evident embarrassment.

"That's hard to say," he said. "We talked French at first. His French wasn't bad, but he had a foreign accent. It didn't sound quite English—a little more like German. I told him he could speak English if he wanted, because I had learned some English in the United States. So he did speak a few words in English. Of course, I don't know the language very well—but it didn't sound quite right to me. And then he shifted back to French. He said he was afraid of attracting attention by speaking English—although his voice was so low no one could possibly have heard him. But that's all I—"

He stopped suddenly, his mouth ajar. Then he slapped his hand hard on his knee, and exclaimed: "*Diable! Que je suis stupide!* How idiotic of me only to remember now!"

"For goodness sake!" I said. "Stop calling yourself names and tell me—what's it all about?"

"I just remembered," Durand said. "I didn't notice it at the time, but I can see it now before my eyes just as plain as if it were lying on that table. That's the strangest thing!"

"Please, Monsieur Durand, before I go mad!" I pleaded. "*What's the strangest thing?*"

"It just struck me," Durand said. "He lit a cigarette while I was talking to him, and I remember now what the pack he took it from looked like. It was a German military cigarette—the kind they issue to soldiers. I'm sure of it. Now how would a British soldier get a pack of those cigarettes?"

I grasped Monsieur Durand's hand across the table.

"Sit tight, Monsieur Durand," I said. "Let me tell you something. Don't show too much surprise. Some one may be watching us. What you have just told me confirms my belief—your Mr. Stowe is a Gestapo man."

Monsieur Durand's healthy reddish face turned a dead white.

"Do you really think so?" he groaned.

"I certainly do," I said. "Just think it over. One of the letters we got for William Gray was signed by a Mr. Stowe. We thought it was a trap and didn't answer it. Now if this man were really a British soldier, he would be afraid of a trap, too. He would hardly walk into your café like this if he got no answer. He would be more cautious. Besides, if he could move about France so easily as to be able to come to Paris alone and hunt up your café, would he need help to escape? I'm sure he's a Gestapo man. You'd better be careful. If he doesn't find his William Gray, he may take it into his head to arrest you. He's been friendly so far, because he hopes to catch his prey by not arousing your suspicions. So he accepted what you said. But if he doesn't succeed, he'll certainly want to know more about your rôle in all this than you've told him."

"What shall I do?" Monsieur Durand asked helplessly. "What is going to happen now?"

"I'll tell you what you can do," I said. "I have travelling permits. You could go to the station now, just as you are, without returning to the café, and cross into the unoccupied zone. I can give you a travel permit and send you to a man who will get you across the border. And that will leave our Gestapo man at a dead end. He will know you were guilty, of course; but you will be out of reach, safe."

"I can't," Durand moaned, looking at me with a piteously terrified expression. "My wife, my children—they would arrest them. Besides, everything I have is here—my home, my business. No, I can't leave. . . . Perhaps it isn't as serious as you think. You may be exaggerating the danger. . . . I know what I'll do. I'm going straight back to the café, and if he's still there, I'll ask him to leave. I'll tell him I can't take the risk of having English soldiers in my place—that I don't know any William Gray, and that I don't want to have anything to do with him."

He said this with a great air of decision, as though his mind were made up. But he made no move to start. I could see that he hadn't convinced himself that he could get rid of his unwelcome customer so easily. Suddenly his face seemed to cloud over, as though he were grappling with an idea difficult to formulate; then it spread into a broad smile, and a cunning look came into his eyes. He said:

"There *is* a way out. A beautiful way. I'm surprised I didn't think of it before. I'm going to phone at once to Gestapo headquarters and report that there's a suspicious Englishman in my place. That clears me. They couldn't possibly suspect me after that."

And before I could say anything, he was in the phone booth at the other end of the room.

Hardly had Durand left the table than I was seized with fear that I had made a terrible mistake. Suppose this Mr. Stowe really were an English soldier? Then I would not only have failed to come to his help when he had turned to us, but I would have been responsible for his capture. I would have converted our advertisement into the trap which he might have feared it was.

I was so tortured by my conscience that I hardly acknowledged Monsieur Durand's good-bye as he hurried off to his café to receive the Gestapo when they arrived. I tried desperately to convince myself that I could have made no mistake. But, to my horror, the deductions which had seemed so unmistakable a moment before, when I had put them to Monsieur Durand, seemed to dissolve into nothingness, and I found myself arguing that he might very well be an Englishman after all.

Suppose Durand didn't think his English very good? After all, as he said himself, he was no judge. And the soldier might have been an Australian or a Yorkshireman. It was natural enough that a soldier in hiding wouldn't want to speak English in public. As for the pack of cigarettes—had Durand really seen them, or just imagined it afterwards? He hadn't noticed them at the time.

And about getting from Rheims to Paris—it wasn't so far, and it would be in the natural direction of escape anyway. If he were desperate, he might risk trying to get in touch with this William Gray, whose advertisement might have provided his only ray of hope.

The torture of these thoughts was too great for me to bear. I had to see what was happening, to reassure myself if I could. I walked to the café, and though it was rather chilly, sat down on the terrace to see what would happen.

I had only been there a few minutes when a German official car drove up. Three men in civilian clothes jumped out.

"That's it!" I thought. "That's the Gestapo!" And I writhed in internal anguish at the thought that I might have put them on the trail of an English soldier.

They couldn't have been in the café more than a minute, when the door opened and they emerged again. Two of the three men who had entered were on either side of another man whom I had not seen before, each one holding one arm. The third man followed behind, as though alert for any attempt to break away. My heart sank. It looked as if I had been wrong.

But as the door swung shut behind them, and they stepped from the terrace into the dusk of the street, the two men let go of the other's arms. All of them broke out into sudden boisterous laughter. They all climbed into the car, and "Mr. Stowe," still laughing, courteously offered the others cigarettes from a package which, I was quite sure now, was German military issue. And off they drove.

I felt better. I thanked God for allowing me to witness this scene, which set at rest a conscience which otherwise would have tormented me all the rest of my days.

CHAPTER NINETEEN

Made in Heaven

ITTY seemed tired and rather depressed when she returned from her trip to the unoccupied zone. I thought she must have failed in her mission. But I was wrong. Her first action was to open her bag, and pull out a sheaf of banknotes, which she tossed onto the table between us.

"Twenty-five thousand francs," she said. "That ought to keep us going for a while. And I've been promised more later if we need it."

The next two weeks were without incident. Father Christian arrived regularly with his young charges, without the slightest difficulties. Chancel called to tell us that he had received word that the first boys we had sent out had arrived in London. Our own troubles were eased by the contribution from Kitty's friend, which enabled us to feed the boys who arrived in Paris as well as any one could, through purchases made on the Black Market.

But though food was not too hard to obtain, given the necessary money, fuel was another matter. With the end of October, bitter cold set in; and Paris was universally unheated. The ration permitted was 55 pounds of coal per family per month—or enough to heat one room about two hours daily. Even this amount usually could not be found.

Persons calling on friends often carried blankets with them to keep themselves warm. I spent one evening at a friend's house sitting before a fireplace where there was no fire. My hostess had ironically tacked her coal card to the wall beside the fireplace, to represent the fuel to which she had a right, but which she couldn't find for sale.

The Germans were not bothered by the coal shortage. They had plenty. Their offices and their apartments were kept well supplied. The sight of coal trucks unloading their precious cargoes into the cellars of German-occupied buildings was one of the things which infuriated freezing Parisians the most.

We did not go out much. For one thing, two, and then three, days a week were pretty well occupied with taking care of Father Christian's boys. And on the days when we were free, we preferred to avoid contacts with other persons, in order to discourage visitors to our own place, who might come at the wrong time. If we didn't want people to come to see us, obviously we had to avoid as much as possible going to see them; and when invitations turned up which we couldn't possibly refuse, we made it a rule that only one would go, leaving the other behind in case of emergencies.

It still happened that close friends would drop in on us without notice occasionally, and in that case, our technique was invariable. If the doorbell rang when the boys were there, they made immediately for the bathroom, the safest hiding place in our apartment, and we did our best to keep the visitor from entering. We didn't expect that our old friends would dash to the police and denounce us even if they did catch us, of course, but we both felt that the fewer persons in our secret, the better. Taking unnecessary chances was not in our plans.

After a little experimentation, our evasive tactics boiled down to one of two methods. If we happened to go to the door dressed in anything suitable for street wear, we would say: "My dear, how glad I am to see you! I was just going out. Are you going my way?"

That occasionally let us in for unplanned walks, but in the frigid days of late October and early November, walking out of doors was a pleasant contrast to stationary freezing in the apartment.

When we were trapped in some costume distinctly impossible for street wear, we adopted our second subterfuge. Making no move to lead the way from the hall into the apartment, we would, as in the first case, express delight at seeing our friend, but then add in a whisper: "Keep your voice low. There's an inspector inside. He says he's come about our taxes, but you never can tell."

This usually got rid of the visitor with the greatest speed. In Paris in those days the ordinarily innocent word "inspector" evoked the image of the Gestapo for every one.

As a rule, whenever we achieved one of these oustings of an old friend, we had to promise a visit of our own; and our method for fulfilling these promises with the least strain on our schedule was to attend occasional gatherings where we knew a number of them would be together. Thus no one realized that we were leading a more secluded life than formerly. What difference there was in our habits they attributed to the changed conditions of war—lack of transportation, necessary preoccupation with securing food, and so forth.

On these sorties, I carried my blanket not only because of the heating problem, but also because I was obliged to spend the night wherever I found myself if I happened to stay too late to get home by ten. The Germans had decreed a rigorous curfew; and as a result, Parisians not only became quite accustomed to spending the night on sofas in strange apartments, but even hardened to sleeping on improvised beds made of two chairs.

Violators of this curfew (later extended to 11 o'clock) were made to sit up all night on the hard wooden benches of the nearest police station. In the morning they were set to work washing the corridors and lavatories of the barracks, polishing the shoes of the German soldiers, peeling potatoes in the military kitchens, and performing similar services until noon, and then released with warnings that a second offense would be more seriously punished. Second offenders were rare.

Under such conditions, social evenings naturally became fewer; and the subjects discussed at these gatherings were very different from those popular before the war. Typical was the first such gathering I attended that winter, at the invitation of so old and so close a friend that I felt I couldn't refuse. Her parties had always been renowned for their glitter and luxury, and the conversational brilliance of her guests. War and occupation had changed all that.

I went alone, of course, for Kitty had to stay home during my absence. The blackout was total, and as it grew dark early at this time of year, I groped my way to her house, my blanket clutched fearfully under my arm. I wasn't quite sure I was even ringing the right doorbell, but after a moment the door opened, and I was able to find my way in by the light of a minute lamp completely encircled in a blue shade.

"That's all the light we dare show," my hostess apologized. "If the German patrol saw the slightest glimmer from outside, we'd pay for it. We only dare keep enough light here to save you from breaking your neck."

When I entered, I found a group which looked quite different from the well-dressed society ordinarily to be found at my friend's house. All had their overcoats on, and the men were even wearing their hats. The women as a rule had their shawls or blankets wrapped around them like hoods.

It was freezing cold in the room, yet a glance at the big stove rigged up before the fireplace showed a faint gleam of fire. Through the transparent door, I could see that the glowing ashes were the remains of the paper balls with which Parisians were reduced to heating their apartments. They were made from newspapers, cardboard boxes and books whose literary value was considered inferior to their worth as fuel. The method was to soak them in water for 24 hours, until the paper turned into a sort of pulp which could be molded into balls. They were then dried, and made fair fuel for stoves—but unfortunately a fuel which burned too quickly to give much warmth.

"German stoves are white-hot compared to this one," a man was saying, as I entered the room. I recognized a well-known Parisian lawyer, who in other days would probably have been discussing the latest legal gossip. "Yet we can't even get the small rations we're entitled to! Of course, it's not enough to heat us even if we did get it. Perhaps that's why the Germans don't consider it worth while to give it to us."

"I met a friend today," some one else spoke up, "who's had a stroke of luck. A Gestapo agent has moved into his house."

"Luck!" a woman exclaimed. "I'd be afraid to sleep at night! What's lucky about it?"

"Why, don't you know?" said the first. "If even a single German state employee moves into an apartment building, the whole building gets enough coal to keep it warm—delivered to the door. Better pray for a German in your place."

That was a prayer I couldn't echo. I would have welcomed more heat in my place, but the last thing I wanted was to have a Gestapo man living in our building, apt to meet our protégés in the hall or the elevator. Heat so acquired, I decided, wasn't among my desires.

And so the conversation went on. Among these people, who on other occasions would have been discussing the arts, or sociological, scientific or professional matters, the level of conversation had been reduced to absorption in the attempt to satisfy the most primitive needs—food and shelter.

One man with a number of small children told how he had burned up all his wooden furniture to keep them warm. There was no longer a chair or a table in his house, he said, and they sat about on rugs like Orientals. A university professor told of gathering twigs in the public gardens to burn in his stove. We heard of a well-known writer who had burned up his valuable library because he could not stand the cold, and of a famous society figure who stayed in bed all day to keep warm.

From heat, the conversation turned to food, and from food to clothes. An exclusively feminine group huddled at one end of the room got started on clothes first—but this time their subject was not style and fashion. These women a few months ago had been among the smartest and best-dressed in the capital; today their conversation swung between the two extremes of meeting the problem of clothing themselves, no matter how, and of nostalgic regret for the luxuries they could find no longer.

There were no mentions of new dresses, as there would have been a few months earlier. The idea of a new dress had become something fantastic and unthinkable. The talk was of the insoluble problems of remodelling old dresses to keep them wearable. There were no thread on the market, no needles, no buttons, no clips. A sewing needle was an object so precious that the most generous woman hesitated to lend it to her best friend. Thread was obtained by unravelling completely worn cloth. Ribbons and loops were employed instead of buttons. The Parisienne's greatest asset was the same as always—her limitless ingenuity.

Many of the women there bewailed the lack of what in happier days they had looked upon as necessities of the toilet—cold cream, face powder, eau de Cologne, soap. Not even ordinary laundry soap was to be had, let alone the delicately perfumed brands to which these ladies had been accustomed.

One of the best known women of Parisian society lamented, almost in tears:

"If only I could get a bar of soap, any soap, that would actually dissolve in water and provide a lather—not the substitutes they give us nowadays, hard as rock and as difficult to dissolve! . . . I think more than anything else, more even than plenty of food, I would like a hot bath with lots of suds!"

And the women about her sighed in unison, moved by this evocation of something which had once seemed to them completely ordinary, but which now had taken its place among the greatest and most unattainable of luxuries.

Because we did not often go about to such gatherings, we were probably less well-informed than most inhabitants of Paris about what was going on in our own city, but we were better informed on the news of northern France in general. The boys Father Christian was bringing to us came from all parts of this region, and many of them had heard reports of the activities of the Germans and the extent of resistance in the various localities of the occupied zone, and even the prohibited zone—which was that part of the territory held by the Germans which was forbidden even to Frenchmen, unless they lived in it. This was composed chiefly of the coastal region, from which the Germans at first hoped to launch their invasion of England, and which later they guarded with equal, if not greater, strictness, for fear the British themselves would invade.

One of the letters we had received at the time of our advertisement in *Paris-Soir* had come from a town within this prohibited region, Bergasse. We had not dared answer it, and since it was in the prohibited region, we could neither visit it nor get any word there. Kitty thought this letter was a genuine one, and our failure to answer it weighed heavily on her conscience. She had mentioned the matter to me several times, but there was no way we could think of to inquire safely for the writer of the letter.

It was on a day when some of the soldiers were lunching at our apartment that Kitty was reminded of the letter from Bergasse by the fact that one of the young men with us that day had succeeded in getting out of the prohibited zone. The thought gave her hope; and she asked Father Christian:

"Tell me, Father, would it be possible for you to make contact with some one in Bergasse?"

"*Mais certainement,*" said the young priest. "Why not?"

"Don't forget that it's in the prohibited zone," Kitty warned.

"And don't forget," Father Christian smiled back, "that the servants of the Church are present wherever human beings gather. The priest of Bergasse is an old friend of mine. I am sure he would be willing to be of any service. And I believe I could get a message to him without any difficulty. What do you want in Bergasse?"

Kitty told him about the letter received from that point, and gave it to him, in the hope that he would be able to check on it in some way.

Three weeks passed. Father Christian didn't mention the matter again, and, to tell the truth, I had forgotten it.

It was a Friday, and we expected Father Christian with a group of the boys again. We planned a special lunch, for we were celebrating the saving of our 150th English soldier. It was Margot who had called attention to the number. On the previous visit of Father Christian, she had asked:

"Father, are you bringing four boys next time as usual?"

"I suppose so," he said. "Why?"

"Because if you are," she said, "I would like to bake a birthday cake. I have been counting up, and that will make exactly 150 we have sent away."

"That *is* an occasion, Margot!" Father Christian said gravely. "I will make it a point to bring four boys, and I will be sure to come with them myself, to help celebrate the occasion."

Even Kitty seemed surprised at the total we had reached. She threw a smile at me.

"Did you hear, Etta?" she asked. "One hundred and fifty boys! Almost a whole company! It mounts up fast, doesn't it?"

"Add the Frenchmen who escorted them out," I said, "and you've got more than your company. Of course, we can't claim full credit for those."

But Margot was thwarted of her desire to make a cake. Materials for it simply didn't exist. Not one of the necessary ingredients could be found—in fact, even candles for it wouldn't have been procurable, if we had ever gotten that far. However, she did get hold of two bottles of excellent Chateau-Neuf du Pape, and we had those on hand for our celebration.

When Father Christian arrived, Margot set the table in gala fashion for ourselves and the boys. She called his attention to the wine, and apologized for not being able to provide the cake.

"Well, never mind about that, Margot," Father Christian consoled her. "I have done a little something myself to provide a special note for this occasion. Mme. Beaurepos, Mme. Shiber, allow me to present Wing Commander John Hitchcock, of Bergasse."

Kitty gasped.

"Father Christian! Without saying a word . . .! Why, this is lovely! That's the most beautiful present I've ever had in my whole life! But how did you do it? Wasn't it terribly hard to get him out of the prohibited zone?"

"Oh, no, no," said Father Christian, deprecatingly. "It was easy enough. Nothing special, really."

The young R.A.F. man, who didn't look as though he could be over twenty, with his candid boyish face (one might almost have said girlish, if his expression had not borne the traces of the hardships he must have endured), disputed this.

"Nothing special!" he said. "I say! It was very special, if you ask me. Do you know what he did? He . . ."

But Kitty's conscience was still troubling her, and without even noticing that she was interrupting, it seemed to me, she burst out with her question.

"Tell me," she said, "when you didn't get any answer to your letter to us—weren't you—well, disappointed?"

His face clouded.

"Oh, yes . . . that letter," he murmured. "Well, to tell you the truth, I was rather down in the mouth when nothing happened. It had picked me up so, you know, when I saw your advertisement. . . . Well, perhaps I'd better tell you the whole story.

"I was at Dunkirk . . . couldn't get onto the boats. I was in the rear guard, and when we got too thin, of course, there was no holding them. They just broke through, and we split up, every man for himself, and took to the woods. I knew one thing, I wasn't going to be taken . . . but I wished I had been for a while, when I ran into a German patrol, and got a bullet in the shoulder. I gave them the slip all right, but then I went out . . . don't know how long. I may have been unconscious for a few hours or a few days. Woke up in a peasant's barn. Seems a peasant girl . . . good looker she was, too; not half bad . . . almost trod on me while she was out picking mushrooms. She told her father, he came out after dark, carried me in, and bedded me down in his hay loft. They got in a doctor, another good chap . . . he would have been for it, of course, too, if they knew what he did for me . . . and he patched me up fairly well. But then the question was, how to get out of there, and back to England.

"Then I saw your ad. I knew what it meant, at once. So I wrote. Then, of course, nothing happened. I'd pinned everything on that letter . . . only hope I had, as far as I could see, of ever getting away. When nothing happened, I had some pretty black days. Even thought of giving myself up, once or twice. But I thought, perhaps something will come of it yet. After all, if it had been a trap, something would have happened by now. It must have been all right. I'll wait. So I waited . . . and finally the Father appeared. He's a wonderful man, Father Christian. . . . But, Father," he said teasingly, "do you think it's right for a priest to make light of the marriage ceremony?"

"If you call it making light to combine a good match with a good deed, I certainly don't," said Father Christian, with a twinkle in his eye. "I'm thoroughly satisfied with everything that happened. And a fine young couple they make, too."

"For goodness sake," I said. "What's all this about a marriage? Did you have to dress up as a bride, Mr. Hitchcock?"

"Well, nearly," Hitchcock grinned. "It seems that Father Christian talked a girl in his village into marrying a peasant boy in Bergasse. Now in that part of the country, when a young man marries a girl from another village, a party goes to fetch her, a group of young men and girls, in gaily decorated carts. The church authorities arranged a collective pass for the party, and I went along to Conchy-sur-Conche as one of the wedding party."

"But didn't the Germans check up on the wedding party?" I asked. "Did you get by without question?"

"That's the best part of it," Hitchcock said, smiling at Father Christian. "They check up very carefully on men of military age, but they don't pay much attention to girls. So I dressed up as a girl, and went in their cart. The collective pass specified twelve girls. All the Germans did was count us. They looked at the individual papers of the men. And on the way back there were still twelve girls, of course; for the bride had taken my place."

"Well, Father Christian," Kitty said playfully, "I didn't think you would turn match-maker to rescue this young man."

"Oh, it wasn't that at all," said Father Christian. "I happened to know that the girl had been engaged to a young man in the Bergasse neighborhood since before the war—so when you mentioned Bergasse, that gave me an idea. I just told her that if she were going to get married, she might just as well do it right away, and she could perform a patriotic service at the same time. I'll guarantee that that marriage was one of the kind that's made in heaven."

CHAPTER TWENTY

Two Scares

O N NOVEMBER 23, Kitty received a letter from the Free Zone. It had been mailed in Paris, so that we knew at once how it had reached us. It was a common thing for people crossing the border secretly to carry mail for friends, posting it after they got into the other zone. It was the only way communication could be maintained between the occupied and unoccupied regions.

Kitty opened the letter, scanned it briefly, and announced:

"I'll have to take another trip."

She tossed it over to me. It was from the same friend who had given her 25,000 francs when she had made her last visit to the unoccupied zone. He wrote that he had succeeded in realizing his plans, and suggested that Kitty get in touch with him at once, since he was leaving soon for North Africa, where he had an estate.

"What does he mean by 'his plans'?" I asked.

"He told me before that he was trying to sell some property he has near the Italian border, and if he succeeded, he could let us have enough money to keep us going indefinitely," Kitty said. "I suppose he didn't want to make it too plain, but that must be what he meant. I had better go at once, if he's leaving the country."

"How long do you expect to be gone?" I asked.

"At least two weeks," she said, "and don't worry if I take three. As long as I'm crossing the border again, I'm going to clean up all our outstanding affairs. First I'll go to Marseilles to see the writer of this letter. Then I'll go to Lyons. Chancel told me yesterday that Captain Handsby—you remember him, the one who was so nervous —has been arrested by the Vichy police, and is being held there. I have some fairly influential friends in Lyons who may be able to do something for him. Then I want to go to Périgueux, where I know a wholesale grocer who has to travel a lot on business. He's offered to help get the boys around in the unoccupied zone."

I probably didn't look too happy at the prospect of being left alone for as long as three weeks, for Kitty added:

"I hope nothing unusual happens while I'm away. But in case anything unexpected does occur, you can always go to Chancel for help."

I tried to mask with a smile the fear I felt at looking forward to the three weeks when I would be left alone again. But I knew Kitty had to go, and there was no point in burdening her with my private fears.

"I'll be all right," I told her. "Everything is running like clockwork. Between Father Christian and Chancel, I'm almost unnecessary. Don't worry, take your time, and I'll manage."

Kitty left the next day, taking the same train as our latest batch of English soldiers. Once again I prepared to settle down to a comparatively calm period; once again I couldn't do it.

It was the Sunday after Kitty left, when I was alone in the apartment (Margot was taking a day off) that Monsieur Durand, the café owner, burst in, a paper in his hand and rage in his face. He slapped the paper down on a table and shouted:

"What are you two up to now? Have you both gone crazy?"

I couldn't imagine what was wrong. I answered calmly:

"Judging from your manner, Monsieur Durand, I should say that it is you who have gone crazy. Would you mind telling me what is the matter?"

Impressed by my tone, Durand became a little quieter; but it was still with considerable excitement that he pointed to the newspaper.

"Excuse me, Madame," he said, "but I think I have a right to be very much annoyed. After the incident of the other day, I thought you would have sufficient discretion not to involve me in your affairs again. But without even asking my permission, you have placed another advertisement. This time I certainly wouldn't have given my consent. It was too near a thing last time."

I read the advertisement on which he was holding a trembling finger. Sure enough, it seemed to be word for word the same as our previous announcement:

> William Gray (formerly of Dunkirk) is looking for his friends and relatives. Address Café Moderne, Rue Rodier, Paris.

"Monsieur Durand," I said, puzzled, "I assure you that we didn't place this advertisement. It seems to be exactly the same as the other one, but we gave no orders that it should be repeated."

"Perhaps Madame Kitty did it without your knowledge," Durand suggested.

"Oh, I'm sure she didn't!" I cried. "In the first place, she would have told me. And in the second, she agreed with me after the other affair that we mustn't use your address again, and, in fact, had better not go near the café ourselves for a while. . . . Goodness! I hope you haven't led the Gestapo here! They must be watching your place! Monsieur Durand, I am afraid it is you who have committed the indiscretion by coming here, not us; for we didn't insert that advertisement."

"But if you didn't, who did?" Durand asked, uncertainly.

"The Gestapo!" I answered. I was certain of it. It had come to me like a flash when I remembered our decision not to go near the café again. "It must have been them. It couldn't have been any one else. We know already that they spotted the announcement and guessed at its meaning. They haven't dropped the case. This is their latest method. Perhaps they inserted that advertisement on purpose to see what you would do, who you would come to when you saw it."

"*Mon Dieu!*" said Monsieur Durand, "What have I done? What can I do now?"

"Nothing," I said. "If they followed you, the damage has already been done. But it may not have been for that at all that they had the ad reprinted. Perhaps they hoped to trap some English boys that way themselves. You may have some one representing himself as William Gray calling at your café for letters."

"And if I get any?"

"You are a good Frenchman, Monsieur Durand," I said. "If William Gray does receive any mail, I'm sure that you will see to it that it isn't delivered to the Gestapo."

Monsieur Durand left, apparently relieved. I had succeeded in convincing him that the Gestapo had wanted to catch English soldiers, not ourselves, and that, as he had previously cleared himself by denouncing their spy, they were probably not watching him. But

I hadn't succeeded in convincing myself. I pictured a Gestapo agent in Monsieur Durand's café watching him as he unfolded the paper, seeing the fear on his face, and following him as he rushed straight to my apartment. I sat at home, alone, quivering with fear, and expecting the peal of the bell at any instant. But as the hours passed I grew a little calmer. I reasoned that if Monsieur Durand had really been followed, we would both have been arrested by now. In fact, the most probable thing would have been that the Gestapo men would have burst in as we were talking together, to catch us red-handed.

Yet my heart was in my mouth all day, and when the bell rang at 9 o'clock, I jumped from my chair with a start, and stood motion-less, in terror, for a moment, afraid to answer the door. But Margot had not yet returned from her day off, and there was nothing to do except go.

There were two young men standing outside the door. One of them said in French, "Where is Madame Kitty?"

I said she was not at home, and made no move to step aside to let them in. But the young man who had spoken simply shouldered me aside and entered, pulling his companion along after him.

Then, suddenly, I recognized him. At least, I thought, this wasn't the Gestapo—but I was almost as displeased to see him as if he had been a German agent. He was a young French seaman with whom we had had an unpleasant experience two weeks earlier. He was one of the escorts provided by Chancel for our English boys, but dis-regarding the instructions that had been given him to pick them up in the street, he had come to the apartment.

"Weren't you told to wait for our boys outside?" Kitty had asked.

"Of course I was," he said insolently. "But I was tired of wander-ing around with no place to go. I'd rather wait here."

"But that isn't the point," Kitty said. "It's dangerous for you to come up here. It's bad enough to have to smuggle the Englishmen into the house without any more persons coming in and out. It might give the whole thing away."

"Are you playing at soldiers, too?" the sailor asked. "I'm sick of orders and discipline. I'm doing what I want now, not what I'm told."

And he threw himself down on the sofa, stretched his legs comfortably out on it, and refused to be budged until the group left at 7 o'clock. Now here he was back again, and I was decidedly not pleased to see him, especially as I was alone in the apartment.

"How do you happen to be here?" I asked him. "Didn't you go to the unoccupied zone with the others?"

"I went all right," he said. "But I came back—with my friend here."

"You came back?" I repeated. "But how did you get across?"

"Same way I went," he grinned. "Your route . . . I couldn't see any sense in staying. Conditions are just as bad as here. No work anywhere."

"Work!" I said. "I didn't know that was why you wanted to cross the line."

"Listen, lady," he said. "Don't make me laugh. You don't think I was such a sap as to go to England to join de Gaulle, do you? The war's over, and I'm glad of it. I'm not fighting for any one, any more. Now—where's Madame Kitty?"

"I've told you that she's not here," I said, becoming angry at his manner. "And in any case, I'm sure there's nothing she wants to see you about."

"There's something I want to see her about, though," the sailor said. "She owes me some money, and I mean to have it."

I was stupefied. It had only begun to dawn on me that both men were drunk. In the ensuing conversation that became very plain, as both of them began to lapse into incoherence. Their argument, as nearly as I could make it out, was that Kitty should pay them for the valuable time they had consumed in escorting her English boys to the unoccupied zone, and also for the time they had "wasted" there. The claim made me furious.

"You're drunk, both of you," I shouted at them, quite beside myself with rage and the nervous tension I had been under all day; and I tried to push them out of the room. But drunk though they were, I hadn't the strength to move them.

Fortunately Margot arrived at this moment. By a combination of her brawn and a barrage of violent Breton French which she poured out at them, mingled with threats to call the police, she finally got them out into the hall, and bolted the door behind them. For a few minutes we could hear them outside, drunkenly cursing at us, and claiming that we owed them "damages"; but finally they went away.

I was a nervous wreck. This incident, coupled with Durand's visit, gave me the impression that a net was closing in around us. The two happenings of the day showed how unexpectedly dangers could arise from our situation. And now I was afraid that the two Frenchmen, who, if they hadn't been so drunk, would have realized very well that we didn't dare call the police, might take their revenge by informing on us. I began to wonder if I shouldn't have given them some money to get rid of them, to keep them quiet. But that would have opened up a prospect of continuous future blackmailing, and I was able to console myself with the realization that this would only have provided a momentary solution to our problem.

I went to bed without supper. I couldn't eat, although in these days of deprivation, I was almost constantly hungry. As usual, I read the paper before going to sleep—and that made sleep impossible.

In heavy display type, I came across this notice in it:

10,000 FRANCS REWARD!

Following the decree establishing the death penalty for all those who hide English soldiers or aid them to escape, the German High Command announces that it will pay 10,000 francs reward to any person providing names and addresses of those engaged in this criminal activity.

I dropped the paper with fear pounding away at my heart. Those two Frenchmen who had just left, I thought—they would turn Judases for the sake of the money they failed to get here. Suppose they see this announcement. Won't they denounce us at once?

I lay in bed with my eyes wide open, unable to sleep. I was too panicky to think intelligently. My mind ran a race with the same thoughts, over and over, never reaching any conclusion or finding any solution, but starting all over again, interminably, at the same point. At 2 o'clock, I gave up the attempt to sleep. I got up, and put some water on the electric grill to make tea. While it was heating, I prowled through the apartment, going through all the closets, opening every drawer, looking underneath even the heaviest pieces of furniture for anything that might be incriminating. I even tore out the fly-leaf from a volume of Byron, which one of the English boys had left behind him, after writing in it a dedication expressing his gratitude for what we had done for him, and burned it.

I drank my tea, and continued my hunt for tell-tale indications. It was 4 o'clock when I finished. Whether it was because I had exhausted myself with my efforts, or because the belief that I had destroyed all evidence against us had settled my mind, I fell into a heavy sleep as soon as I got into bed again.

CHAPTER TWENTY-ONE

The Arrest

IN SPITE of the late hour at which I had gotten to sleep, I was up
before eight the next morning. According to my usual habit, I
was eating my customary breakfast of coffee and toast standing. I
never felt like taking the trouble to sit down to a table to eat breakfast if I were alone.

The door-bell startled me.

"Who could be ringing so early?" I asked myself. Margot had
gone out to the market, so I went to the door myself to see who was
there.

Two men were standing in the hall. They were in civilian clothes,
but both carried briefcases. It had become the mark of their profession, the tell-tale stamp that replaced the uniform. I was sure at once
what they had come for; but, oddly, I was not frightened. Meeting
the emergency was less alarming than wondering when, and how,
it would come.

One of them spoke to me in French:

"Where is Mme. Beaurepos?" he asked.

"She's not at home?" I said.

"Where is she?" he insisted.

"She's gone to Tours," I said. I don't know why I selected Tours.
I knew I mustn't admit that she had left the occupied zone.

"When will she be back?" the man continued.

"Why are you asking all these questions about Mme. Beaurepos?"
I asked—although I knew well enough. But he confirmed my suspicions by producing a badge, uttering at the same time the dread
words:

"German Secret Police."

I was right. It was the Gestapo!

Somehow this scene was a disappointing anti-climax. Ever since
the June day when we had first returned to Paris with William Gray
hidden in our car, now five months past, I had lived in constant

expectation of this scene. Not a single day had passed when I had
not visualized it in some form or other. I had lived in constant dread
of this moment, asking myself how I would behave, and if I would
be able to keep my head. And now that it had come, I was calm and
cool, as though it had been an everyday occurrence. Perhaps it was
because the event seemed so much less spectacular than I had expected—simply two ordinary looking men, in civilian clothes and
carrying briefcases, standing politely at the door of my apartment,
like salesmen. Or perhaps it was because I had milked the situation
dry of all its terrors in advance.

I remember that I looked into the small antique mirror hanging
on the wall of the hall, and was surprised to find that I was smiling.

"Perhaps I ought not to smile," I told myself. "It might annoy
them, under the circumstances. I must be very careful now, and
make no mistakes."

As I look back, it seems to me that I must have acted in the grip
of some cold intensity, a sort of trance. I must have responded to
the demands of the moment like an automaton or a somnambulist,
my mind closed tight to thoughts of the future or to anything except
meeting the immediate emergency. It was with complete composure
that I let the two men in, and followed them into the living room,
towards which they moved at once without waiting for me to indicate the way.

Either they assumed that I did not understand German, or they
were indifferent to my hearing them. At least they seemed to be
talking to one another with entire freedom, completely disregarding
my presence.

"The Englishwoman probably guessed we were onto her," one of
them said. "She's gotten out."

"Maybe not," said the other. "It's quite possible that she's only out
of town, as her friend said, and will be back. How could she know
we had anything on her?"

"Well, if she comes back, that will make it simple. Your job is to
stay here and wait for her. Remember what Pietsch said. Don't leave
the place for an instant, and, don't forget to answer the phone."

He looked about the room, as though reminded of something
by his own words. Locating the phone, he walked across to it, and

with the air of one quite at home, called Gestapo headquarters. When he got the number, he said:

"This is Schulz. Give me Investigation, please. . . . Hello, Captain Pietsch. We're at the Englishwoman's place. Looks as if she smelled something. She's not here. Out of town, her friend says. . . . Yes, Mrs. Shiber. She was here all right."

He listened attentively for a moment.

"*Ja, ja,*" he repeated. "*Jawohl.* That's what I thought."

He hung up, and turned to me, switching back to French.

"You're coming along with me. Pack a few things in a bag. Be sure to put some warm clothing in."

The other man was already sitting at Kitty's desk, calmly and methodically beginning a search of her papers. I was glad I had destroyed everything incriminating that very night. He pulled out the middle drawer, emptied its contents onto the desk, and began going through the papers it contained one by one.

I went into my room and began to pack a suitcase. I put in some toilet articles, warm bathrobe, slippers, a nightgown and a few other things.

I had left the door open, and Schulz was standing in it, watching every move I made. Apparently, I wasn't quick enough for him; for suddenly he said, in English:

"Well, Madam, how long do I have to wait yet?"

"I'll be ready in a minute," I said.

I was trying desperately, as I dawdled with my packing, to think of some way of leaving a warning behind me. Father Christian was due to arrive at noon with four more English soldiers. Chancel hadn't been around for a week, and was likely to drop in at any time. Even Henri might turn up. I thought that if Margot came back in time, I might be able to give her a hint, so that she could keep people away—unless, as was highly probable, they made her a prisoner, too. I knew if I failed to find some way to keep Father Christian, at least, from coming to the apartment, he would simply walk into a trap; for that was what our lovely apartment had become now—a trap to catch any one who came to it.

All I could think of was the story of a man who had been arrested as I was being arrested now, and who informed his friends by writing the word "Gestapo" in soap on his bathroom mirror. But that wouldn't do any good this time, for I had to deliver my warning *before* any one entered the apartment, not after. I tried to think of some place where I might write a similar warning, on the door, perhaps, or in the elevator, but I couldn't think of any way of doing it without the knowledge of my jailer.

"Let's get going," said Schulz impatiently, as I finally closed my bag. I was still without a plan. As we started slowly downward in the self-service elevator, I hoped that we might meet the concierge in the hall, and that I might find some means of making her understand what had happened; but we reached the ground floor, and Madame Beugler was nowhere in sight.

We had reached the sidewalk when suddenly I remembered something—and simultaneously found an excuse for seeing the concierge.

"My dogs!" I gasped. "I forgot about them. I must ask the concierge to take care of them," and I turned and hurried back into the house so quickly that the Gestapo man was left standing alone, bewildered, on the sidewalk.

I almost ran to the concierge's *loge*, and pulled open the door. As luck would have it, Mme. Beugler was just behind it. I had just time to whisper to her, "Don't let any one go to my apartment. The Gestapo is there!" when Schulz appeared behind me. In a louder tone of voice, I said:

"Mme. Beugler—I am going to have to be away for a few days— I don't know how long. Will you take care of the dogs until I come back?"

Mme. Beugler nodded, looking a little bewildered. Schulz took me by the arm, and growled, as he led me out of the building again, "That's enough of this nonsense. You've got more important things than dogs to worry about."

I certainly had. For as Schulz had hurried me out, I had seen a man appear from behind the curtains that masked the doorway in the back of the *loge*; and his fellow resemblance to the two men who had called on me convinced me that he also was of the Gestapo; and that he was waiting there, hidden behind the curtains of the concierge's *loge*, to catch any one who might stop there before going to our apartment.

I got into the car waiting before the door, and Schulz sat down beside me. We started off in the direction of the Etoile. I was shaken by the sight of the third Gestapo man. I didn't know whether he had heard my whispered words to Mme. Beugler. I had spoken so softly, I thought, that probably he had not, and perhaps that was why he had come out of his hiding place.

But since he was there, since Mme. Beugler was being watched too, it seemed unlikely that she would be able to warn Father Christian, or tell any one else to warn him. The trap was still set. I had not been able to unspring it.

The car circled the Arc de Triomphe and stopped a few minutes later before the Hotel Matignon, on the Avenue Matignon.

Before the invasion of Paris, this historic building, which took its name from a former illustrious occupant, Marshal Matignon, had been the residence of the French Premiers. The Germans took it over after the invasion for Gestapo headquarters.

Schulz conducted me into the building between a number of helmeted guards, who flanked the entrance. We went up one flight, passed along a corridor, and finally stopped before a door bearing the name: "Captain Pietsch." He knocked, a voice growled, "*Herein*," and we entered.

The room looked as though it had been used for conferences by the French government, for a long table capable of seating some twenty persons or more stood in the center of it. I was told to sit down at one side of it. Two Germans were in the room, sitting at desks in one corner. One was in uniform, with a scar on his face probably gained from a student duel. Schulz addressed him as Captain Pietsch. The other was a mousy little man who looked like a schoolmaster, with his colorless hair brushed back in pompadour fashion and his tortoise-shell eye-glasses.

Schulz made his report to Captain Pietsch, and left the room. The two men paid no further attention to me. I sat there apprehensively as the minutes ticked by. From time to time one of them answered a phone. Messengers came in and out. Papers were attended to. Finally, Pietsch stepped over to the other man's desk, bent over, and said something to him in too low a tone of voice for me to catch it. The second man nodded, gathered up some papers, and the two of them came over to the table where I was sitting and took their places opposite me.

For what seemed to me several minutes, the two men sat staring at me in silence, as though I were an object of a nature which they couldn't quite understand without careful examination. I supposed this was their invariable technique, designed either to make me nervous (which it did) or to give them a chance to measure their victim and select the methods to use on me.

Finally Captain Pietsch stood up suddenly, fixed a monocle in his eye, and without any preface shouted in French, in so loud a voice that the window panes rattled:

"If you keep one single word from us, if you tell us one single lie, you'll learn how easily we can make suspects talk. Your life is no more important to us than a dog's—a mongrel cur's."

His face was livid with fury. He stared at me for a moment, then brusquely sat down again. Then the other man, whose name I learned later was Dr. Hager, spoke up. He used English, and, quite unlike Captain Pietsch, spoke in a low, almost caressing, voice.

"Mrs. Shiber," he said persuasively, "I really don't think there would be any point in your making matters any more difficult for yourself by denying anything. After all, we do not want to be obliged to imprison a citizen of your great country. Believe me, what we should like to do most of all is to be able to release you at once. If you are a sensible woman, you will simply tell us candidly everything that happened, and I assure you that we shall then be able to let you go."

All of this fitted in perfectly with what I had heard about Gestapo methods—alternation of threats with apparently sympathetic persuasion, the choice between the whip or freedom. The icy calm which had gripped me in my own apartment had disappeared after I had left those familiar surroundings. But it had still not been replaced by the kind of panic which had gripped me in anticipation of my arrest, on so many occasions. Instead, though I was, of course, apprehensive of what might happen to me, my mind was working clearly. I was thinking rapidly and easily. And my reaction to the tactics of my two inquisitors was to say to myself:

"Deny everything! Deny everything, even if they produce the most incontrovertible evidence!"

Dr. Hager was arranging a number of papers, official reports, apparently, before him. I could see some underscorings in red pencil under my name and Kitty's. With a friendly smile on his face, he said:

"All right, now, Mrs. Shiber, we will listen very attentively to your story. You may go right ahead. Tell us everything just as it happened. We know most of it anyway. We know that Mme. Beaurepos was carrying on her activities under cover of her work for the Foyer du Soldat. We know about her little trips. We know that she was smuggling English soldiers across the frontier. In short, we know the whole story, and all we want from you is information on some of the details of the case, which aren't particularly important, but which we want to put in the record for the sake of completeness. Who knows, you might produce some extenuating circumstances which would help your friend."

From the way in which Dr. Hager talked, I suspected that actually he knew nothing. Although to any one familiar with the facts, it sounded as though he had just described our activities, actually he had not shown knowledge of any point except that Kitty worked for the Foyer du Soldat and that she therefore moved about the country. They suspected, of course, that she was smuggling English soldiers out of the country, and had said that they knew it, in order to trap me into an admission. But if they had had more precise details, I was sure he would have mentioned them. It looked to me as though some one had denounced us, but that the Gestapo was not yet sure whether the denunciation was genuine, or whether some personal enemy, anxious for a reward, had made a false accusation.

The raid on our apartment and my questioning, I decided, was not evidence that the Germans had information, but that they wanted to get it. And I repeated to myself, "Deny everything. Perhaps by denying everything, I may still be able to save us; and it's certain that we're lost if I confess."

While these thoughts were going on in my mind, I must have remained silent for a minute or two after Dr. Hager had ceased talking, staring at him across the table. It was he who broke the silence, a little impatiently:

"Come, come, Mrs. Shiber, let's get this over with. Are you ready to tell us everything?"

"Tell you everything?" I repeated. "But I don't know anything. This is all new to me. I don't know anything about any activities of Mme. Beaurepos, and I had no idea why you had me brought here today."

Captain Pietsch turned to Dr. Hager and whispered into his ear:

"I'll leave her to you. . . . Perhaps you're right. Perhaps she's a cultivated, intelligent American woman . . . but she sounds as though she's covering up to me. . . . Go ahead and try your humane methods, if you want to. But when you find you aren't getting anywhere with your sentimental nonsense, I'll take over. I'll guarantee to make her talk."

And with that he got up and left the room, without so much as a glance in my direction.

Although I knew very well how far the Gestapo was willing to go in its questioning of suspects, and so couldn't restrain a chill feeling about the backbone, I was sure this was all play-acting—not only because Captain Pietsch, while pretending to whisper, spoke loudly enough for me to overhear, but also because he spoke in French. I was certain that he wouldn't use this language to a German colleague, unless he wanted me to understand, too; for of course, he didn't know that I also knew German.

As the door closed behind Pietsch, Hager began again:

"I don't think we'll have any need of my colleague, Mrs. Shiber," he said soothingly. "You're an intelligent woman, and you realize that you can't protect your friend from the consequences of her ill-considered acts, so there's absolutely no reason why you should make trouble for yourself by concealment. Our reports show that you are not implicated in any way in this affair of smuggling English soldiers out of occupied territory, and the only charge we could bring against you would be that of failing to inform us of what was going on. I am quite sure our courts would be glad to overlook this matter, on the ground that you are a neutral and therefore on a somewhat different basis from a citizen of belligerent countries on either side—especially if you demonstrated that you were not an accomplice by your willingness to clarify these minor details on which we would like to check our own reports. . . . Now, Mrs. Shiber, on about what date did Mrs. Beaurepos first send English soldiers across the demarcation line?"

"I'm sorry," I said firmly, "but not only must I insist that I know nothing whatsoever about any such activity on the part of Mme. Beaurepos, but I refuse to answer any questions at all until I have the advice of a lawyer appointed by the American Embassy."

I was sure now that they knew very little, or Dr. Hager would not have said that I was not implicated in the escapes.

He looked at me and shook his head sadly.

"I don't know who could have advised you to adopt such a hostile attitude towards us," he said, in the voice of a mother disappointed in one of her cherished children, "but let me, in your own best interests, dissuade you from continuing in it. Perhaps you do not realize, Mrs. Shiber, how grave this case is, and how grave it might prove to be for yourself if your attitude convinced our courts that you were, not a neutral observer, but an approving witness, or even a participant, in the activity of Mme. Beaurepos.

"I am sure any lawyer with your interests at heart would give you the same advice as myself, but in any case, your request for a lawyer cannot be granted. Even if the American Embassy should send a lawyer here, he could not be admitted to this building. This is the headquarters of the German Secret Police, and no lawyers are permitted to meddle in our investigations.

"Your friend has committed a crime which may be punished by death. There is no such charge against you—yet. But if you try to save her, if you continue to maintain silence about what you must have seen while you were living with her, you may convict yourself of having been an accomplice, at least after the fact. And you may share her fate, without having contributed in the least towards helping her. . . . Now, Mrs. Shiber, about how many English soldiers in all did Mme. Beaurepos smuggle out of the country?"

"Deny everything," I repeated again to myself, and aloud I said:

"I'm sorry. With the best intentions in the world, I couldn't answer your question. I don't know the answer. I don't know anything about it. If Mme. Beaurepos was actually doing anything of that kind, it was in secret. I didn't know all her interests. We made it a rule not to interfere with each other's private activities. When I had a visitor, Mme. Beaurepos always retired inconspicuously, and when she had one, I did the same."

Across the room, I saw an electric clock on the wall. It was eleven o'clock. In an hour, Father Christian would be at the apartment. If he followed his usual habit, he would ring the bell, and when it opened would shout joyfully, as was his custom:

"I have a few hungry boys with me. May I bring them in to lunch?"

And, too late, he would notice that an unknown man had opened the door; or, if it was Margot who was sent to open it, that there was a Gestapo agent in the next room.

Dr. Hager changed tactics. He stopped asking direct questions about the English soldiers, and instead began to question me on our private lives. He sat there opposite me, never taking his eyes off me for an instant, and putting question after question on such minute details of our existence that it seemed ridiculous to take them seriously. I had to tell him everything about the beginning of my acquaintance with Kitty, the circumstances of my husband's death, and the reasons why I came to Paris.

It was just after 12 when Dr. Hager collected his papers, and rose from the table. His friendly smile had disappeared. He still looked like a schoolmaster, but now like a bad-tempered one, angry because his pupils had outsmarted him. I congratulated myself that I had been responsible for that. I had answered all of his questions, but whenever they began to get into dangerous waters, I had managed to avoid his traps. I was on my guard, and stubbornly determined that these people, who, I was now sure, knew very little about what we had been doing, should not learn a single name or a single useful fact through me.

The door opened, and Captain Pietsch entered.

"Well, how about it?" he asked. "Did the woman talk?"

To my amazement, Dr. Hager answered:

"Yes, she talked. I'm quite satisfied with the results. The interesting part was not what she said, but what she tried to conceal."

I looked at Dr. Hager with fear and stupefaction. Had I underestimated him? Instead of my outsmarting him, had he outsmarted me? Of course, I thought, he might have said that to confuse me; for though he spoke in German, he had learned from me during the questioning that I understood that language.

But then another thought struck me that drove everything else out of my head. He was talking before me as though he didn't care what I heard. Did that mean that he had no fear that I would ever be able to tell any one else of his methods? And did that mean that I would never be freed?

The Captain looked towards the clock, and mechanically I followed his look. It was ten minutes past twelve. Captain Pietsch put his hat on and went out. I was left alone with Dr. Hager, who was stuffing his papers into his briefcase, evidently preparing to leave also.

Ten minutes past twelve! Father Christian should have arrived at the apartment, but nothing had happened. Perhaps, after all, the concierge had managed to warn him. I began to regain courage once more.

The phone rang.

Dr. Hager picked it up, answered, listened for an instant, then lifted his head, gazed triumphantly at me, nodding his head significantly.

"Bring him here at once," he said finally, and then hastily corrected himself: "No, no! You mustn't move from there. You may have other visitors. I'll send some one over . . ." (he raised his head and looked steadily at me again as he finished) "for the priest."

I tried to show no emotion. I think I succeeded. I was prepared for what he thought might be a surprise, since I knew that Father Christian was expected, and I had already decided how to act if he should walk into the trap.

I heard Hager give orders for some one to go over to our apartment at once and bring over a priest who had been arrested there. Then turning towards me with a self-satisfied smile, he said:

"Have you ever noticed, Mrs. Shiber, that when a string of pearls breaks and one of them drops off, the others invariably follow, one after the other? It seems that we have broken the string."

While we were waiting for Father Christian to arrive, Dr. Hager again tried to impress upon me that the game was up, now that another one of us had been caught, and to urge me to save myself by telling him what I knew while there was still time. But I stuck to my denials.

When Father Christian was announced, Hager had a guard take me out, and at the same time told him to find Captain Pietsch and bring him in. Obviously, they wanted to talk to him alone, in an attempt to wring a confession from him, as they had tried to get one from me. I complained that I was hungry, and was given some ersatz coffee. About two o'clock, I was summoned back to the room. Father Christian was sitting where I had been. As I entered, he said, "How do you do, Mrs. Shiber?"

"Then you recognize her, do you?" Hager said.

"Of course," Father Christian said. "I was trying to call on Mme. Beaurepos and was arrested," he said to me. "I have no idea what this is all about."

That was all I needed to know. He had denied everything also. But, I wondered, what had happened to the boys? They couldn't have been arrested, or there would have been no possibility of Father Christian's denying his guilt. In the hours that followed, it became quite evident that, if Father Christian had brought them to Paris, they had in some way escaped the Gestapo, for there was no mention of them. Instead, we were plied again with question after question, sometimes separately, sometimes alone, sometimes by Dr. Hager, sometimes by Captain Pietsch, sometimes by both together. They tried to get us to contradict each other; but fortunately we both stuck to the simplest version of our relationship, indicated by Father Christian's opening remark to me when I was brought in. He said that he had come to see Mme. Beaurepos. I said the same, and added that I had only seen him in the apartment casually and knew little about him myself, except that Kitty was interested in a fund he was raising to restore his church. They tried to trip us up by asking such questions as when we had first met. Avoiding too great definiteness, I placed it at about the epoch when he had first come to Paris, and he did the same. I followed the system throughout, when I couldn't plead ignorance of a question, of keeping as close as possible to the truth.

That prevented my being contradicted either by ascertainable facts, or by Father Christian.

Again and again during that interminable afternoon, I heard him make virtually the same answer to many questions. He maintained that his connection with Mme. Beaurepos had to do with the church, and whenever the questioners touched on his reasons for coming to see her, he answered invariably:

"I am sorry, but as a member of a disciplined church, I can only account to my superiors for activity connected with my profession."

Although Captain Pietsch, his blood-shot eyes starting from his head, and the veins on his thick neck swelling, shouted at him that the Gestapo had ways of making stubborn people talk, Father Christian calmly refused to change his attitude.

They gave up at six o'clock. Dr. Hager summoned the policeman who had brought me to the Hotel Matignon, and said to him:

"The woman will remain under investigation."

Schulz told me to take my bag, which I had been carrying about with me all day, and come with him. As I left, I heard Dr. Hager reporting over the telephone—whether for our benefit or for his superiors, I wasn't quite sure.

"It seems to be a very well organized gang," he was saying. "They must have three leaders. One is no doubt working in northern France getting the men to Paris. The second, supervising the Paris headquarters, is in our hands." (That must mean me, I thought with a start, since I know they haven't caught Kitty). "The third, the one who helps them get over the frontier, is still at large."

That was all I heard as I was led out the door.

Once again we walked through the long corridor, and started to descend the stairs. Halfway down, I stopped short as a blood-curdling shriek reached my ears. Only a man in mortal terror of death could have uttered such a sound, I thought. I turned instinctively to my guide, my mouth, I think, open, and my face certainly wearing an expression of horror. He was stoical and unmoved.

"Come along," he ordered, taking me by the elbow and urging me on.

The shriek was followed by a succession of rapid screams, ending in a long wail that died suddenly away into nothingness. We had reached a side entrance leading into a courtyard before the terrifying noises stopped.

"Where are you taking me?" I asked, as we stepped out into the courtyard.

"Don't worry, Madame," he answered, with a broad grin. "We're going to a good hotel."

He motioned me to a waiting automobile, and got in beside me. Fifteen minutes later we drew up before the "good hotel." I recognized it at once.

It was the military prison of the Rue du Cherche-Midi.

CHAPTER TWENTY-TWO

Prison

THE SIGHT of the military prison carried me back in thought to the years of my past life, the peaceful, lovely years when Kitty and I had enjoyed Paris as only foreigners could, when we had looked upon it as a museum of history, not as a place where history was still being made—history in which we might become uncomfortably active pawns.

Kitty had brought back one day, from a prowl along the book stalls that lined the Seine, a pamphlet printed soon after the arrest of Captain Dreyfus, of the famous Dreyfus Case. On the title page an illustration showed the captain being led into the military prison on the Rue du Cherche-Midi.

"Let's visit this prison some day, Etta," Kitty said to me, as she showed me the picture. "I love to see the historic settings which are one of the things which make Paris so fascinating. There's hardly a street without some famous name connected with it here! You can live in the house where Molière wrote his plays, or take your coffee where Richelieu used to play chess—perhaps at the same table where Lenin and Trotzky also played three centuries later. I don't know any city where the past is involved with the present as much as in Paris."

So we made a pilgrimage to this famous prison. where we found a guide in a charming old Frenchman who was its warden. He apologized for not being able to show us around the section still used for military prisoners, although it was nearly empty. But he answered all our questions with enthusiasm. It was obvious that he had interested himself whole-heartedly in the past of the building that was in his charge.

"The prison was originally a convent," he told us. "A noble Frenchwoman, Madeleine Ciz, had it built when she was converted from the Protestant to the Catholic faith, and Louis XIV, the Sun King, contributed 1,500 livres to its construction. At the time of the

French Revolution, when the jails became overcrowded, the Revolutionary Committee requisitioned the convent and made it a prison. It's been one ever since."

"But where does it get its odd name?" Kitty asked. "From the street, I suppose—but what gave the street that name?" (Cherche-Midi means "search for noon.")

"On the contrary," said the warden, "the street gets its name from this building. When it was still a convent, the nuns used to provide food for the poor every day at noon. Early in the morning, beggars and destitute people would begin to turn up, and wait patiently in front of the building until the nuns brought out great kettles of soup at noon. So the building and the street got the name of 'the search for noon.' "

We walked about the part of the grounds to which we could be admitted, and admired its old-fashioned architecture, its thick walls and its arched entrances. I remembered particularly the amazing smallness of the windows, not much larger than a sheet of writing paper. That feature of the building depressed me; and I said to Kitty as we left: "How can the warden, a highly civilized man, appear so cheerful in spite of knowing that his prisoners are buried alive in this gloomy, airless tomb, almost without windows? It must be a horrible prison!"

Two years later, I myself entered this tomb.

I think humiliation is the dominant feeling of a prisoner received in a German jail. The absolute indifference to human dignity is horrible for a person used, like myself, to respect and deference through a lifetime. You no longer feel like a human being, like a person, but instead no more than an animal, without personality, whose feelings are considered worth no consideration from any one.

I was handed over first to indifferent women guards, who ordered me to strip to be searched. When I hesitated timidly, hoping that I might be allowed to keep on my last garments, they shouted rudely at me to hurry up, and fairly snatched my underwear from me, leaving me naked and shivering in the bitter cold of the unheated building.

After the minute search, I was taken to the photographer, where full face and profile pictures were taken, of the kind every one has seen on posters describing wanted criminals. I understood now why the faces in these pictures are always so stiff and the eyes of the hunted persons in them so full of fright. As the prison photographer fixed my head in a clamp that prevented me from moving it, I felt frightened and helpless too, and looked at the camera as though it were a gun trained upon me.

Before he took the picture, he pinned a number on my chest. I shall never forget that number. It was 1876. I was no longer Mrs. Etta Shiber, an American lady living in a comfortable apartment in the Etoile quarter, moving in a small and pleasant circle of loved friends and acquaintances. Now I was Number 1876, a record in a card catalogue, a statistic, an inmate of an institution where no one knew my name or cared to know it, where my friends could not find me. Indeed, they could not even know what had become of me. I felt myself cut off irrevocably from that other world in which I had lived, completely in the power of my captors.

The formalities of my reception lasted about an hour. Then the chief guard, a German sergeant major, rang a bell, and when a soldier of about fifty appeared, he said to him:

"Third floor."

I learned later that this was where all the woman prisoners were kept.

"Follow me, 1876," the soldier said.

This was the first time any one had called me by the number, and for a moment I didn't respond. He said roughly: "1876 is you. Don't forget it. Now come along."

We passed through a long corridor, where German soldiers were posted at every cross-corridor. They did not carry their rifles at shoulder arms, like sentries outside official buildings, but their bayonets were fixed, and they were on the alert, ready to use their weapons at a moment's notice.

We climbed winding stairways where nuns had once filed silently to their devotions. On every landing there was an armed sentry.

As we passed under an arched opening into a corridor on the third floor, a foul odor which I had begun to notice downstairs, and which I was sure was responsible for a splitting headache from which I was now suffering, thickened and became more intense.

My guide stopped before a heavy iron-bound door. He pulled open a little slide and looked through the small peep-hole it uncovered into the interior. Satisfied, he pushed a ponderous key into the lock, swung the door open, and unceremoniously shoved me in. The door swung to behind me, the lock clicked, and I was in my cell.

If the odor had been bad outside, it was suffocating here. I thought I would faint, or be violently sick, one or the other. In my first frightened glance about I saw four iron beds, taking up all the space of the cell, leaving barely room to press between them, except for the small area occupied by a table just big enough to support the tin canister standing on it. This was the source of the terrible smell— and again I was nearly sick as I visualized the hundreds of such utensils which must exist throughout this building, each one adding its stench to the horrible atmosphere in which I would have to live for I didn't know how long.

Three of the beds were occupied, although it was only a little after seven o'clock. The women in them turned frightened eyes towards me, but no one spoke. I sank down on the empty cot. I knew I should undress and get into bed, like the others, but I couldn't muster the strength to move. Except for the imitation coffee given me at Gestapo headquarters, I had had nothing to eat since my light breakfast early in the morning. But I didn't feel hungry. Indeed, if I had thought of food at that moment, before I had gotten accustomed to that awful smell, its very image would have revolted me.

The resistance I had maintained all day gave way, and I began to cry. The more I tried to restrain myself, from the last remnants of pride which forbade me to show my weakness before strangers, the more deeply I was shaken by my sobs. I had not wept so bitterly since my husband had died in my arms in New York and, before that, since my brother had died in Paris. But this time, I was weeping for myself.

A young girl in the next bed leaned towards me and whispered gently:

"Did they beat you? They beat every one before they bring them in here. They beat me, too."

I was immediately ashamed of myself. No one had beaten me—at least, not yet. What right had I to cry? The terrible pressure on my chest seemed to be lifted. I stopped weeping, wiped my eyes, and looked about.

My three cell-mates were all gazing at me. I didn't realize yet how much it means to a prisoner when some one else comes into his restricted world from outside, some one who can bring news and remembrance that something does exist outside of prison walls, some life of light and freedom, from which one is not necessarily cut off forever, with which some contact still remains. But I did feel instinctively that I had come into a new world, one entirely different from that which I had left. I began at once to feel a solidarity with these other three inhabitants of the new universe of which I was now also a citizen.

We began talking in low tones, huddled together so that we could hear one another without being audible ourselves outside of the cell, and in a few minutes we knew all about one another.

The young girl who had addressed those first sympathetic words to me was named Mary Bird. She was English, only twenty, and both beautiful and charming. She came from Guernsey, one of the Channel Islands, off the French coast, but belonging to England. The Germans occupied this island after taking the coast opposite it. Four weeks later Mary and twenty-seven other inhabitants of the island were arrested, charged with espionage on behalf of England.

I looked into her clear face and lovely blue eyes.

"Did you really do espionage work?" I asked.

Mary cast a frightened glance towards the neighboring bed, and protested: "Of course not. Neither did the others arrested with me. We did nothing of the kind."

The girl on the other side of me was a Spaniard named Lola. Her crime was having smuggled a French soldier over the Spanish frontier. He got over safely, but she was caught a few feet from the border and brought back.

"How many soldiers did you smuggle over the frontier?" I asked.

She looked at me in surprise.

"Why, only one of course—my boy—Gaston."

I realized at once that my own experiences had caused me to mistake a romantic flight for an organized effort to save soldiers from the Germans, like ours.

Lola's face took on an almost ecstatic expression as she added defiantly:

"They can keep me here as long as they want. Since I know he's safely out of their clutches, I don't care what happens to me. Nothing they can do can make me regret that I saved my man!"

The third occupant of the cell, whose bed was farthest from mine, was an Alsatian woman, Marthe Wenzinger. About thirty-five, she had probably been quite pretty when younger, but she had already lost her good looks. She was tall, with colorless hair and blue eyes. She had apparently managed to take good care of herself—her nails and skin showed that—but the clothes thrown over the foot of her bed seemed cheap and poor.

She told me that she had worked as a translator from French to German and vice versa in Paris. When the Germans came in, they arrested her, accusing her of espionage against Germany and for France before the war.

"Judging from your name, I imagine you must be of German-Alsatian descent," I said.

"That makes it worse. They hold it against me that in spite of my German descent, I was working for the French. But let me tell you something—it's safe for me to say it here, because there are only the four of us, and we're all in the same boat; we won't give one another away—because we Alsatians are of German descent, we understand the Germans better. And so I hate them more than any of you."

And she glared at me with an expression of concentrated hatred on her face. Then suddenly her features relaxed, and she smiled at me.

"And you, Madame. What are you here for?"

I began explaining myself to them—how I had come to Paris in search of a peaceful setting for the last part of my life, and how the war had swept me into its bewildering circle. I must have taken too long telling these preliminary facts, for the Alsatian woman interrupted impatiently:

"But what are you charged with?"

"Helping to smuggle English soldiers across the frontier," I said.

Mary Bird started as though in fright, and began:

"But for that—" and then interrupted herself suddenly, putting her clenched hand quickly to her mouth, as though to stifle what she had started to say. But I knew what the rest of the sentence would have been. She had meant to say: "But for that they can shoot you!"

"And did you really help English soldiers to get away?" the Alsatian woman asked.

I was tempted to answer: "Yes, more than 150 of them," when Mary Bird grasped my arm, saying swiftly: "Quiet! The guard is coming."

Sure enough, we could hear the tramp of heavy boots passing along the corridor. It was eight o'clock—the hour at which the guards checked on the prisoners, and extinguished the faint yellowish lights in the cells. The peep-hole in the door clicked open. Then it shut again, and the light went out. It was pitch dark, and I had not yet undressed or made my bed. I sat down on the side near Mary Bird and started to take off my clothes. Suddenly I felt an arm on mine, then the voice of Mary Bird whispered into my ear:

"Be careful of the Alsatian. She's a stool pigeon!"

CHAPTER TWENTY-THREE

First Day in Prison

I LAY on my back in bed, eyes open, gazing through the pitch dark towards the invisible ceiling. A deep silence had settled over the whole prison. I could hear only the heavy breathing of my three cellmates. They had fallen asleep within a few minutes after the light had been put out. But in spite of my lack of sleep the night before, in spite of all the tiring experiences of the day, I could not sleep. The thoughts raced feverishly through my brain. Once in a while I dozed off for a moment, to start up from the beginning of some nightmare connected with the day's events.

So the Alsatian woman was a stool pigeon! How fortunate that Mary Bird had stopped me in time! I might have told her everything. It had never occurred to me that the Nazis would have placed spies even here, in these putrid cells, living under the same conditions as the prisoners, in order to deceive them into believing that they were their comrades. I saw that I must be more careful, that I must suspect everything and everybody.

But could Mary Bird be mistaken? Suppose this Alsatian woman were just another unfortunate, as miserable as ourselves, locked up either on a false charge, or because she actually had worked for her country against the enemy? Or could Mary Bird herself be a stool pigeon, trying to create confidence in me by accusing another? That, I thought, was completely incredible. I was sure this gentle girl was just what she seemed to be on the surface. But I made one resolve—not to admit the part I had played to any one, even the most sympathetic and the least suspect persons with whom I might come into contact.

I dozed off for a few seconds in the midst of these thoughts, and in a half-dream Father Christian's face floated before my eyes; and then suddenly the horrible screams I had heard in the Hotel Matignon seemed to ring in my ears again, and I thought it was he who was screaming. I was jerked back to consciousness again, my nerves trembling with fright.

What is happening to him now? I wondered. Almost certainly he is in jail somewhere, too, perhaps in this very jail. Will they beat him, torture him? I asked myself. Of one thing I was sure. Whatever they did to him, they would never wring such a shriek of abject terror from his lips. He would die, I was sure, with the same high dignity as he had displayed when Captain Pietsch, his bloodshot eyes starting from his head, roared threats at him. He had made me feel then, unarmed and helpless as he was, that he was stronger than the Gestapo captain, with his revolver strapped to his belt and his henchmen within call.

Into my mind floated Dr. Hager's simile about the string of pearls. Who had broken that string, I wondered. Who had betrayed us?

Could it have been the two French soldiers I had ejected from the apartment? But what else could I have done? When Margot had threatened them with the police, perhaps she had given them the idea of going to the police themselves. Perhaps they had seen the offer of a reward. They wanted money. That was why they had come to our apartment. Maybe they had found another way to get it.

I told myself that this was impossible. The two men had been arrogant and insulting. If Margot had not returned, there is no telling what they would have done. But, after all, they were French. I couldn't imagine them betraying us to the Germans—at least, not intentionally. Perhaps that was it. Perhaps they had given us away without meaning to. They had been drinking. They were talking loudly, swearing; they were in no state to be cautious. Perhaps what they said had caused some prowling Gestapo agent to prick up his ears. Perhaps they had been arrested, and forced to talk . . . But if so, they couldn't have told much; for obviously, they knew more than the Gestapo seemed to know. They knew how the border was crossed, for they had crossed it. Perhaps they weren't the ones who had given us away; or perhaps they had held back all they could, after having betrayed us unwittingly.

That blood-curdling scream I had heard—could it have come from one of them?

Or would any one else have been willing to earn a 10,000-franc reward by denouncing us? The Gestapo agents had arrived only twenty-four hours after the prize was announced. But if so, who could it have been? So few persons knew, and none of them, it seemed, would be likely to have given us away.

Could it have been the owner of the hotel where Father Christian had stayed overnight with his boys? Or Emile, who brought the messages from Monsieur Durand? Or the letter carrier? Or the postal clerk who intercepted letters for "William Gray"? Or Monsieur Durand himself?

I couldn't believe that it was any of these—first of all, because all of them were French. All of them were fighting the same enemy as ourselves.

Then who, who, I asked my aching brain, who could have betrayed us?

I remembered that Dr. Hager had put one question to me again and again, in different forms: who was the person with whom we were in contact in the unoccupied zone? Who was the leader of that group? Could it be possible that our betrayal had originated there, on the other side of the border, from some one who had come into contact with men we had freed? Some one in Chancel's organization, perhaps? No, that seemed less likely, for then Chancel would ha:e been the first to be arrested rather than ourselves.

But the unoccupied zone, we had been told, was full of Gestapo agents, and perhaps one of them had heard something from some of the boys themselves. They might very well have thought that once across the border, the danger was over, and with it the need for caution. They might have talked imprudently. Or it might have been some of the French escorts, rather than the English boys, who had given us away—perhaps in conversation with a friend in a café, a conversation loud enough so that some one could overhear. Especially if they had just reached the unoccupied zone, they might not have learned how well organized the Gestapo was there, too.

If the clue had come from the unoccupied zone, that would explain two things: why Dr. Hager was so obviously groping in the dark, and why he had showed such interest in our connections in the unoccupied zone. Our great mistake, I thought, might have been that we had failed to insist that every one of the boys should promise solemnly not to tell how he escaped until after the war; for even in England, there might be enemy ears listening, ceaselessly listening, to careless talk, everywhere, all the time.

But I had no way of coming to any conclusion. I only hoped that our betrayal had come in some such casual way as an overheard conversation in the unoccupied zone; for in that case, there might be no way in which the Gestapo could pursue its investigation any farther. They might come up against a blank wall, if only all of us remained firm in denial. Perhaps the other pearls would not drop off the string after all. Perhaps they could be, some day, restrung again.

And I dropped finally off to sleep.

Seven-thirty! The knuckles of a heavy hand beat loudly on the cell door. My companions hastily leapt from bed and began putting on their clothes.

I didn't move. I lay there for a moment, blinking, and trying to orient myself, after the deep sleep which had allowed me to forget, momentarily, where I was. Mary shook me by the shoulder, calling:

"Hurry, Mrs. Shiber, hurry, or you'll be punished."

"What do they do to you worse than keeping you penned up in a foul hole like this?" I asked, hurrying all the same, for I knew very well that the German genius for punishment was unlimited.

"They send you to the punishment cell," Mary said. "It's not a cell; it's a tomb. No window, no light, no furniture. They leave you there for days for the slightest offense."

"There must be a bed!" I exclaimed.

"No. There's a bare stone bench. That's all."

Ten minutes later the guard entered with a German officer, making the regular morning inspection. I was dressed, and my bed coverings were folded according to regulations, thanks to Mary's help. It was only when I put my bed in order that I discovered how filthy it was.

At eight A.M. they brought us a drink supposed to be coffee, foul to look at and foul to taste. With it we were supposed to eat bread saved from our ration of the supper of the day previous. But since

I had not been there the day before, I had no bread, and none was brought to me.

We had hardly finished, when the guard came again.

"Number 650," he called. "Examination!"

The Alsatian girl followed him out. As soon as she had gone, Mary Bird said:

"She's going to make her report. They'll ask her if she got anything out of you. I was frightened last night. I was afraid you were going to give yourself away. She doesn't admit it, but she knows English quite well. I said one or two things to make her start, just to find out. She knows Spanish, too."

I looked towards Lola.

"She's all right," Mary said. "You can trust her."

"But are you sure the Alsatian is a spy?" I asked.

"Certain. I've been here three weeks now, and I've noticed that she's always moved around, and whenever they shift her to another cell, a newcomer arrives just afterwards. There were four of us here yesterday. Two of them were shifted, and she was sent in just before you arrived. I was sure we were going to have a new cell-mate before you came, because of that. That's how I knew you were all right, too.

"This makes four times in three weeks that I've been in the same cell with her. I've heard her talk often enough to know that she tries to pump every one. She'll only stay here three or four days. If she hasn't got anything out of you by then, they'll move her somewhere else, to work on another new arrival.

"I could tell you a lot of things about her, but I'll wait till later. She may be back any minute, and before that, I want to tell you what really happened to me. I denied everything last night, of course, because she was listening."

In feverish haste, sometimes leaving a sentence unfinished and rushing on to the next in her anxiety to tell me her story before the spy returned, Mary Bird told me of the adventure of the little island of Guernsey.

Her island, she told me, lies in the Channel some thirty miles from France and eighty from England. It was a haven for English officers retired on pension and former colonial administrators, come there to pass the last years of their lives in calm and quiet.

Typical of the island was the Syms family, whose head was a retired official of the Indian civil service. He had moved to Guernsey when he left active duty, with his wife and son. Mary Bird was engaged to young Syms, and they were to have been married when their plans were upset by the outbreak of the war.

Her fiancé left for England immediately to join the Army. A few months later, the tragic fall of France occurred. The Germans moved onto the undefended island, and established a garrison there.

"One night," Mary continued, "my fiancé knocked on the door of our home. He told me that he had come from England in a small boat with a companion, both of them dressed in civilian clothes, and charged with the mission of getting detailed information about the number of Germans on the island, and the type of defenses they had established. We managed to hide them for a week, but eventually they gave themselves away somehow or other—we never knew just how. A Gestapo detachment came over from the mainland and turned the island upside down looking for them. They finally got them, and every one who had been in contact with them while they were on the island—twenty-eight of us in all. His father and mother are here, and so is he, in this prison."

"Have you seen him since they brought you here?" I asked.

She shook her head sadly.

"No. It's terrible to know that he is here, in this same building, but that I can't speak to him . . . We managed to exchange one or two notes. There was an old guard here, an Austrian, who carried them back and forth. But he was caught, and we haven't seen him since. I don't know what happened to him."

She stopped suddenly. We could hear footsteps in the corridor. Then the door was pulled open suddenly, and the guard shouted: "1876! Examination!"

Once again I forgot for a moment that I was a number now, not a name. Mary touched me on the elbow. Her eyes were full of fright.

"That's you, Mrs. Shiber," she said.

I followed the guard into the corridor.

"Where are you taking me?" I asked.

He didn't answer. I never learned, during my prison stay, whether the guards habitually refused to answer prisoners' questions because that was the order, or whether they had ceased to consider us as human beings, and thought us so far beneath their notice that it would have been as absurd to hold any conversation with us as with a rock or a tree. That was the impression their attitude always gave me—that to them we were inanimate objects with no wills, no feelings, no thoughts of our own.

He led me to the office of the prison warden, the same office where Kitty and I had once been received by the charming old Frenchman who governed the prison then. His place had been taken by a German officer, one of those with the icy eyes and the hard, set, unmoving faces which looked as though they had been carved out of wood. Beside him stood Dr. Hager, my examiner of the day before.

Hager greeted me effusively, as though I were an old and dear friend. He fairly oozed saccharine courtesy.

"My dear Mrs. Shiber," he said, "I can't forgive myself for not having explained more carefully to that stupid Schulz that he should have taken you home yesterday. He misunderstood, and brought you here. I came at once, as soon as I learned what had happened, to beg you to forgive me. Won't you sit down?"

He pointed towards a large blue leather armchair which looked to me like the same one I had occupied two years earlier. I dropped, stunned, into its depths, trying to make some sense of what was happening. I had just begun to adjust myself to the prospect of prison, and here I was being told that it was all a mistake! Were they going to let me go? Somehow that didn't sound like the Gestapo. Had the American Embassy heard of my arrest, and intervened? But how could they have learned of it?—unless some one had come to the apartment, Henri, for instance, and been warned by the concierge.

Dr. Hager sat down opposite me, and began to talk in an ingratiating manner.

"It has been decided that you will be released and allowed to return to the United States. If you wish, I can ring your Embassy and we will inform them, in your hearing, of our decision. Then we can release you in a week or two."

"In a week or two?" I asked, wondering why, if they had really intended to send me home last night, they couldn't do it today.

"Well, we hope we can get it over as quickly as that. You see, it's all a question of finishing the investigation of this unfortunate case. Of course, if it takes us longer to get all the facts together—two or three months, say—we would have to hold you, because, you see, you're an important witness. They do that in your country, too, you know—hold what I believe you call material witnesses. The more quickly we can clean up this case, the more quickly we can let you go.

"Now I have been looking over the evidence, and I have come to the conclusion that you are actually quite innocent—that the principal actors took advantage of your good nature, and your unwillingness, as a neutral, to intervene or to denounce them. Actually, Mrs. Shiber, they were doing you a grave wrong, for without your realizing it, they were working, so to speak, under your unconscious protection. They counted on the fact that you were an American citizen to divert suspicion from them and perhaps to lighten the consequences if they were caught. No doubt they will try to implicate you in the hope that they will thus participate in the leniency which would naturally be extended to a neutral. They have acted shamefully towards you, in risking your liberty, even your life perhaps, for the sake of their own aims, and they certainly do not deserve any consideration on your part. They can hardly expect you to protect them by keeping silent—especially as it is in any case only a matter of time until we will have all the facts, and if you help us by giving us some information that will only mean shortening the investigation slightly, nothing more."

I could see very plainly now what he was getting at. I said nothing, though I thought he expected me to interrupt, and he continued.

"As I said, Mrs. Shiber, I am quite convinced of your own innocence, but I am afraid I cannot say the same for your friend, Mme. Beaurepos. She was the head of this group, but she managed to get away just in time. She knew we were after her. She told you she was going on a trip, but actually she was escaping and leaving you behind to take the punishment. If she had really been your friend, she would have taken you with her. Now do you see how badly you have been treated? Here you are, in prison, and she has escaped, rejoicing in her own liberty, and completely uninterested in your fate.

"Now, Mrs. Shiber, you see what the situation is. You have been the dupe of—I don't like to say this about an old friend of yours, but it happens to be the truth—an unscrupulous woman. Fortunately for you, we have been able to see through her schemes, and to realize that it is not you who are guilty, and so you will be freed as soon as we have completed our investigation. Now as I say, I hope that will only take a week or two; but it may take longer if we have trouble clearing up some of the minor details. So it rests only with you: give us your assistance on these points, and we will be able to do our work more rapidly, and consequently to release you sooner. I know this jail isn't a very pleasant place. I deeply regret the error that put you here in the first place. But now that you have been entered, I can't do anything about it. A discharge order has to be issued by my superiors before you can be freed, and in a case like this, no such order is ever approved until the investigation is completed. So, as you see, I am helpless. It depends only on yourself whether you will be out of here in, say, a week, or perhaps three or four months."

It was all very clear now; it was just what I thought he was leading up to. Dr. Hager was trying to persuade me to tell what I knew by dangling before my eyes the possibility of release. They had given me a little taste of prison in the hopes that the horrible prospect of remaining in jail would weaken my resolution. But I was surer than ever that they still knew very little about our case; otherwise, why would such elaborate measures be necessary to persuade me to talk? As for what they said about Kitty having abandoned me, that I knew simply could not be true. I had known her too long and too well to be taken in by that. It was this part of Dr. Hager's plea as much as anything else which convinced me that everything he said was false, carefully designed to make me betray my friends. Since I knew that could only be a ruse, I was certain the rest of what he said was untrue as well. He was trying to draw me out, I told myself; very well, I will try to draw him out.

"But Dr. Hager," I said, "I have told you I know nothing about this affair. What could I possibly tell you that would help?"

"We believe that your friend has escaped into the unoccupied zone," he said. "It would be natural for her to follow the route over which she sent the English soldiers if she believed she were about to be arrested. No doubt you have addresses of friends of hers there, with whom she might have made contact. Or perhaps you even have an idea what city she may be in. That would give us something to go on. Of course, we couldn't arrest her there. We have no authority in the unoccupied zone. So, if you still are reluctant to cause your friend any harm, even after what she has done to you, you can rest assured. If she is in the unoccupied zone, she is safe."

"But if she is safe there, if you can't arrest her in the unoccupied zone, why do you want to know where she is there?" I asked, with apparent innocence. As a matter of fact, I knew very well, from Henri and others, that the Gestapo operated in the unoccupied zone too, and that French police were often obliged to do their dirty work for them, arresting their own compatriots and handing them over to the Germans.

Dr. Hager shook his head slowly, like a schoolmaster disappointed in a stupid pupil.

"My dear Mrs. Shiber, don't you understand yet? I am trying to close this case, to get it over with—and incidentally, to get you out of here. I am not allowed to let the investigation drop until I have definitely accounted for all the suspects I have been ordered to follow up. Now I have accounted for all but one. Mme. Beaurepos' name is the only one against which we still have to place a question mark. If I can only report, 'Mme. Beaurepos has been located at Marseilles—'" he watched me narrowly as he mentioned the names of these localities, as though casually and at hazard, giving a rising inflection to each name, hoping, I was sure, that a light would come into my eyes at one of them—"'or Lyons—or Cannes—or Nimes—' then I can put down that she is beyond our jurisdiction, and that the investigation is ended."

I wondered how much of this might be true—had they actually arrested every one except Kitty? Were Tissier and Chancel perhaps in their hands? And frightened little bourgeois Monsieur Durand? He would be likely to tell anything he knew, not that he knew a great deal. I decided to make one more test of Dr. Hager.

"Dr. Hager," I said, "you told me a minute ago that you were willing to inform the American Embassy of your decision to release me, in my presence. Would you do that now?"

"Why, of course," Dr. Hager said. He picked up the desk phone, and said, "American Embassy, please."

He looked towards me, almost triumphantly, I thought, as though to say: "There! You didn't think I'd do it, did you?"

I couldn't hear the voice answer on the other end, though I strained my ears in the hope of catching it, but Dr. Hager said: "This is Dr. Hager of the German Secret Police talking. I wish to report the arrest of an American citizen. Would you be kind enough to connect me with the proper person?"

There was a pause. Then Hager identified himself again, and gave my name and address, as though to some one writing it down. Then he continued:

"We have been obliged to arrest and hold Mrs. Shiber in the military prison on the Rue du Cherche-Midi . . . yes, go ahead, take it down . . . Ready again? . . . on a charge of complicity in aiding English soldiers to escape from occupied territory . . . Yes, that's it . . . So far our investigation leads us to believe that Mrs. Shiber was an innocent victim of those actually guilty . . . We are obliged to hold her as a material witness, but we wished to inform you that she will be released as soon as our investigation has been completed . . . How long? We hope in a week or two . . . That depends partly on Mrs. Shiber herself. We think she could help us in locating the woman with whom she shared an apartment—a French citizen, British by birth—who was the ringleader of an organized gang, and as soon as we have discovered where she is, we will be able to close the case . . . Indeed? . . . Is that so? . . . I'm very happy to hear you say that. It is exactly the advice I have been giving Mrs. Shiber myself."

Still holding the phone close enough to his mouth so that any one at the other end could hear what he was saying, he said to me: "Mrs. Shiber, the Embassy tells me that in their opinion, as a neutral, you should avoid taking sides by withholding any information you may be able to give to the authorities in control of the territory on which you happen to live. They advise that you tell whatever you know."

I rose from my chair.

"I'd like to speak to them myself," I said.

Dr. Hager flashed a quick glance at the prison commander at the same time that he said, "Why, certainly, Mrs. Shiber," and rose as though to offer me his place.

The commander intervened quickly.

"I can't permit it, Dr. Hager," he said. "I'm sorry. I have already stretched a point in allowing you to call. Prison regulations are rigid on that point. Prisoners are not allowed to talk on the phone with any one at all. Even you yourself could not talk with a prisoner in that fashion. I am definitely unable to allow Mrs. Shiber to use the phone. It is strictly forbidden."

Dr. Hager shrugged his shoulders and made a gesture of impotence in my direction. He returned to the phone. "Hello . . . Hello," he said, then put down the phone. "They must have hung up," he said.

To me this little scene was conclusive. It had obviously been well rehearsed. I was certain Dr. Hager had not called the American Embassy. That meant that my suspicions were right, and his whole appeal was an elaborate attempt at deception. Once again, I said to myself: "Deny everything! You must continue to deny everything!"

"Well, Mrs. Shiber," said Dr. Hager, with a tone of great relief, as though everything were settled now, "let's get this annoying business over with. Now where do you think is the most likely place to look for Mme. Beaurepos?"

"I've told you already the only thing I know," I said, "that she was going to Tours."

"She didn't go to Tours," said Dr. Hager shortly. "That we know. That is in the occupied zone. Where would she go in the unoccupied zone? Where has she friends?"

"I have no idea," I said. "I told you that we lived completely separate lives. I didn't know her friends, and she didn't know mine."

I can't describe the look that Dr. Hager gave me. Mostly, it seemed to be disgust. There was anger in it, too. He had apparently been certain that he was about to reach his goal, and here he was, back where he started from. He stepped around the desk and exchanged a few whispered words with the prison commander. Then he turned towards me. His face was dark with rage.

"I have been wrong about you, Mrs. Shiber," he shouted at me. "I thought you were innocent. I thought you had been taken advantage of. But now I see that you are as guilty as the rest. That is the only reason you could have for hiding what you know. And such ridiculous excuses! Do you expect me to believe that you don't know the friends of Mme. Beaurepos, with whom you have been living for years? No, Mrs. Shiber! You are lying because you are in it as deep as all the rest! There is only one way out of this prison for you! That is to the scaffold! You know the punishment for your crime—death! You have just proved to me that you deserve it."

He stopped, and then suddenly shifted to a softer tone of voice, though his accents were still hard enough.

"Perhaps it is just that you do not realize the position you are in. Perhaps that is why you are so stubborn, not because you are guilty, or completely guilty, yourself. I will give you one more chance. I will give you until six o'clock this evening. If you haven't become reasonable by then, I will have no option. I shall have to record in my report that I consider you one of the guilty persons."

I can't pretend that I was not shaken at hearing myself threatened openly with the death penalty. But I managed to reply fairly steadily.

"I don't need until six o'clock tonight to make up some story to satisfy you," I said. "Perhaps it is stupid of me, not to try to secure my release by imagining some information which might deceive you into believing I was able to help. But I'm not cut out for such clever rôles. I can only repeat that I don't know anything."

Dr. Hager glared at me again, and the burning eyes behind his thick-lensed glasses frightened me. He rushed towards me, raising his right arm as he did so. Instinctively I backed away.

"Aren't you ashamed of yourself," I cried, "trying to strike a defenseless woman?"

A knock sounded on the door. Dr. Hager dropped his arm.

"*Herein*," the prison commander growled.

The door swung open, and the guard announced:

"Mr. Marvel of the American Quakers."

The Stool Pigeon

I LEARNED later that Mr. Marvel was a frequent visitor to the Cherche-Midi prison. As the Paris representative of the Quakers, he called systematically at the various camps for prisoners of war, the internment camps, and the prisons, and arranged for food and other comforts to be given to the inmates. For some reason, the Quakers had been particularly successful in securing permission from the Germans to carry on their work, and were able, for instance, to enter prisons like mine which even accredited diplomats found it almost impossible to visit. I suspected that one reason why the Germans allowed the American Quakers and certain other American organizations privileges refused to other groups was that the United States was still neutral, and the Germans hoped by cooperating with such non-official bodies to counteract to some extent their bad reputation in the United States.

It was apparent that Mr. Marvel was accustomed to considerable consideration in this prison. The prison commander offered him a chair with exaggerated courtesy, as Dr. Hager slipped unobtrusively out of the room. The guard entered to lead me back, but Mr. Marvel said:

"Excuse me, Major; isn't this Mrs. Shiber?"

"Yes," the commander answered.

"It's about her that I came today," he said. "May she stay?"

The commander ordered the guard to wait in the corridor, and Mr. Marvel turned to me, saying that as soon as he had learned that an American woman was in the prison he had hurried over to inquire about my situation.

"Did the American Embassy send you over?" I asked

Mr. Marvel smiled.

"I'm sorry," he said, "but I am not allowed to talk to you about anything except your physical needs. That is the condition on which I am allowed here."

225

The German Major, who had suddenly stiffened in his chair when I had asked my question, relaxed again.

I was depressed at this rebuff. It seemed almost as though I were still shut off entirely from the world without, since I could not even communicate with this American who had succeeded in reaching me.

Mr. Marvel asked if I had brought enough clothing with me. I answered listlessly that I needed warm underwear, and he promised to send me some. At this point, the phone rang; and while the prison commander was talking, I ventured to say, in a low tone of voice:

"Did the Embassy send you because of a phone call from here this morning?"

"I don't know of any phone call," Mr. Marvel said. "The Embassy was told by a Monsieur Beaurepos that you had been arrested. I have been to several prisons looking for you. Tell me quickly what you are here for, so I can report to the Embassy."

I had only time to tell him the charge when the commander hung up, and Mr. Marvel shifted swiftly back to the subject of clothing and food. I was happy again, for I knew that if Henri had discovered what had happened, he would do his utmost to warn Kitty, and keep her from coming back to the apartment. And it also seemed probable that I had adopted the right course, for it was not Dr. Hager's phone call, as I had thought for a moment, which had brought Mr. Marvel to the prison; and so I was still convinced that it had been a fake. But now the Embassy knew of my plight, and I no longer felt abandoned and alone. Outside the prison walls, friends would be working for my release. I seemed to have grown suddenly much stronger; and for the first time since I had choked down that terrible ersatz coffee, I realized that I was very hungry.

Mr. Marvel said good-bye to me, and I was taken back to my cell. I stepped through the corridors almost light-heartedly. I felt that these horrible men who held me prisoner would no longer dare to raise a hand against me. I was protected now, shielded by the fact that my jailers knew that the great country of which I was a citizen had found out where I was, and would not permit them to mistreat me.

My cell-mates looked curiously at me when I returned, but the Alsatian woman was there again, so none of them asked me any questions. She, however, ignorant of course that I knew she was a spy, set herself to pump me. With a smile that was meant to appear sympathetic, but which had a particularly bad effect on me since it immediately called to mind Dr. Hager's similar expression, she said:

"Don't worry, Madame. America will come into the war soon, and then Germany will be finished. . . . Why did they call you to the office?"

It must have been the exaltation that had resulted from the visit of Mr. Marvel that caused me to answer as I did. The words poured from my mouth without my having thought them at all. It was an instinctive, an automatic reaction. It seemed to me that some power was talking through me, rather than that I myself uttered the words which I was surprised to find myself saying.

"If you are not afraid of earthly justice," I lashed out at her, "if you do not tremble with fear of punishment during your lifetime, for committing the foulest of all crimes, betraying the confidence of the miserable unfortunate persons in this jail, worming their secrets out of them and reporting them to their jailers, then you should fear the Hereafter and the implacable justice of God. What do you get for performing this hangman's job that makes you willing to appear on the Day of Judgment with so heavy a load of guilt upon your soul—money? Much money? Enough to make up for living in filth to do your filthy work, and dying in moral filth, and living in the memory of those who knew you as the lowest and the most abject of human beings?"

I shouted this out in a sudden torrent of white-hot rage and loathing, my eyes fixed on the Alsatian woman's face; and instead of terrifying her, I became terrified myself, as her cheeks flushed bright red, and then were drained suddenly of all their blood until they became dead white, creased with the shadows of her wrinkles. Her eyes took on the expression of a hunted animal, at bay and facing death, and suddenly, with a loud wail, she threw her arms around my neck and began weeping on my shoulder. Her entire body shook in spasmodic convulsions, and the sobs seemed to be wrenched from her by main force.

This sudden torrent of grief disarmed my other two cell-mates as well as myself. Mary and Lola sprang up, put their arms about her, and tried to console her.

We heard footsteps in the corridor. The cover was pulled aside from the peephole, the guard peered in, then indifferently snapped it shut again, and passed on. Only crying women! He had seen enough of that here. That was of no importance.

It was many long minutes before the Alsatian woman stopped crying. She sat on the edge of one of the beds, her face buried in her hands, and from time to time, after we thought she had finally finished, a great dry sob would rack her body. Then, without taking her hands from her face, she began in a low, broken, monotonous tone, to tell her story.

Part of what she had said already was true. An Alsatian speaking perfect French and German, and with an acquaintanceship with several other languages, she had worked up a prosperous little translation business in Paris. In the autumn of 1938, a year before the war broke out, a young German called at her place of business, and said that he had a confidential message for her. She took him into a private office, and without further formality, he said:

"I am in the service of the German Intelligence. We wish you to work for us."

"At first," the Alsatian woman continued, "I could not believe he was serious. It seemed absurd that the German Intelligence Service should recruit agents in so crude, even dangerous, a fashion. But he produced credentials, and quickly made it plain that the offer was a genuine one. I was indignant. I reached for the phone to call the police.

"With perfect assurance, the German said:

"'Don't do anything stupid, Fraulein. Before you use the telephone, read this letter.'

"He pulled a paper out of his pocket and handed it to me. I recognized my mother's handwriting at once. I had not heard from her for several weeks. She had gone to live in St. Polten, Austria, with my uncle, her brother, when my father died.

"The letter began:

"'My dear Marthe: I beseech you to comply with the wishes of the man who gives you this letter, for that will help to ease my terrible situation . . .' I read hastily through the rest of it. My mother was in the notorious Oranienburg concentration camp. I had read of its horrors in the French papers.

"What could I do? To refuse would have meant death or torture for my mother. To accept meant comparative happiness for her. I *had* to give in. I've been working for them ever since—two years that they have been absolute masters of my life, because it is in their power to mistreat my mother. They made me offer my services to the French espionage service, and when I succeeded in getting in, they made me work for them in the very heart of the French Army. Since they came into Paris, I have been assigned to this prison as a Nachrichten Agent."

She raised her face from her hands for the first time.

"No!" she cried, "I'm not doing this for money, or because I like it, or because I don't hate and despise myself every minute for doing it! I've thought of suicide—I've thought of it more than once. But then what would happen to my mother? There isn't any escape. I know. I've thought of everything. I'm condemned to do my work— and to do it well, for they watch me, they know I don't work for them willingly, and they know how to punish if I don't succeed. . . . Blame me if you want. You can't blame me more than I blame myself. But what would you have done? Would any of you have condemned her own mother? Wouldn't you have tried to save her, even at this awful cost?"

"Couldn't you escape?" asked Mary Bird.

"Escape! I could, yes, of course . . . but don't you understand yet how I am held to this work, even forbidden the last resort of leaving life itself? I could escape; but my mother can't escape. There is no escape from Oranienburg. If I saved myself, my mother would pay for it."

"Have you seen your mother since?" I asked.

"That is my chief reward," Marthe answered bitterly. "She is still in Oranienburg, but she is on a privileged regime—when I do good work—and I am allowed to visit her once every three months. She is a wonderful woman, a heroic woman," Marthe's eyes misted with tears again. "The last time I saw her, she urged me to try to get out of France, to go to some other country, America, perhaps, and leave her to her fate. 'I am 74,' she told me. 'I have not long to live any-how. I no longer care what happens to me. I want to go to join your father. He was fortunate enough to die before this rule of anti-

Christ began.' But I couldn't do it. How could I? How can you condemn your own mother to shorten her life even by an hour?"

"If it were my mother," Lola said, "I should have accepted, just as you did; but I would have told them nothing useful. I would have lied to them. I would never have betrayed my cell-mates."

Marthe laughed scornfully.

"You are a baby," she said. "Do you think they are as naïve as that? Do you think they can be deceived so easily? I never know when a trap may be set for me, when some one may be testing me to make sure that nothing is held back. I don't know now whether one of you is not an *agent provocateur*. How do I know whether you, Mrs. Shiber, didn't attack me just now to make me say what I have just said? How do I know that you, or one of the others, won't report me, so that I will be punished, or my mother will suffer? Mrs. Shiber! How did you know I was a spy? Who told you? No one knows but the Germans. Did they send you here to trap me? Are you a spy, too? Are you another one of us?"

I gasped in amazement at the accusation. Marthe was almost hysterical.

"How can you think such a thing?" I exclaimed. "Don't you trust me?"

Marthe suddenly became more calm.

"I trust nobody," she said. "I suppose you're all right. But let me tell you what happened once. The first week I was here, I was put in a cell with a very young girl, who had been arrested for crossing the frontier illegally. She cried all night, and told me a pitiful story about how she had to escape because she had killed a German officer who had tried to assault her. She woke up in the night screaming, and said she saw the murdered man's face in her dreams. I took pity on her, and reported that I couldn't get anything out of her."

Marthe shook her head suddenly as though trying to free it of some hideous thought.

"Would you believe it?" she said. "That girl was an *agent provocateur*. She had been put in the cell to test me. I was confronted with her the next day, and asked why I hadn't reported her story. I tried to excuse myself by saying I had taken pity on her. 'We have no pity in this service,' I was told. They beat me and put me in the punishment cell. Three days later, the guard came and said, 'You are going to see your mother.' I was terrified. I thought perhaps they had killed her. But they had not. No, they had not killed her."

She buried her face in her hands again, and was silent for a moment. Then suddenly, half-crying, she shot out the rest of her story in a burst of sobs, talking at top speed as though to get it over with as quickly as possible:

"No, they hadn't killed her. I saw her in the camp hospital. She was recovering from the effect of solitary confinement in an unlighted, unheated, dark cell. Think of it, an old woman of 74! They told her, 'This is a present from your daughter.' And now I hold nothing back—nothing!"

We looked at one another, Mary, Lola and myself, embarrassed, uneasy, at a loss how to help the tormented enigma of a woman weeping on the bed. But as we watched, her sobs stopped. She sat up, quite calm again, dried her streaming eyes, and said, "I'm sorry. I feel better now—relieved to get it all off my chest. I didn't mean what I just said. You can trust me now. I swear I'll never give any of you away."

But then she stopped and a cloud seemed to come over her face. She spoke hesitantly.

"But Mrs. Shiber . . . tell me . . . how did you know that I was a German agent? Did they tell you downstairs? During your examination?"

I felt Mary's grip tighten on my arm. I knew what she meant. Be careful! Don't give me away!

"They didn't exactly tell me," I said. "I guessed from some things they said. Your name wasn't mentioned, though. . . . Do you know Dr. Hager?"

"Of course. He is assistant chief of the Gestapo investigation bureau."

"He tried to persuade me to help them," I said. "It was something like the offer they made you, but much less general, of course. He wanted me to provide them clues to help them find a friend of mine whom they haven't caught yet."

"And you refused?"

"Yes."

"You could refuse," Marthe said bitterly. "You don't have a mother locked up in a concentration camp. . . . I suppose they offered you some inducement?"

"They promised to free me. They said I could go back to America in a few weeks."

"Yes, yes," Marthe said musingly. "That's quite in the pattern. They wanted you to betray your friend, and they offered you freedom for it. . . . But you refused. How beautiful! . . . I wish I could have done the same! You knew where your friend was, but you wouldn't tell! I would have done the same, if I were free to act as I wanted."

She took my hand, and leaning towards me, said gently:

"Can I help you, Mrs. Shiber? I am allowed a free day tomorrow. I can come and go as I please. I could get word to your friend that she is in danger, that she must be careful. I can tell her where you are. . . . Would you like me to do that?"

I met Mary Bird's eye, and I saw a look of fright in it. What was Marthe really thinking? Did she want to help, or was this another trap? Which was her real self—the woman who had promised not to betray us, who was offering to help me now, or the German stool pigeon? Perhaps her whole story was a fiction. How did we know that she had a mother in a concentration camp? Suspicion and sympathy struggled in my mind, confusing me more and more. But I could see that there was only one safe course. I could not afford to take any risks. There was only one thing to say.

"Thank you, Marthe," I said, as gently as I could. "But the fact is that I don't know any way of getting into contact with my friend. What I told Dr. Hager was the truth. Her present whereabouts is a complete mystery to me."

"You don't trust me," Marthe said, turning away, and sinking onto the bed again. "I can't blame you. But I did think you believed me. I did think you understood."

"I will be perfectly frank with you, Marthe," I said. "I don't trust you. I do believe you. But you are not master of yourself. You have told us that. So I would not tell you anything even if I knew something. As it happens, I know nothing."

"Very well," Marthe snapped. "I suppose I should be grateful to you. You've saved me from committing a blunder—offering to help you. I might have been caught. I was risking more punishment for my mother. I shouldn't have done it. . . . But I was so happy to think some one believed in me again. . . . Oh, what's the use . . . let me alone, will you?"

Despite the rigid prison rule that no one was to lie on her bed during the day, she stretched herself out, pulled the blanket over her and closed her eyes. She seemed to be going off to sleep. But a few minutes later she jumped up from the bed without warning. She rushed at the door, and began kicking and striking at it with all her strength, so that the hollow sound of her feet and fists pounding on the iron resounded through the corridor. I heard the guard's running feet outside, the peephole clicked open. Then the door was flung ajar, the guard seized Marthe by the elbow, and pulled her out.

I never saw her again. But four months later, while our case was on trial, my lawyer told me that among some documents which he was allowed to see was her deposition. It was in my favor.

CHAPTER TWENTY-FIVE

Release!

THE DAYS dragged by in the prison of the Rue du Cherche-Midi with dreary monotony. Its beginning I have already described—wakening by the guard at 7:30, inspection ten minutes later, by which time we had to be dressed and have our beds made according to the prison regulations.

Our "coffee" was distributed at eight. It was black and nearly tasteless, which was fortunate, for what taste there was was unpleasant. What it was made of, I never succeeded in guessing, though I was told, vaguely, that German coffee was a mixture of four different ersatz products. It was sweetened with saccharine instead of sugar.

Lunch came at 11. It was always the same, day in, day out—whale soup. This was not a liquid, as its name indicated, but a sort of jellied mass inside which our meagre daily vegetable ration was included. It was supposed to be made from whale meat. With it came two slices of a rubber-like mass, the proud product of some branch of the German chemical industry, which looked like salami, but tasted like nothing in particular, and certainly had no meat in it at all.

The third and last meal of the day was handed to us at six in the evening. It consisted of a cup of ersatz tea, again sweetened with saccharine, and our daily bread ration, half of a very small round loaf of dark unappetizing bread. This we were supposed to distribute through the three meals of the day.

On this diet, we were constantly hungry.

Persons who have never skipped more than a meal or two can have no conception of the misery that comes with constant, unremitting hunger. Its very nature takes on a different quality. Ordinarily, hunger is a positive thing, which sharpens the appetite and causes a heartier approach to the next meal. But the hunger that fastens upon you when you eat insufficiently, day after day, is a negative feeling, an empty gnawing which is felt as a lack, but which creates no happier acceptance of the coming unpalatable meal, which doesn't contribute to make it more satisfactory—perhaps because you know in advance that it will not be enough, that the hunger which held you in its grip before you began eating will not diminish while you eat, and will still be as strong when you have finished.

It is almost with a sense of shame that I look back today to my prison experience, and realize that my thoughts, like those of my cell-mates, were almost exclusively preoccupied with food. Since there was nothing to do all day, and since four persons locked up together in a narrow room can't talk to each other all day long—particularly when they have no new experiences to talk about—I sat silent on my bed much of the time, day-dreaming and for half an hour or an hour, my thoughts would play with the idea of some simple dish, pork chops, for instance. I would imagine myself buying them in a store, carrying them home, preparing them for broiling, and the delicious aroma of broiling meat would seem to rise in my nostrils and awaken sharp pangs in my stomach. Indeed, there were times when I was not sure whether my imagination had not actually carried me to the point of hallucination, whether thinking of food had not progressed to the point where I actually saw it before my eyes.

The quantity of food the Germans gave us was perhaps one-third of that needed for the normal functioning of the human body. It was not so little that there was danger of dying of malnutrition, but it was not enough to permit ordinary activity.

This systematic starvation quickly deprived us of the greater part of our physical and mental energy. All we could do was sit on the edge of our beds, barely existing, not living. The slightest effort appeared enormous. Often we were too tired even to talk. If an object escaped our relaxed fingers, we would sit still for minutes, trying to muster enough energy to bend down and pick it up.

Was it the general shortage of foodstuffs throughout Europe which obliged the Germans to keep us on such short rations? That did not seem to be the answer. If that had been the only reason, our jailers would have permitted us to receive gifts of food from outside. The Quakers, for instance, wanted to supply us with extra food, but were not permitted to do so. The prison rules prohibited the sending of food to prisoners *while they were still under examination*—and that was the case of all those in the Cherche-Midi prison, none of whom had been tried and sentenced.

This made the German motive quite clear. They desired to weaken the prisoner, to reduce his will power, so that his powers of resistance would be less, so that his reasoning would be dulled. Thus he became clay in the hands of his inquisitors. It made it easier to extort information from him by such methods as those they had used against me. Perhaps if they had waited until I had been in prison two or three weeks, I wouldn't have seen through Dr. Hager's ruses. He made a mistake in tackling me too soon.

Similarly inhuman, it seemed to me, was the system which placed male guards over women prisoners, who had no privacy from them whatsoever. One never knew at what moment the peephole cover would be pulled back, and the guard would look into the cell. Indeed, the prison rules prescribed that guards should peep in at the inmates as often as possible, in order to know what they were doing at every hour of the day.

To me, the most disgusting necessity of all was that of being obliged to perform even the most private of physical functions in the presence of all my cell-mates. The canister I had so unpleasantly noticed when I was first imprisoned was our only toilet, and it was impossible to have any privacy in the use of it. Moreover, it remained in the cell all day long, being removed only at night, when the guard took it away, replacing it with an empty one.

In what other prison could such an incident have happened as that which I witnessed myself—an incident which happened to Lola? She was pregnant when she entered the prison. One morning she was incapable of getting up for the morning inspection. When the German officer arrived, she whispered to him, from white lips drawn tight in a pain-racked face:

"I am with child. I feel very ill."

"Don't lie to me," he snapped, and pulled the bed clothes off her to see for himself that she had spoken the truth.

I had never heard before of a prison whose inmates were not allowed a certain amount of exercise and fresh air daily, even if it was only half an hour in a courtyard. But in all the time I spent in the Cherche-Midi prison, I never left my cell except when I was called to the warden's office.

We could not even walk back and forth in our cells, as wild animals may pace their cages, for the four beds which took up all the space made that impossible.

The ventilation slit in the cell—it didn't deserve to be called a window—was closed by glass, and so far as I know, couldn't be opened. At least, it never was. All day long we had to breathe the filthy air of the never-opened cell.

That was the atmosphere in which I lived, day after interminable day.

How did we spend our time? We spent it doing nothing; there was nothing for us to do. We could not read. We were allowed no books. We could not write. We were allowed no paper or pencils. Absolutely no occupation had been foreseen for the hapless prisoners who had to sit out the dreary hours, day after day, week after week, month after month. If starvation had not dulled our wits, this forced inaction would inevitably have done it sooner or later. The only breaks in the dull monotony were our three meals. In the morning, we drank our coffee, and then, like well-bred children, sat on the edges of our beds with our hands in our laps and waited for lunch.

At 11 o'clock, we had that meal, and then, once more sitting patiently on our beds, waited for supper. We strained our ears for the slightest sound in the corridor. The noise of the footsteps of the guard, passing the door, was an event, one of the few happenings which could distinguish any minute from any other. We knew the walk of every guard in our part of the prison. We usually knew when the peephole would open, for we could hear the guard coming. He would walk six steps, then stop. We would hear a slide click open and shut again. Six more steps. Click, click. Six more—and then it would be ours which would open.

The monotony became so unbearable that if we were left alone for two or three days at a stretch, we would begin to hope to be called for examination, even if a beating were likely to go with it. Anything was better than the unbroken procession of immeasurable time. But our greatest thrill, of course, was the arrival of a new cellmate. Only after I had been in prison for a while did I realize what a great event my arrival must have been for my companions. Then I, too, began to long for the arrival of another prisoner. It didn't occur to me then that that meant I was also hoping that the Gestapo would catch new victims. All I could think of was that I needed desperately some event to break the monotony, something that my mind could take hold of, to prevent it from deserting me completely.

The 6 o'clock meal we saluted gladly, for it meant that we only had to sit idly for another hour. At seven we were permitted to go to bed; and an hour later the lights went out.

The first night I had spent in that awful atmosphere, with the black air pressing upon me, seemingly so heavy and so thick that I felt I could take it in my hand and squeeze it like rubber, had been horrible. But I came to long for the night, because then I could lie down, and if I couldn't sleep, at least I no longer saw the surroundings about me, and I could imagine, through the dark, other scenes than this bare prison cell.

About me in the dark I could hear my companions gasping for air in the putrid atmosphere, but still, in comparison with the day, the night sometimes seemed lovely, allowing me to lie in its silence and its blackness, as though enveloped in a heavy curtain, and float away in imagination, away from the stone walls, and iron-bound doors, and locks and keys of the prison.

In the lightheadedness provoked by insufficient food and lack of occupation to hold the mind down to any reality, it was not necessary to be asleep to dream. I could lie on my bed with my eyes open, staring into the impenetrable dark, and dream while I was still awake. Often, in this stage, halfway between sleep and wakefulness, I imagined suddenly that I was back in New York, and that I had just awakened from a nightmare. Sometimes the feeling would persist until I passed into a genuine dream, only to awake hours later; and sometimes it would pass at once, and I would realize, with despair in my heart, that it was the nightmare which was real, and the relief from it which was the dream.

Thus passed the endless days. Thus passed the welcome nights.

For some days after the disappearance of Marthe Wenzinger, there were only three of us in the cell. Then a new prisoner turned up. This time the newcomer was a Polish girl, whose crime was trying to help members of the Polish Legion, hiding in France, to get to the unoccupied zone. I don't remember her name. She told me what it was more than once but I could never pronounce it, nor imagine how it might be spelled. It sounded as though it were all s's and z's.

She was an untamable girl, incurably optimistic, and though her refusal to accept defeat seemed unrealistic to us, who had become broken to prison life, it was a refreshing change to be in contact with this fighting psychology.

She had a freshly healed wound on her cheek. I asked her how she had gotten it. She smiled as she answered:

"That's a souvenir of the Hotel Matignon."

"The Hotel Matignon?" I repeated stupidly. I would have understood at once earlier, but by now my mental processes had been slowed up by starvation and inactivity.

"Well, wasn't that the route you took to get here?" she asked me. "You ought to know their methods. Of course, I asked for it. I fought back. I wasn't going to stand there like a cow being butchered while they beat me up. That awful Captain hit me and I hit him right back. It was no good, of course. I just got a terrible beating for it. The mark on my face is nothing. You should see my back."

Almost her first question to us was:

"What's the chance of escape?"

It was Mary Bird who answered:

"There isn't any."

The Polish girl was unimpressed.

"Huh!" she snorted. "Has any one ever tried?"

"I don't think so," Mary said. "I've been in five cells now, and seen quite a few prisoners. It's the first time I've heard any one even mention it. There's not a chance of getting out of this place."

"So that's your opinion, is it?" the Polish girl said, with more than a trace of sarcasm in her voice. "What have you done to find out? How about the guard? Have you tried him?"

"No," said Mary wearily. "It wouldn't do any good. The guard we had before this one carried some notes for me. They caught him. So they put a new man on.

"There, you see!" said the Pole, triumphantly. "German guards aren't unapproachable. If you managed to get away with something with the first one, I should think you would have tried again. Let me speak to him. I know the language his kind talks. . . . And how about the hospital? Did you ever play sick to get taken there? No, I can see by your faces none of you even thought of it! No wonder you think you can't escape. You haven't made the slightest effort, you haven't even considered how to go about it! You've just been sitting here like animals, hoping for good luck! Well, that's not my way. I'll show you that there's no such thing as an escape-proof prison."

Her attempt began next day. At lunch, she whispered something in the guard's ear. He didn't answer, but as he went out, our Polish friend sat down to eat her soup with an expression of great satisfaction. She never finished it. She was halfway through when the guard returned with the inspecting officer.

"Number 1902," he said. "Attempting to corrupt a guard. Ten days solitary confinement."

And the man to whom she knew how to talk hustled her away to the punishment cells. Her half-finished bowl of soup was left on the table behind her. As the door closed on her, we looked at one another with a common impulse. Then Mary picked up the bowl, and poured its contents into ours, dividing it as evenly as she could.

I had been arrested on November 26. On December 14, at 11 A.M., we heard the footsteps of the guard outside. It was lunchtime, and we expected him to enter with our soup. But when he swung the door open, he didn't have the pot he usually carried. Instead, he said:

"1876—come with me. You are to be released."

I stared at him stupidly for a minute.

"I—I—what?" I stammered.

"Come along. Hurry up," he ordered. "I've got to get lunch. I can't wait all day for you."

I hurriedly embraced my cell-mates, picked up my bag (it was always packed, for I had nowhere else to keep my few clothes), and followed him along the corridor.

"Are you sure I'm being freed?" I asked. "Isn't it only another examination?"

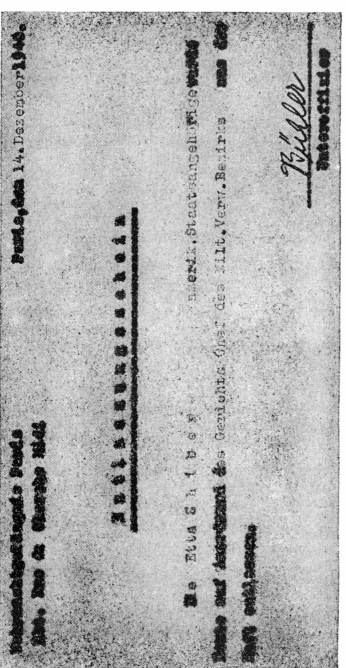

Release order which freed Mrs. Shiber from the Cherche-Midi prison for a short period before her trial.

My tone must have been almost a pleading one, but he gave no answer. He simply hurried along the corridor and then down to the ground floor until we reached the room where I had been received—where my fingerprints had been taken and where I had been searched.

There I was handed a release form which stated that I had been in the Cherche-Midi prison from November 26 to December 14, and on the latter date had been freed. I was told to sign a paper stating that I had been well treated in prison, that the food had been sufficient and of good quality, and that I had no complaint to make of the direction of the prison. I couldn't see any point in protesting. I signed.

Another guard took me to the office of the warden. The Major was standing behind his desk, smiling affably.

"Well, Mrs. Shiber," he said, "it gives me great personal satisfaction to be able to restore your freedom to you. I trust that you will not leave us with too bad an impression. The order to release you has just arrived, and though ordinarily, under prison regulations, all releases occur at 6 in the evening, I made a special exception in your case, in order to let you out at the earliest possible moment."

He picked up a bunch of keys from his desk. I recognized them at once as those which had been taken from me at the Hotel Matignon.

"Here are your keys," he said, handing them to me. "You are free."

Up to this moment, I had been dazed and suspicious. I expected another Nazi trick. But it seemed to be genuine. Still, I couldn't quite believe it yet.

"I'm free?" I murmured, talking to myself as much as to him.

"Yes, Madame. I have had no further instructions concerning your case—simply the order to release you."

"Could I leave the city, for instance?"

"Certainly, if you wish. You may do anything you could have done before your arrest."

He accompanied me to the door of his office, and opened it for me politely. I walked through the antechamber, between the stiff unmoving sentries, across the courtyard, and to the outer gate. An officer just inside looked at my release form, stamped it, and returned it politely. The heavy door was flung open, and, feeling as unreal as though it were all a dream, I walked out into the free air of the Rue du Cherche-Midi.

I stopped on the corner, my knees shaking. I felt I couldn't go any farther until I had had a minute to readjust myself to my new situation, to accustom myself again to free movement, to free exercise of my own will. I breathed in deeply, again and again, feeling the cold sweet air stab its way into the depths of my lungs. I looked about me at what others would have considered ordinary, everyday sights, completely uninteresting. But to me they were the fascinating stirrings of another world—people walking along the streets, moving wherever their own wills directed them; a rare automobile or two passing by; long lines in front of shops across the street; a man stepping from a corner café; a woman leaning out of an opened, unbarred window, shaking a dustcloth.

The scene wavered before my eyes. I could feel the tears welling up in them. I blinked them back, and turned in the direction of the Metro.

It was true. I was free.

CHAPTER TWENTY-SIX

Where Is Kitty?

I HAD turned mechanically towards the subway with the unconscious idea of going home, but then I stopped, wondering if that
was really what I wanted to do first. I must have looked drunk to
passersby, hesitating, wavering, and at the same time breathing in
deeply as though I had just made some great effort.

It occurred to me that I could go to a restaurant, where I would
eat as much as the rationing laws permitted me to buy. I could taste
at last some of those unattainable dishes I had dreamed of in prison.

And then the thought of another luxury came into my mind—a
bath! During all the time I had spent in that dreadful cell, I had
not been able to take one. We were without the simplest facilities
for keeping clean. A common washbasin served for all four of us
in the morning, and there was barely enough water to wet our
faces. And I could go to a hairdresser, too! All these possibilities
made me feel like a child looking ahead to Christmas.

And a newspaper! What had happened since I had been in jail?
We had been completely cut off from all news. I knew nothing of
what had happened while I was imprisoned. I wanted to catch up
with the progress of the world, too—even though I knew all French
newspapers were now controlled by the Germans.

I continued to walk indecisively towards the subway as I tried to
decide what to do first, and in the end it was habit rather than decision which took me home. I knocked on the door of Mme. Beugler's
loge. When she opened it, she seemed for a moment not to recognize
me. But then my dogs rushed forward, barking frantically. They
sprang up and licked my hands, making so much noise that neither
the concierge nor myself could make ourselves heard.

When they finally quieted down, Mme. Beugler's first words
were:

"My God, what have they done to you, Mrs. Shiber?" Only then
did I realize that the experiences of the past weeks must have

marked themselves deeply in my appearance. "But, thank God," the concierge added quickly, "at least you are free again."

"What happened to Margot?" I asked.

"They arrested her, too, but they let her go the next day. She came back here, but the two Germans living in your apartment advised her to look for another job. They told her that her employers probably wouldn't be back. So she went home to her family in Brittany."

"Oh, yes! Those Germans!" I said. "They aren't still there?"

"They left yesterday. They stayed there day and night—two of them in your apartment, and one man always down here in my *loge*. They were waiting for Mme. Kitty. They thought she would return, and they were going to arrest her. They must have decided it was no use, and moved out."

"How did you manage to warn Mme. Kitty's husband?" I asked. The concierge was surprised.

"Monsieur Beaurepos? But I haven't seen him. It's lucky for him he didn't come here. They would have arrested him. They did arrest that good-looking young priest who used to come to see you."

"Yes, I knew that," I said. "But then—how in the world did Monsieur Beaurepos discover that I had been arrested? It was he who told the American Embassy."

I can't describe the joy I felt when I entered my apartment again after my irksome imprisonment. The first thing I did was simply to walk about from one room to another, unable to sit down calmly and rest. I turned the lights on and off, I tried the hot-water faucet to make sure that it was still working, and that I could actually enjoy the luxury of hot water whenever I wanted it.

The bell rang. I hurried happily to the door, wondering which of my friends would turn out to be my first caller.

When I opened the door and saw who it was, I had to steel myself suddenly to keep from fainting. It was Dr. Hager.

I had thought my nightmare was over. But here was the chief actor in it, and no doubt it was beginning again. My freedom was only an illusion, one more of their despicable tricks.

But Dr. Hager was wearing his sympathetic smile again, and using his softest voice.

"Goodness, Madame Shiber, don't look so frightened!" he said. "I only dropped in to ask if the two men who stayed here left everything in order. If they have done any damage, you will be reimbursed, of course. If anything is missing, don't fail to report it. . . . Do you mind if I have a look around to make sure everything is all right?"

He proved to be a thorough inspector. With my guidance, he poked into every closet, examined minutely all the rooms, even looked into the icebox.

"You must excuse my being very minute, Madame," he said to me at one stage in the proceedings. "I am responsible for any damage my men do."

"There doesn't seem to be any," I said, wondering what the real object of his search could be—for it obviously was a search.

"You're a very strange woman, Mme. Shiber," he said, still smiling, as he finished his inspection. "I expected you to ask me how it happened that you were released. One would say you aren't interested in your own case."

"I'm still a little dazed, I guess," I answered.

"That's not surprising, of course," Dr. Hager admitted. "Well, I can tell you, without giving away any official secrets, that the investigation of this case has been concluded—and, as I told you before, that was the only thing holding up your release. The criminals, except your friend, Mme. Beaurepos, are all in jail. The investigation demonstrated that you had taken no active part in any criminal activity, so you have been freed."

He walked to the door. With his hand on the knob, he paused and turned:

"And what do you plan to do now? Are you going to take my advice and go back to the United States?"

"I'd like to," I answered. "But can I? Do you think I would have any difficulties?"

"No, no, none at all," Dr. Hager protested, with a sweeping gesture. "You are entirely your own master. You can stay or leave, as you please. No one has any right to interfere with your plans. . . . Is there anything else I can tell you before I go?"

"Yes, I . . . ." I hesitated a moment. "I wonder if you have found out what happened to Mme. Beaurepos?"

Dr. Hager made an impatient movement.

"Look here, Mme. Shiber," he said, "let me tell you something. The organization to which I belong is badly misjudged. Here in France, and in your country, too, you hear nonsense about the Gestapo taking revenge on persons. That's ridiculous. We have no interest in revenging ourselves on any one. An individual may stoop to that sort of thing, but an organization like ours has more serious purposes.

"No, we don't know where Mme. Beaurepos is, except that we know she has left the occupied zone. That's all we want. Our only purpose was to destroy her organization. We have succeeded. As far as we're concerned, it's entirely immaterial whether Mme. Beaurepos is ever apprehended or not. The case is closed."

He looked at me ponderingly for a moment before continuing.

"Of course, if Mme. Beaurepos should be so stupid as to make any effort to resume her old activity, that would be another matter. In that case, we would be obliged to arrest her. . . . I have a bit of advice for you, Mrs. Shiber. If you still think your friend deserves that you should help her, persuade her to go to America with you. It will keep her out of trouble. If she remains here, she may be tempted to commit a second offense—and I assure you, she would not escape us again."

When Dr. Hager had gone, I sat down and tried to imagine what had been the real purpose of his visit. I was sure that it wasn't to see if any damage had been done. He was certainly looking for something—but what? Surely his men must have inspected the apartment thoroughly while they were there; and I had only been back for a short time.

I gave the riddle up; but I couldn't get rid of the feeling of Dr. Hager's presence so easily. It seemed to me that I could sense him standing behind me, with that false smile of his on his face. For the first time, I was afraid to remain alone in my own apartment. I walked through it, putting the lights on in every room, even the kitchen.

"Goodness," I thought to myself, "I'm afraid of the dark! I'm acting like a child again. I'd better leave Paris. Not until I get as far away as possible can I be at peace again—far away, out of the reach of Dr. Hager and all his gang. I should have started to make arrangements to go today. Who knows—one lost day might still be fatal. The first thing tomorrow I'm going to see what I must do to get back home."

As soon as I got up the following morning, I collected all my documents, put them in my handbag, and set out for the American Embassy.

As I stepped from the elevator on the ground floor, I saw a French policeman in front of the concierge's *loge,* talking to Mme. Beugler.

"Why, here she is now," said Mme. Beugler, waving towards me. The policeman tipped his hat politely, and handed me a piece of paper. It was a request that I should come to the Prefecture at once concerning a traffic violation.

"There must be some mistake!" I objected. "I don't even own an automobile. My friend does, but it's in her name. I have nothing to do with it. I don't even drive!"

The policeman was firm.

"I can't help that, Madame," he said. "My orders are simply to bring you to the Prefecture to answer for this violation. Anything you have to say you will have to tell them there."

With a sinking heart, I preceded him to the door. I knew the charge of having committed a traffic violation while I was locked up in the Cherche-Midi prison was ridiculous, and I suspected that this might have some connection with Dr. Hager's visit of the night before. It was all an elaborate comedy. I had been released by the German police only to be taken over by the French police; and I had heard only too often how the French had been forced to do the dirty work of the Germans.

There had been cases, I knew, of French policemen discharged for refusing to carry out German orders, such as those to arrest Jews: and it was common knowledge that German instructions to the French police were often sabotaged by the very men appointed to carry them out, who might, for instance, warn those they were charged with arresting to get out of sight.

The French police themselves were not immune from feeling the weight of German displeasure. I had heard one story of an incident which occurred in a café on the Champs-Elysées, where two German officers had called the manager and demanded that a man at the next table, evidently Jewish, be told to leave. Obediently, the manager asked his Jewish customer to go to avoid trouble. Instead, he answered in a loud voice:

"Inform these officers that if my presence annoys them, their presence annoys me. I am a Frenchman. This is my country. If they don't like sharing it with those who belong here, we shall be very happy to have them leave."

One of the German officers, in a rage, told the manager that if the Jew did not leave in five minutes, the café would be closed permanently. On the manager's plea that his means of livelihood was being jeopardized, the customer got up and passed before the table of the officers; as he did so, he spat contemptuously on the ground. The officer who had threatened the manager, beside himself with fury, drew his revolver and killed him—and several hours later ten policemen were arrested at random in the district by German soldiers, and told that they would be punished because of the failure of the French police to keep order in that district. They were never heard from again.

I was myself inclined to be skeptical of stories like this one, but it was repeated throughout Paris, and believed by everybody.

Before the war, Parisians had always enjoyed jokes in which the police were held up to ridicule: but at the same time they had a good deal of liking for *monsieur l'agent* in most of his rôles. French police often had an easy and kindly manner. They seemed to represent the spirit of a free country. They were not required to salute Army officers—but when the Germans arrived, all that was changed. They were furnished with the white cuffs which distinguish German policemen and they were ordered to salute German Army officers and stand rigidly at attention when they passed by, or even when a German non-commissioned officer passed.

I witnessed one humiliating spectacle in the Place de l'Opéra, where a German sergeant took his revenge on a French policeman who had pretended not to see him when he passed. He ordered the unfortunate Frenchman to stand at attention, to salute him, and then to run three times around the Place. Parisians watched the representative of their law being put through these paces with expressions of the deepest shame. Finally, when the policeman finished his third round, out of breath, the German ordered: "About face!" and when the policeman obeyed, he gave him a hearty kick which sent him sprawling.

That was too much for the Frenchman. He sprang up and knocked the German over with one blow of his fist. But two sentinels, standing guard with fixed bayonets before the Kommandantur on the corner, ran over and seized the policeman. He was led away between them. I never heard what happened to him.

But most of the French police submitted to the German rules without rebellion—in fact, some of them even overdid it. Thus it was common, when Frenchmen crossed the street before traffic policemen who had been taught the new stiff German gestures, to find him exaggerating them, caricaturing them, in fact—sometimes with a sly wink for an obvious compatriot, as though to say: "This is the way *they* do it. Absurd, aren't they?"

But I knew that the French police had been forced nevertheless to obey the directives of the Germans, so I was sure, as I turned into the great gateway of the Prefecture with my escorting policeman, that it was really on the orders of the Germans that I was being summoned.

I showed my *convocation* at the doorway, and was directed to the traffic department on the second floor. A police lieutenant received me, studied the paper I handed him carefully for a minute, then asked:

"You are Mme. Shiber?"

"I am," I said.

"Can you prove your identity?"

That was easy, since I had all my papers with me. He glanced at them, rose from his desk, and opened a door in the rear wall; and with a polite gesture that would have done credit to a dancing master, said:

'This way, Madame, if you please."

I moved towards the door with a sinking heart, in spite of his courtesy, but as I entered the room, I could barely repress a scream of joy—for there stood Henri Beaurepos!

He stretched out both hands as he came towards me.

"My dear Etta," he said, "I'm so happy to see you again! I hope you weren't frightened by the means I used to get you here. You see, you are under constant observation. The only way I could think of to manage a meeting was to have you brought here by the police. The Germans no doubt know you are here, but if they ask why, we'll simply tell them that it was a mistake. . . . Now—did you know you were being watched?"

"No," I faltered. "No, I didn't. You mean . . . I'm not rid of them yet?"

"I'm afraid not, Etta," Henri said gravely. "That's one reason why I had you brought here—to warn you. I don't know what they told you, but I believe the only reason they gave you your freedom was in the hope that you would lead them to Kitty. They've done everything they could to find her—I know because some inquiries cleared through here—and they haven't succeeded. You're the decoy. They expect you either to lure her back by getting in touch with her, or to lead them to her.

"They're looking for me, too. Fortunately, as you see, my contacts are very good. I know that the Gestapo looked me up. They learned that I didn't see Kitty often, that I hadn't been in touch with her for some time, but just the same they want to arrest me, to find out if I know anything, and perhaps to use me as they want to use you, to help them find Kitty. So this was the only place I dared meet you. They would have been able to follow you anywhere else."

"But, Henri," I asked (this had been puzzling me ever since Mme. Beugler had denied seeing him), "how did you find out about my arrest? I thought at first that you had heard of it from the concierge, but she told me she hadn't heard from you."

"I did get the news from Mme. Beugler," Henri grinned, "only she didn't know it. I had a policeman inquire at your place preparatory to visiting you. . . . That's what we're reduced to nowadays. Before you make a surprise visit to a friend, you have to make sure he's still there, or you may meet a German policeman instead when you get to his apartment. It was when I read that the Germans were offering rewards for information about the escapes of English soldiers that I thought I had better begin taking precautions. It's fortunate that I did."

"What about Kitty?" I asked. "Where is she?"

"Don't you know?" he returned quickly. "I hoped you did. That was another reason why I wanted to talk to you."

I shook my head despairingly.

"Oh, Henri!" I almost wept. "You mean to say you haven't been able to tell her of my arrest—to warn her of her own danger? With all your cleverness, and resourcefulness, and influence—you haven't been able to locate her?"

"No," Henri said grimly. "That's just the trouble. She probably hasn't the slightest inkling that anything is wrong. She's likely to walk into their hands at any minute. While we're talking here, she may be going to the apartment now, under the eyes of the Gestapo man watching the building."

"But, Henri," I protested, feeling the blood leave my cheeks, "I must get back. We don't know what's happening there! I must be there to warn her . . ."

"Keep calm, Etta," Henri said soothingly. "You must keep your head. There's nothing you can do to warn her—in fact, you're one of the greatest dangers to her now, for they're watching every move you make. If she has gotten that far, she's lost anyway. . . . What we have got to try to do is to head her off in time. I have been scouring the unoccupied zone trying to find her—calling on friends of hers, trying every lead I could think of. I thought Marseilles might be a likely place, and I tried there, but no one we knew had seen her. What more could I do? I couldn't put an advertisement in the newspaper, warning her the police were after her. Anything that she would have understood would have been plain to the Gestapo, too."

"How terrible!" I said. "And to think that while you were in Marseilles, she may have been there, too! She said she was going there—and also to Lyons and Périgueux."

"You see, Etta," Henri exclaimed, "you can help me . . . I hope you didn't tell the Germans that?"

"Of course not," I said. "Do you think I'm out of my head? I told them I thought she had gone to Tours."

"Good!" said Henri. "Now—I went to Lyons; no trace there. But

Périgueux sounds like a good lead. That's a smaller place. It ought to be easier to find her, if that's where she is. . . . Now have you any idea who she might have seen?"

I told Henri the story of the friend at Marseilles who was financing our work whom she intended to see, but unfortunately I didn't know his name or address. Henri thought he knew who it might be. I also gave him some addresses of friends of Kitty's in Lyons, and particularly that of the person she intended visiting in Périgueux, which he seemed to think was the best clue of all.

Henri wrote down all the addresses, and put the paper carefully away in his wallet.

"If I have just a little luck," he said, smiling hopefully, "I may be able to catch up with her in time. . . . Now, Etta dear, pardon me for having been so engrossed with Kitty—what are your plans?"

I told him that I had been on my way to the Embassy to try to get back to America when his policeman had picked me up. I said also that I planned to try to get my Spanish and Portuguese visas that very day.

Henri frowned.

"I don't want to worry you unnecessarily, Etta," he said, "but I think you should be prepared for the probability that the Germans won't let you go. You can't leave without an exit visa from them— and they're watching you too closely for you to try to get out of the occupied zone illegally."

I could feel myself turning pale again.

"You mean they would refuse me a visa?" I asked.

"I don't think so—not outright. If I know the Germans, they won't refuse; you just won't get one. They'll put you off from day to day, on one pretext or another. But I don't think they intend that you shall get away. They want you to lead them to Kitty.

"Now this is my advice: Go to the American Embassy at once. Talk to them and ask what they think you should do. My guess is that you should try to get out of the occupied zone at once, if it's at all possible. We may be able to arrange something here, if it's necessary, but it would be easier in a few days, when they may have slacked off a little. I'm going to leave tonight to try to locate Kitty again, but you can come here and ask the officer who received you for assistance: and if it's wise to do so before I get back, he can probably help you get over the frontier. But consult the Embassy first, though perhaps you had better remember that they may be a trifle over-cautious. You know what diplomats are.

"Keep in regular touch with them anyway. If I were you, I'd arrange to check once a day, so that they can set to work to locate you if you fail to put in an appearance at the regular time. And again: you can come here with absolute confidence if you need any help—but don't write or telephone. This is where you will find me when I come back. It will be better for you to come, for we can't use that excuse of the mistaken summons again, very well."

He accompanied me to the door, and took leave of me with a warm handclasp.

"Good-bye, Etta, and good luck," he said. "Keep your chin up! And be on the watch for the Gestapo!"

I remembered his words as I left the Prefecture. I peered keenly about as I walked to the subway station of the Ile de la Cité. It was not too hard to identify my shadow. A young man was following close on my heels. When I got into the train, he entered the same car. When I got out, he followed.

Free? No. I was still a prisoner of the Gestapo. Only, for the moment, I was not supposed to know it.

CHAPTER TWENTY-SEVEN

Travels with a Shadow

I REALIZED now that I was still just as much a prisoner of the Gestapo as when I had been in jail. You can't call yourself free when you know some one is following your every step, charged with making a report on all your movements; and I know few things more nerve-racking than the consciousness that you are being spied on every minute.

During the rest of the day, I made several efforts to elude my shadow, but all of them were unsuccessful. For instance, when I left the American Embassy, which was my first port of call after the Prefecture, I slipped out of the side door on the Rue Boissy d'Anglas instead of the front door of the Avenue Gabriel. I looked about, and failed to see the Gestapo agent. Joyously, I hurried away—but I hadn't reached the next corner before I saw him again, following at a little distance.

They had not been very hopeful at the Embassy about the possibility of my being allowed to leave the occupied zone.

"I think it very improbable," one official there told me, "that they intend to let you get out of Paris. It seems pretty clear that they released you only in the belief that you would lead them to Mme. Beaurepos. You can't get out without a German exit visa, you know, and they aren't likely to give you one."

"In that case," I said, discouraged, "there's no point in bothering about Spanish and Portuguese visas."

"On the contrary," said the Embassy official, "get them, and go through all the other formalities necessary to go to the United States. In the first place, that deprives them of any excuse for refusing you an exit visa on the ground that your other papers are not complete. Secondly, it will demonstrate to them that your only desire is to return to the United States. But be very careful, Mrs. Shiber, that the Gestapo has no reason for deciding that you may be considering escaping into the unoccupied zone without an exit visa, for in that case they would undoubtedly arrest you at once."

Before leaving the Embassy, I inquired about Mr. Marvel. I said that I would like to call on him and thank him for his help.

"Don't do it," the official said, in alarm. "You might compromise his work. He is the only American who has permission to visit the prisons, and he manages it because the Germans are absolutely convinced of the conscientiousness with which he sticks to their restrictions on his activity—that he confine himself to the physical wellbeing of prisoners and refuse to discuss their cases. He is thus our only means of getting any information from the prisons, and if you called on him, they might suspect that he had exceeded his rôle, and bar him from the jails. We'll tell him, though, that you expressed your appreciation to us."

When my shadow reappeared behind me after I left the Embassy, I gave up the attempt to slip away from him up the Rue Boissy d'Anglas, and turned to come out on the Place de la Concorde—which, for me, was always the most beautiful square in the world. With their customary sensitivity, the French have classed it a *"monument historique,"* which means that no architectural innovations can be made in it without permission of the Fine Arts administration. Thus the harmony of the setting is preserved.

When the new American Embassy was built at one corner of the Place de la Concorde, it not only had to be designed to fit in with the rest of the square, but actually completed it as its first designer had laid it out; for he had planned a building on the site purchased by the Embassy in the same style as that opposite it, but it had never been built. The American Embassy thus brought to fruition at last the plan originally conceived for the square.

The aesthetic scruples of both the French and the American governments were not shared by the Germans. They moved into the Hotel Crillon, across the street from the American Embassy, and also took over the third of the three buildings forming the North side of the square, the French Navy Ministry. For their convenience, they then constructed a horrible temporary wooden bridge above the street connecting the two buildings, spoiling the whole harmony of the square.

Poor Paris! I thought as I passed it, with an inward shudder, what are you going to look like if the Germans honor you much longer with their presence?

I walked up the majestic Rue Royale, blocked at its far end by the Madeleine, turned into the Boulevard de la Madeleine and continued into the Boulevard des Capucines, one of the most lovely stretches of the Grands Boulevards. Once this street had been lively with traffic; now there were no automobiles to be seen, with the exception of an occasional German official car marked with the swastika. Instead of the brightly colored taxis, with their ebullient chauffeurs, there were bicycle taxis, powered by haggard perspiring human motors, pedaling away with all their might, in order to transport themselves and a passenger riding in a two-wheeled cart behind the bicycle. It made me think of the Chinese coolies and their jinrikishas. I shuddered to see Europeans—Parisians—slaving away in this fashion, at a sort of labor against which Europeans in China had once objected on the ground that it was too degrading to human dignity.

I couldn't resist stopping at the Café de la Paix to rest for a few minutes in the spot where Kitty and I had spent so many happy hours in a time relatively near, but which seemed to have receded deep into the past. This had been one of our favorite spots—as it was, indeed, a favorite spot of all tourists, of whom few failed to visit this landmark of Parisian living, located at the corner where the Boulevard des Capucines opens into the Place de l'Opéra.

Apparently the Germans agreed with the other tourists, for they were there in force. They had invaded it as they had invaded France. The terrace was crowded with German officers and the Frauleins they had imported to do the office work of the many German government bureaus and business offices. It was easy to tell which ones were the Germans, even those who were not in uniform. They were loud, arrogant and boisterous, self-satisfied, impertinent, prosperous. Obviously they were, unlike the French, well fed and well paid. Here and there you would see an elderly gentleman, sitting quietly at a table, reading a paper. Those were the Frenchmen. They seemed almost to apologize for being there, tranquil islands of good taste and good manners in the tumultuous sea of noisy, self-assertive conquerors.

I suppose it was because the proportion of German customers was so high that the Café de la Paix had been able to get charcoal for its braziers. I always loved the tall cast-iron stoves which appeared in Paris with the first cold weather, set up behind glass screens, to make it possible to sit outside in spite of the temperature. I sat down next to one of them, feeling the pleasant warmth exuding from it, and watched, without displeasure, I must admit, my shivering shadow take up a position against a lamp post in the cold December wind that was whipping through the streets. In order to watch both entrances of the café, he had to post himself on the corner, exposed to all the breezes that blew through the Place de l'Opéra from the half-dozen streets that empty into it. He looked very uncomfortable, and I am afraid I sat there a little longer than I might have otherwise, trying to freeze him out. But he didn't budge, and he didn't come inside himself to watch me from warmer quarters. Perhaps he was afraid that I might slip out suddenly, leaving him to be intercepted by an indignant waiter if he tried to follow without taking time to pay his bill.

My next stop was the Louvre department store, where I made a few purchases. They were necessarily few, for there was almost nothing to be bought in the stores. Whatever one did succeed in buying had to be carried home, for there was no delivery service at all.

As I came out, a boy of 14 or thereabouts spoke to me.

"May I carry your parcels home for you, Madame?" he asked.

His manners were good, and he was obviously well brought up; but he seemed embarrassed, and I judged that offering himself for such services was still new to him.

"I'm sorry," I said, "but I'm not going straight home. I have to have lunch first."

"That doesn't matter, Madame," he said. "I can wait, if you want."

"How about you?" I asked. "Have you had lunch yet?"

He blushed, and answered shyly, "Not yet."

He was an appealing little chap, and I felt sorry for him; it seemed so obvious that he had been obliged, after a sheltered childhood, to seek this means of earning a little something to help out a diminished family budget.

"How would you like to have lunch with me?" I proposed.

He became a shade redder, and returned, confusedly:

"Well, you see, Madame . . . that is . . . I haven't any money. . . . I—"

"Oh, that's all right," I said. "I was inviting you. I don't like to eat alone. You can keep me company. . . . Only—do you know any place near here where it's possible to eat without ration cards?"

"Yes, Madame," he said, his eyes lighting up at the prospect of lunch. But then his voice took on a duller tone, as he continued. "But it's very expensive. All the cheaper places ask for cards."

"I think I can afford it," I said, smiling at the thought of how unlikely it was that he could suspect what I meant. "I haven't had to spend very much for food lately."

At the restaurant, my young friend got over his shyness. His eyes sparkling as he dug into a lunch probably much better than he had recently been accustomed to (for the restaurants which didn't bother about ration cards also violated the regulations by buying on the Black Market), he confirmed my suspicions. He did belong to a family which had been well-off before the war, but now had been ruined. His father, head of a manufacturing concern, could have been described as rich; but now he was a prisoner of war in Germany. The little fellow (Pierre was his name) lived alone with his mother, in their beautiful home in the luxurious residential district of Auteuil. Now it was bare of most of its objects of value, which had been sold at a fraction of their real worth, no doubt to be resold to Germans. Their only income was the few francs Pierre was able to make by such jobs as the carrying of parcels.

"Some of my friends sell newspapers," Pierre said. "There's more money in that. But I don't believe in it. It's spreading German propaganda."

He said it so stoutly that I looked at him with admiration, thinking that this fourteen-year-old lad could give lessons to many of his elders, who had accepted cooperation with the Germans because it promoted their businesses and their personal well-being. If Pierre is typical of the youngest generation, I thought, France is not yet lost. Her future will be assured by him and his fellows.

"Do you think, Madame," Pierre asked politely, with a grave concern beyond his age, "that these conditions can last much longer? I'm worried most about my father. What will he think when he comes home and finds out wnat we have been through? And how long will it be, do you think, before they will let him go? The war's over, isn't it? Why don't they send him home?"

"I'm sure he'll be home soon, Pierre," I consoled him, although actually I wasn't sure at all. It seemed plain by then that the Germans were deliberately holding the prisoners of war as a means of pressure on France—and also because that kept the birth-rate down and reduced the number of men she would have available to oppose to Germany in future years.

But Pierre took my assurance at its face value, and told me about his work as a carrier of packages. As a rule, he didn't try stores, he said, because there were few persons who came out of them with packages cumbrous enough so that they didn't want to carry them themselves. But railroad stations were profitable posts, for in the absence of taxis, arrivals had to go to their hotels on foot, and were glad to have some one help them with their luggage.

Pierre's chief trouble, he told me, was that he remained at the stations until closing time, and as many of his customers lived some distance away, he was often caught on the streets at the curfew hour, and had to dodge the German patrols on the way home.

"But it's easy," he told me. "You can hear them coming before you can see them, their heavy boots clump along so, and of course the blackout makes it easy not to get caught. When I hear a patrol, I ring the nearest doorbell. The concierges never mind opening when I tell them I'm hiding from the patrol."

He seemed to be turning something over in his little head for a moment. Then, with a grave smile, he said:

"It's funny, isn't it, Madame? Before the war, I couldn't go out in the streets alone, even in the daytime, without my governess or the chauffeur. Now I stay out alone, even at night, hiding from the German patrols. War makes changes in people's lives, doesn't it?"

"Yes, Pierre," I said, "war makes very great changes in people's lives."

Mme. Beugler came out of her *loge* to meet me when I returned home.

"Mme. Shiber," she said, "the concierge across the street told me something that might interest you. She says that some strange persons have moved into one of her apartments. They're Germans, and one of the things that struck her as odd is that they didn't bring any furniture in—only a sofa and two armchairs. She says they seem to do nothing except sit at the window all day, watching this house. I thought it might be about you."

"It probably is," I sighed, wearily. "They're having me followed, I know."

"Or perhaps it's for Mme. Kitty," the concierge suggested. "They don't want to leave any men here, so you won't suspect, but they still want to catch her if she should return."

I thanked her, and went up to my apartment. I sank into a chair and sought to organize my thoughts, to get a clear view of the situation. There could no longer be any doubt that I had been released simply because they still wanted to catch Kitty. All of Dr. Hager's talk about his lack of interest in catching individuals, about the case being closed, was intended only to pull the wool over my eyes.

It was plain now why he had advised that I should take Kitty to America. He thought that would send me to her at once, if I knew where she was. Then they would arrest her, and probably re-arrest me, too, as well. There was only one thing for me to do.

I must escape. I must get away while there was still time.

I went to the window and looked down into the street. The young man who had been following me all day was standing in front of the house. This time I felt almost sorry for him. He must have been cold. He kept his hands thrust deep into his pockets, except when, from time to time, he wanted to take his cigarette out of his mouth, or light another one.

I gazed across the street at the house opposite, trying to spot the Gestapo agents there, watching our building. I saw nothing suspicious. But then, I didn't even know which windows hid them. Were they perhaps on the same level with our apartment? Perhaps they had glasses with which they could actually look into my rooms, and see me moving about! I shivered, and closed the curtains.

Sunday morning I had a phone call from Mr. Marvel. He said that he was happy to learn that I had been released, and from the reserved manner in which he spoke I assumed that he realized that my phone had been tapped, and that the Gestapo was listening to whatever we said.

"I'd be very much obliged to you, Mme. Shiber," he said, "if you would be kind enough to return the warm clothing I brought to you at the prison. Fortunately, you don't need it any longer, but there are others who do, and our supplies are very limited."

"I'll be very glad to do so, of course," I said. "Where can I bring it?"

I imagined that he wanted an excuse for meeting me, as well as to get the clothing back. By thus calling me on a telephone which he was sure was being watched, he was disarming any suspicions the Gestapo might have about our meeting in advance. We arranged to meet in the lobby of the Hotel Ritz at 7 o'clock that evening—not exactly the favorite place for delivering used clothing, perhaps, but in these wartime days no one bothered any longer about such inelegancies as carrying bundles into luxury hotels.

Hanging up the phone, I decided to go back to the Prefecture and see the officer to whom Henri had recommended me. I wanted to lose no time in getting away, and Henri had said that he might be able to slip me over the demarcation line in spite of the Gestapo shadowers.

As I left the house, I looked about for my faithful follower. He was standing in the doorway of the neighboring house, shabbily dressed as always, waiting patiently for my appearance. I don't know what got into me, but I couldn't resist walking over to him and saying: "To save you trouble, I might as well tell you that I'm going to take the subway to the Prefecture, and after that I'm coming back to the Place de la Concorde, to go to the American Embassy."

He looked startled. Embarrassed, he stammered:

"I—I—I don't understand, Madame. What . . . ?"

"Oh, never mind the play-acting," I said. "You've been following me ever since I was let out. You know the way. Come along."

And off I went, leaving him standing there. After a moment, I looked over my shoulder. There he was, padding along behind me, reminding me of a beaten dog following its master.

At the Etoile subway station, he sidled up to me in the waiting crowd, and whispered pleadingly:

"Excuse me, Madame . . . could I ask you, please . . . if you would be so kind . . . don't let my superiors know you spotted me?"

"Don't worry," I said. "I shan't mention it."

He looked immensely relieved. Inwardly, I felt a great desire to laugh. Yesterday, his presence had kept my nerves on edge. Now he had suddenly become ludicrous, even pitiful—a poorly paid hireling of the Gestapo, afraid that the person he was stalking would cause him to lose his job.

I found Henri's friend in the office I had visited before, in spite of its being a Sunday, and learned that Henri had, as planned, left for the unoccupied zone to look for Kitty. I told him that I had become convinced that I must try to get away as quickly as possible.

"Getting you across the demarcation line is simple enough," he told me. "The real job is to elude the people who are watching you. Once we have done that, the rest is easy. You can go by train to a certain town, where you will be met and taken across the border."

"I think there is only one man shadowing me when I move about town," I said. "I've identified him. He's outside now. But there are others watching the apartment from across the street, so it would be more difficult to start from there."

"The thing to do then," said the French police officer, "is to start you off from some point in your normal movements about town. You must leave just as you are, dressed in ordinary street clothes. Take no luggage. If you are seen leaving your house with a bag, you will never get out of the city. . . . Now as to your shadow. You say he's outside. . . . I could arrest him now, of course, for suspicious loitering about the Prefecture. . . However, the train you want doesn't leave until nine tonight, and we couldn't hold him very long. He will have identification, of course, and though you could get away while we were checking and apologizing, all the stations would be watched before you could take a train. Besides, it would look a little too obvious; the Gestapo might be able to pin it on us. Let me see . . . what's the best way to work it?"

He rose, and walked across the room, his hands clasped behind his back. Then he turned, and said:

"It's always the same man who follows you? There's no likelihood that another man, whom you don't know, will be on the job say an hour or two before your train is due to leave?"

"I've only seen one," I said. "He was on duty all day yesterday, and he turned up again today."

"Good. Where will you be between seven and eight this evening?"

"I have an appointment in the lobby of the Ritz Hotel at seven," I answered. "I don't suppose it will last more than half an hour."

"Very convenient," said my officer friend, with satisfaction. "Here's what we'll do. When you've finished with your appointment in the Ritz, sometime between half-past seven and eight, say, pretend to notice that your purse has disappeared. Make a little agitation about it. Look about nervously for it, to collect a few witnesses. Then point at the man who is shadowing you, and say, 'I think that man stole it. He's been following me everywhere.' I'll have a couple of plainclothesmen there, and they will arrest him. At the same time, they will tell you that you must accompany them also.

"I don't think he'll protest in public, as long as he sees you are coming along, too. He will prefer to show his credentials in the privacy of the police station. We will stall him along as long as we can; and after he's identified himself, we'll do some long-winded apologizing. One way or another, I guarantee that he won't be able to give the alarm until after nine o'clock. By then you'll be on your way. We may be reprimanded for having been stupid enough to fall for your ruse, but that's about as far as they can go. I don't think they'll suspect us of anything more."

"Well," I said laughingly, "I'm not much of an actress; but since it's so important, I'm sure I'll be able to give a finished performance."

And I took my leave lighter in heart, and with confidence that I was as good as saved.

To allay the slightest suspicion of the Gestapo, I decided to make a second call at the German office on the Rue Galilée, where permits to go to the unoccupied zone were delivered. The day before I had made my application for an *Ausweis,* as these exit visas were called. I was sure I wouldn't get one, but I felt that it would seem less suspicious if I pretended to believe that I would.

There was a long line waiting to get exit visas, a group of the most motley sort, including almost all types and classes imaginable. What impressed me most was the silence of the crowd. These usually voluble Frenchmen had nothing to say to one another. I felt a sense of restraint, which I judged came from their consciousness of being within hearing of the enemy. Once in a while an impatient remark would reveal that some of them had been waiting for days or weeks or even months to get their permits to escape from German-ruled territory.

There was a Frenchwoman in line before me. At one refusal of a request, she turned to me and whispered that she also had little hope of getting the permit which she had been trying to get for two weeks. I was sympathetic, and she explained her case further. She said that she had asked for permission to visit her sick mother at Bergerac. She had been refused without explanation. Then, when she received news that her mother was dying, she had renewed her appeal, and had been told that she would have to present a medical certificate on her mother's condition before the *Ausweis* would be issued. She had learned that the only way to get this would be through the services of the Vichy government, since private communications were very limited, and when she tried to arrange for such a certificate, she was told that it would take weeks. Now her mother had died, and she was returning once more to ask permission to attend the funeral.

"I know what they'll say," she said resignedly. "They'll say there's no point in my going there, because she'll be buried before I arrive . . . They don't understand human feelings, these monsters!"

Behind me in the line was a Catholic priest. He had his identity card in his hand, and I saw on it a big letter "J." That meant that he was Jewish, and I was just trying to work up courage to ask a priest how he could be Jewish when the woman behind him did it before me.

"*Chère Madame,*" the priest explained, "my mother was Jewish. In the eyes of the Germans, that makes me Jewish as well, though I was born in the Catholic faith, and am a consecrated priest of the Catholic Church. I'm by no means the only Catholic priest in that situation. I know several others. If they introduce into France the same rule they have in Germany, that Jews must wear a yellow Star of David on their chests, then I will have to sew that on my priest's soutane. There's been talk of it."

"But how does that affect your work, *Monsieur le Curé?*" the woman asked.

"Not at all," he smiled. "I still remain the priest of my parish, in Passy—and I assure you, I have not lost one parishioner because of this stamp on my identity card. I am sure that I shan't lose one either if I should be obliged later to wear the Jewish star."

When I finally reached the head of the line, the official in charge thumbed through a card index file to find the record of my application. Looking at me in what seemed to me a curious fashion, he said: "Just a minute, Madame," and disappeared into an office in the rear, taking my papers with him—to consult a superior, I presumed. He came back immediately, and said:

"You must be patient, Madame. You only filed this application yesterday. Others have been waiting for weeks. We can't make exceptions, you know. You have to wait your turn."

"But I want to go to America," I said. "The boat won't wait."

The official shrugged his shoulders, and turned to the next applicant. But I refused to let him off so easily.

"When do you think I should come back?" I asked.

"I don't know. In a week or so."

I turned away, absolutely convinced that they would never give me an *Ausweis*.

It was 1 o'clock. The day was cold, but sunny. I decided to walk over to the Champs-Elysées, to see that beautiful avenue for the last time before leaving Paris. I wanted to carry the memory of it away with me. It was to be my good-bye to the beloved capital.

"Paris sera toujours Paris." That was what they had been singing only a few months ago—Paris will always be Paris. But how changed it seemed as I walked along! The exterior was the same, but the spirit had been crushed. The faces of the people looked strange, like the faces of dead friends, whose features remain the same, but give a different impression when the animation which inspired them has disappeared. Silent, and like mourners passing through a cemetery, the French passed sadly through their own streets. The

blue uniforms of their soldiers were no longer to be seen. The gray-green of Germany had replaced them. And there were more of those uniforms than there had ever been of French ones. They were everywhere one looked.

The Germans must have stationed enormous numbers of soldiers in Paris to keep its population under control. There must have been tens of thousands of them. They were everywhere. The big hotels and the luxurious apartment houses had been taken over by officers, who had no hesitation in ordering their owners to vacate without delay. Soldiers were quartered in barracks and in smaller hotels throughout the city.

Frenchmen were not even allowed to walk past the hotels occupied by German officers. Police or German soldiers stood guard before all of them. Certain streets, entirely given over to the Germans, were closed to traffic entirely—like the important Avenue Montaigne. Even trucks carrying their own soldiers were not allowed to pass here. It seemed that the noise might disturb the conquerors.

But there was a curious thing about the German private soldiers. They always seemed sad, depressed. Hitler, proud in his victory over France, had promised that every German should have a chance to see Paris. And thousands of German soldiers on leave took advantage of the occasion to visit the French capital, arriving daily to drive around the city in great sight-seeing buses. But they gazed stolidly and without visible pleasure at the spectacle about them. They never indulged in any of the gay pranks common to soldiers and sailors all over the world. I heard German soldiers singing only when ordered to do so on the march by their officers. By themselves, they never walked singing through the streets. Whether their air of constant melancholy came with them from their own country or whether it was produced by the hostile atmosphere about them, I had no idea.

I had reached the George V subway station (the one at which Frenchmen in occupied Paris always used to rise from their seats and stand at attention in tribute to the British), when I made an unexpected, and, in those circumstances, undesirable encounter.

Chancel came out of the subway entrance and moved towards me. My first reaction was joy. "So Chancel is still free!" I told myself exultantly. "It wasn't true when they said they had every one except Kitty. He is at large, too. Perhaps he can tell me where she is. Perhaps he can advise me about my present difficulties."

He had changed considerably since I had last seen him, but he was still recognizable. His beard, which had been only a scant growth when he first came back to Paris, was now thick and luxuriant. It changed his appearance considerably.

But immediately I remembered that I couldn't speak to him. My shadow, following dutifully behind, would certainly spot him and check up on him! I mustn't permit him to show recognition of me. I had become a danger to my old friends, walking about the city in this way, likely to draw unwelcome attention on any one I met. Thank God I would be out of it all in a few hours!

Chancel saw me. His eyes lighted up and he smiled. I turned aside a little as we approached, and whispered sharply as I passed:

"Careful! I'm being followed! Don't recognize me!"

And I swept by, increasing my pace a little with the intention of drawing my shadow along at greater speed, and giving him no time to pay any attention to Chancel, if he had noted his first signs of recognition. I hurried on for half a block, then looked back furtively over my shoulder. I couldn't see the man who had been following me; but a little crowd had suddenly gathered near the subway exit, and I heard a police whistle blowing.

I stood there, rooted to the spot, gazing towards the small knot of people, unable to approach, and unable to move away. A man left the group and walked in my direction. As he reached me, I couldn't help asking:

"What's happening?"

With a disgusted gesture, the man answered:

"Another Gestapo arrest. I don't know why."

I suddenly felt so weak that I had to stumble across the sidewalk and sit down at a café terrace. Poor Chancel! I had led them to him. They hadn't found Kitty through me, but they had got one fish in their net. It was the first reward for their release of me. I determined there shouldn't be another. I was going straight home, to stay there until it was time to keep my appointment with Mr. Marvel.

I spent the afternoon at home, growing increasingly more nervous as the minutes before the moment of escape moved slowly by. There was nothing in particular that I could do. There were no preparations to make, for I couldn't take anything with me. I mustn't arouse suspicions by leaving the house with any baggage, or even dressed for traveling. And I was too nervous to sit down and read a book.

I did, however, have to carry one package—warm underwear for Mr. Marvel. The Germans knew that I was supposed to meet him with these things, for they had heard my conversation with him over the phone. So I packed up the flannel underthings he had provided for me while I was in jail, and paced about waiting for the time to come to go to the Ritz and play the scene which I could not help rehearsing over and over in my imagination. I kept looking at my watch, sometimes at such short intervals that I had to watch the second-hand to convince myself that it hadn't stopped. At 6 o'clock my nervous tension was unbearable. I was then sitting, for a moment, in the living room. The dogs were lying at my feet, occasionally whining mournfully. They had sensed something was wrong with me.

I sprang suddenly to my feet. I would take the dogs for one last walk, before leaving them forever. They barked joyously as I put them on the leash and started out the door with them. The self-service elevator was rising in the shaft as I reached it. It stopped at my floor. Out of it stepped Schulz, the man who had arrested me before.

"Good evening, Mme. Shiber," he greeted me.

"What is it?" I asked, frightened.

"They want to see you at headquarters," he said. "You'll have to come along with me."

My bubble of hope collapsed. There went my chances for escape! Re-arrested already, just when I had expected to get away! But what could I do? Protests or a scene would have been useless. Silently, I opened the door of my apartment and led the dogs back in. They began whining again, disappointed of their outing, as I closed the door behind them. I picked up the parcel of warm underwear and took it along. I thought I might need it again.

But perhaps, I thought, as I got into the elevator with Schulz, perhaps I'm not going back to jail. Perhaps they just want to talk to me because of Chancel's arrest. If he said something that linked him with our case, they might have called me as a witness only. Perhaps I would still get another chance to escape.

But my hope was very slight as I left the building. I looked at my watch. Six-thirty. In half an hour, Mr. Marvel would be at the Ritz to meet me, in vain. In an hour, my friends of the French police would be there, ready to play the comedy whose heroine would be missing. And an hour later, the train that was to have taken me to freedom would puff out of the station, and I would not be on it.

At least, I hoped, my failure to appear should give the alarm. Mr. Marvel should realize what had happened.

CHAPTER TWENTY-EIGHT

Prison Again

ONCE AGAIN in the Hotel Matignon I faced Dr. Hager—this time in his third incarnation. I had already met the pleasant, sympathizing, smiling Dr. Hager and the angry, vituperative, threatening Dr. Hager. Now I made acquaintance with the ironic, superior Dr. Hager.

"Well, the comedy is over," he said, with a satiric smile, as he opened his examination of me. "We now have the last two members of the gang. We got Monsieur Corbier this afternoon, thanks to you, Mrs. Shiber. And I have just received word that Mme. Beaurepos was arrested in Bordeaux two hours ago. So there really wasn't any reason to allow you to wander around the streets any longer, was there?"

He smiled, as though with infinite appreciation of his own cleverness, and continued:

"You were not very wise, Mrs. Shiber. Do you remember when I told you that you might leave for America if you cooperated with us and told us what you knew? If you had not been so obstinate, you would be on your way to your own country now. As it is, you refused to accept the escape we offered you, and now it is too late. We are not going to make you any more such offers. You will have to stand trial now with the others."

One thing I noted with relief—they still did not know everything, since he had not mentioned Chancel's real name. But when he told me that Kitty had been arrested, the thought of Chancel was driven out of my head. So they had her at last—at Bordeaux; that must have been just after she crossed the line on her way back. Henri had failed to intercept her. Poor Kitty! What would become of her now?

My examination this time was very different from the first. There were no clever attempts to trick me, no veiled threats from Captain Pietsch (he wasn't even present). A clerk was called in to take down everything I said. This was to be my official deposition for the court records. Dr. Hager put precise questions, to which I was required to give precise answers. He showed no annoyance, one might almost say practically no interest, in the fact that I told the same story as before. I was still following my old principle: "Deny everything!" But he didn't seem to care. It frightened me and impressed me more than his previous examinations, which were meant to frighten and impress me, had done. His lack of insistence on confession made it seem clear to me that he no longer needed one. Now, I thought, he really knows something, so he no longer has to pretend he knows everything.

It took a long while to answer the hundreds of questions he put to me. At midnight, Dr. Hager called a recess while he sent out for refreshments for himself and the clerk. They gave me a cup of tea and a ham sandwich. It was the last decent food I was to have for seventeen months.

After this break, the questions and answers began again. I continued to take care to give nothing away, to say nothing that would be useful against Kitty, Father Christian, Chancel or any one else. When I had finished, there was a long wait while the deposition was typed, during which I half-dozed off from time to time. It was finally brought in for me to sign. I read it carefully—ten long single-spaced pages—fearing a trick, but everything in it was exactly what I had said. I signed my name to the bottom of each sheet. When I handed it back, it was nine in the morning.

Schulz was called in to take me back to the Cherche-Midi prison. As I prepared to leave, Dr. Hager addressed to me what I think was the cruelest sentence I had ever heard in my life.

It was this:

"It will be two or three months before your case comes up for trial, Mrs. Shiber. That isn't very long. Therefore I advise you to start preparing yourself. You should try to get accustomed to the idea that for the crime which you have committed, it is mandatory for the court to impose the death sentence. Good-bye, Mrs. Shiber."

And he bowed me out with a tooth-baring smile.

I followed Schulz in a daze. The death sentence *mandatory!* I had supposed that it was the maximum punishment! The subtle cruelty with which he had planted that poisoned barb in my prison, to torture me mentally for the weeks that would elapse before my trial, seemed to me more viciously sadistic than the brutal physical beatings which I knew some of his men administered to their helpless victims. Nor did I think any better of Dr. Hager after the trial, when I learned that he had not told the truth, and that the anguish he had inflicted on me was inspired by simple malice— his revenge, I suppose, for my failure to tell all he wanted to know.

My second arrest occurred on December 22, 1940. The process of entering the prison was less complicated than on the first occasion, for it was unnecessary to repeat some of the routine, such as the photographing. Indeed, the attitude of those who received me seemed to be that this was not a new imprisonment, but simply a continuation of the earlier one, which, indeed, it was. No doubt they had known very well that I would soon be back. The trick played on me had probably been used often enough before on others.

Somehow I did not feel this return to prison after my brief taste of liberty as bitterly as I would have expected if I had been told in advance what was going to happen. I seemed to re-enter immediately the atmosphere I had left. The intervening period was wiped away cleanly, as though by a sponge. Five minutes after I had set foot in the prison again, I felt as though I had never left it.

The three women who occupied the cell into which I was put this time were all French. One of them was a conspicuously beautiful girl, who had been cashier in the famous Paris restaurant, Chez Maxims, at the time of her arrest.

Maxims had become a favorite of German officers after the occupation, like most of the famous restaurants and places of entertainment in Paris. It quickly became known as the headquarters of a curious type of Black Market—that which dealt in prisoners of war.

Certain German officers who were able to secure the release of prisoners made their headquarters there, and it was possible to make deals with them for the freedom of relatives. Maxims was not the only place where this could be arranged; but it was the surest. At one or two other rendezvous, cut-rate bargains could be made. Releases were promised at from 20,000 to 50,000 francs. But there were numerous cases in which the amount was paid, and the prisoner was never freed. This never happened at Maxims, where more honorable corruption was the rule. But there the price ranged from 50,000 to 100,000 francs. Half the amount was paid at once, and the other half when the prisoner reached France.

The first problem of hapless French families with the price to ransom their relatives was to find the correct officer to approach. It would have been too bewildering simply to enter the restaurant and try to find the broker in human beings by guesswork; it was too thickly thronged with elegant officers in smartly-cut spick-and-span uniforms, which certainly did not look as though they had ever been exposed to the rigors of battle. It was necessary to know the password. Whispered to the headwaiter, it would lead to an introduction to the negotiator (not always the same officer), who would proportion his sympathy to the amount of money available as ransom. He would also explain very meticulously that in case the prisoner had already died, the money could not be returned.

The girl whose beauty had struck me when I first entered the cell was named Genevieve. Her father, she told me, was in a prison camp. She knew, of course, like all the employees of Maxims, who handled the liberation of prisoners, and she hoped to profit by the fact that she saw these officers every day (and often had to smile and show herself agreeable at their flirtatious sallies) to get a better bargain than was available to strangers. One of them finally agreed to secure her father's release at the rock-bottom minimum, not usually acceptable at Maxims, 20,000 francs, and to allow it to be paid in instalments of 2,000 francs at a time.

Her family had already paid five instalments when a letter which she had written to her father was returned with the word "Deceased" stamped across it. Some time later, the girl went to the German officer, told him that her father had died, and asked him, since her family was desperately poor, if he could return the 10,000 francs. He said he would do so the next day.

But the following morning, she was arrested and taken to the Cherche-Midi prison. No explanation was given her, and she only learned the reason later. The German officer, evidently unwilling to return the money, and equally unwilling to be embarrassed in his favorite restaurant by the sight of the girl who had dared ask for it, had simply reported that she was planning to cross the demarcation line surreptitiously to get to London via Lisbon. She left her mother in hysterics, in spite of an assurance from the police that she would be back in a few days, after questioning. She had now been there three months, without trial, and so far as she knew, without any likelihood of being tried—imprisoned on the simple unsupported denunciation of a corrupt Nazi Army officer!

The second of my three new companions was dark-haired, tall, sad-eyed Maria, a woman of 35, who wept most of the day and night, apparently unable, like the rest of us, to resign herself to prison life.

Her tale was one of almost continuous trouble. Her husband had fought in one of the international brigades in the Spanish civil war, and had suffered a spinal injury which paralyzed his legs. He had been returned to their small Paris home, and his wife went to work to take care of him and their two children, who were eight and ten.

When the Germans began closing in on Paris, Maria tried to arrange to take her husband south, out of their reach, but it was hard enough for a person in the best of health to get away at that time, and there was no way to transport a helpless person. So Maria sent her two children off with friends to stay in the south, and remained in Paris with her husband.

Shortly after the Germans arrived, an order was issued that all persons who had fought against Franco should report to the German authorities. Common belief was that they were to be turned over to Spain, for trial and punishment by her military courts. Sure that he would be discovered, the paralyzed man bowed to this last stroke of misfortune, and committed suicide by taking an overdose of the sleeping pills which were always left by his bed.

Her husband dead, Maria decided to try to get to southern France to rejoin her children. For weeks, she stormed the Rue Galilée, trying to get a permit. Then she received word that the younger child was seriously ill. She made for the demarcation line, and without help, without knowing how it might be crossed safely, tried to get across at night, alone. She was arrested, and it was for that banal offense that she was being held in prison. Her weeping centered about the fate of her children, especially the one who had been taken ill; for she had no way, of course, of knowing what had been its fate, nor did her friends know what had happened to her.

The last of the trio was also about 35. She looked as though she would have been very impressive in the elegant toilettes which were probably her accustomed costume, but was much less so in the dark-blue ski suit which she had been wearing when captured. She spoke a little English and very good German; but neither in those languages nor in her native French did she have anything much to say—though she was the most talkative of the group. She didn't seem to mind prison any more than the luxurious apartment which she said she had been occupying in the exclusive Avenue Henri-Martin, one of the most beautiful streets in Paris. Why she had been arrested she didn't seem to know, or very much care. She said only that she had been about to marry the man who had set her up in the de luxe apartment, and had been arrested while he was away in Vichy on business. She chattered incessantly, but the measure of how unimportant her talk was is the fact that today I can't remember what any of it was about. After three weeks, she was released, apparently with as little reason as she had been arrested.

Perhaps my failure to remember what she said was partly due, however, to my own mental condition. I spent ten weeks this time in the Cherche-Midi prison, and after only a few days of the old starvation rations and the monotonous routine of nothing to do, my mind became so blank that there were long stretches I couldn't remember at all. For instance, when I met Mr. Marvel recently in New York, he referred to a visit to me in my cell at the prison which I couldn't recall.

"You seemed very odd to me, Mrs. Shiber," he told me, trying to stir my recollection of the scene. "You sat there on your bed in a half stupor, your eyes neither quite open nor quite closed, hardly answering my questions. I had the feeling that you were there only in body, not in spirit."

But his prompting stirred no memory of the visit. It must have occurred at the period through which I moved like an automaton, going through the daily routine mechanically and without conscious volition. I sat for hour after hour in complete apathy, and though I was always tortured by hunger, my cell-mates often had to prod me to eat, or I would not have noticed that my food was there before me.

There is one period I remember clearly, however, which began with the very unusual distinction of a visit to my cell by the Major who was the warden of the prison. I don't suppose he came exclusively on my account; he seemed to be making a general tour of inspection. But he said to me: "It occurs to me that perhaps you would be more comfortable if I had you placed in the same cell with some other English-speaking person." I looked up at him in surprise, and indicated that I would like such a change. It was the only instance I had witnessed, or even heard of, in which any such trace of human feeling was evidenced by any of our jailors, and I didn't understand it. Was it perhaps that some one had reported my curious apathy, and the warden didn't want a conceivably important witness to lose her mind before trial?

However, the reason wasn't important, I thought. Any change was a welcome relief to the monotony. I was taken to the far end of the same corridor, and put in a cell with only one other occupant, an old woman whose features showed the strain of long mental torment.

When I entered the cell, I received a cold and suspicious reception which my experience with Marthe Wenziger enabled me to understand. But after a few minutes, she told me her name was Mrs. Syms, and I realized at once who she was—the mother of Mary Bird's fiancé. I told her about my previous experience as Mary's cell-mate, and she melted at once. Tears appeared in her eyes.

"Poor Mary," she murmured, "Do you think those beasts have told her what happened? . . . Oh, John, John . . ." And she burst into wild weeping, but almost without making a sound. It was more frightening than loud wails. Only the convulsive shaking of her fragile body betrayed the fact that she was sobbing hysterically, utterly unable to control herself. It took her some time to regain her calm, and then she told me what had happened.

John was her husband's name. He had been caught in the act of trying to signal to Mary, whom he had glimpsed from his window, and had been sentenced to a month in a dark cell.

He was already in bad physical condition. The prospect of a month alone in a windowless cell must have ended his hopes of survival; and he no doubt preferred that the end should come quickly. He succeeded in breaking the tin cover of his toilet pail over the stone bench, and drew the jagged end across his neck. They found him dead, his head resting on an open Bible, which, with a candle to read it by, was the one privilege allowed him to alleviate his month of solitary confinement. The remains of the candle, burned to the end, showed that he had placed it beside the book, where he had apparently sought final consolation as his life ebbed slowly away.

The suicide seemed to be considered a grave matter by the prison authorities, for though they showed so little consideration for their charges, it was their duty to keep them alive for eventual trial— this being a prison only for those who had not yet been permanently sentenced. It was considered bad for the morale of the other prisoners, and, besides that, a blot on the record of the prison administration. The warden himself came to Mrs. Syms' cell and told her what had happened. He even went so far as to express his sorrow.

"You needn't be sorry for me," she said. "If John thought that was the right thing to do, it must have been. He has always seen clearly, and he has always done what was right. My duty now is to follow him."

"When did you tell the warden that?" I asked.

"Today," she said, "not very long ago. It was only today that I heard . . ." She didn't finish the sentence.

Now I understood why I had been moved. The warden didn't want another suicide among his prisoners, and he counted on my presence to prevent Mrs. Syms from attempting to follow her husband. For once, I agreed with a German.

"My dear Mrs. Syms," I told her, taking one of her hands between mine. "You mustn't think of such things . . . Remember your son. He has lost one parent. You mustn't deprive him of the other. And how about Mary, who always talked of you with so much love and respect?"

Mrs. Syms did not answer at once. She looked into the hazy

dimness of the cell with unseeing eyes, and then murmured under her breath:

"I will have to go. John is calling me."

I spent two weeks with Mrs. Syms in our cell, laboring with her to rid her of the obsession of suicide. It was a benefit to myself which I hardly realized at the time. In reasoning with her, I forgot my own troubles—and I had an object at last, that of saving Mrs. Syms. It was almost with disappointment that on January 17, I heard the guard say to Mrs. Syms "You are to be released. Come with me."

"What about the others?" Mrs. Syms asked. "What about my son? What about Mary? Will all of them be freed?"

"No questions," the guard said shortly. "Get your things."

Mrs. Syms nervously gathered together her few possessions. Suddenly she straightened up, pointed her arm with outstretched finger straight at the guard, and said with an air of wonderful energy and authority:

"I demand an answer. What about the others?"

To my great surprise, her commanding attitude melted the guard. He answered obediently, if gruffly:

"All freed. Your son and his accomplice are prisoners of war. They will go to a prison camp. The rest of you can return home."

For once, it was the truth. I learned later through the prison grapevine that this was, indeed, the decision that had been made for the prisoners from Guernsey. We all thought that the suicide had precipitated this action.

With the departure of Mrs. Syms, I was again moved to another cell, and again I succumbed to the lethargy engendered by monotony and malnutrition. There were moments when my numbness turned into impotent rage, a sort of maniacal frenzy, and I could understand why maddened prisoners ran at their jailers and tried to strangle them, or beat their heads against the wall in desperate suicide attempts, as two of the inmates in our prison had done.

My greatest worry, in my more lucid moments, was that though I knew Kitty had been arrested. and was perhaps in this very jail, perhaps even in the next cell, only two feet away, I knew nothing of what had happened to her. Ignorance of her fate was one of my greatest tortures.

During this time, I received several visits from Mr. Marvel—visits which I did remember. Each time the guard opened the door for him, I hoped he would be able to give me some word from Kitty; but he was never allowed to enter the cell alone. He was always accompanied by two German soldier interpreters, one for English and one for French. Since Mr. Marvel spoke both languages perfectly, it was obvious that the "interpreters" were really listeners, sent along to make sure that he didn't transgress the rules restricting the subjects on which he could talk.

I thought he might try to convey some hidden message to me, and after each visit I would sit for hours, trying to remember his exact words and pondering on any hidden meaning they might have. It was a hopeless attempt, for he told me afterwards that they had none. But I think the effort helped save my sanity, for the fact of having some mental problem with which to struggle broke in on the awful sameness of my days. His visits were the only break in them. If I had not been able to look forward to them, I believe I would have collapsed, physically and mentally.

And then one day I got news of Kitty!

CHAPTER TWENTY-NINE

Kitty

M Y FIRST tidings about Kitty since my arrest were provided by the prison authorities, though they had no intention of assuaging my thirst for news about her—in fact, it certainly never occurred to them to consider the effect on me when they sent it out.

It happened at the evening distribution of food during the second month of my imprisonment. The guard gave us our evening measure of coffee and our portion of bread, but instead of handing over our daily ration of fat (so-called whale meat, which probably came from a chemical factory instead of a whale), he passed us a mimeographed notice, and went out, slamming the door behind him.

I looked at my cell-mates in dismay, for small as our fat ration was, we felt the need of it. The explanation for its absence was on the sheet of paper:

Prisoners will be deprived of their daily ration of fat today as punishment for the attempted escape of an Englishwoman, French by marriage, charged with helping English soldiers to escape from France. Her effort was foiled, and she has been sentenced to 30 days solitary confinement, as has her cell-mate, who failed to report her attempt. Prisoners are warned that any further escape attempts will be even more severely punished, and any prisoner undertaking such futile measures must realize that he is condemning his fellows to disciplining as well as himself.

I had no doubt from the description, and from my knowledge of her character, that this was Kitty, my indomitable Kitty, who refused to be confined even by the bars of a prison without trying to break through them. It made me wonder, too, if she hadn't become slightly maddened by confinement, for she had always had a tendency to claustrophobia. How often I had seen her moving about the room, throwing open one window after another, saying: "The air is so close, I feel as though I were in prison!" Now my poor Kitty, who loved air and freedom so much, *was* in prison, and sentenced to the worst imprisonment of all, a whole month, thirty endless days, in a dark tomb where she would feel herself buried alive!

I was beginning my third month in Cherche-Midi when I fell sick of some horrible infection. The inside of my mouth felt as though it were lined with canker sores. The German military doctor who served the prison took one look at it, and ordered me transferred to the hospital.

The order was the most welcome one I could possibly have heard. I dreamed in ecstasy of a clean hospital bed, of being able to wash, of better food, of the luxury of stretching out in bed in the daytime, instead of sitting rigid on its edge hour after hour. But the reality was not like that.

Though the prison was in the center of Paris, where there are dozens of fine hospitals, I was taken to the hospital of the prison of Fresnes, 70 miles away. I was placed on the driver's seat of a truck, on a cold windy day. Beside me, the driver sat stolidly, silent and sullen. Inside the truck, guarded from the full force of the cold, rode the two healthy men with me—a guard and an officer. I, the sick woman, was allotted the exposed cab of the truck.

I remember nothing of the ride except my constant discomfort and the fact that it seemed as though our journey would never end. I had a high fever, and I think I must have been a little out of my head. I had brought nothing with me from Paris so the prison hospital gave me one of their gowns, and put me to bed between sheets cold as ice.

The hospital was worse than the prison. I was in a cell, just as I had been before, but now I was alone, and the monotony was greater than ever. I saw the doctor once or twice. The sister who attended me washed out my mouth three times a day, and once in a while a cleaning woman came in. Otherwise, I saw no one.

I couldn't eat. The soup and coffee they offered me was execrable; I couldn't force it down, even after what I had been accustomed to in Cherche-Midi. The room was so cold I couldn't keep my hands over the covers, which were thin and inadequate.

Order committing Mrs. Shiber to the prison hospital of Fresnes for treatment. The slip states that she is suffering from running sores in the mouth. Note that the forms used in this Paris prison taken over by the Gestapo are in German, imported from Leipzig, as the printer's mark shows.

The only break in the monotony was the occasional opportunity to talk to the cleaning woman, who was an inmate of the prison. From her I learned that Kitty had been there a few days before. The black cell had been too much for her, and she had been brought to the hospital in a state of collapse before her month was up. She had made frantic efforts to obtain her transfer to a real hospital, offering to pay all costs if it could be arranged, but of course without success. She had asked for sleeping pills at night, but instead of taking them, had hidden them until she accumulated what she thought would be enough, and then had taken them all at once. It had made her very ill, and that was all. Shortly afterwards she had been returned to Cherche-Midi.

The pain in my mouth began to decrease. It must have run its course naturally, for the hospital was practically without medicine, and I couldn't see that they did anything for it, except to wash out my mouth with what seemed to be ordinary water. I begged to be returned to prison. So I rode back, locked in the Black Maria (the French call it *panier à salade*—salad basket).

When I got back to Cherche-Midi, I was so thin and weak that the guard had to help me up the stairs. I couldn't make it alone.

It was shortly after my return from the hospital that I was called to the warden's office, where I found Dr. Hager waiting for me.

"I have come to inform you," he said, "that your case has been put down for trial on March 7. You see that we have wasted no time. I said it might take three months, but we have done a little better than that. I have also come to give you a last warning. It appears that there is still time for you to modify your attitude and thereby, perhaps, to profit by the leniency of the court, which may be willing, after all, not to impose the supreme sentence . . . Mme. Beaurepos has made a complete confession, and therefore can expect to receive consideration from her judges. Your stubbornness in denial is likely to arouse their hostility. In any case, you cannot, under the circumstances, expect any clemency—unless, of course, you follow the example of your friend."

My instinct whispered to me: "Another trick! Deny everything!"

But Dr. Hager had come prepared. He opened his brief-case and drew out a bundle of documents.

INFIRMERIE CENTRALE

Bulletin d'Exeat

La nommée Schiper Itta
actuellement en traitement à l'Infirmerie
centrale pour
peut rejoindre sa Maison d'origine

Fresnes le 21 Février 1941
Le Médecin

Mrs. Shiber's discharge from the prison hospital of Fresnes. The personnel here was French, and the form is therefore in that language also. Misspelling her name as Itta Schiper (she was committed with a less marked error as Ettah Shiber), the prison doctor notes that she is to be returned to the prison she came from (maison d'origine).

"This is the prosecutor's brief," he said. "Would you like to see Mme. Beaurepos' confession?"

He looked through the documents, drew out one of 12 or 15 pages, and handed it to me.

I leafed through it. Each paragraph began with the words, "I confess . . ." and it seemed to contain a fairly complete account of our activities. I was thunderstruck. How could Kitty have done such a thing? How could she have handed us all over to the mercy of the Gestapo?

"Well, you see," said Dr. Hager, triumphantly, taking back the confession. "Mme. Beaurepos has saved herself. Now how about your confession?"

I remained silent. Dr. Hager raised his voice:

"Come, come, Mrs. Shiber, this is ridiculous! You will only provoke the anger of the court. I came here to save you from the result of your own stubbornness. These documents are to be sent to the court at once. It contains the deposition in which you obstinately deny all knowledge of this affair. It was very childish of you to adopt so obviously false an attitude. If you wish to change it, there is still time. I can replace it by your confession, and I assure you, it will increase your chances immensely at the trial. You will be considered by the judges as cooperative, rather than hostile. I am acting only in your own interest."

Dr. Hager would have done better if he had omitted that last sentence. I thought I knew him too well to believe that, and it convinced me that he was still playing a double game. He seemed to have all his evidence, so what more did he want of me? Whatever it was, I was sure it would be to my disadvantage. I said simply: "I have nothing to add to my original deposition."

Dr. Hager shrugged his shoulders with the air of washing his hands of the whole affair, and stuffed his papers back into his brief-case. I was led back to my cell.

At 8 o'clock on the morning of March 7, the guard ordered me to accompany him for trial. I followed him through the long corridors till we came to the head of the staircase. There he stopped, peered through the peephole into a cell, jerked open the door, and called:

"Number 2017—for trial!"

A woman appeared in the door of the cell. It was Kitty.

My heart bounded suddenly in my chest and then began thumping so hard it seemed to me that it must be audible. Kitty had hardly changed at all during her ordeal of imprisonment. She had on the same coat she had been wearing when she left for the unoccupied zone, when I had last seen her. Her face was pale, and there were deep shadows under her eyes; but she did not seem broken either in body or spirit.

She looked towards me, and I thought I detected the shadow of a smile as she said softly, "Hello, Etta."

"Silence!" the guard roared. "Prisoners must not talk."

And so, forbidden to say anything to my old friend to ease my bursting heart, I walked silently with her to the ground floor, and out into the courtyard, where we were turned over to other guards.

We heard a car draw up outside the gate, and then it was thrown open. A green-painted convict transport van stood at the curb. The guard opened the door and Kitty got in. I followed her. The door was locked behind us, and with a lurch the van started.

Alone with Kitty, I raised my arms to hug her, but I let them fall in astonishment when she looked at me reproachfully as she said: "How could you have given us all away, Etta? How could you have had the weakness to tell everything to those people?"

"I . . . I . . . ?" I stammered, so taken back that I couldn't get the words out before she continued:

"They must have terrorized you, Etta . . . but you should have been firm. I ought to be angry at you. God knows you deserve it. But I just can't be angry at you. Anyway, what does it matter now?"

"But, Kitty," I exclaimed, recovering my power of speech, "I didn't tell them anything—not a thing. I swear to you that I have always denied everything—even a few days ago, when Dr. Hager came to the jail and urged me once more to confess."

"But, Etta," Kitty protested, "I saw your confession with my own eyes. It was a ten-page deposition, signed by you. I recognized your handwriting."

"I made a ten-page deposition," I said, "and I signed it, but it was a denial, not a confession. If you saw anything else, it was a forgery."

"My God!" said Kitty. "I believed in it—and I *did* confess."

"Tell me," I asked, "when Dr. Hager showed you my forged confession, did he tell you that there was no sense in continuing your denials, that I had earned the clemency of the court, and that you should do likewise?"

"Something like that," Kitty said.

"That was what he said to me," I said, "when he showed me your confession. But I didn't trust him. I continued to deny it."

Hastily we compared dates and notes. As nearly as we could make out, Dr. Hager had tried the same trick on both of us on the same day, one after the other. I had come first, so that the confession I had seen had also been a forgery—but then Kitty had failed to see through the ruse and had given him a real one.

"It's awful, awful," Kitty moaned. "I was the one who gave us away! And I accused you! Oh, how could I have been so stupid?" I put my arm around her shoulder.

"It wasn't your fault, Kitty," I said. "That devil would have tricked any one."

"What are we going to do now?" Kitty asked.

"What I have been doing right along," I said. "Deny everything."

Kitty shook her head slowly.

"It's too late, Etta," she said. "What they put in the forged confessions may have been fairly complete, but the confession I made has everything in it—everything! They questioned me for hours. They have fifteen pages of the most minute details—names, dates, places, everything. It wouldn't do any good for me to stand up now and say that I made it all up. With the information I gave them, they will be able to verify everything. We're lost, Etta, lost . . . and it was all my fault!"

The car jolted to a stop, Kitty threw her head up proudly, brushed her hair back with her hand, and smoothed out the wrinkles of her dress.

"Heads up, Etta!" she said. "Don't let these Germans see we're afraid of them! Don't give them that satisfaction, whatever happens."

We heard the key turn in the lock, and the door of the van was swung open. I saw where we were at once—in the Rue St.

Dominique, in front of the military tribunal, established in an 18th century mansion of the St. Germain quarter.

I got out, and Kitty followed. Dr. Hager was standing at the door. When he saw us he rushed towards us, and seizing the guard by the collar of his tunic, began shaking him in a rage, twisting his collar till the guard's bobbing face became crimson, and shouting at him in the most violent German abuse:

"You fool! You idiot! You dog! What do you mean by leaving these two women alone together before the trial? Why weren't you sitting inside with them? . . . You're through being a guard, my fine fellow, but you're not through with prisons. I'll see that you find out what prisons are for."

And suddenly he aimed a vicious kick at the guard, then stalked off into the courtroom.

The guard, dropping his head like a beaten dog, led us around to a side entrance. He was too dispirited to object when we whispered to each other.

"Kitty," I said under my breath, "how long do you think we'll get?"

"A year or two, perhaps," she said, "but the war may end sooner, and then we'll get out."

"But, Kitty!" I protested. "The death sentence!"

"Oh, Etta," Kitty said. "Don't be melodramatic. How can they condemn two women to death? Don't worry. There's no chance of that."

CHAPTER THIRTY

The Trial

OUR GUARD led us up one flight, past files of helmeted sentinels. Two stiff-faced German soldiers also stood at either side of the courtroom door.

The room itself was a magnificent 18th century salon with tapestried walls, priceless draperies and sparkling crystal chandeliers. It looked as though it had been a ballroom, and, indeed, there was still a grand piano standing majestically in one corner of this high-ceilinged room. "This looks as if we had been invited to a reception, not a trial," I said to myself as we entered. But the disposition of the rest of the furniture was more businesslike.

In the center of the room was a long table, behind which were several high-backed chairs, for the judges. On it lay thick bundles of documents, tied with cords. They were, I assumed, the papers concerning our case.

Opposite this table was a long bench for the defendants. We were seated there, and a moment later Monsieur Tissier was brought in. He was dressed in his Sunday best, as he had been when he called on us in Paris. But how different it looked now! During his long imprisonment, his suit had become wrinkled and torn. It had lost the air of having just been removed from the mothballs which it had so plainly worn when we had seen it before.

When he spied us, Tissier stopped uncertainly, apparently wondering whether he would be allowed to greet us. Then he made up his mind to risk it, stepped up to us, and held out his hand. We both shook hands with him, and then he sat down at the edge of the bench, first dusting it off carefully. After all, this was still his Sunday suit.

Next to appear in the courtroom door, accompanied by a guard, was Father Christian. He strode forward quickly and firmly, apparently unaffected by his months of imprisonment. He seemed fresh and alert, and his eyes moved quickly over the room with evident interest in the scene. He greeted us with a faint smile as he sat down beside Tissier. It was the first time the two men had met, but they could hardly be in doubt of each other's identity. They shook hands.

Chancel was the last to arrive. He took his place between Father Christian and myself, greeting us only with a slight nod, as a well-bred person sitting down beside strangers might have done. He gazed grimly at the floor, and when I threw a sidewise glance in his direction, he looked quickly away. I thought he might be angry with me, that perhaps he attributed his arrest to me—which would have been accurate enough, except that it was not my fault. That, however, was not his reason. I was to find out later why he adopted this attitude.

I watched the door anxiously, expecting to see Monsieur Durand enter at any moment. But no one else appeared. "Good," I thought, "they didn't get him."

Next to arrive were our lawyers. The Germans had permitted us each to select a lawyer, but it was an empty formality. Before the German Military Court lawyers were not permitted to examine witnesses, and they were therefore little more than spectators of the proceedings. They could not even talk to their clients. They were, however, allowed to sum up at the end of the trial.

Mr. Marvel had procured a lawyer for me—no simple task, for in the first place it was necessary to find a Frenchman who knew perfect German, and also, to satisfy the requirements of the court, one who could prove that none of his four grandparents were Jewish.

It was exactly ten by the bronze grandfather's clock which stood against one of the walls when the judges entered the courtroom. They were preceded by their president, a man of about 50, wearing a colonel's uniform. His eyes were a cold, icy blue, and his face seemed to have been chiseled from granite.

Two officers of lower rank, the so-called "voting judges," followed their presiding officer. Both wore eye-glasses, and looked as though they had been poured from the same mold. They were blond, colorless, and with a tendency to stoutness.

Last to enter was the prosecutor.

I could hardly restrain a shriek when he entered the room.

Kitty nudged me inconspicuously, and I realized that she had recognized him too.

It was Captain Weber, the German officer who had ridden back with us, when we were traveling from Doullens to Paris with a soldier in our luggage carrier, who had later come to our apartment with an obvious interest in getting better acquainted with Kitty. He walked in a calm, dignified manner to the left end of the long table, where a chair had been placed for him, and sat down. He glanced in our direction, but showed no surprise. I judged that he had already gathered from the documents in our case who we were. He had had plenty of time to prepare for this encounter; but for us it was an unexpected shock. How would his presence affect our case? Would he be better, or worse, disposed to us than a complete stranger?

There was no way of telling. After his single glance in our direction, Captain Weber became immersed in the documents before him and paid us no more attention.

It was then that we were astounded by an almost comic spectacle. Six German privates marched stiffly into the room. I noticed, with the curious fixity on unimportant detail that sometimes seizes upon one at such moments, that their broad leather belts had round buckles on which was inscribed, *Gott mit uns*. Behind them came an interpreter.

The six marched up to the judges' table, halted before it, right-faced towards the judges, saluted, and shouted, "Heil Hitler" in unison. An oath was read to them, which I suppose was the equivalent of our own swearing in of a jury. They saluted again, left-faced back into single file, marched solemnly to a rank of six chairs standing at one side of the room, swung around simultaneously, and plumped down on their chairs in unison. The whole thing was so well-drilled that it was obvious that it must have been rehearsed with the greatest of care. This was our "jury," and it was clear that they could be counted on not to upset any of the calculations of the court.

I couldn't help smiling at this catering to democratic ideas by a burlesque of a jury trial. As I was to discover later, their rôle was to sit there, listening to proceedings like any genuine jury, and after the trial, when the judges left the room to confer, to march out also in the unlikely case, I supposed, that the judges should desire to ask their opinion. But the sight of them sitting there, in the correct attitude prescribed by military regulations, each with his cap balanced at an identical angle on his right knee, was sufficient to convince any one that they would hardly presume to disagree with the colonel and the two captains sitting at the judges' bench. My impulse to laugh at this parody of a court of justice was quickly checked by the realization that it held my life in its hands.

I looked towards Kitty, wondering if this spectacle had affected her in the same way. The expression on her face didn't accord with the encouraging words she had uttered to me as we entered the building. I had seen it before, stoical and fixed, but only when she was in grave trouble. I tried to analyze my own feelings, and found I didn't seem to have any. I was stonily calm, even indifferent.

"Frau Kitty Beaurepos," the presiding justice called.

A guard touched Kitty on the elbow. She rose, and was led before the long table.

The first questions put to her were the usual formal ones: name, address, age, place of birth, nationality, religion, and so forth. Then the presiding judge put the first real question to her:

"Do you feel conscious of your guilt?"

"Certainly not," Kitty answered. "I should have felt guilty to have acted in any other way. I am an Englishwoman. My conscience told me that it was my duty to help English soldiers."

"Permit me to inform you," the judge said in a cutting tone, "that no account of these proceedings will be published in the newspapers. It is therefore unnecessary to make speeches. If your diatribe was addressed to England, it was quite futile. It will not reach that far. If it was your aim to convert the prosecutor or myself to Anglophilia, I think I can assure you that in that also you are hardly likely to succeed."

He picked up one of the papers in front of him, and said:

"Moreover, you are not an Englishwoman. You married a French citizen, Henri Beaurepos. You are therefore French."

Turning towards the prosecutor, he added:

"Why is this man Beaurepos not among the prisoners? Has anything been done to apprehend him?"

Kitty answered first.

"I married Monsieur Beaurepos ten years ago. We have not lived together for the last five years. I have taken steps in Lyons to divorce him."

This last I knew was untrue. Kitty was evidently trying to prevent any suspicion from being shed on Henri. She did not know, of course, that the Germans were looking for him, but that his caution, and his friends in the French police, had saved him from capture.

Somewhat to my surprise, neither the judge nor the prosecutor added anything to this—the latter, perhaps, because Kitty had saved him from confessing a failure on the part of the police. The judge consulted his papers again, and said:

"Frau Beaurepos, you are charged with having conspired with Mme. Shiber, Monsieur Christian Ravier, Monsieur Tissier and Monsieur Corbier for the purpose of smuggling English soldiers out of the country."

"That is inexact," said Kitty, in a clear voice.

"Indeed!" said the judge sarcastically. "That is very curious, considering that I have your signed confession before me. I presume you intend to retract it. I fear you are going to cause us to waste valuable time. Who gave you the very bad advice to deny what you have already admitted?"

"I have had advice from no one," Kitty said steadily. "I am not retracting my confession. But there is no reason why these others should be here with me. They were not involved in my activities."

"In the course of my duties as a military judge," the German colonel said, "I have heard a number of curious and, shall I say, incredible, stories told by prisoners, but few as difficult to believe as that Frau Shiber, for instance, who occupied the same apartment with you, failed to notice that it was a sort of way station for escaping soldiers. She must have been singularly obtuse."

"Nevertheless," Kitty insisted, "she knew nothing of my activities. I was careful to keep them secret from her. My greatest crime is that I have involved an innocent woman in this affair."

"Ah, yes," said the judge, still in that same sarcastic tone, "And Monsieur Tissier? I note that you used his estate to cross the boundary line. That was accomplished while he was looking the other way, I presume?"

"We did not ask his permission," Kitty said. "We picked it because of its position. Then we simply crossed it. That was all."

"Better and better," said the judge. "Now, Monsieur Ravier. What interesting excuse have you prepared for him?"

"I used him as a cloak," Kitty said. "He thought I was traveling about the country to help him collect funds for the restoration of his church. That pretext was valuable to me to explain my movements."

I listened to Kitty with mingled admiration and pity. It was splendid of her to try to save the rest of us, at her own expense, but her story was so pitifully thin that it couldn't possibly have stood up, even before a less biased court than this one.

"Well, we have one left," the judge said. "What about Monsieur Corbier?" And immediately, without waiting for her to answer, he continued, mimicking her voice, "Monsieur Corbier is completely innocent, and I met him only to discuss with him the present death agonies of the British Empire."

Captain Weber broke into raucous laughter, followed quickly by the other judges and the interpreter. The six soldiers of the "jury" seemed a little disconcerted. They stared at one another for a moment, then, deciding that when a colonel makes a joke, a private should laugh, they burst out simultaneously into a sort of snort, stopping short with the same unison with which they had begun. It couldn't have been more exact if it had been rehearsed.

When the merriment had subsided, Kitty answered quietly:

"I do not know Monsieur Corbier."

I realized that she had spotted the same detail that I had. Chancel was still being addressed as Corbier. That explained why he had pretended not to know us. The Gestapo, which had sought him before as Chancel, and no doubt was still seeking him, now had him in their power without realizing his real identity. It was probable that they knew less about his activities than about ours.

"You are very noble," the judge said, with an even heavier overlay of sarcasm than before, "but, of course, childish and clumsy.

Your efforts to save your co-defendants will be of no avail, and I am surprised that you should have been so stupid as to make the attempt. As far as you yourself are concerned, you have admitted the crimes charged against you. You made a confession, and you have just stated that you do not retract 'it. That is all we need hear from you. We will allow the others to convict themselves, as you, Frau Beaurepos, have just done."

He made a gesture of dismissal, and Kitty was led back to her seat. He called the next name

"Frau Etta Shiber!"

It was my turn. I took my place before the table, and went through the preliminary questions. Then came the first important one.

"You know the charges against you," the judge said. "Are you guilty?"

"I am guilty . . ." I said.

The judge looked up startled.

"Another curious one!" he said. "The first confesses her guilt in 15 pages, and then claims she has committed no crime—and that when she committed the crime she says she didn't commit, nobody helped her." He looked around, but got only a titter from Captain Weber. "Now this woman, who has declared in 10 pages that she is innocent admits at once that she is guilty."

"I hadn't finished," I said. "I started to say that I am guilty only of not persuading my friend to come to America with me when the war broke out. She was emotionally disturbed by the fact that thousands of soldiers from her country were in danger. I should have realized that she was not capable of understanding the situation clearly, and should have persuaded her to come away."

Captain Weber rose from his place.

"Mr. President," he said, "is this a conspiracy to make a mockery of this trial? Are we to sit here while the defendants make speeches defending one another!"

"Do not be alarmed, Mr. Prosecutor," the judge said. "The court has not yet heard anything which impresses it as being describable as a defense. The reactions of the prisoners are curious, but not effective . . . Frau Shiber, I see, is by way of being an amateur lawyer. She is filing an insanity plea for Frau Beaurepos. I regret to inform you, Frau Shiber, that insanity is not considered as alleviating, but as aggravating, the offense in this court. In the degenerate democratic system lunatics may be considered as comparatively desirable members of the community, and thus worth saving from punishment, but we do not regard the matter from quite the same viewpoint. However, it's quite evident that Frau Beaurepos is in full possession of her senses . . . I may add that you are in deep water yourself, Frau Shiber, so that you would do better to attend to your own defense than to seek excuses for your friend. Her hearing is over. We are on yours now. Suppose we keep to the subject. Do you recognize your guilt of the crimes with which you are charged?"

"I am innocent," I said.

"So you intend to continue denying everything?" the judge asked.

"It is not a question of denying anything," I said. "I am innocent. There's nothing to deny."

The judge turned his cold steely eyes on me for a minute, without moving or speaking. Then suddenly he thumped his fist on the table before him so hard that the piles of papers jumped from the wood.

"Nonsense!" he roared. "Innocent! How dare you claim to be innocent! Why, this business went on before your eyes, under your nose. The apartment where you lived was constantly filled with escaping soldiers. This dastardly secretive activity went on in your presence. Of course, you were second in command of this band of criminals! Of course, you took part in every activity of Frau Beaurepos! You participated in every discussion! You accompanied your friend on her clandestine trips! You are guilty, Frau Shiber! There is no use trying to hide it! The court will take note of your attitude!"

He had roared all this out in a single breath, in a paroxysm of fury. I stood transfixed, hypnotized by his gaze and his words.

"If that is all you came to tell us today, Frau Shiber," the judge ended, resuming a calmer tone, though still a severe one, marked by only a trace of his habitual sarcasm, "you might as well have stayed in your cell. I have already read your deposition. I knew already that you claimed to be as innocent as a newborn lamb. If you have nothing to add to that statement, you might as well take your seat."

I stumbled back to the bench. If I had had any hope after Kitty's testimony, it had disappeared now. This court was not going to worry about proof. It was true, of course, that I was guilty; but it was quite evident that if I had been innocent, the result would have been the same. As long as they believed I was guilty, that was enough. The tribunal was not going to waste time making the prosecution establish guilt.

CHAPTER THIRTY-ONE

Captain Weber Speaks

WHEN MONSIEUR TISSIER in his turn moved up to the long table and stood before his judges, I experienced a curious reaction. For a split second, the scene before me seemed to flatten out, as though it were a painting on a flat surface—a painting by Daumier. I seemed to see before me, as I might have seen it on a canvas, in the deep shadows which Honoré Daumier would have given it, this pathetic-grotesque picture of a humble old man facing the leering faces, not of his prosecutors, but of his persecutors. Then the sudden perception of how this scene might have been transmitted to canvas by one of the most savage of France's painters vanished, and I was again part of the scene, not a spectator of it, in a courtroom, not looking at a painting of it.

But I remained impressed by the symbolism of the scene. This dignified old man, in the shabby, wrinkled, black suit which had been his Sunday best, humble and helpless, confronting those implacable judges who were unwilling to forgive even the conquered, seemed to me to represent France, beaten and despoiled. The simple innate dignity which animated him seemed also to have been felt by the presiding judge, who resented it, and sought to break it down by a petty attack on the old man.

During his study of the documents in the case, he had noticed one detail which, he thought, gave him a chance to heap ridicule on Tissier; and as soon as the preliminaries had been disposed of, he hastened to take advantage of it.

"I notice that you signed your deposition with a cross instead of your name," he said. "Is it possible that you can't write your own name?"

"No," said Tissier calmly, "I cannot."

"Well, well!" said the judge sarcastically. "How very revealing! In this country which prides itself on its literacy, a man who, as his papers show, has been elected mayor of his community three times in succession, can't even sign his name! What ignoramuses the others must be! No wonder a country which chooses illiterates to lead it is too weak to defend itself! Don't you think, Monsieur Tissier, that there should be schools in France to teach mayors how to read and write?"

"I did not say I do not know how to read and write," Tissier said. He raised his right arm and held it out before him.

"I know how to write," he said, "but I cannot hold a pen because a German bullet tore my hand on the Marne in 1914 and my fingers have been paralyzed ever since."

As Tissier held out his hand, with its stiff, bent fingers, it was obvious what he must be saying, and the judge, his face reddening, hastily put the next question without waiting for the interpreter to translate. Tissier's examination was short. He admitted that he had allowed any one who wanted to do so to cross his estate, because, he said, he did not admit the right of foreigners to make regulations binding Frenchmen in France.

Father Christian followed Tissier. I wish I had a stenographic record of his testimony, for, ignoring legal questions, he put our moral defense in clear, simple terms more eloquent than any reproduction of them which I can set down here from memory. As nearly as I can remember, the way he summed up his attitude was this:

"France is still at war with Germany. The generals surrendered to you, but the people did not. The war is still being fought, not on military fronts this time, but in the cities, the towns, the villages, in the homes of humble individuals. What we did was to fight one of the minor skirmishes in that war. You have won this skirmish, but you have not won the war, and you will never win the war. How many are you in France? A million? Two million? There are *forty* million against you!

"When a soldier fights in battle, he knows that he may be killed. But he knows that as long as the fight continues, his death may not be in vain. We knew, too, that we might be killed in this battle. But we know also that our deaths will not be in vain. You cannot stamp out resistance by imprisoning or executing the few individuals you surprise here and there. Their fellows will only be inspired to avenge them.

"I am a priest, but in this war I have been a soldier, and a soldier who has not surrendered. For I was fighting for more than a military decision between two powers, rivals for control over the same parcel of land. I was fighting for justice, and in this war, I could see only one kind of justice, a justice partaking at the same time of the human and the divine. I do not expect to find that justice, or any justice, in this court. But I know that in the end, divine justice will prevail; and the verdict of God will be pronounced, not against us, but against you, who presume to judge us."

I was surprised that Father Christian was allowed to talk so long, uninterruptedly, pausing after each phrase while the interpreter translated it—quite faithfully, as far as my own imperfect German allowed me to judge. Dr. Weber had stepped behind the presiding judge's chair and was whispering to him. Perhaps it was absorption in their conversation which caused him to allow Father Christian to continue, or perhaps his speech was the subject of their whisperings. I imagined that Weber was urging him to cut Father Christian off, and that the judge, perhaps, was saying: "Let him talk. He's only convicting himself."

Last to be called was Chancel, and once more he was addressed under the name of Corbier. It was obvious now that the Germans actually did not know whom they had in their power, that they were ignorant of the fact that the man they had sought even before our activities began was actually before them. Kitty must have been overjoyed to realize that she had taken the right line in denying that she knew Chancel, when he said, in answer to the judge's stock question as to whether he were guilty:

"Of course not. I have never seen the other defendants before, and have no connection with them."

"You seem to forget," the judge said, "that you were arrested because you were seen to greet Mme. Shiber."

"I greeted no one," Chancel said. "I recall that just before I was arrested, the lady whom I learned here today is Mme. Shiber came towards me on the street. From a little distance, she looked like a friend, and I started to lift my hat. But as she came closer,

I realized I had mistaken her for some one else. I told that to the Gestapo any number of times. Is it a crime to make a mistake in identity these days?"

"It is a crime to have things like this in your possession," the judge rapped out suddenly, and drew out a picture postcard from the documents before him. "This was found in your apartment! A caricature of the Fuehrer, with, 'Vive la France! A bas les Boches!' written on it! That stamps you as an enemy, of the same vile type as the other defendants! How do you explain that?"

I was astounded at the sudden anger displayed by the judge at the production of this exhibit, which he must nevertheless have seen several times before. He seemed as irate as if he had just come upon it for the first time. I could only explain it by the rage with which the Germans always encountered the word "Boche," which they considered the worst term that could possibly be applied to them.

"There must have been thousands of cards like that in circulation," Chancel said. "I received that one in the mail. I can't help what people send me. It might have been posted by your own police to manufacture evidence against me, since they hadn't anything else. How do I know?"

"But you kept it!" the judge roared. "You kept it! That is the proof of your guilt. That is all we need to know! That is enough for us! You are stamped as an enemy of the Reich! And for our enemies we have no pity! You may sit down!"

Chancel turned and walked back to his place. As his eyes met mine, I saw in them a quick flash of recognition, as though he wanted to tell us, "Thanks. I can't say more now."

It was the prosecutor's turn. I wondered what he could have to do, for it seemed to me that the judge had played his rôle for him already. It turned out that there was to be no further examination of witnesses. The Gestapo had done all that. The records of their researches had been placed before the judges, and that was all that was necessary. It was not even considered important that we should know what testimony had been given against us, or who had given it. The few questions the judge had asked us constituted our entire trial. Now the prosecutor was to ask that we be sentenced, in the name of Hitler.

Unnecessary though it seemed, Captain Weber was not going to miss the opportunity to make a long speech. He arranged a heap of documents before him, poured a glass of water from a bottle and gulped it down, and then proceeded to launch himself into an amazing and jumbled discourse, in which known facts were thrown together with guesses and possibilities, without the slightest distinction being made among them. The mere assertion of any detail by the prosecutor seemed to be considered by him as sufficient evidence of its truth—an assumption in which the court evidently concurred.

"Sitting here before us," Weber began, "caught red-handed in their felonious activity in behalf of the enemy who attacked our peaceful nation without provocation and is now being justly punished for it, are the members of an English spy ring. The unceasing vigilance of our military authorities and of the Gestapo has foiled their criminal plans. We have here all the principal traitors to our Fuehrer with one exception—the tailor Chancel, who is still a fugitive, but who will not escape us.

"Mme. Beaurepos took the vilest advantage of our good nature and our clemency towards the conquered, whose treachery in attacking us we were so willing to forget, by operating under the veil of a charitable organization which we permitted to function among our prisoners. She brought English soldiers—our sworn enemies—to her Paris apartment, and returned them to England, together with French soldiers, that they might take up arms against us again, and destroy the lives of Germans. She is as much a murderer as if she herself had fired the shots into the defenseless backs of our brave men. She gave tools and explosives to others to permit them to sabotage our efforts to restore peace and calm to this territory which we hold by the right of conquest."

I looked at Kitty as he said this, an entirely new charge which hadn't been hinted at before. She simply lifted her eyebrows and shrugged her shoulders slightly, as though to say, "What's the use?"

"According to the data in my possession," Weber continued, waving vaguely to the papers before him, "more than 500 English soldiers were returned to service in England. These men were transported to Paris by Christian Ravier, who abused his priestly robes by using them as a shield for the men he brought to the apartment of

Mme. Beaurepos. By this act, he has himself defiled the office he holds, and deserves no consideration because of it.

"Chancel, the fugitive, transported these men to the estate of Tissier, who smuggled them across the border into the free zone. Mme. Shiber supplied the money necessary to carry on this work. Monsieur Corbier was one of the liaison men of this organization. That is the general outline of their rôles. I will now explain their exact activities, one by one."

And he did so for nearly an hour, mingling correct details with pure imagination in the most fantastic manner. I found myself again and again listening to his account as if it had been a story told of other persons, it had so little relation to the facts. I judged that actually they had been able to find out little except what Kitty had confessed; for all the details he mentioned which were exact were such as she might have confessed, incriminating herself, but involving the rest of us only as she was forced to give explanations of our relations with her.

In dealing with Kitty, Weber laid emphasis on the assertion that she was a spy, for which, of course, there was no shred of evidence, and couldn't be, for the accusation was completely untrue. The English soldiers she had sent back to England, he asserted, had carried information about the strength of German garrisons in the towns she had visited, maps showing the emplacement of gun positions, photographs of war plants for the use of the R.A.F.

Father Christian was described first as a dangerous anarchist, then as a Communist. Tissier was set down as an avaricious old man who charged 50 francs a head for smuggling prisoners out of occupied territory. (Who gave them that detail, I wondered? That didn't sound like Kitty). Besides, Tissier wanted to revenge himself on Germany because of his crippled hand, which was a light punishment for his crime of having fought against Germany once before.

At one point, Weber admitted by implication how flimsy was the chain of evidence by depicting Chancel as one of the ringleaders and predicting that when he was caught, much more would be known about our operations. But when he came to Corbier in his speech, being completely without facts, he dwelt upon his diabolical cunning in refusing to admit the known fact that he had shown signs of recognizing me on the street, and that he had succeeded in destroying all evidence against himself except, by a fatal oversight, that damning postcard—"this evidence, gentlemen, that he was a personal enemy of our Fuehrer, Adolf Hitler!"

But what astounded me most was his description of myself.

"And now we come to Mrs. Shiber," he thundered, "an American millionaire, the perfect product of the Anglo-Saxon pluto-democracies, where the rich grind the faces of the poor into the ground, and fatten on their sweat and their labor. By the ill-gotten gains of the sweat-shops that furnished her with her millions, Mrs. Shiber was able to live a life of sybaritic luxury in Paris, far from the harsh and uncivilized atmosphere of the United States. And to what use did she put those millions? To the succor and comfort of our enemies. Seventeen million francs were consumed in these evil machinations——"

I gasped. I couldn't help myself. I had no idea how many dollars were represented by 17,000,000 francs, but I was certain it was more money than I had ever seen in my life. Somehow the precision of this particular lie impressed me more strongly than the curious description of myself which had preceded it.

Dr. Weber took time out to swallow another glass of water. Then he launched into the peroration of his speech.

"But what," he demanded, "is the greatest crime of these defendants? Is it that they have been responsible for the loss of more lives of the soldiers of the Fuehrer? No. That is grave, but it is not the gravest of all. The Fuehrer's soldiers are happy to give their lives that the world may be reborn, strengthened and regenerated, that the New Order may reign for a thousand years to come, under the benevolent guidance of our blessed German nation! The great sin of these defendants is that they have tried to dam the wave of the future, that they have ignorantly and viciously tried to rob the whole world and all its people of the blessings of the future realm of strength and joy for which we Germans have been ready to sacrifice everything.

"This criminal opposition to the great projects of Adolf Hitler is the greatest of all crimes. It is that principle which clarifies the issue before us. What does it matter if we have no complete record of the connection of the defendant Corbier with the others? That would attest only to his minor crime, to his crime of detail. The postcard we found in his house is the proof of his major crime, the crime which transcends all others, his unalterable enmity to the great revolution of our time, to the greatest revolution of history. And of all these others, too, we know—we have heard from their own lips—that they, too, would stand in the way of this great regeneration of a corrupt world. What if they have been clever enough to hide their traces here and there? Must the guilty be freed because we cannot prove exactly when and where and how they sinned, though we know that they are the enemies of the human race? No, *meine Herren!* The guilty must accept their punishment, without equivocation, without quibbling! What right have they to demand that we prove in detail their ignominious acts, into which we deign to pry too far, for fear of coating ourselves with the mire in which they live! They must be lopped off, like diseased members, from the body of the community which they would infect, because they are the bitter enemies of mankind, of Germany, of our great leader, Adolf Hitler!"

He sat down. Judges, attendants, guards, "jury"—every one except ourselves—raised their arms in unison, and shouted, "Heil Hitler!" Weber rose again, a piece of paper in his hand. From it, he read:

"I demand the sentence of death for Frau Beaurepos, Frau Shiber and Herr Ravier. I demand seven years at hard labor for Herr Tissier. I demand three years at hard labor for Herr Corbier. In my opinion this is the just penalty they merit under the law."

CHAPTER THIRTY-TWO

The Sentence

I DIDN'T hear the lawyers for the defense, who were allowed to speak for fifteen minutes apiece. I couldn't follow what they were saying, for the words kept echoing through my head, "I demand the sentence of death for . . . Frau Shiber!"

It wasn't so much that I was frightened, at the moment, or even surprised, for I had been more or less prepared; it was just that this thought monopolized my attention to the exclusion of everything else. I told myself that I would prefer death to years in such a prison as that which I had left. After all, I was no longer young. I had nothing to look forward to except death in prison, or perhaps being freed after my sentence, broken in health, and able to do nothing except await the release of death.

But I had to adjust myself to this idea, which had suddenly become more real than ever before. My mind seemed to be trying to struggle out of a sort of apathy to a new arrangement of values and outlook.

Through the confusion of conflicting ideas which struggled within my brain to reach a new clarity, I remember noticing Captain Weber, sitting at the end of the table, his chin on his hand, and then the presiding judge, and remarking that both seemed cut out of the same pattern, as though one were only another incarnation of the other. What Weber had asked, it seemed to me, the judge would certainly grant. They were too much alike to disagree. One had demanded the death sentence. The other would pronounce it.

I looked towards Kitty. She, too, seemed not to be hearing the drone of the defense lawyers. There was a faraway look in her eyes, and I realized that she must be struggling as I was to bring this new idea into the focus of reality.

I cannot recall a word of what any of the defense attorneys said. I did not even realize when they stopped speaking, for I was only brought back to awareness of the scene about me by the sharp raps of his gavel with which the presiding judge announced that he and his two associates would retire to discuss the verdict. But just as they rose to leave the room, the door opened, and Dr. Hager appeared, out of breath, and apparently highly excited. He went straight up to the presiding judge, opening his brief-case as he approached him. Arrived at the table, he pulled out a folder containing some papers, and handed it to him, talking rapidly, but in a low voice, as he did so.

The judge beckoned to Weber. He and the other two judges put their heads together for a moment. Then there was a great nodding, as though a group of automatic figures had been set in motion all at the same time, and every one sat down again. The judge rapped once more with his gavel.

"I declare this trial reopened," he said. "Important new evidence has just been brought to the attention of the court . . . Monsieur Chancel, stand up!"

Chancel! Then they had discovered whom they had captured!

I had to admire Chancel's presence of mind. He remained perfectly motionless at this unexpected pronouncing of his name. But he was the only one who was not trapped. All our heads swung around towards him.

"Dear me, Herr Chancel," the judge said ironically, "I see that if you have forgotten your name, your friends have not. And I notice that they *do* seem to know you, suddenly. You might as well abandon the comedy, Herr Chancel—or Herr Corbier, if you prefer."

I bit my lip. My only consolation was that I had not been the only one to be caught. In any case, I told myself, the game was up. They knew his identity anyway. It really made no difference, now.

Chancel rose and walked again towards the table. Dr. Hager beamed as he approached. He was obviously very much pleased with himself.

"So it appears that we did have the other ringleader, after all," said the judge. "It seems, Herr Chancel, that you were incautious enough not to destroy your genuine papers, and also to leave them, together with some in the name of Corbier, with one of your friends, who has had the misfortune to be apprehended. Would you like to modify your statement that you don't know the defendants and had nothing to do with their activities?"

"If you are so well informed already," said Chancel, "it seems unnecessary that I should add anything."

"Perhaps you are right," said the presiding judge. "It is quite unnecessary. We know already what your attitude is. Nothing you could say would be likely to change our opinion. It is a matter of indifference to this court whether you admit or continue to deny your obvious connection with this criminal conspiracy."

Captain Weber rose:

"I should like to modify my recommendations to the court," he said, "to include the name of Herr Chancel among those for whom the death penalty is demanded."

"The alteration is noted," the judge said. "You may sit down, Herr Chancel."

Chancel's defense attorney immediately sprang to his feet. The incident had restored my ability to pay attention to what was going on, and this time I listened to the plea, which was based on the fact that Chancel was a member of the Gueules Cassées, the group composed of men wounded in the face during the last war. Chancel's lawyer appealed to the court as a military body to show the respect paid by one soldier to another who had performed his duty and sacrificed his well-being for his country, and pointed out the deference which the German government had often shown towards this organization. For this reason, he concluded, he asked the court not to pronounce the death sentence.

He spoke in German, a language which Chancel did not understand. While his lawyer was speaking, Chancel sat quietly on the bench, staring blankly in front of him, as though indifferent to the whole proceedings.

With the end of his speech, the interrupted program was resumed. The judges filed out of the room, followed, with the same military precision with which they had entered it, by the "jurors." For the first time, now that the case was over, our lawyers were allowed to talk to us. They moved over to our bench, and we talked over the case, at the same time munching some sandwiches and drinking a little red wine, for which one of them sent out. I could hardly refrain from tearing at my sandwich, the first decent food I had seen since my re-arrest, but the first sip of the wine, to which I had become completely unaccustomed, made me dizzy, and I didn't dare take any more.

Chancel, the moment the proceedings were over, turned to us, and said, "Permit me, ladies and gentlemen, to apologize for my tardiness in greeting you. I know that you all understood why."

Father Christian seemed unmoved by the sentence of death asked against him.

"I am quite happy," he told me, "because they didn't get the boys who were with me when I was arrested. I saw them as the Gestapo car which took me away rounded the corner, waiting in different doorways, where I had left them. They looked to me as though they wanted to spring on the car and wrest me away from the Gestapo. Perhaps they would have, if they'd had time to think. But of course we were gone almost as soon as they saw us."

"What happened to them, do you think?" I asked.

"I'm sure they're all right," said Father Christian, "I had given them precise instructions in case of such an accident."

"You mean," I said, "that you had expected that some day you would ring our bell, only to be arrested?"

"Of course," he said. "Why, otherwise, would I have taken the precaution to come first without the boys? We are all in the hand of God, and his ways are mysterious. I had not to question the fate he might decree for me. But in the meantime, 'God helps him who helps himself,' and so I took my precautions."

"What did you tell the boys to do?" I asked.

"They were instructed to go to the hotel where we stayed one night—the one of which I told you," he said. "Its proprietress is a clever woman. I'm sure they're out of the country, like the others."

Monsieur Tissier sat beside us on the bench, saying nothing. His hands were clasped in his lap, and he seemed pondering deeply. I felt guilty for his fate, responsible that he was now in this courtroom, waiting to hear his doom. I turned towards him, and began to try to tell him how sorry I was that we had gotten him into this fix.

"It's not your fault, Madame," he said. "Please don't disturb yourself about me. I assure you, I am not worried about myself."

"But you are so silent," I said. "You seem so downcast."

"I was thinking about my vines," he said. "It is March. I should be trimming the stalks. And the roots should be covered with earth, and channels cut so that the melting snow will drain off the land and not flood my vines. There are a thousand things to do in a vineyard, Madame. I wonder who will care for mine?"

Our lawyers got into an argument among themselves about the probable sentences. One of them said pessimistically, forgetting probably that we were within hearing, that no doubt the sentences had been decided upon before court convened, and that probably the prosecutor's requests would be granted.

"On the contrary," my lawyer said, "I don't think there will be any death sentences at all. I don't believe they will dare sentence Mrs. Shiber to death, since she's an American citizen. The Germans don't want to take any action which would irritate the United States. And if Mrs. Shiber is not given a death sentence, it won't be easy to impose one on any one else. Father Christian would probably escape the death punishment, too, as a priest."

"Yes, but how about my client?" asked Kitty's lawyer.

"Well, the fact that she was born English and is French by marriage ought to help," my lawyer answered. "If she were either all English or all French, it would probably be worse."

"That," Kitty whispered in my ear, "is about the thinnest argument I've ever heard. If that's the only hope he has for me, I might as well give up."

The minutes dragged by, and the judges did not reappear. Conversation died down, and we all sat nervously on our bench, our eyes on the door. One of the lawyers looked at his watch.

"They've been out an hour," he said.

"It couldn't have been any previously prepared sentence, then," one of the others said. "They must really be discussing the case."

But at that moment Chancel's lawyer, who had gone out to see what was happening, came back and dispelled that illusion.

"They aren't discussing the sentence," he said. "They're having lunch. I saw them from the corridor. They left the door half-open. They're stuffing themselves like pigs, and having a high old time while they're about it."

It was two o'clock when the doors opened and the judges filed ceremoniously back into the courtroom. It couldn't have taken more than a few seconds for them to take their places again, but to me it seemed hours before the presiding judge rose from his seat, picked up a sheet of paper, and read the sentences. They were:

For Kitty, death; for Father Christian, death; for Chancel, five years at hard labor; for Tissier, four years at hard labor; for myself, three years at hard labor.

The thought of three more years of prison surged through my mind and overcame me with horror. I half-opened my mouth to cry: "Kill me, too—but not three more years of that terrible prison. I'll die there!"

But Kitty caught me by the arm, and whispered into my ear:

"Control yourself, Etta. Don't let these Germans see us lose our dignity. Don't cry. You don't want them to have the satisfaction of making an American cry."

I was at once profoundly ashamed of myself. I had received the lightest sentence of all, and when it was pronounced, I had for a moment thought only of myself. And Kitty—Kitty, who had just heard herself condemned to death—was consoling me, encouraging me! I squeezed her hand hard, and choked down the sobs I had felt welling up within me.

Now that the trial was over, no one worried any more about our being together, and once more we were locked into the prison van together, without a guard, for the trip back to the Cherche-Midi. Both of us realized that this would probably be the last time we would ever see each other, in this jouncing, evil-smelling vehicle in which we were being carried back to jail like freight. I broke down, and laying my head on Kitty's chest, wept bitterly, but this time it was more for her than for myself, and for sorrow at our parting. Kitty smoothed my hair, and said:

"Cry now, Etta, if you like. You'll feel better for it. But promise me to be strong before the Germans. Never weep where they can see you. If you must cry, hold your tears back until night, when no one will hear or see you. That is what I did in prison, Etta. I was not weeping for myself, but because I had brought you into this fatal adventure. I should have made you go home when there was still time. Believe me, your sentence hurts me more than mine.

"Don't worry about me. Promise me that you will never think of me sadly. I am not sad. I did what I had to do. I knew the price, and I am willing to pay it. I have given England back 150 lives for the one she is losing now. Think of that when you think of me. Remember that I was not one who failed, but who succeeded, who won a 150-to-one victory against the Germans. Smile when my name comes to your mind, as you used to smile at me in the old days. Forget the troubles and the worries of the past months, and remember only the strong young boys with the brave hearts whom we sent home again . . .

"There was a time when I was terrified at the thought of death; but not now. I have become accustomed to that thought now. Millions will have died before this war is over, and one more death will make little difference—especially when by that death I have purchased renewed life for so many others . . . Perhaps death comes easier if it comes unexpectedly, in action, when a bullet strikes without even being noticed. But even though its coming has been announced to me in advance, I can look it in the face and not be afraid. I have done my task. I have earned my rest."

She was silent for a moment, and then she smiled sadly, and said to me, so softly that I could hardly hear her over the noise of the van, as though she were speaking to herself:

"And when the war is over, go to England, and walk along the embankment of the Thames, in the spring, where I always used to walk. I will be with you . . . See if you can find some of the boys we sent to England. Tell them that as I once helped them, now they must help me. They must carry on the work I can no longer do by continuing to be what they have always been—the loyal and unwavering defenders of England."

The van came to a clanking stop. We had reached the prison.

CHAPTER THIRTY-THREE

Cut Rate for Freedom

I REMAINED in the Cherche-Midi prison until May 16, when I was
sent, with twenty-five other women who had been sentenced to
prison terms, to the prison of Fresnes—the same whose hospital had
appeared so horrible to me.

It was a large jail, five stories high, which reminded me of pictures
I had seen of Sing Sing. It surrounded a small courtyard, where I
learned that prisoners were allowed to spend two hours each day in
the afternoon, and I looked forward to getting the air which had
been denied me at Cherche-Midi. But I was to have no such luck.

My sentence, which called for hard labor, should actually have
worked out in practice to solitary confinement, for there was in fact
no hard labor which a woman of my age could perform at Fresnes.
But the warden found it impossible even to keep me in solitary confinement, for the prison was too crowded to allow a single prisoner
to have a whole cell to herself. All he could do, therefore, was to rule
that I must remain indoors when the others went out.

Although I missed the opportunity to get fresh air and to move
about a bit, I nevertheless found the two hours when I was left
to myself the pleasantest of the whole day. Continuous solitary confinement would no doubt have had a very bad effect on me; but
since I was cooped up day and night with other cell-mates, the two
hours when I was left alone provided a blissful change. I cannot hope
to describe the intense yearning for a few minutes' privacy which
besets prisoners forced to live day in, day out in the constant presence
of other persons, as I had to do at Cherche-Midi. My daily two hours
alone in the cell were so welcome to me that I was actually afraid I
might be permitted to go out into the courtyard with the others. It
was worth the loss of exercise and fresh air. I was very careful never
to admit to any one how I felt about it, for fear my routine would
be changed.

314

Fresnes had one advantage over Cherche-Midi—a prison for women alone, it had women guards. But the food was simply indescribable—much worse than at Cherche-Midi, a thing which I would have thought impossible before I made the change. I could hardly choke it down, though I was always hungry. In quantity, the rations here, as at Cherche-Midi, were starvation portions—certainly not enough to keep an adult healthy for any considerable period.

"Breakfast" came at 8:30 A.M. It consisted of a coffee substitute made from barley. Lunch was at eleven—a colorless liquid concoction with a nauseating odor, accompanied by ice-cold smelly potatoes. The first time I tasted that soup, I promptly threw it up. I had a chance to try again at five in the afternoon. That was the last meal of the day, and it consisted also of the vile-tasting soup.

I do not think that I could have survived six months at Fresnes if it had not been for the Quakers, who managed to get me extra items of food from time to time. Realizing that something was wrong when I failed to meet him at the Ritz, Mr. Marvel had traced me again, and during all the time I was at Fresnes, he saw to it that I received parcels from his organization. I am sure that I owe my life to that aid. It was malnutrition, certainly, which was responsible for the high death rate at Fresnes. Almost daily I heard the bells of the tiny prison chapel toll for funerals. Very often, in moments of depression, I heard that sound and told myself that one day it would sound for me, that I would never leave Fresnes alive.

There was only one bed in my cell, for three of us. Because I was the oldest, I was allowed to sleep in it. The other two had to sleep on the floor.

One of my two inmates was a rather remarkable woman, Mme. Berthet, tall, blonde and with expressive blue eyes. She was about forty-five, with an American mother and an Alsatian father. She had been born in Alsace while it was under German rule, but her thinking was French, not German. She told me that it was because of a cousin that she found herself in jail. He had been a prisoner of war in Germany, and had succeeded in escaping. She hid him, and both were arrested. She got two years for aiding an escaped prisoner.

Mme. Berthet was a woman of exceptional accomplishments. She had studied law in Germany, and had practised as a consulting lawyer in Paris. She was also a legal interpreter, being equally conversant with French, German and English.

She had already served eleven months of her sentence when I arrived at Fresnes, and had hopes of being released shortly. She told me that her husband had influential connections with important German officials, and, indeed, either she or he must have had some friends in high places, for the first Friday I spent in jail, she said to me, "Well, I'll see you Monday. I'm going home for the week-end."

"What?" I exclaimed incredulously.

"Oh, I always spend the week-ends at home," she said lightly. "I'm the only prisoner in Fresnes who takes the week-ends off."

I thought she was joking, but a few minutes later a guard came for her, and sure enough, she didn't return until Monday morning.

When she returned, I couldn't refrain from expressing my surprise at such a curious procedure.

"I know one thing," I said to her, "and that is that the Germans don't allow any one such privileges unless they get something in return for it. I don't know what you do in exchange for your weekends of freedom—but I've had an experience like this before, and I know what I suspect."

Mme. Berthet looked at me teasingly, apparently not in the least perturbed by what I had said.

"Well, now," she said mockingly, "what do you suspect?"

I told her about Marthe Wenzinger, "an Alsatian like yourself," I explained. Mme. Berthet listened with an amused smile on her lips, and burst into a little chuckle when I had finished.

"So you think I'm a spy, too, do you, Mrs. Shiber?" she laughed. "To begin with, you've already been sentenced. Why should the Gestapo bother about wasting a spy's time on you now? You're dead right about one thing, though. The Germans don't hand out any privileges without compensation. I pay for my week-ends out—or rather my husband does; but it's not the kind of transaction you think. It's just an ordinary business arrangement. He pays cash."

"You mean your husband pays somebody to let you spend the week-ends at home?" I gasped.

"Exactly," said Mme. Berthet. "Everything has its price, you know, especially in Nazidom. You may remember how we used to hear about the incorruptibility of Nazi civil servants? Don't believe it. They'll sell anything. It's costing my husband a pretty penny now for my weekly vacations, and he's trying to settle the matter once and for all by buying me out of here entirely. I imagine he'll succeed."

She was right. Only two weeks later she was released, and I said good-bye to her, thinking that I wouldn't see her again.

But some ten days after she had left, a guard came to the cell and told me there was a visitor to see me. She took me, not to the usual visitors' room, where wire screens separated the prisoners from those who came to see them, but to a small office, where she left me alone with—Madame Berthet! She was completely transformed, now that she was no longer a jail-bird, elegantly dressed, her hair elaborately arranged, and in appearance quite a different person from my former cell-mate.

"I don't imagine you expected to see me, Mrs. Shiber," she said, "but you see, I haven't forgotten you. How would you like to get out of here?"

"Of course I'd like to get out," I said. "But how?" I was suspicious of her again. There was something curious about all this, and about her ability to arrange a private interview with me so easily.

"The same way I did," Mme. Berthet said. "I've been talking to my husband about your case. He thinks it can be arranged."

"I don't know what to say," I said confusedly. "Just what is your husband's means of influence with the Germans? How does he arrange all this? What do they want me to do?—for I'm sure that I won't be allowed out of jail for nothing."

"Oh, dear, Mrs. Shiber!" Mme. Berthet said. "You still suspect me of trickery, don't you? Well, now, I'll tell you how my husband got his influence. It's a long story and it has nothing to do with the case; but you asked for it, so here it is. You'll see that you needn't worry.

"My husband owned a factory making agricultural machinery before the war. Shortly after the occupation, he was visited by a representative of a German concern which asked him if he would consider selling his factory. He refused; and immediately he began to find it impossible to operate. He couldn't get raw materials, of which the supply was controlled by the Germans; work was constantly being hampered by visits of officials for 'inspections,' followed by impositions of irksome regulations; his workers were subjected to pressure to move to other employment; and he found himself facing the prospect of having to shut up shop. The Germans let him taste about a month of this treatment, and then their man came back again. There was nothing else to do. He sold out. Incidentally, all this occurred about the time I was arrested, and perhaps my sentence would have been lighter if they hadn't been working on him at the time.

"You have to give them credit for one thing—they paid a good price. They have plenty of money, of course; they get it from us for nothing. . . . Well, there was my husband, an active man all his life, left with nothing to do. He was chafing at his inactivity, and finally he hit upon a plan.

"I suppose it was what had happened to himself that gave him the idea. He paid particular attention to the effort the Germans were making to acquire majority interests in all French business. The object was pretty plain. While they had unlimited amounts of money at their disposition, and unlimited means of coercion, the Germans planned to buy up all French businesses, in perfectly legal form and according to French procedure. Thus, after the war, when the occupation of France will have to end, Germany will *own* France. She will have economic control over the country which can't be broken. Even if she loses the war, she will still have won France."

"But certainly, if Germany loses the war, she will have to give back what she has taken," I objected.

"How?" Mme. Berthet asked. "It may seem easy to you, Mrs. Shiber, but remember that all these transactions were perfectly legal ones, under French law. The businesses will have been bought and paid for. Ownership of stock often can't be traced, because most French stocks, unlike your American ones, are made out to the bearer, not to any particular person. Sometimes French citizens are used to represent the Germans, who are the real owners of a business that seems to be in French hands. And remember that every one of these changes will have been consecrated by further contracts and developments made since on the faith that the first transfers are valid. To try to untangle the structure after the war might mean wrecking the whole economic system of the country, or tearing down the legal principles on which the forced exchanges were based.

"Now my husband reasoned that the Germans needed Frenchmen to act as agents, and dummy owners, and acquirers of stock in these affairs, so he offered his services. That is the origin of his influence with the Germans. He has done them great services in securing important transfers of French businesses to German ownership. He receives heavy commissions for each such transaction, and has amassed quite a considerable fortune. This activity has also put him in touch with many influential Nazis, and that is how he was able to find the right persons to approach, first to let me get out of jail during week-ends, and finally to buy me out of prison altogether. He may be able to do the same for you."

"I am afraid," I said coldly, "that I would prefer not to have any dealings with a man who is selling out his own countrymen to the enemy."

"Oh, come now," Mme. Berthet laughed, "don't be so stiff-necked. My husband says some one is going to do it, so it might as well be he."

"Not long ago," I said, "I met a fourteen-year-old boy who had to support himself and his mother because his father was a prisoner in Germany. He refused to sell papers, the easiest way for him to make money, because it was spreading German propaganda. He could have made the same excuse as your husband."

Mme. Berthet glanced furtively about the room. Then she came closer, and whispered, as though she were afraid of being heard outside the room.

"Mme. Shiber," she said, "I think I can trust you. I must tell you the real reason why my husband is doing this. He is keeping duplicate records of every transaction with which he is concerned, and of the means of coercion used to force sales. After the war, it will be easier to annul the sales he has handled than most of the others. He is pretending to help the Germans in order to be able to undo their work afterwards. He will be one of the principal witnesses

against the Germans when these transactions are reviewed later. Now
do you understand, Mrs. Shiber?"

She looked straight into my eyes with those clear expressive eyes
of her own, and I was convinced, for the moment at least, that she
was telling the truth.

"Yes," I said, "now I understand. But what do you think you can
do for me?"

"I spoke of your case to my husband," she said, "and he took it
up with some of his German connections. They said yours is not
nearly as simple as mine, partly because you are a foreigner, partly
because political considerations are involved, partly because your
offense was much graver. But he finally got them to name a price.
To get me out, he paid 100,000 francs. They will free you for one
million."

"A million francs!" I said. "Goodness! That sounds like a lot of
money! What is it in dollars?"

"At forty francs to the dollar, just $25,000."

"I could never raise that much," I said. "All I have in the world
is a few thousand francs in the prison office, and $1,000 which was
sent to me at the American Embassy while I was in jail."

"That doesn't matter," Mme. Berthet said. "My husband would
be glad to advance you the million francs. All you need do is deposit
$25,000 in his name in an American bank."

"You don't understand," I explained. "I haven't $25,000 in America
or anywhere else. I've never in my life had that much money at one
time."

"You must be joking!" Mme. Berthet said. "My husband made inquiries, and the Germans told him you spent millions financing the
escapes of the English soldiers. You surely don't expect me to believe
that you haven't $25,000 to free yourself?

"Look! I'll put all my cards on the table. It wasn't only because
of interest in your case that I took the trouble of trying to arrange
this way out for you. My husband, as I told you, has plenty of money
now—in francs and in Paris—but who knows what it will be worth
after the war? He's very anxious to find some way to convert some
of it into dollars, in a New York bank—and this provides a means.
Now don't you see, Mrs. Shiber, how advantageous this will be for

all of us? You get your freedom, my husband is enabled to insure our future. I'm sure it's worth $25,000 to you to be out of this hole."

She opened her bag and drew out a sheaf of papers.

"Here," she said, "everything is prepared. All you have to do is to sign this document authorizing your bank to transfer $25,000 to an account in my husband's name—we have left a blank here, where you can fill in the name of the correct bank—and we will have you out of here in a few days."

"But, really, I'm telling you the truth," I protested. "I'm not a millionaire, whatever the Germans said. I haven't that much money."

Mme. Berthet looked at me for a moment with a curious twisted smile. Then she lifted her eyebrows, sighed, and stuffed the papers back into her bag.

"Oh, well," she said, "I see how it is. You think the price is too high. You are saying to yourself, I suppose, that since my husband wants dollars in New York, he has no interest in beating the Germans down. I assure you, Mrs. Shiber, you can't bargain with these people. They set their price, and that's all there is to it. We can't do any better for you.

"Think it over. If you change your mind, you will be allowed to communicate with me through the prison officials. They will send for me if you ask them to. I will give you a few days before my husband has to tell the officials with whom he dealt that you value your money more than your freedom. It may create some difficulties for us. I'm sure we wouldn't have gone so far if we had dreamed that you wouldn't be anxious to accept and grateful to us for helping you.

"But I advise you not to hesitate too long. People are saying that America may enter the war soon. In that case, you won't be able to get out, at any price."

I went back to my cell in a daze. Mme. Berthet's proposition had left me in a curious frame of mind. I couldn't make out where, in her curiously mixed character, self-interest ended and a genuine desire to be helpful began. She had evidently carried away a very false idea of me, too, since she believed that I had plenty of money, but would rather stay in jail than part with it. How happy I would have been to pay the last penny I owned to leave this prison! But when she said $25,000, she might as well have said a million. One was as impossible for me to get as the other.

Was it really true that America might enter the war? Then what would happen to me? The American Embassy would close, Mr. Marvel and the Quakers would no longer be able to help me—and I would be alone and a prisoner in an enemy land!

Mme. Berthet's visit certainly did not cheer me up.

CHAPTER THIRTY-FOUR

Micheline

M<small>Y OTHER</small> cell-mate at Fresnes was Micheline Seurat, a widow of thirty, pretty and frail, now serving her second sentence. Both had been for the same offense—referring to the Germans as "Boches." The first time they had given her six months. This time it was a year.

"But, Micheline," I asked her, "after you had gone to jail for using that word once, why weren't you more careful thereafter?"

Micheline shrugged her little shoulders.

"*C'était plus fort que moi.* I couldn't control myself. It just escaped me. You would have done the same. It was at that Gaumont-Palace affair."

"What Gaumont-Palace affair?" I asked. I hadn't heard anything about it. I knew the Gaumont-Palace, of course, the largest moving picture theatre in Paris, holding some five to six thousand people.

"Why, it was in all the papers," Micheline said. "But then, you must have been in jail at the time. It was like this. I went to see a picture there one evening and there was a newsreel which consisted of nothing but pictures of Hitler—the Fuehrer visiting the front lines, the Fuehrer pinning the Iron Cross on a soldier's tunic, the Fuehrer inspecting a munitions plant, the Fuehrer surrounded by school children, the Fuehrer this and the Fuehrer that. It was disgusting! Let the Germans make a God of him if they want to, but why should they try to ram him down our throats? Naturally every one began whistling and booing." (In France, it should be explained, whistling is a sign of disapproval, not of approval). "The film was stopped, the lights were put on, and a Gestapo officer came out on the stage and said the film would be shown again, from the beginning, and if there were any further disturbances, we would have to take the consequences. So they started again, and the whistling began again. The show was stopped, and the audience told to leave.

"We all filed out, most of us not at all put out at not seeing the rest of the show. We were pleased with having stopped the Hitler picture. But as we came out of the theatre, we found German police at every exit. They were arresting every fiftieth person to come out, man, woman or child, to be punished for the insult to the Fuehrer.

"It was really terrible. There they had us pinned in, in single file, between two lines of Germans, and at the head an officer was counting the people as they filed out, to himself, so you couldn't guess how near you were to the fatal number. He would say, '*Fünfzig,*' and the guards would pull the fiftieth person out of the line and hustle him off to one side. I would have been all right, for they took a young man just three places in front of me, so I couldn't possibly have been caught, but I got angry when they pulled him away, and said, '*Sales Boches,*' just a little too loud. So here I am."

A few weeks in the same cell with Micheline, and I became almost a member of her family. She told me all the gossip about her relatives, which ones were nice, which were not, who had money, who had divorced. I shared her admiration of some and her indignation of others. And naturally, in my turn, I began to tell her about my own past life, and my friends—chiefly, of course, Kitty. I told her often how painful it was not to have had any news of her, not to know whether she was still alive or whether the sentence of execution had already been carried out. One day, when I was talking of Kitty, Micheline said,

"I have been thinking about your friend, and I believe I have thought of a scheme to get news of her."

"How?" I asked.

"Well, since she was not transferred here when you were, she probably stayed at the Cherche-Midi prison. Now, whenever any of their prisoners are ill, they send them to the hospital here."

"I know," I said. "I was here once myself."

"Well, if we could get in touch with any prisoners from Cherche-Midi, we might be able to find out something about your friend. There are almost always some of them here. The cleaning in the hospital is done by woman prisoners. At the exercise hour, I will try to find one of them who may be able to ask a few questions for us."

But it was only three days later that Micheline succeeded in locating one of the cleaning women.

"You should see the girl I found," Micheline said. "I don't believe you could understand a word she says, though. She's as tough as they come, a *fille du milieu* from Montmartre, and she talks underworld slang exclusively. She's been here since before the war. Her gang murdered an informer and she got four years as an accomplice. Her name is Titi. She'll see what she can find out, and all she asks is that you get her some '*mégots*.'"

"Some what?" I asked.

"I told you you wouldn't understand her," Micheline said triumphantly. "That means cigarettes."

"I'd be glad to," I said, "but how can I?"

"Oh, you can get them all right," Micheline said. "Ask the guard to buy you some out of your money in the prison office. Then I'll take them to Titi. Of course, you'll have to pay Black Market prices, and throw in a good tip for the guard."

For the next week there was no news. Micheline returned every day from the exercise period to report that no one in the hospital knew anything about Kitty. There were a dozen Cherche-Midi patients there at the time, and I thought it an ominous sign that with so many of them at Fresnes, none had even heard Kitty's name.

But finally, Micheline returned triumphant.

"I've good news for you," she said. "Your friend is still at Cherche-Midi. And do you know what Titi is doing? Really, you should get her a mountain of cigarettes! She is trying to arrange a meeting between you!"

"A meeting!" I said. "How can that be?"

"One of the patients in the hospital here now works in the Cherche-Midi laundry," Micheline explained. "She is returning in a few days. She was the one who knew Kitty was there, because she distributes the laundry to the prisoners. She will take a message to Kitty to pretend to be ill so that she can be sent here, and then you will pretend to be ill also, and have to go to the hospital as well. Titi will see to it that you are put in adjoining beds. What do you say?"

"I'd love to see Kitty again," I said with a sigh. "But I doubt if it will work. You have to be much more than really sick to be sent to the hospital here. If the prison doctor were concerned about his charges, I would be there now. My health is bad as it is. I've always had high blood pressure, and I can feel that my heart is not functioning well now."

This was the strict truth, for the bad food and my emotional reactions to prison life had had a deleterious effect on my health. I often lay awake all night, because of the irregularity of my heartbeat. I had not complained of it, because my experience with the hospital had been that it was no improvement over a cell, but now, I thought, if by any chance Kitty should be brought here, I would have a real illness to complain of, and perhaps I could see my dearest friend once more.

I went to sleep that night quite happy. I thought Titi's scheme fantastic and impractical, but even the little ray of hope it gave me tranquilized me: and for the first time for several nights, I went easily off to sleep, to dream that Kitty and I were back together in our beloved apartment, before the shadow of war had fallen over it.

CHAPTER THIRTY-FIVE

A New Cell-Mate

MR. MARVEL paid me another visit, bringing with him a welcome parcel containing several cans of food, potato salad, tuna fish, bread and sugar. He was accompanied by a snub-nosed bespectacled German, whose job was to listen to everything he said, to make sure that he didn't exceed his privileges.

The German's presence infuriated me, for there were two questions I particularly wanted to ask. One was whether he knew anything about Kitty. The other was if it were true that America was about to enter the war.

I asked outright about Kitty, but the German immediately intervened.

"You know you have no right to ask such questions," he said. "You should not bother Mr. Marvel with them."

I looked in despair towards Micheline, and it seemed to me that I saw her lips pouting to pronounce the fatal word. I frowned sternly at her.

A few minutes later I tried to phrase my second question so that the German wouldn't realize what I was trying to find out.

"Thank you again for coming to see me, Mr. Marvel," I said. "Do you expect to stay on even if America enters the war?"

But the German was on the alert.

"If you persist in putting improper questions to Mr. Marvel," he said sternly, "we cannot permit him to continue to visit you."

We could hardly wait for the cell door to close before we pounced upon the food Mr. Marvel had brought, wolfing it down gluttonously.

"Thank you for that murderous look," Micheline murmured through a full mouth, as soon as the excitement of getting real food had subsided a bit. "I was just going to say 'Boche' once more. They're so stupid! What harm would it do for you to know what has happened to your friend? Is that going to upset their sacred Fuehrer?"

At the exercise period that day, Micheline's talk with Titi brought real news. As soon as she had been locked into the cell again with me, she threw her arms around my neck and whispered in my ear: "Guess what? A message from your friend!"

"No!" I squealed. "What did she say?"

"She's going to try to get into the hospital here!" said Micheline.

"Oh, if only she can!" I said fervently. Looking back, I don't know why I wanted so strongly to see Kitty again, under the circumstances. But I did. It wasn't reasonable, perhaps, but then sentiment rarely is.

"How did you find out?" I asked.

"A new patient from Cherche-Midi had a message from the laundry woman," Micheline explained. "The laundry woman saw Kitty and told her of the plan, and Kitty said that she would do her best if—Oh!"

Micheline's little exclamation told me at once that she had stopped herself just as she was about to say something she hadn't intended I should hear. It wasn't difficult to imagine what it would have been. Kitty would try to do it if her sentence wasn't carried out in the meantime.

I began figuring how much time had elapsed since the trial. It was almost exactly three months after March 7, the date of our trial. I knew the death sentence had to be approved by the military Kommandantur of Paris, and if Kitty's lawyer were energetic, I assumed that he might be able to appeal her case all the way up to Berlin. Even so, considering how cavalierly the Germans dealt with procedure, it seemed that Kitty couldn't count on much more time.

And as I made this calculation, suddenly, without warning, I burst into a spasm of weeping. The thought of Kitty's execution, which had gradually passed into the background of my mind, again occupied the first place in my thoughts. The hope of seeing her again had suddenly been routed by the realization that at any moment, even now, she might be paying the supreme penalty for her acts. And in addition to the sorrow for Kitty which swept over me like a wave, I was overcome by a feeling of guilt because I had given so little thought to her plight since I had been in prison. Once again, I had been pitying myself, the luckiest of all of us.

Micheline sat beside me on our one bed, and put her arm around my shoulders.

"Don't cry for the evil that is going to happen," she said softly. "Perhaps it may never come. My mother always used to tell me, when I was a little girl, and cried in anticipation of something I feared, that it was soon enough to meet trouble when it came, and that there was no point in crying ahead of time, for there would be plenty of opportunity for tears when the bad news really came . . . Besides, I don't think your friend is going to be executed. The Germans don't wait three months to carry out their sentences. If they had meant to kill your friend, they would have done it already."

"Do you really think so, Micheline?" I asked. "You aren't saying that only to console me?"

"No, it's true," she said. "I was in Lille when some persons were sentenced to death at noon, and we heard the firing squads an hour later."

On Mr. Marvel's next visit, he had with him, not only the German guide, but also a Frenchman, whom he introduced to me by saying:

"As I am obliged to return to the United States, I wanted to present to you Mr. Maurice Fleury, who will take over my work. He will come to see you from time to time, just as I did, on behalf of the Quakers."

This announcement was a heavy blow to me. Mr. Marvel represented not only my sole contact with the outside world, but also, to me, America. No matter how assiduous his French successor might be, he could not possibly mean as much to me as one of my own countrymen. While Mr. Marvel was still visiting me, I could tell myself that I was not entirely cut off from my own country, a prisoner in a foreign land. But with his departure I would feel deserted and alone.

I saw that my expression had made him realize how much his announcement had affected me, but he could say nothing to console me, for the German was actually watching our lips, ready to pounce upon us for uttering unpermitted thoughts even before they had been made audible. Nor could I ask the question which rose in my mind immediately: What of America and the war? This time, however, it was hardly necessary. I could guess the answer from the news I had just heard. America could not yet be at war, or Mr. Marvel would not be able to return to the United States; but that event was probably considered imminent, or he would not be leaving.

All we could do was to exchange sympathetic glances. Then the three men left the cell, and I remained alone with my thoughts, for it was the exercise hour, and the other prisoners were all in the courtyard.

For a brief moment, I was seized by a giddy feeling of panic. America is preparing to enter the war, I thought, and all Americans are returning home. The American Embassy, my last hope, the final refuge to which I might cling, will close. Even the faint moral support its existence gave me will disappear now. I will be entirely in the power of the enemy. Who knows how long the war will last? If it goes on longer than my term, I will remain a prisoner. I will never escape alive from the horrible captivity, I told myself in despair.

But then the thought of Kitty came to my mind, and once more gave me strength.

"Why am I complaining," I said to myself, "when she is bearing so bravely a lot much more desperate than mine?"

Perhaps it was because I had lost hope of early release that I set to work now to compile my prison almanac. All the prisoners had their private calendars, on which they checked off the days they had served, but so far I had not made one. I had a sort of unexpressed superstitious belief in some miracle, which would bring about my release suddenly and unexpectedly. With the departure of Mr. Marvel and my fear that soon all Americans would have left France, that naïve hope faded away; and I accepted resignedly the conclusion that I would have to serve my full term.

I therefore prepared my prison calendar, with a line for each day of the three years I would have to serve, and each night crossed off one of the lines. Micheline saw me at it, and one day glanced idly at my calendar.

"You've shortened your sentence by one day, my friend," she observed, tossing it back to me.

"How?" I asked, as dismayed by the prospect of one day more in jail as though it made much difference in the dreary reach of three long years.

"Because," said Micheline, "you are unlucky enough to be serving until March 7, 1944. And 1944 happens to be a leap year, so that February will have twenty-nine days."

Silently, I added one more line to my calendar, making it 1,096 days I would have to serve instead of 1,095. I felt, as I did it, an absurd resentment at the judge who had cheated me of an extra day of freedom, by making my sentence extend just one week beyond that extra day.

Thirty days had been crossed off on my calendar since the message from Kitty, and there had been no further news. Had she been unsuccessful in her attempt to simulate sickness? Or—but I didn't dare think of the possible alternative.

Day after day Micheline returned from the exercise period only to report that Titi had no more news. Prisoners from the Cherche-Midi jail arrived constantly at the Fresnes hospital, but none of them had any word from her.

"Perhaps," I said to Micheline one day, "the Germans discovered that messages could be carried between the two prisons. Or it may be that the laundress was moved to other work, and can't keep in touch with the other prisoners any more."

"I tell you what I'll do," Micheline said. "When I see Titi this afternoon, I'm going to ask her to try to get word back by some other patient returning to Cherche-Midi. If our laundress has failed us, perhaps we can get another messenger."

I waited anxiously for her return, but when the exercise period ended, Micheline did not return. I heard the other prisoners entering their cells at four, as usual, but my cell-mate did not come back. I could hardly take my eyes off the door, and I jumped at the slightest noise outside. But at six, Micheline was still missing.

When the guard came in with the big pot full of the disgusting liquid referred to in the prison as soup, I couldn't refrain from asking about Micheline.

"My cell-mate didn't come back rrom her afternoon exercise," I said. "Do you know what happened to her?"

The guard looked at me stolidly as she ladled my portion of soup out into my bowl, picked up her pot and walked out without a word. I wanted to throw the bowl of soup after her, I was so furious.

I didn't sleep all night, worrying about Micheline's fate, and also because her disappearance, if it was permanent, meant cutting me off from Titi and possible news from Kitty. At seven in the morning, when a key grated in the lock, I was still awake. I jumped up quickly, thinking Micheline was being brought back. Perhaps she had been overheard talking to Titi and had spent a night in the punishment cell.

But no! The door opened, and the guard pushed a strange woman into the cell, then came in behind her, and began gathering up Micheline's few poor belongings—a nightgown, a thin cloak, some underwear, a few toilet articles. She tied them up into a bundle, and went out without a word. Obviously Micheline was not coming back; and I was left alone in the cell with the stranger.

How I hated my new cell-mate! It was not her fault, but the resentment I felt against the sudden disappearance of Micheline, at this moment when I was torn with anxiety about Kitty and counted desperately on her to get me news, was transferred to the woman who had had the bad luck to replace her.

The new arrival was about 50. She sat down easily on the end of my bed, as though she felt quite at home in prison. I decided that she had not just entered it, for her hair had been dyed blond, but since the last opportunity she had had to care for it, some two inches of a grayish-dark layer had grown beneath the dyed portion. Her face was worn and flabby, and there were heavy pockets under her eyes. She looked like a woman worn out by a hectic and probably none too savory past.

She cast a glance at my calendar, which I had attached to the wall. "Three years, *hein*?" she said. "What was that for—stealing?"

I was indignant. Then it occurred to me that, after all, it wasn't particularly surprising that a jail-bird should be suspected of theft. I didn't feel like confiding in her, either. So I simply said, "No, not stealing."

"Embezzlement?"

"No."

"Well, don't tell me," she said sarcastically, "I love to play guessing games."

She looked me over carefully, then inspected the clothes I had hung against the wall, and said, disappointedly:

"I get it now. You're just one of those politicals they've got crowding the prisons these days. Right?"

I nodded. The tone of her voice indicated that she considered me an impostor, practically without any right to be in jail at all. She obviously had nothing but contempt for "politicals," who got into jail fraudulently, without committing any of the crimes more honest criminals had to perpetrate to gain admission.

And Louise Dallon was, indeed, familiar with prisons. She had already, she told me, served six sentences, totalling twelve years. She specialized in a particular type of stealing. She would take a job as a cook under a false name in some wealthy household, and at the first favorable opportunity would make off with everything valuable she could carry away.

"I got off easy this time, considering my record," she said casually. "Only a year. I'm sure if I'd worked it a little more cleverly I could have gotten off entirely. They've got so many politicals like you in the jails, they haven't any room for us any more. You'd be surprised how many people up on light charges are acquitted just because there's no place to put them."

She shook her head wonderingly.

"These are funny times," she said. "You don't meet the same kind of people any more. You politicals aren't so much fun, if you don't mind my saying so. Sort of stuffy. . . . Now take the Black Maria that brought me here from Rouen. Six of us there were in it. And would you believe it, I was the only legitimate one? Mine was the usual—I cleaned out an apartment. But the others! No business to be there at all. Babes in the wood, all of them! We were all one-year people. I did something for it. I had a right to be there. But the others! Well, I wouldn't let them put any airs on with me—calling themselves prisoners! One of them had drawn capital V's on the walls of houses; another one had shouted, 'Vive de Gaulle!' Then there was a woman who had some English leaflets dropped from airplanes in her house, and another who was arrested for listening to the London broadcasts. The most desperate criminal in the lot was a woman who refused to serve a German soldier in a grocery store! What's the country coming to when people like that can call themselves criminals?"

And without the slightest transition, she switched to:

"How's the grub here?"

"Terrible," I said. "But I get special parcels every once in a while, and I'll share with you, if you'll do something for me."

The idea had come to me while she was talking that an old hand at jail life like herself might make an even better go-between than Micheline. If there was any way to get around prison regulations, she ought to know it.

I told her that I wasn't allowed to leave the cell, and that I wanted her to find out for me what had happened to Micheline, and to get in touch with Titi again for me.

"Titi?" she exclaimed. "Which Titi? Not Titi of the Place du Tertre?"

"I don't know," I said. "All I know is that she's from Montmartre, and got four years because she belonged to a gang that killed a man."

"That's the one!" she said. "That's Titi, all right."

And just as I thought everything was working out beautifully, and that she would be the ideal person to get in touch with an old acquaintance, she exploded:

"*Eh non, madame! Jamais!* Talk to Titi of the Place du Tertre! Never! I wouldn't stoop to speak to her if she were the last person on earth. The likes of me speak to the likes of her! I ought to scratch your eyes out for asking it."

I shrank back, half-terrified and half-bewildered at the rigidity of the criminal hierarchy. But then Louise laughed hoarsely.

"Oh, well, you don't know any better," she said. "You're only a political. But talk to Titi for you! *Non, ma 'tite 'dame. Ça, jamais!*"

CHAPTER THIRTY-SIX

Louise Clears Up a Mystery

IN THE next few days, my conversations with Louise gave me a glimpse into a strange new world, whose conceptions were very different from those I had been used to, but which was no less hemmed in by rigid conventions than my own. One of the most astonishing features of her underworld thinking to me, who had been accustomed to think of criminals as persons who had rejected ordinary morality, was that, on the contrary, her moral scruples remained, and even, one might say, were enhanced, by the fact that in justifying her own way of living she was obliged to assert her own blamelessness all the more violently.

Thus, when I ventured to ask her if she believed in religion, she almost jumped down my throat, violently insulted that I had even presumed to suggest that she might not be deeply religious. She informed me that she never missed church on Sunday.

"Well, then," I said, "you must believe in the Ten Commandments."

"Of course I do," she answered aggressively. "Why?"

"Even the seventh commandment?" I asked.

"Which one is that?" she asked suspiciously.

"Thou shalt not steal," I reminded her.

"I see what you're driving at," she said. "You're like the lawyers. You call it stealing, what I do. Well, it isn't stealing. The rich people only call it that because they've got the law on their side. But how did they get their fine things? By cheating other people, didn't they —people who weren't smart enough to protect themselves? They call that business. Well, I call it business, too. If they aren't smart enough to be careful who they're hiring, or to keep watch on what they've got—well, that's their bad luck. They don't have to take me in. That's their mistake. I'm out to do them, like they're out to do other people in business. They ought to be careful. If they aren't, they deserve to lose out. When I lose out, what happens? They put

335

me in jail. Do I go whining around about it? Not on your life. That's the game we're playing.

"I'll tell you what stealing is. If I took things for my own use, because I liked them, that would be stealing. But I don't. It's straight business with me. I don't take anything that can't be turned into cash. Even if I pick up something I take a fancy to, I don't keep it. That wouldn't be right. I stick to business. I'm a serious, dependable person.

"There's all kinds make their living that way, Madame, just as there's all kinds in your set. Take that Titi, for instance. There's a bad one, that'll do you a mean trick any time she gets the chance. But you ask any one that knows me, and they'll tell you you can count on Louise. They'll tell you I never told a lie in my life."

"Is that why you spent twelve years in prison?" I asked her.

"Oh my God," said Louise. "You still don't know what I'm talking about! You're thinking of what I tell the police or the judge. I tell 'em anything I think they'll believe. What else can you do? That's not lying. That's part of the job. You have to keep out of jail if you can. They know you're trying to do that, anyway. They don't expect you to give yourself away—wouldn't believe you if you did. That doesn't count. I'm talking about my private life. I wouldn't tell a lie to a friend, not for a million francs. That's the kind I am."

Louise, I discovered, was resentful at the presence of "politicals" in the jails. She seemed to feel about us in much the same way that steerage passengers feel about the gay parties from first class who sometimes go slumming in their part of the ship in evening dress after a good dinner. She classed us with "the high class dames" who occasionally got into prison before the war for kleptomania, whose mental processes she heartily condemned. What she did wasn't stealing, from her moral viewpoint, but what they did was, because it didn't serve any useful purpose. It wasn't business with them. It was plain, simple, inexcusable vice. As for those of us who were foolish enough to get put into jail for expressing their political opinions, well— "Couldn't they keep to their place and stay out of here?" Louise asked hotly.

"But there's a war on," I said. "All of us are fighting it now."

"Not me," said Louise. "That's the bunk. War is for big shots. It's got nothing to do with us."

"But, Louise," I said. "You're a Frenchwoman. The Germans have invaded your country. Don't you want to see them out of here?"

"What difference does it make to me whether I get chased by French cops, or German cops?" Louise asked. "I end up in the same jail, don't I? What difference does it make to the big shots either? You don't think this is a real war, do you? Maybe it was different last time, but you can't make me think the German army pushed us over in six weeks. It was all fixed in advance. Some of the rich people fixed it up. It's their racket. I steal a little silverware here and there, and you try to preach to me. The big shots steal the whole country, and you think you ought to get into trouble trying to save it. Wake up, kiddo. You weren't born yesterday, were you?"

Set a thief to catch a thief, I remembered. Maybe Louise wasn't so far wrong. Maybe some persons inside the French state had done what she did from inside a family. The same thing on a bigger scale. Getting away with the furniture. Only the furniture of a state included not only its resources and its political power, but things like liberty and justice. Thieves had gotten away with those.

It was curious, I thought, how a woman could drift into Louise's sort of life, and still retain all the conventional moral principles. All she had to do was to readjust her thinking to persuade herself that she wasn't violating them, and she could continue to apply them strictly to every one else. I remembered how the street-girls of Paris used to be called *lorettes* because there was a special early-morning mass for them at the little church of Notre Dame de Lorette. They didn't feel either that their way of living made them moral outlaws. Perhaps, I thought, criminals often just happen. Perhaps Louise slipped as unconsciously into her way of life as I had slipped unconsciously into helping Kitty smuggle her English soldiers out of the country. After all, though I didn't agree with the law that called me a criminal, and did agree with the law that called her one, our legal positions were just the same. We were both considered equally guilty of crime, and the proof was that we were in the same cell. In fact, my fault was considered the more heinous, for I had been sentenced to three times as long a term as Louise. I didn't feel myself a criminal,

I didn't regret what I had done—but then, neither did she. Had I, I asked myself, any right to take a superior attitude towards Louise? Wasn't it perhaps bad luck rather than immorality that had shaped her lot?

Once or twice I tried again to bring up the question of speaking to Titi, but Louise was so violent on that subject, that I never dared press the matter. Finally, one day, I managed to get far enough to explain how anxious I was to try to arrange a meeting with my friend in the hospital.

"What's so important ,about that?" Louise asked. "There's no hurry, is there? How long's she in for?"

"She was sentenced to death," I said.

Louise stared at me, terrified. I was astounded at the effect the words had on her. Apparently, to this hardened frequenter of jails, a death sentence was still highly impressive.

"Death!" she repeated. "Death?" Then: "Why didn't you tell me before. That's different. All right, I'll talk to Titi for you. She's not in my class, mind, but if that's the only way you can get in touch with your pal, all right. Tell me about it. What's Titi got to do with it?"

I explained to her what had gone on up to then.

"I'll try to locate her this afternoon, and find out what goes," Louise said. "I dunno if she's around. I ain't seen her since I got here."

Louise came back from the courtyard. As the door clanged shut behind her, she·dropped onto the bed, and said: "Well, I found out what happened. I told you that Titi was a louse."

"Why," I said, "what did she say?"

"She didn't say anything," Louise said, with satisfaction. "She's in solitary. That's why I ain't seen her. Thirty days! So's your old cellmate."

"Micheline?" I exclaimed.

"Yeh," Louise said. "Hair pulling. They got into a fight. On account o' you and your friend. Plenty of the girls heard what it was all about. I got the whole story."

"On account of me!" I echoed. "Louise—tell me what happened!"

"Titi got sore because Micheline was nagging her about not getting any more news from your friend," Louise reported. "Finally she said, 'Quit worrying me about her. They took her away from Cherche-Midi three weeks ago.' Micheline asked why she hadn't told her before. She said, 'Would your American have given me any more cigarettes if she knew her friend wasn't there any more? I wanted to keep on getting them.' That made Micheline so mad she slapped Titi. And that Titi—she's a bad one. She shouldn't have hit her. She jumped at Micheline, and they had a terrible fight. The girls told me they never saw nothin' like it. So they both got thirty days."

I hardly heard the last words.

"Kitty!" I gasped. "They took her away! Then they've executed her! She must be dead by now!"

Even Louise seemed shaken by the expression on my face.

"Wait a minute, Madame," she begged. "Don't take it so hard. I don't think they took her away to be executed. They just moved her to another prison."

"Why do you think so?" I asked faintly.

"They did more talking than I told you yet before the fight broke out," Louise said. "Titi told her that some German police took her away. They took all her things with her, and a day's rations. They wouldn't do that if they were going to shoot her. They do their shooting at Vincennes. That's only in the suburbs. They wouldn't need a day's rations to go there. Besides, they took two other women with her who had long sentences, but not death. Titi thought they might have moved them to the prisons at Nancy or Dijon."

I was saddened at the thought that Kitty was again out of reach, but at least I felt better at the thought that she was probably still alive.

"Thank you, Louise," I said. "Would you do something else for me? See if you can find out anything about Kitty—maybe from new prisoners coming here from Cherche-Midi."

"I'll try," Louise said. "More likely we might find out if any one is transferred here from whatever other jail they sent her to. It used to be pretty easy in the old days. Even in St. Nazaire, we could find out in a couple of weeks anything we wanted to know about any other pen. But since the Germans took over it's been tougher. I'll send out the grapevine call for your friend though. Maybe we'll get something."

CHAPTER THIRTY-SEVEN

A New Prison

THE first cold snap of winter came suddenly. The thermometer dropped to freezing overnight, and the steel and cement mantrap of Fresnes turned into a refrigerator. Remembering the misery caused by the cold at Cherche-Midi, I looked ahead with apprehension to the prospect of passing another winter in prison—and in a jail that seemed likely to be colder than Cherche-Midi had been.

Cherche-Midi was a medieval building. Its walls were a yard thick, and the minute windows which gave so little light did have the advantage of keeping the cold out, too. Huddled together, four in a cell, we could at least warm the air slightly with the heat of our bodies. But Fresnes was a modern prison, a structure whose cells, tier on tier, were steel cages apparently suspended from the girders above, planned to be kept at a livable temperature by its central heating system. And Louise had brought back the news, gleaned at the exercise period, that there would be no coal for the furnaces. Even the warden's office, and the quarters for the German members of the prison staff, would be heated only by small stoves.

Louise, muffled up in her overcoat, a shawl knotted around her neck, her gloves on her hands and her hands in her pockets, said grimly, "There's no doubt about it, *ma p'tite dame,* we'll just freeze to death here unless some miracle happens."

It seemed to me that the cement floor and the iron door and bars, far from providing any protection from the cold, actually transmitted it. I followed Louise's example, putting on all the clothes I had, and sitting muffled up in the biting cold of the cell, praying for Louise's miracle.

The afternoon exercise period, hitherto Louise's delight, because of the opportunity it afforded her to talk to the other prisoners, now became a source of terror, and she envied me the regime which made it unnecessary for me to go out. She came back from the cold breezes of the courtyard with blue lips and chattering teeth, gazing longingly at the cot into which she was not allowed to get during the daytime.

"If only I dared slip under the bed covers to get warm!" she said. "But if they catch me, I'll go to the punishment cell, and that will be worse. . . . If this cold keeps up, I'm going to pretend I'm sick and get sent to the hospital. At least I can cover myself up in bed there."

During these freezing days, Louise and I usually huddled up together, sometimes with our arms around one another, for warmth. I hadn't entirely abandoned my idea of trying to reform her, and I tried to persuade her that honest work would be preferable to the kind of life she led. I actually got her to the point where she wouldn't interrupt me impatiently at the first few words, and I did my best to convince her that there was more satisfaction in the accomplishment of a given task than in outwitting an unsuspecting employer, and that the world was a pleasanter place to live in if it wasn't necessary always to be dodging policemen.

I finished one such lecture with no interruption, but at the end, Louise said sarcastically:

"And what do I live on?"

"Live on what you can make honestly," I said. "When you get a job as a cook, work at it. Instead of robbing the place, stay there and do what you are hired to do."

"Huh!" Louise snorted. "Work from seven in the morning till eleven at night for 400 francs a month, when I can make fifty times that in a few days, and take life easy for three or four months until it's time to do another job? Take orders from a stupid woman who's never satisfied? Live in a little cubbyhole up under the roof, and have the family prying into my private business all the time? No, thank you! None of that for me. And what else can I do, especially at my age, with no education? I live better the way I manage now."

"Do you call this good living here?" I asked her.

Louise shrugged her shoulders.

"I don't always get caught," she said. "And when I do, it don't last forever."

My efforts to shift Louise's point of view were so little successful that on the one occasion when I thought I had made some progress, I was quite taken aback to discover what she really had in mind. One day, when we had been sitting side by side for some time without saying anything, she said suddenly, out of a blue sky:

"Madame, how would you like to teach me English?"

"I'd be glad to," I said. "We can start right away if you want Why?"

I hoped she would say that she wanted to learn the language because it might increase her ability to earn an honest living.

"I want to go to America," she said. "I hear there are a lot of rich people there—and that they like French cooks. If I got into one of those families, I could make a real haul. . . . And they tell me the prisons are better, too, if you get caught. Yes, I'd like to go to the United States."

"Well, there's not much chance of your getting there," I said, "even if the war ends. They don't let people with prison records into the country."

"Why not?" asked Louise. "Americans get put in prison too, don't they?"

Early in November, a German commission arrived to inspect the prison. They looked into every cell, and I felt like an animal being sized up for slaughter by butchers under their searching, unfriendly glances. We didn't know what the inspection was all about, but that it was something very much out of the ordinary seemed indicated by the suppression that day of the regular exercise period.

Louise came back from the courtyard with the answer the next day.

"Remember I told you it would take a miracle to get us out of this icebox?" she asked. "Well, the miracle has happened. We're all going to be transferred to other prisons. The Gestapo finds the Cherche-Midi prison too small. It's going to take over this one, too. We'll be split up among the different provincial prisons. I hope they send me to Dijon. That's a fine place. No trouble about heat there. They keep the men working in the forest all day, cutting wood. The women don't do anything except sit in nice warm cells. . . . I might come across your friend Kitty there. If I do, and if we're sent to different places, I'll get word to you somehow. Trust me to find a way."

"Do you think that's where she is?" I asked.

"How should I know? . . . But I tell you what. We can probably get a message to her wherever she is. Since we're probably all going to different places, I'll just spread the word around, and one of us will be sure to reach the same prison. She can tell your friend where you are, if they let us know before we go. I'll pick out some girls who know the ropes and tell them what to do."

A week later, I left the prison of Fresnes. There was no previous official notice. At seven in the morning, we were told to assemble in the courtyard, each with all her belongings in a bundle. We knew at once that that meant we wouldn't be returning to our cells. I took down my calendar from the wall, and put it in my bundle. It was the only souvenir I carried away from Fresnes.

In the courtyard, the prisoners were lined up in long rows. I looked about for Micheline, and finally caught a glimpse of her in a group already passing out of the gate under the escort of French gendarmes. She waved to me, and I waved back. That was all we could do. I would have given anything to have been able to say good-bye to her properly.

Apparently no arrangements had been made to send any particular individuals to any special prison, for instead of forming the groups by name, the officer in charge simply moved down the line counting. When he had reached 200, he ordered those prisoners to keep together, and said to a guard beside him:

"This group is for Troyes. Line them up in fours, and start them off. You only have an hour before the train leaves."

Louise and I were in this group. When Louise heard where we were going, she said: "Troyes? I'm not going there. There's no prison there—only the county jail attached to the court house. They can't be planning to put 200 people there. I'm not taking any of their makeshift accommodations. I'll take my chances with some other group."

"How will you manage that?" I asked.

Louise winked.

"Just keep your eye on me," she said.

The gendarmes bustled about, trying to get us into fours. Louise became separated from me in the process. She seemed to be falling towards the rear, purposely I imagined. They finally got us into some semblance of order, and with gendarmes in front, behind, and on both sides, we started to move towards the gate. I heard little screams behind, and turned. A woman was lying on the ground. I wasn't surprised to see that it was Louise. Two of the gendarmes tried to get her up, but she hung limp and relaxed in their arms. The German officer in charge beckoned to a woman not yet included in any group.

"Get in there," he said, pointing to the place left vacant by Louise; and to a guard, "Call the doctor."

We started forward again, leaving Louise behind. She had won. She wasn't going to Troyes. But what made her think, I wondered, that the place she would draw instead would be any better?

I realized what a sorry sight we must present from the faces of the people we met in the streets. Some of their expressions seemed shocked, others terrified. We must have been a pitiful caravan, women young and old, thin and gaunt from our existence in prison, trudging through the streets with our bundles, surrounded by gendarmes.

I think the people who saw us realized that most of us were not ordinary criminals, for there seemed to be too much sympathy in their eyes for that.

Reaching the railroad station, we passed through lines of German soldiers surrounding it. It was clear that they had no intention of letting any one escape in the confusion of boarding the train.

Three cars were waiting for us on a siding. I climbed into one of them, a third-class coach with hard wooden benches. Some of the gendarmes got aboard also. They warned us not to try to attempt to escape, for if any one did, they would be obliged to fire. Not trusting to talk alone, they locked the doors and windows.

Our cars were hooked onto a train, and we pulled slowly out of the station. The bleak November countryside seemed to coincide with the hopelessness of our situation, as our moving jail cut across the land. Through the window I saw the leafless trees bending before the strong, cold wind. I felt more a prisoner than ever, because I could see the outside world from which I was shut away. Somehow it was worse to pass across it, to have it before one's sight, and to know that one couldn't enter it, than to be shut away from it behind stone walls, and know only in one's mind that it was there, nearby but unattainable.

To make it worse, our coaches had been attached to an ordinary passenger train, and as we stopped at the different stations (it was a local, which seemed to stop every few minutes), we could see passengers getting freely in and out of the ordinary passenger coaches. At each station, the gendarmes posted themselves at the doors of our coaches, locked though they were. It was obvious that the train service wasn't anywhere near equal to the demands on it, for there were crowds at even the smallest stations, and almost everywhere, some of them were left standing on the platform, unable to get aboard, when we pulled out. We saw them again and again storm the locked doors of our coaches, only to be waved back by the gendarmes standing behind them. Most of them looked up puzzled at the windows behind which we were imprisoned as they sought places elsewhere.

As we paused at these stations, I thought—and so, I soon discovered, did many of the others—that we would never be likely to have so good a chance of escape as now. If only one of the doors were left unlocked! If only the gendarmes failed to guard it! I didn't dare express my thought out loud—but others did.

"What a shame," a woman near me said suddenly, loud enough to be overheard by the gendarme seated at the end of one of the benches of our compartment, "that French police should be set to guarding French people, sentenced by the Germans! How can they do their dirty work for the Boches, I'd like to know?"

An elderly gray-haired woman of cultured appearance, sitting across the way, said: "It's disgraceful! If I were a man in the place of any of these gendarmes, I'd leave the door open at the next station."

The gendarme sat silently in his place, looking down at his feet, as though he hadn't heard. But the woman sitting next to him nudged him violently, and said: "Aren't you ashamed of yourself—you, a Frenchman—acting as a German stool pigeon? I'd rather beg than make my living taking orders from the Germans. You're not a Frenchman!"

The gendarme turned towards her.

"What am I to do, Madame? I have a wife and three children. I have been a policeman all my life. I don't know how to do anything else. How could I get a new job today, in times like these? This isn't my regular job. I work for the French government, not for the Germans. I have to do what I am ordered to do."

"The French government! Vichy! Phew! It has to do what it's ordered to do, too—by the Boches," some one else cried.

"*Mesdames*! Please! This is doing you no good," the gendarme pleaded, very much on the defensive. "I don't want to report you. I'm a Frenchman, too. I'm only doing my duty."

"You call yourself a Frenchman!" said the woman next to him again, "but you take us to jail when you know very well we've been sentenced by the Germans."

"Don't forget," said the gendarme. "Some of you have been condemned by the Germans; but there are common criminals here too. I'm not the judge. I can't decide which of you are political prisoners and which aren't."

"All of us here are political prisoners," one woman said, and jumped up. "Ladies—if there are any of you who are not political prisoners, hold up your hands."

One woman alone raised her hand. She didn't look like a criminal. She was a modest looking woman in her thirties, and she seemed embarrassed.

"And what did you do, Madame?"

In an almost inaudible voice, she confessed:

"I forged a food ration card—but it was for my baby."

"That's not what I mean," the first woman said. "You're no criminal. Is there any one here for theft, or robbery, or assault?"

No one raised her hand. Perhaps there may have been some ordinary criminals among us who didn't choose to admit it, but no one was in a frame of mind to go into that. The fury broke on the unfortunate gendarme from all sides. Another one hurried along the corridor to our compartment.

"What's going on here?" he demanded sternly.

His colleague tried to tell him, not without difficulty, for by now the shouting women threatened to drown out his voice entirely.

As soon as the newcomer had seized the situation, he bellowed above the tumult: "Ladies! Ladies! You forget we would be punished if we let you escape!"

"Come with us," one of them shouted. "Let your job go!"

And realizing that this half-hearted defense was almost a compliance, the women redoubled their efforts. This time they shifted their tactics, praising the men as real Frenchmen, unwilling to see French women jailed by the invader. The second gendarme gazed at the women for a moment, then walked slowly to the front of the coach, unlocked the door, and then beckoned to his fellow, who walked with him to the back, leaving the open door unguarded.

Almost unable to believe in their success, the women gazed at each other with wide open mouths, in silence. Then they began hastily gathering up their bundles, and crowding into the corridor, ready to get out as soon as the next station was reached.

It was none too soon. I could see that we were nearing Paris. The next stop would probably be the last before the capital, for we were in its suburbs.

I was thinking feverishly myself. As soon as I got off the train, I told myself, I must get to the Paris Prefecture in some way, and get in touch with Henri's officer friend. This time no one would be following me, and he ought to be able to get me across into the unoccupied zone.

The train was slowing up. I left my bundle in the luggage rack. It would only be an incumbrance, and a dangerous distinguishing mark. I took my place in the corridor with the others.

The women in front had pulled open the door before the train quite came to a stop. There was a forward surge—and then a backward wave. From where I stood, I couldn't see what was going on. "Why didn't they get off?" I wondered.

Those in front pushed violently to the rear again. I slipped back into the compartment to escape the crush. Through the window I saw the answer. The platform was filled with German police. As the disappointed women were shoved back into the car, a German officer leaped aboard and began berating the French gendarmes for their carelessness. They had come to take over before we reached Paris, figuring, no doubt, that that would be the most dangerous place from the point of view of escapes. Our opportunity had passed. We sat depressed and silent while our coaches remained on a siding in Paris, and while they were attached to the train for Troyes. And hardly a word was spoken before our arrival there at three P.M.

CHAPTER THIRTY-EIGHT

Prison at Troyes

WE WERE tired after our long journey, but no one thought of suggesting any rest for us after the trip. We had no sooner alighted from the train than we were lined up and marched towards our destination. It was two miles, and all of us, weakened by the privations of prison life, were exhausted when we reached our new home. When we saw it, we looked at one another in dismay.

The building was still unfinished. Scaffolding covered it, and piles of brick lay about on the ground. One of us, who came from the region, identified it as a building originally intended for a hospital. Work had been interrupted on it when the war came, but the Germans had used it to house internees temporarily until their permanent internment camps were ready. Now it was to be our prison.

Inside it was even more evident than outside that the building was only half-finished. We climbed the stairs single file, clinging close to the naked unplastered walls in order not to fall off the narrow winding staircase, which had no banister. Most of the walls showed the bare brick. The only sign of plumbing I saw was one unconnected pipe projecting from a wall.

What about heat? was my first thought.

There was no sign of any heating system as we filed through the corridors, nor did I see any means of heating the room into which I was pushed with four others. There was no furniture—just five sacks of straw heaped up in a corner. These, laid on the floor, were to be our beds.

Louise was right, I thought, as I gazed with dismay about this cheerless cell. I was far from changing my mind a little later when I laid my straw sack on the floor, and tried to make myself as comfortable as I could under the single thin blanket which had been given me in the meantime.

At Fresnes, when the cold weather began, I had longed for the stuffy but warmer air of Cherche-Midi. Here I yearned for the bed I had slept in at Fresnes. In spite of my exhaustion, I lay awake half the night; the other half was filled with nightmares from which I kept awaking with a start, my body protesting at the hardness and coldness of the cement floor, which I could feel clear through the straw.

"This must be temporary," I thought. "They'll do something about this tomorrow. Even the Germans can't expect any one to live in such conditions."

But nothing was done on the morrow, or the next day, or the next. Our jailers seemed quite satisfied that they had done their full duty towards us. There was not the slightest heat in the prison, and every day the weather grew colder. We had one pitcher of water a day in our cell which was supposed to serve five of us for both drinking and washing—but as the water in it was customarily frozen, and we had no means of melting it, we had to do without both.

It must have been because they realized there was danger of our dying from cold that we were allowed here one privilege which had not been permitted elsewhere. We could stay in bed all day if we wanted—if you could call resting on the straw sack under the scanty blanket staying in bed. What we did on the coldest days was to place the sacks side by side, so that the five of us could lie on three of the sacks, keeping as close together as possible for warmth, with the other two sacks over us as well as the five blankets and all the spare clothing we had, including even the cloth bags one or two of us kept their clothes in. We got into this communal bed fully dressed, of course, and with shawls or towels tied around our necks and feet, or transformed into improvised mittens. During the coldest spells, we spent most of the twenty-four hours of the day in this fashion, clambering out only when we had to, to get our food or for other reasons, and scurrying shivering back into our artificial burrow as quickly as we could.

We were more avaricious of heat than the primitive peoples who never let their fires go out because they have no means of kindling new ones. The only heat we had to conserve was that manufactured by our own bodies, and we were misers about that. If one of us carelessly disturbed a blanket so that a little cold air came in, she was due for immediate simultaneous scolding from the other four. We regarded the heat generated by each one of us as common property, which no one had a right to waste.

One of the minor annoyances that preyed on us at Troyes was that for weeks at a time, though there was a large window in our cell, we could not see out of it. It was covered with an impenetrable layer of frost. This increased our idle boredom. There was nothing to distract us, nothing to do except lie all day on our sacks. The afternoons seemed endless, and the nights interminable.

Usually, when a guard appeared with our food, on the cold days when we were huddled together under our pile of clothing, only one of us would creep out to get it—and she would be assailed by a stream of complaints if her manner of getting out of our bed let too much air in. The unlucky person who had to get out served the others, who thus enjoyed the questionable luxury of taking their meals in bed.

Under these conditions, it can hardly be said that we lived individual lives. We were all units in one life, and that no very eventful one, like the microscopic animals which live in colonies, the smaller individuals constituting one larger one. Perhaps it was partly to maintain our sense of individuality in spite of this that we talked to each other so much about ourselves, and about our pasts. Lying in the heap of straw and clothing, I learned quickly the life stories of all my companions.

The intellectual of our group was Mme. Ragomin, an Argentine of Spanish origin who had lived in Paris for many years. A dentist by profession, she was also somewhat of a linguist, speaking English, French and German besides her native Spanish. She didn't speak them too well, however.

It took a good listener to get all the details of Mme. Ragomin's stories, for she mixed up her languages, and whatever she had to say came out in a mixture of all four. Her conversation always made me think of a juggler keeping a number of objects in the air at the same time. That was the way she tossed her four languages about.

Her first confession gave me a shock. She admitted that she had worked for the German Intelligence Service. When she saw the effect produced on us, she went on (I'm not going to try to reproduce her mixed language):

"Don't be afraid. Haven't you ever heard of an *agent double?* That's what I was. I was sending information to the British Intelligence Service all the time. That's the only reason why I was working for the Germans. I had to do it to get inside information for the British. The Germans got suspicious, set a trap for me, and I was caught, red-handed. I didn't have a chance of getting out of it. . . . What I can't understand is why they didn't shoot me. That's what usually happens to a spy who works for the wrong side."

Also on the intellectual side was Mme. Santot, a bony-faced French spinster of about fifty, who had been a school-teacher all her life, and looked it. She was bitter, not against the Germans, but against the Vichy government. It was Vichy that had sentenced her, because she refused to follow the instructions given her to conduct her classes in the spirit of the new directives of Marshal Pétain, who replaced the splendid motto of France, "Liberté, Egalité, Fraternité," by "Travail, Famille, Patrie" (Work, Family, Country).

Mme. Santot evidently had the obstinacy that characterizes many spinsters, who become increasingly uncompromising as the years roll on, unshared with any one with whom some mental accommodation might be necessary. When she received the new instructions, she read them to her pupils, and then attacked Pétain for replacing liberty by the sort of work which amounts to slave labor; the unselfish ideal of fraternity, which implies that all men are brothers, by the narrower concept of family, which concentrates on the self-interest of a small unit; and equality by country, because he desired blind obedience to the sort of country he was creating, in which equality would no longer have any place. For that, she had been sentenced to a year in prison.

"One year?" echoed Mlle. Blanc, a young woman of 22, when Mme. Santot told us her story. "Why, I got a year for only—well, see for yourself."

In spite of the cold, she crept out from under the blanket, unbuttoned the overcoat she was wearing, and pulling her chemise out from under her blouse, showed us a small pin, like those so common before the occupation—crossed French and British flags.

"I got a year just for wearing this," she said, "or rather, for wearing another just like it. They took away the one I had on my coat. But I had another in my bag, and I have always managed to keep them from finding it. I had it pinned on my underwear while the judge was sentencing me for wearing it. And I wear it still."

Climbing back under the covers, she told us the details of her arrest. It was shortly after the German occupation when a German soldier spoke to her on the street, telling her, she realized afterwards, to take off the pin. But as she knew no German, she didn't understand him. He called a patrol and she was arrested. Not until she appeared before a military court, one of whose officers spoke French, forty-eight hours later, did she discover that it was her pin that had caused all the trouble.

"I was so angry at being kept in a dirty cell for 48 hours just because of a pin," she said, "that I lost control of myself. I called them some names, I guess. I told them it was idiotic to keep any one locked up for two days for such a trifle. Well, I should have held my tongue. Instead of two days, I got three hundred and sixty-five."

The fifth person in the cell was the woman who had confessed in the train to having forged a food ticket. She still seemed to have a sense of guilt about it, for she didn't tell us her story until she had been urged by all of us. She was a humble person, who seemed to think that we were all heroines of romantic legends, while for herself she accepted the thesis of her judges that she had committed an ignominious crime. But after she had told us what she had gone to jail for, we all felt, in spite of her protestations, that she was the best of us all.

Her name was Mme. Otto. She had six children. Her husband was a prisoner of war in Germany, and she was left alone to struggle with the problem of getting food for her family in a country where even the wealthiest found it difficult to get enough to eat. In an attempt to increase her children's meagre portions of food, she had applied for a ration card in her husband's name—one more ration, she hoped, to divide among the six. Her deception was discovered, and she was sentenced to six months in jail.

She cried softly as she told us her story, particularly when she spoke of her children, whose fate she didn't know. She had been allowed no news of them since she had been in jail. And yet, with her mother's heart torn daily by anxiety over the fate of her children, she had remained uncomplaining, unembittered, feeling herself almost justly punished for a guilty attempt to gain food rations which, perhaps, she thought, might have been needed more badly by some one else than by her own starving brood.

"You can't have much longer to serve now," I said. "When will you get out?"

"About Christmas," Mme. Otto said. "I was sentenced June 23."

"And what's the date today?" Mme. Ragomin demanded.

None of us could figure it out. I reached for my calendar and started to check the days.

"How can any one remember the date," said the school-teacher, "when the days are all the same, when nothing special ever happens to distinguish one from the others."

And as I worked it out, she continued, "Today is a dead, dull, drab day like the others, which will pass like all the other meaningless days on which nothing has happened into the well of history and be forgotten."

I had finished my calculation.

"Today," I said, "is December 7, 1941."

CHAPTER THIRTY-NINE

Pearl Harbor: Axis Report

THE guard who brought our "breakfast" the next morning was not the usual one. Instead of stopping in the door, measuring out our portion of the ominous-looking liquid referred to as coffee, and then moving on without speaking, she actually came into our cell, and filled the cups there. Then, advancing towards us, she said: "Which one of you is the American?"

"I am," I answered, wondering why in the world she wanted to know. I didn't like her expression. It boded me no good.

"Oh, so it's you, is it?" she answered, and regarded me for what seemed an eternity. It was obvious that she had something to say, and obvious also that she was in no hurry to say it.

Finally she decided to speak.

"I've got news for you," she said. "America is in the war."

All of us started. To the others, that meant one thing: the certain defeat of Germany. Europeans had all clung to that hope. They remembered that the entry of the United States had been the beginning of the end before. They were sure it would be that way again. I suppose the others looked happier about it than I did; for to me, it meant, of course, that the awful aloneness that I had anticipated had become a fact.

"Yes," said the guard slowly, "America's in the war—and they say she's out again, already."

"Out again?" I gasped. "What do you mean?"

"Out! Knocked out! She's lost the war already, that's what I mean," she said.

"It's not possible!" Mme. Ragomin spoke up.

"Oh, yes it is!" the guard retorted. "How can she fight without a navy? And she hasn't got any navy, any more. It was all sunk— all of it. The Japs attacked Pearl Harbor, and didn't leave a single ship afloat. What are the Yankees going to do now?"

She picked up her pot of coffee and stalked to the door.

"The radio says they're expecting Roosevelt to ask for peace terms any hour now," she said, and slammed the door behind her.

We looked at one another in dismay. We were so upset we forgot to drink our coffee, which usually we gulped down as soon as we got it, in order not to lose any of its precious heat.

"It can't be true," Mlle. Blanc said. "How could the Americans be surprised like that?"

"Of course it isn't," Mme. Ragomin chimed in. "It's just one more of their Nazi lies. Don't you think so?" she asked the school-teacher.

Mme. Santot was less certain.

"I never believe more than half they say," she said. "No doubt it's exaggerated. But they must have some basis for it. What do you think, Mrs. Shiber?"

"If it's only half true, that would be terrible," I said. "It wouldn't surprise me if America has entered the war—but if the Japanese sunk the fleet, or even half of it, that would be an incredible tragedy. I don't believe we could have been caught napping like that."

We talked of little else all morning, and when a call came for Mme. Otto to report to the prison office, she volunteered at once to try to find out if it were true. She jumped out of bed and went through the curious reverse process we had to follow if we left the cell—instead of dressing to go out, we undressed; that is, we took off the odd garments we might be wearing over our regular clothes for warmth.

She was gone about half an hour. When she returned, there was a curious expression on her face. She seemed worried and uncertain. In fact, I had almost the impression that she was afraid of us when she entered.

Thinking only of what the guard had told us that morning, I said at once: "What's the matter? Bad news?"

"No," she said, "on the contrary. Rather good news, I think."

And as all of us turned to her expecting some report on America's entry into the war, she came out with something entirely different. "I am being released at once."

This was an event, and for the moment we forgot about Pearl Harbor, too.

"Released?" Mme. Ragomin cried. "Then why look so sad about it? You ought to be happy. Or are you going to miss our collective bed so much?"

"No," Mme. Otto said miserably. "It's not that. It's—well, I'm not going home. I've got to go to Germany. I don't know—if I'll like it there.

"I have to join my husband," Mme. Otto explained. "You see, he's a machinist. He makes precision instruments. It seems they need skilled workers in their factories. They offered to let him out, and me, too, if he'd go to work for them. So he said, Yes. . . . We'll have the children with us, you know."

She proffered the last sentence apologetically, as if in extenuation.

"So you're going?" said Mlle. Blanc. There was a touch of scorn in her voice.

"What else can I do?" Mme. Otto said helplessly. "It doesn't depend on me. My husband arranged it all. . . . We get the same food rations as the Germans do. . . . That will be better for the children."

"When do you go?"

"Right away. They're preparing my release papers. I just came back to get my things."

She started to gather up her few pitiful belongings and make a bundle of them.

"I think your husband is just a rotten collaborationist," said Mlle. Blanc, aggressively.

"Please!" said Mme. Otto, plaintively, as though some one had struck her in the face. Tears welled slowly from her eyes and began running down her cheeks.

"Perhaps the poor man was thinking of the children," Mme. Ragomin said, coming to her defense. "Perhaps he wanted to get his wife out of jail. You can't blame him for that."

"Nonsense!" said Mme. Santot sharply. "She was getting out in two or three weeks anyway. He's selling himself for bigger rations, that's all. Probably making a bad bargain, too—out of a prison camp into slavery. The man's a fool as well as a traitor! I'd starve before I'd work for the Germans!"

Mme. Otto timidly said: "Please!" again. The tears were flowing faster now, but she was not sobbing. They seemed to be streaming out of her eyes and running down her cheeks of their own volition, without her knowledge.

"He's a good man," she said. "He doesn't mean any harm. He doesn't know what it's like in France—what they've done here."

But Mme. Santot was not the sort to relent.

"You agree with me yourself, don't you?" she pursued her victim. "That's why you looked so sad when you came in, isn't it? You don't approve, do you?"

Mme. Otto shook her head slowly through her tears.

"I wish he hadn't done it," she said. "But how do I know why? It must have been for the children."

She gathered up her belongings and moved slowly to the door. Then she stopped, and, with the tears still flowing down her cheeks, she said:

"Mrs. Shiber—I almost forgot. It's true what they said. There was a radio on in the office. It said the Japanese had sunk the whole American fleet."

The key grated in the lock, and the door opened.

"Come on," said the guard.

"Good-bye," said Mme. Otto timidly. I answered her, and so did Mme. Ragomin. The other two were silent. Mme. Otto cast them an anguished look, and the tears fell faster as she passed out of the door.

Mme. Otto's news, on top of the intense embarrassment and pity I had felt at the scene which accompanied the departure of this simple, humble little woman, threw me into the deepest depression. My cell-mates seemed to react in the same fashion.

"What's going to happen to France?" Mme. Santot asked. "Our only hope since our defeat has been America's intervention. If America has been beaten already . . ." her voice trailed away.

"We can't be beaten already," I said. "I'm sure of that. Even if we have lost all our fleet, I know my countrymen. They won't accept defeat. It will make it harder. But I'm sure we'll win all the same, in the end, fleet or no fleet. We've never lost a war yet! And think of all our factories! Think of the planes, and the tanks, and the guns we can build! How could we be beaten so easily? The British weren't beaten after Dunkirk were they—or even after the fall of France? If they could hold on, almost alone, for a year and a half, why should America give up so easily? No, Mme. Santot, I'm sure of one thing—if America is in the war, America will win it."

"After all," said Mme. Ragomin, "there's no more reason for believing the radio than the guard. It tells more lies than she could ever imagine."

The enervating prison regime began to tell on me, and again, as once before in Cherche-Midi, I began to lose track of what was going on around me. I remained for hours, even days, in a state of half-consciousness, something like the waking sleep which sometimes precedes real slumber, in which dream and reality merge inextricably into each other. It was during this period that Mme. Santot and Mme. Ragomin fell out. How their quarrel originated, I never could make out. Probably the source of it was nothing else than irritation at being confined so long together; but whatever started it, they quarreled all day long, from the moment they woke up until we all went to sleep.

Mlle. Blanc and I tried to reduce the argument by occupying the two middle places in the common bed, but their tart remarks were then only fired back and forth over our heads, in a constant barrage of verbal machine gun fire. Most of it I heard only intermittently, as a sort of dull distant chatter which made no sense, as I lay with closed eyes, sometimes losing consciousness of my surroundings for an hour or more, sometimes achieving a sharper focus again, when my invariable thought was: "Thank goodness; there's a little more of my time gone without my noticing it."

I could feel again that there was great irregularity in my heartbeat, and from the discomfort it caused me, I knew that my blood-pressure must again be dangerously high. I wondered if I should report sick, and if so, what kind of treatment I could expect. If it were like the hospital at Fresnes, it wouldn't be worth troubling about. I needed a warm room, food fit to eat, facilities for keeping clean. Would I get them? I was so apathetic that my doubt about this possibility was sufficient to keep me from making any, decision, affirmative or even negative, about asking for the doctor.

But as I lay long hours in my cell, while the constant battle of my two cell-mates went on over my head, I began to accept as a certainty the idea that I would not live through the more than two years which still remained of my sentence. So far, I had survived on the residue of the strength built up in the years of good living. Now there was no reserve left. I felt as if all strength had been drained from me.

Now, I thought, the parcels from the Quakers will probably stop coming. They were all that kept me going. And these long spells of semi-consciousness could mean only one thing—the approach of the end.

I put my hand on my thumping heart, and its irregular beat convinced me that it would be the first of my organs to give way. Perhaps it would stop some day quite suddenly and unexpectedly, and my two quarrelsome neighbors would continue their dispute over my unhearing ears, until suddenly they would discover with horror and surprise that one of their companions had escaped forever.

CHAPTER FORTY

A New Arrival

Afew days before Christmas, a new prisoner was assigned to our cell to replace Mme. Otto. When the guard shoved her in and slammed the door behind her, she took a few faltering steps towards us, and then stopped in obvious amazement.

I could understand her surprise. To us, our system of huddling together in our common bed had become habitual and quite commonplace, but to a newcomer it must have seemed odd to find us all bundled up together under our pile of variegated coverings. She stood staring at us, and our four pairs of eyes looked up at her. We saw a really beautiful woman of about 35, with the noble profile and the jet-black hair which denoted Mediterranean origin. Her excellent figure was set off by well-cut clothes of good quality—in fact, she presented an elegant appearance, of a nature to which we were no longer accustomed.

She broke the silence first.

"Do you lie there on your backs like that all day?" she asked.

"We do," said Mme. Ragomin, "and you'd better put on everything you've got and join us if you don't want to freeze to death. There's no heat in this place."

"That's not my idea of a solution for that problem, ladies," said the newcomer. (Her name, we learned shortly, was Marguerite Moyat). "You aren't planning to spend all winter in that attitude, are you? It's only December now; it will be colder before it's warmer, and it won't be warm until April at the earliest. You must insist on heat."

"Don't be ridiculous," Mme. Santot snorted. "You must be very green to talk about insisting on anything."

"Pardon me," said Marguerite, "but may I ask you one question: has it occurred to any one of you to protest against the lack of heat?"

We looked at one another in amazement.

"Protest!" Mlle. Blanc repeated. "What's the good of that? The Germans have all the coal. A lot they care whether we freeze or not."

"And I don't care whether they care or not," Marguerite said. "I just insist on the regulations. We were sentenced to prison, but not to a cold cell . . . I'm not as green as you think. I've already served three months, and I've got things out of the Germans that no one else ever dared ask. You don't know how to go about it. If you ask for any favors, if you ask for any human treatment, you won't get it. Don't ask. Demand. They understand that. Tell them freezing isn't in the rules. They have an unholy respect for the rules. Threaten them. Tell them you intend to report them to their superiors. Do you know they won't dare refuse you the right to do it? Browbeat them! It's the only way. They have no sympathy for the weak, but they're afraid of the strong. . . . So you admit you haven't tried protesting? All right, I'm going to protest!"

"That's all very interesting," said Mme. Ragomin, "but how are you going to make your protest? The guard won't even answer our questions. How are you going to persuade her to take your complaint to the warden or the German commander?"

"Persuade? I'm not going to persuade any one. I'm going to order her. She doesn't have to answer me. An order doesn't require an answer. She'll take my message to the warden. You'll see. I happen to know that prison regulations oblige the warden to receive the complaint of any prisoner who wishes to make one. And if the prisoner isn't satisfied with the result, he can appeal to the military commander of the region in which the prison is located. . . . So I'm going to file a complaint in my name at least. Do you authorize me to make it in yours also?"

We consulted one another, and agreed that it was worth taking the risk. We told her she might speak for all of us—if she got a chance to speak at all.

While we were waiting for the next round of the guard, Marguerite told us her story. She had been the secretary to a manufacturer of canned food. When the Germans came in, her employer got away to unoccupied territory, leaving her behind to keep an eye on the business.

Not long after the occupation, she received a letter from him, carried in by a messenger who had crossed the demarcation line surreptitiously. In it, her employer informed her that he wanted to begin manufacturing in North Africa, and asked if it would be possible for her to get out with the company's funds, so that he could resume business. Marguerite started to collect the firm's assets in preparation for following these instructions, and had turned several million francs into cash, ready to take them out with her, when the Germans arrested her. Her employer's letter, which she had foolishly failed to destroy, was evidence of her intention of getting the money out of the occupied zone, so she was sentenced to 18 months.

The guard arrived not long after she had finished telling her story, and Marguerite put her theories to the test.

"Guard," she said peremptorily. "You will tell the warden that I wish to see him or the German commander at once to make a complaint in accordance with the general prison regulations governing prisoners' rights."

And she turned her back immediately and walked to the other side of the cell, as though that ended the matter.

The guard remained imperturbable as usual, and clanked away with her soup pot without making any answer.

"See?" said Mlle. Blanc. "That's the last of that."

"I will make you a little bet," Marguerite said, "or I would if either of us had anything to bet, that that is not the end of that. The guard won't dare not to report to the warden a request made according to the rules."

And sure enough, half an hour later the guard returned, and said gruffly:

"The commander will see you now."

Marguerite left the cell with a triumphant glance in our direction.

"She can look like that now," said Mlle. Blanc, "but how will she come back? Or will she come back? Have they got punishment cells here?"

But Marguerite was back, and in fifteen minutes.

"It was easy!" she said. "You know who commands this place— an Austrian! I spotted his accent the moment he opened his mouth. His place is so hot I could hardly stand it. When I told him the cells were freezing, I looked hard at the big stove in the middle of his office—and he started apologizing! He told me he had already made a report about it, but he couldn't fix up anything because the building had been designed for central heating and had no fireplaces or chimney outlets in the separate rooms. He said it's impossible to get enough stoves for the cells—but he's trying to get a few for the corridors, to dry out the walls—if he can get coal for them. Anyway, ..e's promised to get us heavier blankets by Christmas."

We all brightened up; all, that is, except Mlle. Blanc, who wasn't willing to give up yet.

"You got promises," she said, "but I'll wait till I see something done before I celebrate. What good will stoves in the corridors do? No heat will get into these ice-boxes. As for blankets—remind me when we get them."

And she turned out to be right. The blankets never came. Nor did we ever get any stoves, even in the corridor.

On that first day, Marguerite continued to brave the cold outside our common nest. She only joined us in bed at night; and in the morning, she alone crept out and picked up the water pitcher. When she saw the water in it was frozen, she gave up, and came quietly back into bed with the rest of us. From that time on, we were five once more in our share-the-heat community.

Marguerite's place in the bed was next to me, and as she talked rather good English, we got into the habit of talking together in that language, becoming close friends. I quickly discovered the one weakness in her intellectual armor. She believed the future could be foretold from playing-cards. She had managed to bring a dog-eared pack in with her, somehow or other, and she could consume hours reading the cards. No one discouraged her, for it helped pass the time, but when I tried to argue with her about it, and showed that I did not really take her results seriously, she became quite heated.

"Oh, I know you sceptics!" she snorted. "You take a very superior attitude about the cards, but what explanation do you advance for unusual happenings? You have a mystic idea of your own, which is so familiar to you that it never occurs to you how odd it is. You ascribe everything to an unknown force you call 'accident.' If a brick happens to fall on your head, it's an accident. If a bridge collapses when you walk over it, it's an accident. But why did the brick drop at the precise instant when you passed by, and not a second sooner or later? Why did the bridge collapse just when you happened to be passing over it, and not some one else? You can believe that's all caused by your mysterious 'accident,' if you want. I believe there aren't any accidents. Everything is planned ahead, everything is foreordained. And if that is so, why shouldn't we be able to look into the future? I know the cards tell us what is to come, because they have told me, many times, and they have been right!"

"But that's just coincidence," I said. "They must have been wrong pretty often, too."

"Not at all," said Marguerite, hotly. "All the things I've read in the cards haven't happened yet—but it takes time for everything to be fulfilled. Your 'coincidence' is just 'accident' again, under another name. . . . Wait! I'll prove to you that the cards don't lie. I'll ask them about your immediate future. Then wait and see if it doesn't turn out as they say."

She took an unconscionable time with her cards this time, laying them out, studying them, and then beginning the whole process again, until finally she turned to me with the greatest seriousness, and said, "Mrs. Shiber, you are going to be released soon."

I shook my head doubtfully.

"But it must be so!" Marguerite said. "I did it three times. I got the same result each time. I tell you, you will be out of here soon."

I thought it was no use continuing the argument about the validity of fortunes told by playing cards. I just said:

"It sounds impossible. I have more than two years to serve still, and I don't see any possibility of release."

"I don't see any likelihood of it either," Marguerite said. "But I know you will be released. It's in the cards. They say you will be released before me. . . . Look! I am going to give you the address of my cleaning woman. She has the keys to my apartment. You can stay there when you get out."

I didn't try to argue with her. She wrote a note then and there to her *femme de ménage*, acting at once on what she thought she had seen in her cards. I took it as though I believed in it, too, tucked it away in a pocket, and promptly forgot about it.

My first bad heart attack came in February.

It was signalled by a sharp pain, and the sensation that a giant fist was squeezing my heart inexorably. I suppose it was because of my weakness as a result of privation that I lost consciousness almost immediately, which was a relief, for it freed me from the pain. When I came to, my cell-mates were bending over me, their faces absolutely colorless.

That was the first of a series of spasms, which were spread over a period of twenty-four hours. Almost always I lost consciousness. The prison doctor was called in three times, but didn't order my transfer to the hospital, because there was no one who could watch me constantly, while in the cell the others could take care of me.

When the series of attacks passed, and I showed signs of feeling better, Marguerite said,

"You frightened the others. They thought it was the end. But I knew you couldn't die here, because the cards promised you freedom."

"Perhaps that's what they meant," I said. "There's more than one kind of release, you know."

Marguerite shook her head decidedly.

"No, that's not possible," she said. "If it were death, the cards would have showed it. The ten of spades is the death card. It never appeared in your fortune. You watch!"

And she went through her rigmarole again, laying out her cards in the prescribed pattern. Sure enough, the ten of spades did not turn up among them.

Perhaps it was because I had ceased to argue with Marguerite about her belief in cards that she dared resort to them once again on my behalf. I had talked with her often about Kitty, expressing the fear that haunted me that she must have been executed by now.

"Would you like to know what has happened to her?" Marguerite asked.

"Of course," I said, wondering how she proposed to get that information. But then she produced her cards, and my hopes sank. However, I was too tired of the subject to continue to argue the point, so I made no protest. Finally, after Marguerite had laid out her cards and studied them, she turned to me and said, "Your friend is alive!"

No doubt she expected me to express joy, but when she saw that the news had no effect on me, she realized at once why that was.

"I see you still don't believe in my cards," she said. "All right! You will some day. Remember, when you get out of here—and it can't be very long now; the cards say so—remember that I read it here. Then, perhaps, you will believe also that the cards were right when they told me that your friend is still alive."

Spring came late that year. Not until the middle of March was it warm enough for us to abandon our common bed. From our cell window, we could see the fields turning green. We opened the windows, and breathed in the spring air, with its scent of young grass and of fresh-turned earth in the ploughed fields we could see between the bars. We heard the chirping of the birds outside. Even in prison, spring seemed to mean an awakening, a refreshing, a rebirth of life.

My periods of lethargy lessened. I felt once again that, after all, I might not die in prison. I might still live to be able, one day, to walk through the green fields unhampered, to move about at my own will, as freely as the birds which played outside our window in the first warm sunshine.

CHAPTER FORTY-ONE

Spring

SPRING brought a welcome change into the lives of the cooped-up inmates of Troyes. A space behind our building was fenced off with barbed wire, and we were allowed to spend two hours daily in the fresh air, walking about or sunning ourselves. This time, I was anxious, after so long a period of indoor life, to get out and enjoy the warm weather. Fortunately, the prohibition against my joining the other prisoners had apparently been lost sight of between Fresnes and Troyes. When the first exercise period was announced, I lined up with the others, and no one prevented me from going out with them.

It was the middle of April. The trees were showing the tender green of their first leaves. There was a fragrant warm breeze, with only the slightest touch of chill in it, refreshing and invigorating. I walked briskly up and down, enjoying the air—enjoying it, perhaps, too much. I was conscious of my heart pounding away, but I was too happy to pay much attention to it.

I must have overdone it. Halfway up the stairs, I suddenly collapsed, losing consciousness immediately. It's a wonder I was not killed, for I might have pitched right over the unprotected edge of the banisterless stairs. Mme. Ragomin told me afterwards that she caught me as I was falling, or I might have done so.

When I came to, I was back in my cell. The prison doctor, who was French, was standing over me, which didn't surprise me, but what was astonishing was that the Austrian Major who commanded us was there too. He smiled at me sympathetically—which put me at once on my guard. So far, it had never boded me any good when a German showed signs of sympathy.

"*Gott sei dank,*" he said. "I am happy to see that you are better. The doctor tells me that you have had these attacks before. Why did you not report them to me? I could have seen to it that you were allowed certain privileges which would improve your state of health."

I looked towards the French doctor in astonishment. I assumed that he had reported my previous attacks as a matter of routine, and I was surprised to hear the Major profess ignorance of my condition —and quite as surprised at his solicitude, which, after my previous experiences, rang very false. There had been one occasion when the prison doctor had sent to Troyes for a specialist to examine my heart. Surely the warden must have known of that! And if he had allowed me to go untended during those freezing winter months, why was he so suddenly concerned now?

His next remark surprised me even more.

"Don't you know, Madame," he asked, "that prison regulations permit you, in consideration of the state of your health, to petition for parole in order to get private treatment until you are completely recovered? All you require is a certificate from the prison doctor that your state of health necessitates it. What is your opinion on that, doctor?"

"I think definitely," the French doctor said, "that Madame is in no condition to remain here."

"How long a leave do you think she would require to recover normal health? Three months, perhaps?"

The doctor considered for a moment. Then he shook his head.

"Six, I should say."

"*Meinetwegen,* six months it is then. . . . You doctors are incorrigible—always taking the part of the prisoners against the administration. Well, then, doctor, if you will be good enough to prepare the medical certificate, I will send the petition through the Kommandantur. I hope, Madame, that you will shortly be able to enjoy a little vacation."

He smiled so broadly that the sunlight filtering through the window sparkled on his gold teeth, and left the cell followed by the guard, who had been standing stiffly at attention in the doorway during this conversation.

The doctor remained behind, and as soon as the door had closed, I said to him:

"Please tell me, doctor, just how bad my condition is. You are a

Frenchman so I can say to you that I am surprised at so much solicitude from the Germans. Is it because he's afraid I might die on his hands?"

"Not at all, Madame!" the doctor said. "Don't alarm yourself unnecessarily. This regime is very bad for your health. That goes without saying. But living a normal life, with proper care, you have nothing to worry about. You have many long years ahead of you. But since you're lucky enough to get this chance of clemency, by all means, take it."

"Clemency!" I said. "It's the *mot juste,* doctor! But why is clemency being offered to me, in particular? It's not a German habit, you know. And why now, when conditions are improving, after I spent all winter freezing here? What's behind it all, doctor?"

The doctor made a helpless gesture.

"How should I know, Madame? I'm not in their confidence. I'm only the doctor—and French to boot. They don't tell me what their motives are. . . . It's not usual, I know that. But it's fortunate for you, and I see no reason in the world why you shouldn't take advantage of it."

The moment the doctor left, Marguerite said, "Well, Mrs. Shiber, what do you think of the cards now? Weren't they telling the truth?"

"What I'd like to know," I answered evasively, "is whether the Germans are telling the truth. Is it only because they're so concerned with my health that they're willing to let me go?"

"What other reason could they have?" asked Mlle. Blanc. "Unless, of course, they want to be lenient with you because you're an American."

"She was an American last December, too," Mme. Santot broke in drily, "when we were all lying here like corpses in a morgue ice-box—if you'll permit the comparison. She didn't become an American this afternoon. Besides, now that America is in the war, there's less reason than ever for her to get special treatment. I admit I don't understand it."

"It's quite simple," Mme. Ragomin opined. "There's no sense hunting for complicated explanations. Today's attack on the staircase—in public, where it made more of an impression than those you had in here—has frightened the commander. He likes to submit a good report at the end of the year, and the fewer deaths on it, the better. He probably thinks your condition is much worse than the doctor says it is, and he prefers to have you out of here."

"I don't believe it," the school-teacher said. "They don't care that much about deaths. That may have been true of pre-war civilian prisons, but not of these German military jails. There's a woman on the third floor with asthma so bad she can hardly breathe. She has frequent bad attacks, and the doctor has asked her transfer to a hospital several times, but she's still there. Here on' our own floor there's a woman with a bad case of tuberculosis, with a recurrent high fever. She hasn't been offered any parole either. There's something funny about this, but I certainly can't figure it out. I'm going to talk to some of the more experienced prisoners tomorrow and see if any one can explain it."

I found it difficult to go to sleep that night. I lay awake, thinking of the joy of returning to my apartment once more. . . . But then, I wondered, what will happen when the six months are up? It will be November then. Will I have to go back to finish my term, just at the worst time of year? Can I perhaps get an extension? And is the six months considered as part of my term, or will I have to spend six months more in jail when I return to make up for it?

Mlle. Blanc was lying on the sack next to me.

"Mme. Shiber," she whispered, "are you still awake?"

"Yes," I said. "Why?"

"Would you do me a great favor?" she asked. "You will be going to Paris soon. Would you go to see my mother when you get there?"

"Of course, my child," I said. I reached over to pat her cheek. It was wet. She had been crying.

"Certainly I will," I said. "What do you want me to tell her?"

"Just that I am very lonely without her, and that I think of her constantly . . . and that I have taken her advice. Can you remember that?"

"Yes," I said. "Where does she live?"

"3, Rue Washington," she said. "Mme. Blanc, of course. . . . You won't forget it?"

"I'll write it down in the morning," I said, "to make sure. Remind me then."

"No, no," she said. "Please don't wait until morning. Memorize it now. Do you remember it still?"

"3, Rue Washington," I said. "Now are you happy?"

"Yes," she said, very softly. "Now I am happy. . . . You're sure you won't forget it before morning?"

"I'm sure I won't," I said. "Now try to go to sleep, dear. You need rest."

"Yes," she said. "I do need rest. I'm going to sleep now."

Poor child, I thought, prison life has been harder on her than on any of the rest of us—perhaps because she is younger, and less able to resign herself placidly to her fate. I had noticed she had grown thinner and paler in the weeks we had been together. I wondered if she didn't really need a parole more than I did.

It must have been the result of having been out in the open air for the first time in months the previous day that accounted for none of us waking until the guard banged on the door with our morning "coffee."

We sprang sleepily out of our blankets, and had our cups filled with the hot liquid. Mlle. Blanc still lay quietly under the covers.

Mme. Santot bent over her.

"Wake up before your coffee gets cold," she called, and shook her by the shoulder, then jerked her hand away as if she had been stung.

"She's so cold," she exclaimed, "and stiff! I think she's dead!"

We froze suddenly in our tracks. I remember noticing that Mme. Ragomin, who was just about to drink her "coffee," stopped with the cup poised in mid-air, as though unable either to continue the motion, or put the cup down.

Summoning up all her courage, Mme. Santot turned the girl over. We could all see the rigidity of her body now. She pulled up an eyelid. It did not close. One eye remained open, staring blankly and horribly at us.

It was too much for Marguerite. She ran to the door and began pounding on it, shouting for the guard. We could hear her come running down the corridor, the pot banging against her knees as she ran. She jerked the door open.

"What's going on in here?" she demanded harshly. Then, catching sight of the motionless figure on the bed, she asked, *"Morte?"*

Mme. Santot nodded.

"Touch nothing," she ordered. "I'll get the doctor."

She was back in an instant with the same physician who had cared for me. The doctor gave one glance at the body, and nodded.

"Probably before midnight last night," he said. "Hmm!"

He bent over swiftly, looked closely at the girl's lips and chin, then sniffed the air sharply. Then, kneeling beside the sack, he started hunting through the bed-clothes. In a moment he straightened up. He had a small phial in his hand. There was still a little of a colorless liquid in it.

"Now where in the world did she get that?" he asked himself. He turned to the guard.

"Get some one to take the body to the morgue," he said. "Notify the commander. I'll wait here till you get back."

The guard went out. The doctor turned to us.

"Did she have any special reason for committing suicide?" he asked. "Do any of you know why she did it?"

Mme. Santot shrugged her shoulders.

"She was young and she was in prison," she said.

"But she had only eighteen months to serve!" said Mme. Ragomin. "Couldn't she have stood it that long?"

"She was murdered by the spring," Marguerite said. "I think it was the contrast between the fresh breeze, and the green outside, and her own imprisonment."

I didn't say anything. I could hear her soft voice, with a little note of pleading, saying to me in the night: "3, Rue Washington. . . . Please don't wait until morning. . . . Now I am happy. . . . I'm going to sleep now."

CHAPTER FORTY-TWO

Parole

M<small>ME. SANTOT</small> was as good as her word. She succeeded in finding
out the reason why parole had been offered me, through one
of the inmates who had been a stenographer and had been put to
work in the prison office.

According to her, she had seen a letter in the files from the Kommandantur of Paris, informing the warden that there was a possibility that I might be exchanged for a very important German prisoner held in the United States. Immediately after she had seen that
letter, the commander had called the doctor in, and said:

"I see that Mme. Shiber has had several heart attacks. In your
opinion, doctor, how bad is her condition?"

"It is not grave," the doctor said, "but naturally prison regime is
particularly hard on a woman in her condition."

"But there is no danger of death?"

"I couldn't answer for that if she remains in prison," the doctor
had answered. "Under normal conditions, with a reasonable amount
of food, rest and comfort, she would be quite all right."

That was the morning of the day when I fainted on the stairway.
It was easy to piece the rest of it together; the commander, impressed
by the fact that I might be of value to the Germans for an exchange,
and fearing from the doctor's statement that I might die if I remained in prison, had suggested the parole in order to make sure
that I would be on hand if and when I would be useful to them.

"Now I understand," I said, when Mme. Santot had finished. "I
didn't think the Germans would worry about the death of a prisoner
unless they saw some advantage in keeping her alive. . . . But I
don't see why I should be important enough for any one to be
exchanged for me. . . . Probably the whole thing will fall through.
I'm not going to believe it until it happens. That way I won't be
disappointed."

But it did happen, and the very next day. When the guard came
in as usual in the morning, and doled out our portion of "coffee," I

had no reason for thinking that this would be the last time I would have to swallow that horrible potion. When the sergeant of the guard arrived in the middle of the morning, this unexpected interruption raised my hopes for a moment, but he motioned four men into the cell. They searched it minutely, going over the straw sacks especially, inch by inch. We guessed what they were hunting for—they wanted to find out if any more poison were hidden in the cell. But they found nothing. We heard them go into the next cell after ours. Apparently Mlle. Blanc's suicide had stimulated a prison-wide search.

When the door opened at the usual hour for lunch, I was expecting nothing out of the ordinary. But the guard entered without her pot of soup, and said to me, "Come to the office, please."

I stared at her. It was the first time I had ever heard her, or any of the guards, say, "Please." She didn't even shout at me to hurry. Instead, she went on, "And bring your belongings."

"Bring your belongings!" It's true, I thought, they must be letting me out! I hastily gathered up my things, saying as I did so:

"My friends! Perhaps my petition for a parole has been granted! Don't you think so?"

"Don't hope for too much yet, Mme. Shiber," Mme. Ragomin said kindly. "There's hardly been time for action on that. They are probably moving you to the ground floor so you won't have to walk up and down stairs. We'll see you in the yard this afternoon. . . . *Au 'voir.*"

"*Au revoir,* ladies," I said, and followed the guard. Mme. Ragomin's explanation was probably correct, I told myself. Forty-eight hours wasn't time enough for my parole to have been granted. But still that "please" of the guard stuck in my mind, and I still hoped.

I went down the banisterless stairway very slowly and cautiously, and the guard patiently slowed her step to accommodate mine. I hoped with all my pounding heart that it would be release, not transfer, which would mean that I would have to adjust myself to a new set of cell-mates, very probably much less congenial than those I had grown to like in the hard days we had spent together.

The guard stopped with me outside the door of the warden's office. The sentry told her to wait; the Major was busy for the moment.

Also standing outside the door was an elegantly dressed woman, wearing an expensive coat and a fashionable hat, a veritable fashion plate. She was evidently in the custody of the French gendarme who stood beside her. I didn't recognize her until she spoke:

"Mme. Shiber, I believe," she said. "We have met before."

It was Mme. Berthet, from Fresnes!

"What are you doing here?" I asked. "Did you have anything to do with getting me paroled?"

"I?" she laughed. "Goodness, no! I'm going back to jail myself. . . . I ought to be very angry with you. It's all your fault."

"*My* fault?" I echoed, surprised.

She glanced at the gendarme. He seemed to have no objection to our talking, and my guard, for once, was courtesy itself.

"Yes, because if you had accepted my proposal, I wouldn't have tried to smuggle some of my husband's money out into Switzerland. They caught me. They got the money and I got a year."

"You don't have to worry," I said to her. "Your husband will no doubt be able to get you out once more—or at least get you weekends off again."

"My husband!" she exclaimed harshly. "That stinker! Do you know what he testified at the trial? That I had stolen the money from him, and was trying to get away with it! And do you know what I said?"

I never found out what Mme. Berthet had said. At that moment the door opened, and the guard motioned to me to come in.

The Commandant rose politely when I entered.

"Won't you sit down, Mrs. Shiber?" he said, and sat down again himself only after I had done so.

"Mrs. Shiber," he began with unction, "I have good news for you. I have received a favorable answer to your petition for a six months' parole. You see that we lose no time here. I had a special messenger take the petition to Paris, and I received an answer by telegraph. . . . Now, Madame, you understand that since you are still technically in custody, we must keep tabs on you. Therefore, I must ask you where you desire to pass this time?"

"In Paris," I said.

"That is quite permissible," the major returned. "But you understand that your freedom is conditional, and that you must comply with certain regulations. If you violate them, we will be obliged to bring you back here. I do not think you will find them very onerous. On arriving in Paris, you will report to the Kommandantur, and you must not go elsewhere without securing prior permission. During your residence in Paris, you must present yourself in person daily, and report any changes of address."

"Every day?" I asked, rather surprised at this requirement.

"Yes," he answered, somewhat stiffly. "I think this privilege should be worth that much to you. . . . And now, Madame, a pleasant journey to you, and better health, I hope."

The momentary stiffness gone, he accompanied me to the door and opened it for me to pass through. My guard took me over again and conducted me to the quartermaster's office, where I was given a release certificate stating the conditions of my parole, and asked to sign for an envelope containing the money I had had with me when I entered.

"We have made certain deductions for items you were allowed to buy during your imprisonment," I was told. "You will find an accounting for them with the money."

"Yes, yes," I murmured. "That's perfectly all right."

I was too anxious to get outside the prison gates even to look in the envelope. I signed the receipt, and a moment later the doors swung out before me. For the second time I tasted the ecstatic joy of freedom after imprisonment.

The railroad station was, I knew, some two miles from the prison. I remembered the direction from which we had come on arriving, and started out on foot. But I had overestimated my strength. I was able to walk only a couple of hundred yards when I felt so tired that I didn't dare continue. I sat down on a boulder by the side of the road, and waited for some vehicle to pass. The first arrival turned out to be a peasant with an ox-cart. When I told him I wanted to get to Troyes, but was too weak to walk, he helped me up onto the low cart, and walked along beside me, guiding the oxen with occasional light blows from a long stick he carried.

"Coming from there?" he asked, jerking his thumb back over his shoulder towards the prison.

"Yes," I said, suddenly ashamed for the first time of having been in prison, before some one who didn't know why.

"How'd they treat you there?"

"Well," I said, "it's run by the Germans but the guards are French. They treated us all right—no worse than they treat any one else, I suppose."

"You're a foreigner, aren't you?" he asked, suspiciously.

"I'm an American."

"American!" he said, and stopped short. So did the oxen, no doubt habituated to copying his movements. Then he started forward again, the oxen obediently resuming their slow placid gait.

"I don't suppose there's any chance of your getting back to America now?" he said.

"I don't know," I said. "There may be. I think that's why they let me out. I hope they're going to exchange me."

The peasant seemed to have gained new energy.

"Listen, Madame," he said, "if you get back to your country, give your countrymen this message from an old French peasant—and tell them he knew that he was speaking for forty million Frenchmen. Tell them not to delay. Tell them not to wait too long. Tell them they needn't bother to put off their coming until they are able to do the job all alone. For they won't have to do it alone. We will fight with them, just as we did last time. We expect them. We are biding our time. But we are ready. We have our arms. They are hidden—well hidden. We are waiting for your countrymen to come to bring them out. And then, together, we'll drive the Boche out of *la belle France* as we did once before. . . . But tell them to hurry. Tell them that we are weakening every day. The sooner they come, the stronger we will be to help them. . . . Will you tell them that, Madame?"

"I will tell them," I said. "I won't forget."

The railroad station was a bewildering place for me, with crowds hurrying back and forth, free to move in any direction, unregimented and, so it seemed after prison, disorderly. It is going to take me some time, I thought, before I will be able to resume my normal place in society and get used to people again.

I went into the ticket office to get a ticket for Paris, and for the first time opened the envelope that contained my money. It had held 12,000 francs when I had handed it over. Now there were only about 8,000 left.

I sat down on a bench to examine the document listing the Gebühren—the "deductions." I had been charged for the one or two small items I had been allowed to buy through the prison office—a comb, pins, and other trifles—at a ridiculous rate, and there was even a charge for the doctor who had been called in for me from town (quite without my knowledge, for I was unconscious at the time). But the heaviest charge was for "medicine," and for a moment I was puzzled. Then I realized suddenly what it must be. It was under that form that the cigarettes I had bought for Titi were entered.

At the ticket window, I stood before a man smoking a cigarette. I caught a whiff of the smoke, and immediately my head began to turn and I felt giddy—although before my arrest, I had often smoked as many as twenty a day. It was, I supposed, partly lack of habit and partly the weakness resulting from malnutrition.

I learned as I bought my ticket that there would be no train for Paris for another hour. I wandered aimlessly across the street and walked into the first small restaurant I came across, thinking to eat something before taking the train—for I had left the prison without lunch—not that that would have made much difference.

It was like every little French restaurant, run, I assumed, by a man and his wife, the former waiting on the customers, the latter doing the cooking. As I entered it I glanced at a mirror hanging on the wall near the entrance and stopped short. We had had no mirrors in prison, and I had not seen my own face for months. I didn't recognize myself.

My unkempt hair had grown stringy and was now almost all white. My face was yellow and sickly, and lined with wrinkles. And my clothes! The hat which had come from one of the best shops of Paris was a formless mass of felt and cloth. My tailored suit, of excellent material and perfect cut—well, it looked as if it had been slept in, not once, but every day for months—as it had.

The proprietor saw my startled look when I glanced into the

mirror. Putting it together with my disheveled appearance, he said, politely and with an understanding smile:

"I suppose, Madame, you come from the hospital—that is, from the prison."

"Yes," I said. "I would like something to eat, but of course I have no ration card."

"Naturally," he said. "It is too bad, but—really, Madame, I can't serve you without a card. You realize my situation. I would do it gladly, but if I am caught, they would close me up."

"I understand," I said dully. "It's not your fault, of course."

"From your accent, Madame, I should judge you were English or American?" he pursued.

"American," I said.

"American?" he repeated. Then, switching to not bad English, he went on, "So they had an American in jail there! Look, Madame —I was a waiter for a while on the French Line—the *paquebots,* you know. Then I worked for a little while in New York. I am very fond of Americans, Madame. I cannot sell you anything—but perhaps if you would like to be my personal guest? They cannot prevent me from sharing my own rations with you."

I tried to protest, politely, though it was only a gesture. I was too anxious to change from prison fare to be too meticulous about not depriving any one else of their rations. I let him lead me through the kitchen to his private apartment.

"Sit down," he said, pushing a chair up to the table. "Excuse me just a minute." And I heard him back in the kitchen, saying excitedly to his wife: "*Figurez-vous!* An American in their dirty jail! Watch the dining room while I get her something to eat."

He returned with what to me was a banquet—a piece of roast meat, salad, cheese. There was even a small piece of butter for the bread. The proprietor sat with me, drinking a glass of red wine—I didn't dare touch it yet—and talking with me, chiefly about the last war.

"You remember, Madame," he said, "what your General Pershing said when he arrived in 1917 'Lafayette, we are here!' The Americans saved France then, and we know they will save us again. That is our last hope, and our only hope, Madame—your country. We know she will not fail the people of France."

CHAPTER FORTY-THREE

Father Christian

IT WAS 9 o'clock in the evening when I reached Paris. I stepped from the *Gare de l'Est* into the street with a feeling of apprehension. So many times before I had come out of this station into the gayly lighted square before it, with its rows of brilliant cafés and the happy, laughing crowds thronging their terraces. Now it was gloomy and deserted, and the few persons hurrying by wore expressions which convinced me that the city was feeling the oppression of the invader even more bitterly than when I had last left it.

I went at once to my apartment. This time it was I who almost failed to recognize Mme. Beugler. She had lost weight, and now the bones of her head showed plainly under the sunken flesh of her once plump face.

"Have you been ill?" I asked, after we had exchanged greetings.

"No," she said, with a tired smile. "I know I've changed. I'm much thinner than when you saw me last. It's the food situation. It's very bad here now. Much worse than when you were here. One of the tenants was calculating the other day that the French people altogether have lost 400,000,000 kilograms in weight. That's figuring an average loss of 10 kilos per person—and I've lost 15 myself. I used to weigh 65, now I weigh 50 [1] . . . Has Mme. Kitty been released also?"

The question pained me so much, I couldn't explain completely at once. I said only:

"I don't know, Mme. Beugler. You see, we haven't been together."

"What a pity! I always supposed you were in the same cell, and could console one another."

I couldn't bring myself to tell her of Kitty's death sentence; and I had learned already from what she had said that she knew nothing of what might have happened to her. I changed the subject:

"What happened to our dogs?"

[1] A kilogram is 2.2 pounds.

381

"They aren't here any more," Mme. Beugler said uneasily. "I don't know if you noticed, Madame. There isn't a dog in Paris any more. When there isn't even enough to eat for human beings, what can you do about dogs?"

"You didn't *eat* them, did you?" I almost screamed.

"Goodness, no!" Mme. Beugler said vehemently. "No, Madame, that isn't what I meant. I wouldn't do a thing like that—although, I tell you, there are people who ate their dogs. That's a fact. Their cats, too. . . . I couldn't feed the dogs, Madame. What could I do? I had to turn them over to the Society for Prevention of Cruelty to Animals. They put them out of the way painlessly. I assure you, Madame, it was the best way."

"I suppose it was," I answered wearily, saddened by this news, though on my already dulled senses it fell with less of an impact than it would have done at other times. "I'm tired. I think I'll go to bed." And I reached out mechanically to the board where our keys used to hang.

"But, Madame," the concierge said, surprised. "Surely you didn't expect to find your apartment intact when you returned!"

"Why, yes . . . I did," I faltered. "I hadn't thought about it. . . . You mean . . . it's not mine any more?"

"*Voilà!* In March, the Germans came with a big moving van. They said you had been convicted of smuggling English soldiers out of the country, and your property was to be confiscated. They took everything away—everything! You never saw anything like it. They even pulled nails out of the walls, and saved them. I had to telephone the landlord to keep them from taking the curtain rods and other fixtures that belonged to the building."

"Then it's empty!" I said. "Our things are gone!"

"Wait!" said Mme. Beugler. "You haven't heard the oddest thing of all yet. Two days afterwards they came back, and showed me an order that your apartment was to be turned over to a German officer. And they brought back the identical furnishings they had taken out. Your own things! And moved them right back in again! Now what kind of sense does that make, I ask you? If the Germans were going to hand the apartment over to one of their officers, why did they move everything out and then back again?"

"So a German officer is living with all our lovely things now!" I said, feeling as though I were likely to burst into tears at any moment.

"Yes," Mme. Beugler answered. "A military prosecutor—Captain Weber is his name."

Weber! Now I understood the curious story Mme. Beugler had told about the removal and return of our furniture. I remembered Weber looking about and complimenting us about the taste with which we had fixed up our apartment. No doubt the furniture had been taken out while he was arranging to get our place for himself, and was put back in at his request.

"Thank you, Mme. Beugler," I said. "I'm very tired. I must find a place to sleep before curfew. Au 'voir."

I walked out into the dark streets. I felt as though I had just been present at the funeral of my past.

Finding a place to sleep was not too easy. I tried one or two small hotels and found them filled. It was after 10. If I failed to find a place before 11, I would be picked up by the patrol, and would spend my first night outside of prison in the police station! Suddenly I remembered the hotel where Father Christian had left his boys one night. He had given me its address when he tried to get me to come to visit the proprietress. I determined to go there.

As I entered the hotel, I found myself in a sort of lobby deserted of all guests. The only person in sight was a middle-aged woman at the hotel desk, working at the books. As I approached, she gave a fleeting glance at my bedraggled clothes, and said coldly:

"Sorry. We have no vacant rooms."

"Please," I said, "try to squeeze me in somehow. I'm very tired and it's nearly curfew. I don't blame you for finding me rather unprepossessing, but I can't help my appearance. You see, I've just come out of a German prison."

She took off her glasses and looked at me without them, with a more human interest, I thought.

"A German prison?" she repeated. "Why were you there?"

"You're Mme. Henri, aren't you?" I asked, without answering her question.

"Why, yes. How do you know my name?"

"Father Christian told me," I said. "I am Mrs. Shiber."

"Mrs. Shiber! The American? The one who wouldn't come to see me?"

"I'm afraid so," I said. "I didn't want to let any more people than I could help in on our secret. As you see, I had reason to be afraid."

"I don't hold it against you," said Mme. Henri, smiling broadly. "I understand. But now you trust me more, *n'est-ce pas?*"

"Father Christian guaranteed that you could be depended upon," I said, "so I came here when I found that they had confiscated my apartment."

"*Les cochons!*" Mme. Henri exclaimed. Then suddenly, a look of distrust came into her eyes. "Excuse me," she said, "but can you prove you are Mrs. Shiber?"

I showed her my papers and my prison discharge.

"Excuse me, Mrs. Shiber," she said. "I just happened to think suddenly—after all, I do not know her, and it could be a trick. . . . It is 11. Just a minute. I must close."

She locked the door. I thought that in hundreds of thousands of other buildings at the same moment, Paris was simultaneously locking itself up for the night. Animation was suspended now until morning.

Mme. Henri led me to a room, with a little embarrassment at having to admit that she had intended to bar me at first on the grounds of my appearance, which did not, I confess, make me appear a desirable guest. It was clean and cozy, with a tiny bathroom attached to it. Not many months ago I would have found it ordinary enough, but now, after the prison of Troyes, it seemed the height of luxury. I even reveled in the wall-paper, of that curious purple violence found only in low-priced French hotels.

An hour later, fresh from a bath, my hair combed, and my face feeling clean for the first time in months, I was reclining in my soft bed, ravenously devouring a slice of cold meat which Mme. Henri had brought up to me. She was sitting on the edge of the bed, questioning me on my prison experiences. I told her of the last report I had had from Kitty—that she had been transferred from the Cherche-Midi prison, but that I didn't know where.

"If only I knew!" I exclaimed. "Perhaps then I could find out whether she is . . . I mean, what has happened to her."

"From what I have heard," Mme. Henri said, "she has probably been moved to Germany. I'm afraid that makes it impossible to expect to get any news of her."

"Germany?" I exclaimed. "But how did you learn that?"

"Father Christian told me."

"Father Christian!" I almost shouted. "You have seen Father Christian? How? Where? When?"

"Two weeks ago, in this room."

"I don't understand," I said. "He was condemned to death, too."

"Of course, you couldn't know, just coming from prison," said Mme. Henri. "It was stupid of me. I should have told you at once. But I was so busy asking you questions that I forgot what you would like to know. Here's what happened. Four weeks after he was sentenced, the prison was notified that officers from the Château de Vincennes would call for him on a certain day, his execution having been set for dawn the day after. Sure enough, two officers arrived with an order for his delivery, signed a receipt taking over his custody, and took him away. . . . There must have been a fine scene at the prison an hour or so later when the *real* officers arrived."

"Then the men who got him were—?"

"From the British Intelligence Service! They had learned the exact time when the transfer was to be made, and called themselves just an hour earlier."

"But that was a long while ago," I said. "You say you saw him only two weeks ago. Didn't he get away to England then?"

Mme. Henri laughed.

"Not he," she said, "not Father Christian. That was the idea of the Englishmen who got him out, but he said, 'I was resigned to the fact that my life was over, and so this extra life I have been granted is clear gain; in risking it, I risk nothing. Besides, God has snatched me from death once, and he can do it again, if he so wills.' And he went back to smuggling soldiers out of the country. That isn't all. He's also working with friends, publishing secret papers, sending information to the British, and so forth. He's a brave man, Father Christian!"

"I would so like to see him again," I said. "Do you think it would be possible?"

"Perhaps," said Mme. Henri, "but we had better be very careful.

We must make sure first that you are not watched, for instance. I don't know how to reach him, but he communicates with me fairly regularly, and I will tell him about you. But he will probably know already that you have been released. Through his underground connections, he has followed the fate of all those who were convicted with him. That was how he learned that Kitty had been sent away to Germany."

"Has he told you anything about the others?" I asked. "Chancel and Tissier, I mean?"

"Both in the prison of Dijon. Chancel could have gotten out. The Gueules Cassées interceded for him, and he was offered his liberty if he would sign a guarantee never to oppose the Germans again. He refused to sign, so he's still in jail."

I left Mme. Henri's hotel the next morning, for I was obliged to report my address to the police, and I thought it would be better not to stay there, since they might check up to find out if my new address had any connection with my past activities. I told her that I would not come back to the hotel for several days, in order to have time to discover whether or not I was being followed, and that if I were, I wouldn't come back at all. But I arranged with her to have dinner at the same restaurant every night, where she was to come also whenever she heard from Father Christian. There we agreed that we would strike up a conversation as though we were strangers, in order to communicate with one another without being suspected, in case I should be provided, once more, with a shadow.

CHAPTER FORTY-FOUR

Last Days in Paris

IT WAS only when I put my hand into my coat pocket as I left the hotel and touched a slip of paper that I remembered something which had completely slipped my mind the previous day—I had Marguerite's note to her *femme de ménage* telling her to let me occupy her apartment. I went to the address it gave, fearing that it, too, might have been taken over by the Germans, but this time I was in luck. Before noon, I found myself established in a pleasant little Left Bank studio. My first care was to make my required appearance before the police, where I was given something very necessary—ration books. My next act was to get some new clothes. I found it almost impossible to find anything very attractive. The stores were bare of merchandise. But it wasn't hard to improve on what I was wearing, and I felt that I had regained some of my self respect when I was able at last to change the garments which I had worn day after day for so many months (and during the winter, without ever taking them off).

My first visit was to 3, Rue Washington, to keep the promise I had made to poor little Mlle. Blanc. I was very nervous as I rang the bell. I knew I had a painful ordeal before me, and as I waited at the door, I tried to phrase the sentences in which I would have to tell Mme. Blanc of the last hours of her daughter.

In the end, I am afraid I blurted it out rather badly, but Mme. Blanc helped me by maintaining an iron composure. There was a tightness on her face and a hardness in her voice which betrayed the grip she was holding on her soul to prevent her emotions from breaking through, but she reined herself in before the stranger who had entered her life once, briefly, to bring her evil tidings.

When I repeated her daughter's message: "Tell her that I am lonely without her, that I think of her constantly, and that I have taken her advice," Mme. Blanc said quietly, but with that curious tautness in her voice: "That was not the way I foresaw it."

387

I tried to frame an apology for us, her cell-mates, and especially for myself, who had not realized her intention, in spite of the strange way she had spoken to me. If we had dreamed that she had poison, I said, we would have taken it from her. But who would have imagined that she could have gotten it in prison?

"She took it with her," her mother said. "I gave it to her." Her voice was dull and without inflections.

"*You* gave it to her?" I repeated, thunderstruck.

"Yes," said Mme. Blanc, still in that expressionless monotone. "Perhaps you will not understand me. I may have been wrong. I did not want to let the Germans take her away without giving her the means to escape if what they might do became unbearable to her. How could I tell what might happen to her? They might have beaten her. They might have tortured her. You see, I was thinking of helping her to escape ill-treatment. I didn't think that it would happen like that—that the drab days, and the privation, and the confinement would be too much for her . . . and the time so short until she could have come back to me. . . ."

For the first time, her voice quavered.

"Thank you, Mrs. Shiber," she said. "Would you mind going now? I'd like to be alone."

It was ten nights before Mme. Henri appeared at the restaurant where I had dined faithfully day after day, arriving with the first customers and leaving with the last. She came up to my table, and saying to me, *"Permettez-vous?"* as though she were a complete stranger asking if she might sit at the same table, she took a seat and continued to act as though she did not know me.

I could see that she was purposely dragging out the meal, and I did the same. Once or twice, she asked me to pass the salt, or hand her the bill of fare. She was still playing the part of the stranger, but paving the way by these routine remarks to be able to speak to me naturally later.

By the time she thought it safe, there was no one left but the proprietor and a lone waiter who evidently wished that we would get out and let him go home. Mme. Henri waited until the last customer had gone, and then, still taking the precaution of appearing to be addressing me casually, she said, "I have seen Father Christian."

"Wonderful!" I exclaimed. "When can I see him?"

"Not at all, I'm afraid," she replied. "He asked me to say to you that he regrets it deeply, but that he has reason to believe from underground reports that although you do not seem to be shadowed regularly, they are keeping close tabs on you. It would be dangerous to both of you for you to try to see him. He would be recognized, no doubt, and it would appear as though you intended to resume your old activities. He said to tell you that he hopes to see you again after the war, when there will be no more Germans in Paris."

"Did you ask him about Kitty?"

"Yes; but he knows nothing new. He says he does not believe she has been executed yet, because they would probably have learned of that. They have agents even in Germany, and they are still trying to find out what happened to her. He suggests that you ask permission to write to her at the Kommandantur. If she has already been executed, they will probably tell you so. If not, they may even give you the prison address."

I was at the Kommandantur at noon. I handed my release papers to the officer in charge to have him stamp it with the date, as he did daily, and was about to ask if I could send a letter to Kitty, when he said:

"So you are Mme. Shiber? We have just sent a messenger to your apartment to look for you."

"What's the matter?" I asked, with a sinking feeling. Once again, I thought, my temporary freedom is illusory. I am going back to jail again. Is it because of my meeting with Mme. Henri? Have I led the German police to another victim, and am I being returned again, now that I have served my purpose as a danger to all who meet me?

"Nothing's the matter, Madame. You must leave Paris today, that's all."

"Today? But why?"

"You are going to America, Madame," he said, and a broad grin appeared on his face. I imagined that he had enjoyed my evident fear, and had amused himself for a few seconds by delaying this announcement.

I was conducted to the office of a German colonel, who informed me that in accordance with an agreement between the United States and Germany, I was about to be exchanged. He told me that I was to return to my apartment, pack anything I wanted to take with me, and wait there for a Gestapo escort who would take me to Juvisy, where I would board a train for Lisbon at 5 o'clock that afternoon.

I listened in a daze, but in spite of my bewilderment and elation, I didn't forget my anxiety for news of Kitty.

"May I make one request, Colonel?" I asked. "I would like to send a farewell message to my friend who was arrested with me before I leave Europe. She is in prison, but I do not know where."

"What is her name?"

"Kitty Beaurepos," I breathed.

"Excuse me a moment," he said politely, and stepped into the outer office. I waited tensely for the result. In a few moments he was back.

"Yes," he said. "You can write to Mme. Beaurepos. Address the letter to her at the *Politische Zivil Gefangenen Stelle,* and it will be forwarded."

"Then she's still alive!" I couldn't help exclaiming. "Thank God for that!"

The Colonel looked at me with a quizzical smile.

"So that was what you wanted to know," he said. "Why didn't you say so? I could have told you that here in Paris we have no way of knowing that. All we have here is that address. You can send your letter there, and it will be forwarded—if she is still alive. But whether she is or not, I am afraid we cannot guarantee."

And so I come to the end of my story. You know the rest—how I was exchanged for Johanna Hoffmann, how I boarded the refugee train at Juvisy, the journey to Lisbon, and finally my return aboard the *Drottningholm* to the free soil of my own country. In this new atmosphere of a country which, though at war, had not yet tasted nor realized what war meant, the experiences I have related receded into a distance which each day seemed to grow more unreal and more dreamlike. At times, it seemed to me quite impossible that all this should have happened to me, that I should have been caught up into these toils—I, an ordinary woman with no particular taste for adventure.

My only desire now was to forget all that had happened to me; but as the days went by, and the first joy of release passed, I was overcome with a new anguish—one which was associated with the period which I had hoped to put behind me. It was, oddly enough, the result of the width of the gap between my new life and the events through which I had just passed. For, all about me, I saw people leading their normal calm existences, unaware, apparently, of the importance of the enemy threat. I had been a part of the war, although a small part, and I could not regard it with detachment myself, or remain unmoved when I saw others doing so.

Sometimes I would look about me in the streets, at the carefree crowds, and say to myself: "And yet we are at war!"

For me, that fact had changed a whole existence. For millions of others, it had also changed—or cancelled—existences; and while those about me seemed so unhurried, I knew that other thousands were striving and dying, and that every minute lost to help them would mean for them, not sixty seconds more of discomfort, but the end of life itself.

I couldn't forget the faces of those I had left behind me—Kitty, Father Christian, Tissier, Chancel, all the others, with whom I had lived an existence so different from that I know at present. With them, almost against my own will, I had been able to save some few lives—but how many more who could be saved still remain in peril! How many in France and in other countries under the heel of the oppressor suffer, struggle and die!

The indifference I meet everywhere frightens me. I believe in human solidarity—but so many live unconcerned with the pains of their millions of brothers under the yoke! I believe in divine justice —even in our materialistic world—but I know it works through the instrumentality of human beings sufficiently in tune with it to strive for its execution. And as I see how many there are who put their own comfort above the efforts necessary to save millions of helpless beings, I feel guilty myself—guilty for being here now, in a place of safety, busied with matters of no importance, while this clash of the forces of good and evil is shaking the world.

Yes, I am troubled by a sense of guilt. Some who are alive today may be shot tomorrow; and how can any one rest knowing that he might be able to contribute to saving precious human lives, if he is not doing so?

Is it only quieting my conscience if I say to myself that when God desires that we should act, He shows us the way, tells us what to do—lest they die?